A Modular Calculus for the
Average Cost of Data Structuring

A Modular Calculus for the Average Cost of Data Structuring

by

Michel Schellekens

University College Cork-National University of Ireland
Ireland

 Springer

Michel Schellekens
University College Cork (UCC)
National University of Ireland, Cork
Department of Computer Science
Centre for Efficiency-Oriented Languages
Western Road
Cork, Ireland
Email: m.schellekens@cs.ucc.ie

Cover art:
Title of art work: This little light of mine

Tapestry artist: Pascale De Coninck
www.pascaledeconinck.com

Photographer: Dori O'Connell
www.dorioconnell.com

Tutorial CD:
CALVIN AND HOBBES ©1986 Watterson.
Dist. By UNIVERSAL PRESS SYNDICATE.
Reprinted with permission. All rights reserved.

Additional material to this book can be downloaded from http://extra.springer.com

ISBN 978-1-4899-9906-1   ISBN 978-0-387-73384-5 (eBook)

Printed on acid-free paper

9 8 7 6 5 4 3 2 1

springer.com

To my wife, Pascale De Coninck, and parents, Yvan and Yvonne Schellekens.

Foreword

As of June 2008 it will have been 50 years since the award of my Princeton Ph.D. During that academic year, aside from my research in symbolic logic, I worked on the von Neumann computer at the Institute for Advanced Study to program a small combinatorial puzzle. It took some collaboration, a little special coding, many hours of trial and error, and the use of punched cards to get the correct sequence of computations done on that machine. Today the problem is an exercise for undergraduate classes.

The IAS computer was the prototype of machines built by IBM that were expensive and very power hungry. They were as big as dinosaurs — and nearly as slow! The progress in computer architecture over that half century since 57/58 (and even over the last 25 years) has been truly astonishing. Now, for a fairly modest price, I have sitting here on my desk an Intel Core Duo laptop running at a processor speed of 2.16 GHz, with an L2 cache of 2 MB, an on-chip memory of 1 GB, and a bus speed of 667 MHz. The hard disk has a capacity of over 93 GB, and the external back-up disk can store nearly 300 GB. The laptop itself has wireless I can use at the coffee house down the street, a CD and DVD player, video output for lectures (or movies I can show at home), and an internet connection via a high-speed cable modem here on my desk. At the moment as I write I am listening to classical baroque music over internet radio, but I can get literally hundreds of sound connections for all kinds of music and talk radio. People would have killed for such personal computing power only 20 years ago. And as the clerk at the computer store reminded me last week, my laptop is even now somewhat outdated! By comparison the old IAS machine — now standing as a sad, dead fossil at the Smithsonian Institution Museum in Washington, D.C. — seems a rather small, baby dinosaur.

Let us also note that in less than a decade another dinosaur, the supercomputer, has had a remarkable reincarnation. Genetic research, cryptography, and astronomy — to name only a few areas — today would be all but unthinkable without the use of supercomputers. A widely circulated news report this week told us:

> A recent IBM research project that aims to replace electricity with pulses of light to make data transfer between processor cores up to 100 times faster could lead to laptop-sized supercomputers and drastically improved power consumption. The technology, called silicon

nanophotonics, replaces electronic wires with pulses of light in optical fibers for faster and
more efficient data transfers between cores on a chip.

Not only are the reports of the death of Moore's Law from 1965 much exaggerated,
as the alternatives to the older silicon technology are coming forward, but the multi-
core design will require a complete rethinking of algorithm development to take
advantage of on-chip parallelism.

And here is another news report that just came to me this hour via an e-mail list:

Intel has announced one of the smallest flash-memory drives that could give handheld devices
the power of desktop computers. The chip will compete with similar chips from Samsung,
which are used in gadgets such as Apple's iPod and iPhone, but Intel's chip comes with
a built-in standard electronics controller, which makes it easy and inexpensive to combine
multiple chips into a single, high-capacity hard drive. Since being introduced in the late
1990s, flash memory has revolutionized consumer electronics due to flash-memory chips
being smaller, more durable, and more energy efficient than magnetic hard disks, making
them the ideal replacement for hard drives in handheld devices such as MP3 players, mobile
phones, and even some high-end laptops.

Clearly we live in very exciting (computer) times!

I do not know whether I will still be alive to see the practical realization of quantum
computing, but I do know that I myself cannot even begin to take advantage of the
computing power sitting right here before me today. Of course, experts are indeed
putting the new machines through their paces and doing great new science; but I also
believe we have very, very much to learn still about crafting efficient algorithms. No
matter what new machine is produced, it is always possible to invent a nasty problem
beyond its capacity in memory and/or speed. But that does not mean that the new
facilities cannot produce excellent and improved results on older problems – if we
know how to take advantage of the new architectures and improved capabilities.

This brings us to the question of algorithm analysis, the topic of the present monograph. Let us note first that worst-case analysis need not hold back good algorithm
development. An early success was Linear Programming: though there can be very
tough problems, current algorithms work very, very well in practical applications. A
somewhat related example is the problem of solving Boolean equations. The general
question is NP-complete, but recent implementations are having remarkable success.
Here is a quotation from the Wikipedia entry for the "Boolean satisfiability problem":

Modern SAT solvers (developed in the last ten years) come in two flavours: "conflict-driven"
and "look-ahead". Conflict-driven solvers augment the basic DPLL search algorithm with
efficient conflict analysis, clause learning, non-chronological backtracking (aka backjump-
ing), as well as "two-watched-literals" unit propagation, adaptive branching, and random
restarts. These "extras" to the basic systematic search have been empirically shown to be
essential for handling the large SAT instances that arise in Electronic Design Automation
(EDA). Look-ahead solvers have especially strengthened reductions (going beyond unit-
clause propagation) and the heuristics, and they are generally stronger than conflict-driven
solvers on hard instances (while conflict-driven solvers can be much better on large instances
which have inside actually an easy instance).

Modern SAT solvers are also having significant impact on the fields of software verifi-
cation, constraint solving in artificial intelligence, and operations research, among others.
Powerful solvers are readily available in the public domain, and are remarkably easy to use.
In particular, MiniSAT, which was relatively successful at the 2005 SAT competition, only

has about 600 lines of code. Minisat is an example of a conflict driven solver, and an example for look-ahead solvers is march_dl, which won a prize at the 2007 SAT competition.

The point here, it seems to me, is that clever heuristics can have huge pay-offs. The rub is that the finding of good heuristics is an art: past success may yield clues and inspiration for attacking future problems, but continuing success is by no means assured.

In the book before us, Michel Schellekens reports on work by him and with his collaborators on a systematic method for doing the average-case analyses of a wide class of algorithms.

He explains how the new approach builds on traditional methods, while solving new problems in a new way. He makes a strong case for the effectiveness of the scientific and mathematical foundations introduced for giving greater analysis accuracy and re-use adaptability to the algorithm designer.

As the author outlines in the concluding Chapter 11, exploiting features assuring modularity always seems to be good design advice. The language $\mathcal{MOQA}$ offers both serious examples of how to achieve modularity as well as some interesting theoretical problems to be explored. The parallel facilities of the language also open up other possible areas for study which could impact both future software and hardware design.

The basics set out here so clearly should lead to many new investigations and results.

Berkeley, California, December 2007 *Dana S. Scott*

Foreword

Every human on the planet routinely, daily, grapples with estimating the relationship between best-case, average-case, and worst-case times for a myriad of issues. How long will the drive to the airport take? How long will I be in labor? How long will the monsoons last? When will I get through the checkout line? Will this professor ever stop talking? Typically, we humans deal with these estimates with aplomb, easily exploring the space of probabilities and consequences to come up with a daily schedule that is mostly right. However, some of us, maybe as a group, scientists and engineers, but certainly myself, often look too deep. It is of no end of annoyance to my spouse that I normally arrive at an airport very early. Typically, early enough to get a meal and get some work done. Traffic on Hwy 101 along the San Francisco Bay Peninsula, which I take to get to the San Francisco airport from my home in Palo Alto, is notorious for having a very wide distribution of transit times. And, not wanting to be rushed, I estimate near-worst-case and arrive, really, too early. What is the actual worst-cast travel time from Palo Alto to San Francisco? Well, if an earthquake struck nearby it could be days or weeks. So, my estimate of travel time doesn't really consider the actual worst-case but incorporates some level of probabilistic analysis to come up with a typical worst-case. My spouse, on the other hand, likely estimates toward best-case and really isn't too often too late. She just ignores more outliers than I do and things generally work out. Most humans, I assume, proceed similarly.

When we move into the realm of real-time scheduling, ignoring outliers is no longer possible. Definitive mechanisms have to be in place to accommodate all outcomes (except those of complete system failure). For systems in which computation must occur before a specified deadline the analysis must include a value for what is typically called worst-case execution time (WCET). The literature contains much work on WCET, how to measure it and how to constrain it, for every conceivable programming language, runtime, and environment. It is a very difficult problem. And, a miscalculation can cause system-wide failures.

In my role as specification lead of the expert group for Java Specification Request 001, The Real-Time Specification for Java (RTSJ), one of the most important areas, to me, was to provide the RTSJ platform with fundamental semantics and interfaces which would allow developers to manage WCET miscalculations with more ease that in typical real-time development environments. The RTSJ includes a subsystem called, 'cost enforcement'. 'Cost' is the term used in real-time scheduling analysis to mean the amount of time a task needs to use the processor. WCET is often used as the value for cost. Cost enforcement in the RTSJ looks at the cost parameter not only as information for the real-time scheduling analysis but also as a contract with the system. The system will not allow a task to use more processor time than the value given in the cost parameter. If a task does attempt to exceed this value it is stopped. In systems without such a mechanism what may happen is that an errant task, or a task for which WCET was miscalculated, can cause a cascade of deadline misses often resulting in a system-wide failure. With cost enforcement the errant task is stopped and the system has the opportunity to dynamically correct the situation. It is my belief, and also of the JSR-001 expert group, that any modern, serious real-time system requires a mechanism like cost enforcement. The point I wish to make here is that because WCET is so difficult to predict yet crucial to correct system function designers must often go to great lengths to accommodate the inherent inaccuracies.

So we come to the work of Michel Schellekens, the subject of this book. I first interacted with Michel on the advice of the Director of University Relations at Sun Microsystems, Inc., where I am a Distinguished Engineer and lead the Real-Time Java effort. Michel's work immediately interested me because he was attempting to shed new light onto an area previously thought to be, by the best minds in computer science and computational theory, essentially opaque. Michel and I have kept in touch over the years. I strongly supported him with the founding of the Center for Efficiency Oriented Languages (CEOL), including a donation of the RTSJ platform on Sun servers, and attended the opening in Cork on November 10, 2003.

Michel's work attacks, head on, the problem: Is there a way to obtain a theoretical upper bound on the average time complexity of an algorithm given average inputs. This is not trivial. Algorithmic time complexity, although difficult, often yields concrete results for best and worst case situations. One inspects the algorithm and imagines an input set which will cause the algorithm to do the least or most work, respectively. However, even thinking about what is an average case set of inputs, how to identify such a set in a general way and to track such sets throughout the computation to derive an upper bound on average time complexity is truly amazing in scope.

The work in this book clearly shows that the full story on best-, average-, and worst-case execution time is not yet fully written. I fully expect Michel's work to move from the algorithmic domain into the execution domain and thence into useful commercial products. It's only a matter of time. When this happens it will be interesting to note that the computer scientists, computational theorists and computer system practitioners have taken over five decades to produce systems which deal with the relationship between best-, average-, and worst-case times as easily as my spouse does on every trip to the airport.

Palo Alto, California, November 2007   *Greg Bollella*

Preface

The Analysis of Algorithms is a core Computer Science area which provides information on the expected, i.e. the average-case, performance of algorithms. Such information is useful in a variety of applications, including power estimation and resource budgetting in a real-time context. The Analysis of Algorithms also provides fundamental insights in the design of efficient software. Hence, both from an applied and a theoretical perspective, the investigation of improved methods and tools for static average-case analysis is a worthwhile goal.

Average-Case Analysis involves a variety of techniques which, typically, do not allow for automation. Currently algorithms must be analyzed on a case-by-case basis and it is not feasible in general to statically derive the average number of basic steps carried out by an algorithm during its execution. Various bottle-neck problems have been high-lighted in the literature and some well-known algorithms escape analysis.

In view of the status of the field, the ultimate aim to provide a unified foundation for average-case analysis motivated the work of many authors including [Knu73, FS95, Ram96, Vui80]. As pointed out in [Vui80]:

> A progress in our understanding of these questions should drastically affect the way in which we discover and explain the fundamental algorithms, as catalogued by Knuth [Knu73] and Aho et al [AHU87].

The aim of this work is to present a new approach to the Average-Case Analysis of Algorithms, based on the novel notion of random bags and their preservation. The view presented here is that the notion of a random bag may serve as a unifying model for abstract data structures and their data distribution, while random bag preservation enables the constructive tracking of the distribution during computations. The approach inspired novel algorithms and considerably simplified their average-case analysis.

The work presents a modular calculus for static average-case analysis which drastically simplifies the analysis and opens up the way for novel explorations on static timing tools. Random bags also contribute a visual way to represent data and their distributions, which, in addition to facilitating average-case analysis, provides a useful teaching aid.

A parallel between the role of Static Analysis in Software Engineering and the role of Calculus in "real" Engineering may be helpful to illustrate the motivation behind the research. Engineering offers the capacity to analyse the strength of a construction, such as a bridge, by analyzing its blue prints, rather than subjecting it to heavy loads to test its limits. This approach should ideally find a natural parallel in Software Engineering via Static Program Analysis. Rather than executing a program on a large selection of inputs to experimentally derive information on its average-case behaviour, the goal is to derive this information statically via an analysis of the program's source code. Calculus supports the analysis of blue-prints in Engineering. Similarly, the aim of this work is to provide a foundation for a Calculus supporting Static Average-Case Analysis of a program's source code. This is a major challenge and our aim is not to provide an all-encompassing answer. Instead, we focus on the introduction of new advances in this area as a basis for a simplified and unified theory of average-case analysis and as a potential platform on which to build future improved modular static analysis tools.

A central aspect of the novel approach, which distinguishes it from prior approaches to Average-Case Analysis, is the use of randomness preservation to ensure the compositionality property, well-known from the Semantics and the Real-Time Language areas, in the context of the Analysis of Algorithms. Compositionality can rightfully be referred to as the "golden key" to static analysis, witnessed by its central role in static worst-case time analysis. A main theme of this work is that compositionality, combined with the capacity for tracking data distributions, unlocks a novel technique for modular average-case analysis. This approach provides the inspiration for the $\mathcal{MOQA}$[1] "language". The language essentially consists of a suite of random bag preserving data-structuring operations together with conditionals, for-loops and recursion and hence can be incorporated in *any* traditional programming language, importing all of its benefits in a familiar context[2].

A key feature of $\mathcal{MOQA}$ is that its operations have been purpose designed to ensure the capacity for a compositional static average-case analysis of $\mathcal{MOQA}$ code. The guaranteed compositionality property of $\mathcal{MOQA}$ programs brings a strong advantage for the programmer. The capacity to combine parts of code, where the average-time is simply the sum of the times of the parts, is a helpful advantage in static analysis. Moreover, re-use is a key factor in our approach: once the average time is determined for a piece of code, then this time will hold in any context. Hence it can be re-used and the timing impact is always the same. Compositionality also improves precision of static average-case analysis, supporting the determination of accurate estimates on the average number of basic operations of programs.

It is a main theme of the current work to introduce the new foundation for average-case analysis and to illustrate its applicability, as well as to motivate and specify the $\mathcal{MOQA}$ language and discuss its associated static average-case timing tool *Distri-Track*.

---

[1] MOdular Quantitative Analysis.

[2] $\mathcal{MOQA}$ is implemented at CEOL in Java 5.0 as $\mathcal{MOQA}$-Java.

The work is carried out at the intersection of several areas: Analysis of Algorithms and Random Structures, Semantics, Real-Time Languages, Static Program Analysis, Modular Design and the mathematical theories of Finite Partial Orders, Linear Extensions, Multi-Sets and Probability Theory. Hence the material may be useful for a variety of researchers and students, with interests in Computer Science, Electrical Engineering or Mathematics.

We provide an overview of the chapters in this work.

Chapter 1 provides an introduction to the new techniques for average-case analysis and focuses on a motivation of the central notions involved. This includes a motivation of compositionality as the "golden key" to static timing and the need for novel language design to reach compositionality, including the related concept of an Efficiency-Oriented Language.

The chapter provides a brief introduction to the $\mathcal{MOQA}$ language, for which static average-case timing can be achieved in a modular way through the tracking of distributions. Random bags are introduced as concise ways to capture data and their distribution and distribution tracking is incorporated via the concept of random bag preservation. The split operation, well-known from algorithms such as Quicksort and Quickselect, is provided as an example of a random bag preserving operation. This example also serves to illustrate the tracking of distributions in $\mathcal{MOQA}$ and the use of the notion of a separative function to establish random bag preservation.

The chapter also discusses the central Linear-Compositionality Theorem, which forms the basis for the static derivation of the average-case time of $\mathcal{MOQA}$ programs. Advantages of the $\mathcal{MOQA}$ approach are outlined and the chapter concludes with a discussion of the related area of bridging Semantics and Complexity and the area of Real-Time Languages.

Chapter 2 presents introductory notions, including partial orders, series-parallel orders, trees, heaps and bags. A brief overview of some basic sorting algorithms is provided as well as an introduction to standard timing measures, including exact time, total time, worst-case, best-case and average-case time.

Chapter 3 introduces the central notion of compositionality, including IO-compositionality. Worst-case time is shown to be semi-IO-compositional while average-case time is shown to be IO-compositional. The Average-Case Time Paradox is discussed in this context. This paradox regards the fact that even though average-case time is shown to have better compositionality properties than worst-case time, in practice the derivation of average-case time is known to be much more difficult than worst-case time. The paradox is shown to be linked to the potential lack of randomness preservation of standard algorithms, including well-known examples such as Bubblesort and Heapsort. Moreover, the chapter motivates how IO-compositionality of the average-case time measure can be used, in combination with randomness preservation, to obtain linear-compositionality. This greatly facilitates average-case time analysis and overcomes the Average-Case Time Paradox.

Chapter 4 revisits in a slightly more general context, the fundamental notions of random structures, random bags and their preservation, which have been introduced in Chapter 1. The State Theorem is presented which enables an interpretation of states in random structures as "generalized permutations". Chapter 4 also introduces the central notion of an isolated subset. An isolated subset forms a subset of a partial order such that the restriction of the random structure over this partial order to the isolated subset is guaranteed to yield a new random structure. A simplified definition of an isolated subset is obtained for the case of series-parallel orders. The chapter concludes with the Extension Theorem, which demonstrates that it is sufficient to define random bag preserving operations locally on an isolated subset, where the extension of the operation to the entire random structure is obtained in a natural way.

Chapter 5 introduces the basic $\mathcal{MOQA}$ operations, including the Random Product, the Random Deletion and Percolation, the Random Projection, the Random Split and the Top and Bot operations. Each of these $\mathcal{MOQA}$ operations is shown to be random bag preserving. Deletion operations typically are not included in the context of automated average-case analysis, since the analysis of deletions with respect to average-case time is well-known to be problematic, even in the context of traditional average-case analysis. Hence the Random Deletion opens up the way for the inclusion of novel algorithms, such as Percolating Heapsort and Treapsort, which are analyzed in Chapter 9. The Extension Theorem of Chapter 4 is applied to extend these operations from local applications on isolated subsets to applications over the entire random structure. Uniformly random bag preserving operations are singled out as of particular interest, since this type of operations enables simplifications of probability computations in later chapters. The $\mathcal{MOQA}$ operations are shown to preserve series-parallel data structures which yields a characterization of the so-called $\mathcal{MOQA}$ atomic-constructible data structures as series-parallel orders. Finally, some simplifications for the series-parallel case are obtained in the context of the computation of cardinalities of random structures. Such simplifications for series-parallel orders will also be useful in the context of Chapter 6, which regards the average-case analysis of the basic $\mathcal{MOQA}$ operations.

Chapter 6, joint with D. Early, presents the detailed average-case analysis of the basic $\mathcal{MOQA}$ operations, resulting in the formulas obtained by D. Early. As shown in Chapter 7, $\mathcal{MOQA}$ programs are Linearly-Compositional with respect to the average-case time, i.e. their average-case time can be expressed as linear combinations of the average-case times of more basic components. Hence, ultimately, a successful average-case time derivation yields the average-case time of $\mathcal{MOQA}$ programs, expressed in terms of the average-case times of the basic $\mathcal{MOQA}$ operations. Formulas for the average-case times of basic $\mathcal{MOQA}$ operations are obtained in Chapter 6 and simplified formulas are derived for the case of series-parallel orders. These formulas are systematically applied in Chapter 9, which presents examples of compositional average-case time derivations of $\mathcal{MOQA}$ programs. Finally, the formulas of this chapter are illustrated via basic applications involving inductively defined data structures, such as linear orders and complete binary trees. Chapter 6 concludes with a demonstration of combinatorial identities used in the derivation of the average-case time formulas.

Chapter 7 provides the specifications for the $\mathcal{MOQA}$ language, with special attention given to conditionals and recursion, which typically form a challenge for static timing analysis. The random bag preservation of $\mathcal{MOQA}$ programs is demonstrated and the method for the linear-compositional derivation of the average-time of $\mathcal{MOQA}$ programs is outlined.

Chapter 8 provides examples of well-known sorting and search algorithms implemented in $\mathcal{MOQA}$. It also includes examples of two novel algorithms, Percolating Heapsort, the first randomness preserving version of the Heapsort algorithm, and Treapsort, a sorting algorithm over treaps; both of which are essentially based on the Random Deletion operation of Chapter 5.

Chapter 9 provides the compositional average-case time derivation of the programs discussed in Chapter 8, with a main focus on illustrating the use of random bags in this context. The chapter in particular presents the first exact average-case time analysis of a heapsort variant via an analysis of Percolating Heapsort. Compositional average-case time derivations, whenever appropriate, rely on the formulas obtained in Chapter 6. The derivations obtained in this chapter illustrate the basic techniques involved in the static timing tool *Distri-Track*.

Chapter 10, joint with D. Hickey and M. Boubekeur, discusses in more detail the static timing tool *Distri-Track*, developed by D. Hickey. *Distri-Track* analyses $\mathcal{MOQA}$ algorithms programmed in Java, using an implementation of $\mathcal{MOQA}$ by J. Townley. *Distri-Track* enables the automated static derivation of average-case time of most of the $\mathcal{MOQA}$ programs presented in Chapter 8. Experiments, including comparisons with time derivations relying on a Java profiler, are discussed, as well as potential implications for Real-Time Languages. Finally, Chapter 11 presents the conclusion and some potential future work.

The book is accompanied by a software tutorial "Static average-case analysis of programs: a beginner's guide to successful tracking". The tutorial requires Adobe Flash Player, which is freely available online at http://www.adobe.com/. The tutorial provides an introduction to the main concepts used in this work as well as videos illustrating the basic $\mathcal{MOQA}$ operations and a selection of $\mathcal{MOQA}$ programs. The reader is advised to read Chapters 1 and 3, followed by a viewing of the tutorial, before proceeding with later chapters in this work.

Cork, Ireland, December 2007   *Michel Schellekens*

Acknowledgements

Sincere thanks to the CEOL-team for helpful comments on the presentation of the work and countless hours of interesting discussions. It has been a pleasure to work with excellent, critical and inquisitive students. Warm thanks to colleagues Joseph Manning and Emanuel Popovici for their friendship and support. Special thanks to Chantal Berline who reviewed some of the earlier drafts and provided several PPS students "on loan" to CEOL. Steve Brookes suggested the relation with pomsets. Schloß Dagstuhl and DAAD supported a research stay during which some early ideas were explored. Science Foundation Ireland's strong support[3] enabled the full exploration of the approach, the implementation of the $\mathcal{MOQA}$ language and the associated static timing tool *Distri-Track*, as well as the Flash implementation of the $\mathcal{MOQA}$ tutorial. My thanks to the following researchers, both from academia and industry, who were supportive from the start and whose kind words made a difference in challenging times: Chantal Berline, Greg Bollella, Steve Brookes, Roberto di Cosmo, Gordon Plotkin, Dana Scott and Dave Vernon. Also thanks to Rob Esser, Philippe Flajolet, Don Knuth and Peter Puschner for encouraging comments on the nature of the work. The following researchers co-authored chapters in this work: Diarmuid Early co-authored Chapter 6, "Average-Case Time of Basic $\mathcal{MOQA}$ Operations" and Dave Hickey and Menouer Boubekeur co-authored Chapter 10, "Distri-Track". David Devlin and Yin Jie Chen developed the Flash implementation of the $\mathcal{MOQA}$ tutorial, which accompanies this work.

---

[3] SFI Investigator Award 02/IN.1/181.

Contents

Chapter 1
Introduction

Modularity is a crucial property in Computer Science, as clarified succinctly by T. Maibaum in [Mai00]:

> The only effective method for dealing with the complexity of software based systems is decomposition. Modularity is a property of systems, which reflects the extent to which it is decomposable into parts, from the properties of which we are able to predict the properties of the whole. *Languages that do not have sufficiently strong modularity properties are doomed to failure, in so far as predictable design is concerned.*

Achieving modularity is a main challenge in the context of the static derivation of quantitative information from software code, such as execution time or power-use. Quantitative information in practice typically is captured via two types of measures: the worst-case and the average-case measure. While we will refer to the worst-case measure on occasion, a main theme of this work is to propose a novel foundation for modular static *average-case* analysis.

Modularity in this context can be captured in a natural way via the notion of compositionality. This property brings a strong advantage for the programmer. The capacity to combine parts of code, where the average-time is simply the sum of the times of the parts, is a very helpful advantage in static analysis, something which is not available in current languages, and moreover brings the possibility of re-use of code.

Compositionality for average-case is however subtle and one may easily be tempted to conclude that the average-case summation property "comes for free". For genuine compositional reasoning one needs to be able to track data *and* their distribution throughout computations; a non-trivial problem. Indeed, the lack of an efficient method to track distributions affected all prior static average-case analysis approaches. The core ideas presented in the monograph enable the finitary representation and tracking of the distribution of data states throughout computations. This in turn enables one to unlock the potential of compositional reasoning and in particular supports the design of the programming language $\mathcal{MOQA}$. A key feature of this language is that the average-case time complexity is "Linearly-Compositional" for $\mathcal{MOQA}$ programs. In other words, the average-case time of $\mathcal{MOQA}$-programs can be expressed as *linear combinations* of the average-case time of their basic components [Sch09]. This considerably simplifies the average-case time analysis of $\mathcal{MOQA}$-programs and opens the way for (semi-)automation via modular timing. The visual aspect of the distribution representation in this approach has a pedagogical advantage, providing students with useful insights in the nature of algorithms and their analysis.

Before proceeding with a general overview of the language, we clarify some fundamental issues which have motivated its development.

1.1 Static Average-Case Analysis

1.1.1 The Need for Static Average-Case Analysis Tools

Static average-case analysis merits independent exploration in view of its core Computer Science nature [Knu73, CLR96]. From a practical point of view, static average-case analysis tools have the potential to contribute to a variety of areas. Average-case execution time (ACET) is a key measure in estimating heat-dissipation/power consumption, since it provides information on "typical" input behaviour [UK03, QND04]. Static average-case analysis also provides crucial information complementing worst-case execution time (WCET) information. Such complementary information can potentially aid better budgeting of resources in a Real-Time context [MP97]. However, at this stage there are no widely applicable static average-case analysis tools available. Industry needs to rely on simulation, i.e. the execution of code on a (sufficiently large) selection of data to experimentally derive information on the average-case behaviour. This entails imprecision as sample spaces are not necessarily representative and implies an extra cost factor as simulation is time consuming. The simulation problems affect both software and hardware analysis. Our aim is to present a new approach which potentially can provide a basis for novel modular static analysis tools to address this need. The focus of this monograph however will be on the presentation of this new method for modular average-case analysis, where the exploration of applications in the above mentioned areas is regarded as a separate matter.

1.1.2 Compositionality: the Golden Key to Static Analysis

To understand why the compositionality principle is a crucial static timing principle, a comparison with static worst-case timing is useful. It is well-known that static worst-case timing techniques have been successfully developed and a variety of tools have been developed as a result. There are a multitude of these of which we only report a limited selection, ranging from academic approaches, e.g. [KFG93, HBW02], to commercial ones such as Absint's WCET analyzers. The principle which enables the development of static worst-case timing tools is a *partial* compositionality principle which lies at the heart of all current static worst-case timing tools. This principle essentially states that the worst-case time of the sequential execution of two programs is *bounded* by the sum of the worst-case times of these programs, which enables WCET estimation. This allows real-time engineers for instance to estimate the worst-case time of a for-loop in terms of a summation over the worst-case times of the executions of the for-loop body. Note that the worst-case measure is only *partially* compositional, in that we cannot get the *exact* determination of the worst-case time, only an *upper bound* of this time. For a tentative framework developed to address full compositionality for WCET, we refer the interested reader to [BP02].

Similar to the usefulness of a (partial) compositionality principle in a WCET context, the availability of a compositionality principle for average-case time can pave the way for static average-case timing tools.

For this one needs to address the following central question: given the average-case time of two programs P_1 and P_2, how can this information be used to determine the average-case time of the sequential execution of $P_1; P_2$?

Unless this sequential compositionality question is resolved, static average-case tools remain beyond reach.

1.1.3 The Main Bottleneck for Static Average-Case Analysis

It is easy to see why the above compositionality question proves problematic to answer: the average-case time of P_2, in the context of the sequential execution $P_1; P_2$, depends on the distribution of the input data for P_2. This distribution however in practice is typically not known since it will depend on the computation determined by P_1. Assume for instance that we know the distribution of the input data for P_1 and say we denote these input data by the collection I_1. The actual computation of P_1 over these input data I_1 will produce the new input data for P_2, say I_2. However, one typically *cannot* track the distribution throughout the computation, i.e. one cannot, in general, compute the distribution over I_2 from the distribution over I_1. Results have appeared on distribution transformations [Koz81], but these methods remain purely mathematical and do not lend themselves to a concrete method for *effectively computing* new distributions from prior ones. Probabilistic attribute grammars have been proposed as one remedy to *represent* standard distributions in an effective (computable) way [HC88], but again, no systematic method for efficiently tracking these grammars throughout the computations is offered. Attribute grammars give rise to useful ways to determine additional quantitative information such as standard deviation [Mis03].

The compositionality problem for average-case analysis has been overcome via the $\mathcal{MOQA}$ approach, as outlined below. In a nutshell, the static average-case analysis tool *Distri-Track* statically tracks the distribution of the data during the computation of $\mathcal{MOQA}$ programs. This tracking is achieved through a finitary representation of the distribution, referred to as a "random bag", and through a careful design of the basic operations to ensure that such finitary distribution representations are preserved throughout the computation.

1.2 Removing the Bottleneck for Static Average-Case Analysis

1.2.1 The Need for Novel Language Design

Automated average-case analysis is concerned with the design of domain specific languages for which the average-case time can be statically derived from program code. This field, and the general field of the Analysis of Algorithms, has been plagued by problems related to the fact that a lack of randomness preservation of standard operations prevented the analysis of well-known algorithms. Randomness preservation as we will see is tightly linked to the capacity to track data distributions.

The concrete problems facing (automated) average-case analysis been concisely summarized in "Automatic Average-Case Analysis of Algorithms", by P. Flajolet, B. Salvy and P. Zimmerman [FSZ91]:

> *"Judging from the entirety of the analyses contained in Knuth's volume on sorting and searching, the only algorithms that we know how to analyse are those whose complexity is equivalent to a parameter of a static structure. No general method is known in order to analyse intrinsically "dynamic" algorithms."* As reported on page 64 of [FSZ91]: *"examples that typically leave us helpless are heapsort and balanced trees that modify either an ordered array structure or a tree structure."*.

The impasse to progress is directly related, as pointed out above, to the current state of knowledge in the analysis of algorithms.

The core obstacle to extend static average-case timing tools is that certain well-known classical data structuring operations, such as the delete operation, fail to exhibit compositional behaviour w.r.t. the average-case time measure. This led to the consideration of the redesign of standard data structuring operations and more generally novel language design to address the problem. This aim is captured by the notion of an "Efficiency-Oriented Language".

1.2.2 Efficiency-Oriented Languages

Efficiency-Oriented Languages[1] (EO-languages) are languages which have *purpose designed* operations to enable the *modular* (i.e. compositional) static extraction of quantitative information, such as time or power use. In case traditional language constructs fail to be modular, novel language constructs are used to replace the original language constructs to ensure modularity. This allows Efficiency-Oriented "languages" to be naturally embedded in traditional programming languages. The design of EO-languages is a major challenge. Yet two examples of such languages currently exist which illustrate that there is scope for further development in this area.

---

[1] A terminology coined by CEOL.

A first example is provided by the Burns-Puschner approach which achieves compositionality, as opposed to partial compositionality, for the worst-case measure. This approach involves a purpose designed conditional statement [BP02].

The programming language $\mathcal{MOQA}$ is a new language to enable the compositional determination of the average-case number of basic instructions of its programs based on the notion of randomness preservation. We remark that its constructs have been designed to incorporate the traditional data structuring operations, replacing non-compositional standard data structuring operations whenever needed. $\mathcal{MOQA}$ has been specified and implemented in Java at CEOL[2].

It is important to distinguish EO-languages from standard Real-Time languages. Both languages share a similar goal, namely to enable the derivation of quantitative information on programs written in the language. Standard Real-Time languages are typically obtained from existing programming languages by restrictions which guarantee termination, such as exclusions of while-loops and by placing restrictions, e.g. on nested conditionals, to make worst-case analysis practical. Real-Time Languages typically do not significantly alter existing language constructs. This has the advantage that RT-languages remain close in spirit to traditional programming languages[3].

The disadvantage of this approach is that compositionality can not be certified for traditional RT-languages. This has two significant implications: a loss of precision, clear from the fact that worst-case estimates typically overshoot the real worst-case time through upper bounds, and lack of re-use of prior estimates in case of a change in code. Hence traceability is typically lost in this context. EO-languages address this problem through novel language construct design, according to need, in order to guarantee compositionality.

In designing EO-languages, it is important that novel constructs do not drastically increase the complexity of standard constructs which they replace. The novel conditional statement introduced in [BP02], does tend to increase time. The RT-language area accepts moderate slow-downs if increased predictability results. For the case of [BP02] care needs to be taken since the slow-down can be drastic and methods are discussed on how to potentially avoid this problem. For $\mathcal{MOQA}$, constructs typically have equal or improved speed when compared to traditional counter parts, when one ignores the book keeping involved to enable the tracking of distributions, while an increase by a constant factor is typically involved in the book keeping.

1.2.3 The Meaning of Static Timing in our Context

Before continuing with a discussion of the $\mathcal{MOQA}$ language we clarify the meaning of static timing. Static timing as usual refers to the capacity to estimate the time which a program would take upon execution, directly from an analysis of the program's

---

[2] Implementation by J. Manning, J. Townley.

[3] With some exceptions to this rule in the context of RT-Java which also needs to account for time involved in garbage collection.

code, as opposed to deriving information on the time from an actual running of the program (simulation).

To clarify the meaning of "time" in our context, we remark that we will focus on data structuring algorithms which are comparison-based, i.e. for which each action (data-reorganization) is based on a prior comparison between data. The average-case time $\overline{T}_A(n)$ of an algorithm A is then defined as the average number of comparisons carried out over inputs of size n. This is in line with the standard approach in the average-case analysis area [Knu73, FSZ91]. To fine-tune the static analysis further, other primitive operations (such as swaps and assignments) can be accounted for as discussed in [BHS06].

A few issues need to be clarified in this context. As observed, the definition of "time" in terms of the number of primitive operations is consistent with the standard definition of average-case "time" for algorithms [AHU87]. In practice of course, in order to obtain an appropriate estimate of the *execution* time of an algorithm for a given processor one needs to take into account (an upper bound of) the actual time it takes to execute a primitive operation on the processor. Preliminary tests have indicated that this approach can yield results which are quite close to results obtained on the average-case execution time using a Java profiler [BHS06]. This is discussed in more detail in Chapter 10.

Rather than referring to the number of primitive operations as "time" in our context, perhaps it might better be to refer to this number as "cost". Indeed, the number of primitive operations can be used to help estimating various quantitative cost aspects of the code, such as execution time, but also possibly power consumption. Again, one needs to take into account the actual execution time or power consumption of the primitive operations on a particular processor. Since it is customary to refer to the number of primitive operations as "time" rather than "cost", we will continue to use the terminology "time" in the following. The reader should however keep the intended meaning of this terminology firmly in mind.

The $\mathcal{MOQA}$ language will involve high-level basic operations, which can involve a number of primitive operations. In the context of this work, these primitive operations typically will be comparisons. The "time" of a basic operation is the number of primitive operations executed in the basic operation. The "time" of a program will typically be expressed via linear combinations over the times of the basic operations.

1.3 The $\mathcal{MOQA}$ Language

1.3.1 General Description

We will provide a general overview, focusing on an intuitive introduction which minimizes formality, where key notions will be revisited later in this work.

$\mathcal{MOQA}$ nature and scope

The $\mathcal{MOQA}$ language is a special-purpose high-level language. The $\mathcal{MOQA}$ data structuring operations were originally designed to incorporate the standard operations over abstract data types [MR95]. $\mathcal{MOQA}$ has extensive programming capacity in the sense that it incorporates for-loops, (terminating) recursion, and conditionals. This approach enables the programming of a variety of data structuring algorithms, including most sorting and searching algorithms.

We remark that $\mathcal{MOQA}$ can be viewed as a suite of data structuring operations, which can be implemented in *any* existing general purpose programming language. Note that we do not propose $\mathcal{MOQA}$ as a stand alone novel language. Instead we advocate its use in a variety of contexts through appropriate implementation of the basic operations in accordance with $\mathcal{MOQA}$ principles.

A first example of such an implementation is $\mathcal{MOQA}$-Java, implemented in Java 5.0 at CEOL. Currently, $\mathcal{MOQA}$'s applicability is restricted to data structuring contexts. Investigations are ongoing at CEOL to extend the scope to include modulo computations and more general graph based applications.

$\mathcal{MOQA}$ data structures and data-labelings

The $\mathcal{MOQA}$ *data structures* consist of a finite number of finite partial orders, represented by Hasse diagrams. A Hasse diagram represents the immediate directed links between elements, omitting transitive and reflexive links [DP90]. Hence a wide variety of standard data structures can be incorporated in this context. The nodes in these graphs are interpreted as variables storing data.

The $\mathcal{MOQA}$ *data* are labelings of the partial orders in the data structures.

A *data-labeling* is simply an assignment of a finite number of values, one value per node of the data structure. These labels can be any value, e.g. natural numbers, real numbers or words, or even paired data or other data structures containing data, etc. Two conditions need to be satisfied in this context:

1. *Label-comparability:* Any two labels need to be comparable with respect to a given order on labels[4]. For instance, natural numbers are always comparable and so are real numbers, words,...
2. *Order-consistency:* In assigning labels as values to the nodes of a data structure, the directed links of the data structure need to be respected. In other words, if there is a directed link from a node x to a node y, then the label assigned to x must be less than or equal to the label assigned to y.

We refer to any assignment of labels to all nodes of the data structure, respecting the above order-consistency condition, as a *data-labeling*.

We remark that $\mathcal{MOQA}$ programs compute over data-labelings and transform data-labelings to new data-labelings at each stage of the computation.

---

[4] Labels are totally ordered.

We briefly discuss the treatment of repeated labels in our context. At this stage we remark that one approach to deal with repeated labels is to assume that *each* label, repeated or not, comes equipped with a special tie-breaker value. During computations this index value is used as a tie-breaker to decide an outcome of a comparison between identical labels. This of course amounts to considering all labels distinct and hence our analysis, which is carried out on states and under the assumption of distinct labels, will yield the correct result.

Hence from here on we will modify the definition of a data-labeling to be an increasing bijection or in other words, an increasing function where label values are pairwise distinct.

Definition 1.1. A *data-labeling* F is a function from a finite partial order $(X, \sqsubseteq)$ to a countable totally ordered set of labels $\mathcal{L}^*$ such that F is an increasing bijection.

Definition 1.2. Consider a data structure determined by a finite partial order $(X, \sqsubseteq)$ and a linearly ordered collection of labels $\mathcal{L}^*$. $\mathcal{D}_{\mathcal{L}^*}(X, \sqsubseteq)$ denotes the collection of all data-labelings over the partial order $(X, \sqsubseteq)$.

Example 1.1. We consider the example of the discrete partial order of size 3, denoted by Δ_3 and the collection of natural number labels $\mathcal{L}^* = \mathcal{N}$. $\mathcal{D}_{\mathcal{N}}(\Delta_3)$ consists of all lists of size 3 which take distinct natural number values.

Example 1.2. We consider an example of a data structure which is a tree T_4 of size 4, where the tree T_4 is determined by the Hasse diagram displayed on the left below.

Three examples of data-labelings of the tree T_4 are displayed: the data-labeling F_1 with the labels $\{1, 4, 6, 10\}$, a second data-labeling F_2 with the labels $\{2, 4, 6, 9\}$ and a third data-labeling F_3 with the labels $\{5, 9, 22, 35\}$. Note that the data-labelings of the collection $\mathcal{D}_{\mathcal{L}}(T_4)$ are "heaps" in the traditional meaning of this data structure [AHU87].

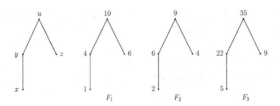

$\mathcal{MOQA}$ states

To enable the timing of computations it is important to identify the *states* that data-labelings can be in. Essentially, states reflect the *relative order* that the labels can be in on any given data structure. The values of the labels are irrelevant in this context, only their relative order is captured.

Consider for instance data-labelings F_1 and F_2 of Example 1.2. These data-labelings are in different states since the order between the labels of y and z differs, i.e. for data-labeling F_1 the label for y is smaller than the label for z, while for data-labeling F_2 the opposite holds. Note that data-labelings F_2 and F_3 are considered to be in the same state since the relative order between labels is the same for both data-labelings.

In the context of so-called comparison-based algorithms, i.e. algorithms for which each action is based on a prior comparison, the computation time can be reliably estimated by the number of comparisons performed during a computation. This number can then be multiplied by the expected time it takes to carry out actions following a comparison, to produce a reasonable estimate of the execution time. In this context data-labelings which are in the same state will lead to the same number of comparisons during a computation. Hence, for the purpose of the analysis and under the assumption that data are equally likely to occur in any of the states, it suffices to carry out the analysis on states as opposed to on general data-labelings. This reduces the data to be considered from a potentially infinite space to a finite space, which enables the average-case analysis.

This type of reduction is a natural approach consistent with standard algorithms analysis [AHU87] and will be formalized and generalized in our context via the notion of a "random structure", which essentially captures the finite state space. We will provide further examples and a formalization of this notion below.

As usual in the analysis of algorithms, to simplify the analysis, we will assume that there are no repeated labels involved in the states. Since, as observed earlier on, data-labelings are assumed not to have repeated labels, the approach is a reasonable one in our context.

To further illustrate the notion of a state, consider a simple example of unordered lists of size 3. These can be represented in $\mathcal{MOQA}$ as data-labelings of a discrete partial order of size 3. We recall from Example 1.1 that this order is denoted by Δ_3. Note that there can be infinitely many data-labelings. Consider for instance the infinite sub-collection of lists of size 3, consisting of a particular selection of sorted lists, say:

$$(1, 2, 3), (2, 3, 4), (3, 4, 5), \ldots (n, n + 1, n + 2), \ldots$$

Despite the possibility of infinitely many data-labelings, in practice each data-labeling will occur in a unique state. Moreover, there will only be finitely many such states. For instance, each of the above data-labelings is sorted, and hence occurs in the unique *sorted state*. Similarly there are infinitely many reverse sorted lists, all of which are in the *reverse sorted state*. To represent all states a list of size 3 can be in, we fix three labels. Any three labels will do for this purpose, say the labels 1,2,3.

The six possible states for a list of size 3 can hence be represented by the 3! possible data-labelings using only the 3 fixed labels 1,2 and 3:

$$\{(1, 2, 3), (1, 3, 2), (2, 1, 3), (2, 3, 1), (3, 1, 2), (3, 2, 1)\}.$$

We illustrate this further with the data-labelings for the tree T_4 in Example 1.2. We recall that these data-labelings are heaps of size 4. If we use four distinct values, say 1,2,3,4, to represent the states then we have only three possible states as displayed.

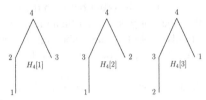

Returning to Example 1.2, note that the first heap, data-labeling F_1, is in state $H_4[1]$. The second and third heap, i.e. data-labelings F_2 and F_3, are in state $H_4[2]$.

Random structures to capture states

States are obtained by identifying data-labelings in case their relative order is the same. This can be formally captured by the notion of a labeling-isomorphism.

Definition 1.3. Consider two partial orders $(X_1, \sqsubseteq_1)$ and $(X_2, \sqsubseteq_2)$.

A function $\Psi \colon X_1 \to X_2$ is *increasing* if $\forall x, y \in X_1.\, x \sqsubseteq_1 y \Rightarrow \Psi(x) \sqsubseteq_2 \Psi(y)$. Consider data-labelings $F_1 \in \mathcal{D}_{\mathcal{L}_1^*}(X_1, \sqsubseteq_1)$ and $F_2 \in \mathcal{D}_{\mathcal{L}_2^*}(X_2, \sqsubseteq_2)$. Let $\leq_1$ and $\leq_2$ represent the linear orders on the label sets $\mathcal{L}_1^*$ and $\mathcal{L}_2^*$ respectively.

Data-labelings $F_1 \colon X_1 \to \mathcal{L}_1^*$ and $F_2 \colon X_2 \to \mathcal{L}_2^*$ are *labeling-isomorphic* iff

1. the underlying orders are isomorphic; there exists an increasing bijection Ψ from X_1 to X_2 which has an increasing inverse.
2. the bijection Ψ respects the ordering on labels, i.e.

$$(*) \quad \forall x, y \in X_1.\, F_1(x) \leq_1 F_1(y) \Leftrightarrow F_2(\Psi(x)) \leq_2 F_2(\Psi(y)).$$

In case F_1 and F_2 are labeling-isomorphic, we denote this by $F_1 \approx F_2$.

To simplify the presentation, we assume that we only consider data-labelings over a single data structure, i.e. over a single partial order. We revisit the case of multiple data structures in Section 1.4.2.

In case the finite partial orders $(X_1, \sqsubseteq_1)$ and $(X_2, \sqsubseteq_2)$ coincide, it suffices to consider the bijection in the definition of labeling-isomorphic to be the identity function, while $(*)$ reduces to:

$$(**) \quad \forall x, y \in X_1.\, F_1(x) \leq_1 F_1(y) \Leftrightarrow F_2(x) \leq_2 F_2(y).$$

To distinguish this case from the general one, we define the following equivalence relation on data-labelings $F_1 \in \mathcal{D}_{\mathcal{L}_1^*}(X_1, \sqsubseteq_1)$ and $F_2 \in \mathcal{D}_{\mathcal{L}_2^*}(X_2, \sqsubseteq_2)$:

$$F_1 \approx^* F_2 \Leftrightarrow (X_1, \sqsubseteq_1) \text{ and } (X_2, \sqsubseteq_2) \text{ coincide and } (**) \text{ holds.}$$

The collection of states over a single data structure can be captured via the notion of a random structure.

Definition 1.4. A random structure $\mathcal{R}(X, \sqsubseteq)$ for a given set of data-labelings, say $\mathcal{D}_{\mathcal{L}^*}(X, \sqsubseteq)$, is defined to be the quotient of this set by the labeling-equivalence relation $\approx$, i.e.

$$\mathcal{R}(X, \sqsubseteq) = \mathcal{D}_{\mathcal{L}^*}(X, \sqsubseteq)/\approx.$$

Remark 1.1. Representatives of the equivalence classes (i.e. "states") can be picked by fixing a fixed set of labels $\mathcal{L} \subseteq \mathcal{L}^*$ with same cardinality as the finite partial order $(X, \sqsubseteq)$. Any such choice of labels $\mathcal{L}$ will do. Representatives, i.e. states, are then obtained by considering the collection of data-labelings which only have pairwise-distinct labels from the selected subset of labels[5]. We will continue to work in the following with the collection of representatives (states) as opposed to the collection of equivalence classes, where we denote this collection of representatives chosen w.r.t to a set of labels $\mathcal{L}$ by $R_{\mathcal{L}}(X, \sqsubseteq)$. We will refer to this collection, with some abuse of terminology, as a random structure.

Random structures capture the states over a given data structure and represent the fact that each data-labeling is assumed to occur with equal probability in any of the states of the random structure.

In summary:

In $\mathcal{MOQA}$, the data-labelings of a given data structure occur in finitely many states. Each data-labeling will occur in one of these finitely many unique states at any given time. Moreover, data-labelings have equal chance to occur in one of these states. The finite collection of data states is referred to as a random structure.

For data structures, such as lists and heaps, we use the following notation, where we work modulo identification up to labeling-isomorphic copies: $\mathcal{A}_n$ denotes the set of $n!$ non-isomorphic lists of size n with pairwise distinct elements, $\mathcal{H}_n$ denotes the set of non-isomorphic heaps of size n with pairwise distinct elements. Also, we let $\mathcal{S}_n$ denote the set consisting of the single sorted list of size n.

We discuss probability distributions in more detail below.

---

[5] Labelings of a partial order using labels from finite linearly ordered set of same cardinality as the partial order correspond to the well-known mathematical notion of *linear extensions* of a partial order. In Computer Science, this notion is also referred to as a *topological sort*.

1.4 Tracking Distributions

In $\mathcal{MOQA}$, we will make the implicit assumption that $\mathcal{MOQA}$ data are produced from random list inputs via $\mathcal{MOQA}$ operations. I.e. each data-labeling is assumed to be priorly constructed via $\mathcal{MOQA}$ operations from a random input list.

The $\mathcal{MOQA}$ operations however will in general *not* preserve the uniform distribution, but will, as discussed in Section 1.4.2, lead to a more general type of distribution.

In the context of $\mathcal{MOQA}$, we will typically work under one of following two assumptions on the random input lists from which other data are generated. In the first case, based on a prior analysis of input data, the input data can be considered to be random, i.e. of uniform distribution. In the second case, where there is no guarantee of random inputs, data are randomized prior to processing, reducing the analysis to the first case.

At this stage we briefly revisit the issue of repeated labels, before continuing with a discussion of the two types of distributions.

Though repeated labels are allowed in $\mathcal{MOQA}$, for the purpose of the time analysis labels can be assumed to be distinct. This is due to the following approach.

Consider the case of random input lists, produced by case 2) above, i.e. via randomization. In that case, for each list of size n, say with elements $x_1, \ldots, x_n$, a data-labeling which assigns the labels $a_1, \ldots, a_n$ (possibly with repetitions) to these elements, is transformed to a new data-labeling, determined by the application of a random permutation σ applied to $a_1, \ldots, a_n$. I.e. the new values assigned to $x_1, \ldots, x_n$ are $a_{\sigma(1)}, \ldots, a_{\sigma(n)}$. In subsequent processing, when a comparison is made between two identical labels, say $a_{\sigma(i)}$ and $a_{\sigma(j)}$, a tie-breaker can be applied as follows. If $a_{\sigma(i)} = a_k$ and $a_{\sigma(j)} = a_l$, where $a_k = a_l$, then the comparison between $a_{\sigma(i)}$ and $a_{\sigma(j)}$ is decided based on the comparison between the indices k and l. This implies that the list inputs, following randomization, can be viewed as copies of the random lists of same size, *which have pairwise distinct labels.*

In case 1), the input lists (with repeated labels) are random from the start and a similar method can be applied, where tie-breaker indices are randomly assigned to all elements of the list. The random assignment is applied to all elements of the list (as in case 2) above) as opposed to only the identical ones, since pre-processing to identify identical labels would involve e.g. a sorting algorithm which would drastically increase the computation time.

1.4.1 The Uniform Distribution

Static analysis techniques for average-case analysis have focused on random data to provide information on "typical", i.e. average running time. This is for instance the case for sorting algorithms such as Quicksort, for which the overall performance on average, with respect to the uniform distribution on input lists, is determined to be optimal. The performance will of course depend on the actual collection of inputs provided for a particular application. The performance under the assumption of uniform data distributions is used as an indicator of the typical time the algorithm will take on arbitrary data. The analysis under the assumption of uniform input data distribution is of course also reasonable in the context of randomized input data.

The assumption of random data amounts to considering inputs equally likely to occur in any of a given number of finite states. Though our method transcends this assumption through the use of "random bags", we note at this stage that random data can be concisely captured via the notion of a *random structure*. The intuition behind a random structure is that it determines a *uniform distribution*.

Consider for instance the random structure over Δ_3 corresponding to Example 1.1:

$$R(\Delta_3) = \{(1,2,3),(1,3,2),(2,1,3),(2,3,1),(3,1,2),(3,2,1)\}.$$

The random structure $R(\Delta_3)$ represents the fact that all data-labelings over Δ_3 are assumed to be equally likely to occur, i.e. each list of size 3 has equal probability of $\frac{1}{6}$ to occur in each of these 6 states. In other words, the distribution is uniform.

Another example of a random structure is the collection of the three states for the tree partial order discussed in Example 1.2, i.e.

$$R(T_4) = \{H_4[1], H_4[2], H_4[3]\}.$$

All data-labelings (heaps) of size 4 are equally likely to occur, with probability $\frac{1}{3}$, in one of these three states.

Finally, we discuss the extreme case of the "random" structure over the linear partial order of size 3. This linear partial order is denoted by S_3, where "S" is used for "Sorted". This random structure only has one possible state. It is "random" in the sense that it contains *all* states allowed by the partial order. Its unique state is the sorted list of size 3, which for the label collection $\{1,2,3\}$ yields:

$$R(S_3) = \{(1,2,3)\}.$$

All data-labelings for the linear partial order are equally likely, with probability 1, to occur in the single sorted state.

1.4.2 S-Distributions

In practice of course there may be several data structures corresponding to a given collection of inputs. To represent this, the notion of a random bag[6] is introduced. A *random bag* represents the data structures involved as well as the distribution of the data-labelings via the relative distribution of the random structures in the random bag.

---

[6] The concept of a bag (also called multi-set) is recalled in Chapter 2.

Definition 1.5. A *random bag* consists of finitely many random structures, say R_1, ..., R_n, each of which has a multiplicity. A multiplicity K_i is a natural number indicating the frequency with which data states occur for a particular random structure R_i, relative to the other random structures. This enables a representation of distributions via a random bag $\{(R_1, K_1), \ldots, (R_n, K_n)\}$. A *strict random bag* $\{(R_1, K_1), \ldots, (R_n, K_n)\}$ is a random bag in which all data structures (i.e. partial orders) are distinct.

Note that for a strict random bag, a data-labeling F has the following probability to be in one of the states of the random structure R_i:

$$Prob[F \in R_i] = \frac{K_i|R_i|}{\sum_{i=1}^{n} K_i|R_i|} = \frac{K_i|R_i|}{|R|},$$

where $F \in R_i$ indicates that the data-labeling F has a state belonging to R_i.

We denote this probability in the following by $Prob_i$.

In case the random structures in the random bag are not distinct, a similar formula can be obtained where one groups identical random structures together and sums up their multiplicities.

Note that the above distribution is more general than the uniform one, since the probability for the uniform case, per data-labeling F, would be $\frac{1}{|R|}$. We refer to such distributions in the following as *S-distributions* and the associated probability as the *S-probability*.

A random bag captures the above concepts in a concise way. The diagram below illustrates the S-distribution corresponding to the random bag

$$\{(R_1, 2), (R_2, 1), (R_3, 5), (R_4, 3)\}.$$

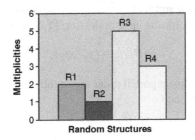

1.5 Random Bag Preservation

We introduce the central notion of random bag preservation, which implies the capacity for the tracking of S-distributions during the computations. Though the study of randomness preservation was pioneered earlier in the literature [Knu77], the formalization of the notion of random bag preservation is new.

The reference to "randomness" preservation may lead one to believe that the aim is to preserve "chaos". Quite to the contrary, the aim is to preserve a specific distribution of the original inputs and hence to impose a very particular structure on the outcomes of each computational step. As opposed to being *chaotic*, the type of randomness preservation which we will formalize is very much *controlled*, and aimed at preserving and tracking S-distributions.

Initially, we will simply view $\mathcal{MOQA}$ operations as transforming data-labelings to new data-labelings. The collection of all possible data-labelings is defined in the following.

Definition 1.6. We use the following notation: $\mathcal{U}$, referred to as the *universe*, is a countable list of variables, say $\mathcal{U} = \{x_n \mid n \in \mathcal{N}\}$. These variables are referred to as *universal variables*. We denote the set of all finite partial orders over $\mathcal{U}$ by

$$\mathcal{PO}_{fin}(\mathcal{U}) = \{(X, \sqsubseteq) \mid X \subseteq \mathcal{U} \text{ and } (X, \sqsubseteq) \text{ is a finite partial order.}\}.$$

The set of all data-labelings over partial orders from $\mathcal{PO}_{fin}(\mathcal{U})$ is denoted by $\mathcal{F}$, i.e.:

$$\mathcal{F} = \{F \mid F \colon (X, \sqsubseteq) \to \mathcal{L}^*, (X, \sqsubseteq) \in \mathcal{PO}_{fin}(\mathcal{U}) \text{ and } F \text{ is a data-labeling}\}.$$

We make the following assumption on data-labelings:

Two data-labelings F_1 and F_2 are distinct in case they differ when interpreted as pairs $(F_1, (X_1, \sqsubseteq_1))$ and $(F_2, (X_2, \sqsubseteq_2))$, for which the underlying order is explicitly taken into account. I.e. two data-labelings differ in case

1) their underlying partial orders are distinct (i.e. set or binary order differ), or
2) in case the underlying partial orders are identical to a partial order $(X, \sqsubseteq)$ and $\exists x \in X.\, F(x) \neq G(x)$.

We call the partial order $(X_2, \sqsubseteq_2)$ a refinement of the partial order $(X_1, \sqsubseteq_1)$ in case $X_2 \subseteq X_1$ and $\forall x, y \in X_2.\, x \sqsubseteq_1 y \Rightarrow x \sqsubseteq_2 y$. In other words a new partial order refines a first one, in case its underlying set is included in the underlying set of the first one and all order relations of the first partial order are still satisfied in the new partial order.

$\mathcal{MOQA}$ computations will involve operations which systematically refine orders under consideration. For instance, a sorting algorithm will gradually introduce more order and hence will refine the ordering under consideration. Other operations may simply leave the original order intact, which is interpreted as a trivial refinement.

Next, we introduce the notion of a refining function and of a labeling-invariant function. The concept of a labeling-invariant function reflects the fact that comparison-based algorithms involve operations which behave in exactly the same way on data-labelings for which the relative order between the labels is identical.

Definition 1.7. Consider a collection of data-labelings $\mathcal{D}_{\mathcal{L}^*}(X, \sqsubseteq)$.
A function $\Psi \colon \mathcal{D}_{\mathcal{L}^*}(X, \sqsubseteq) \to \mathcal{F}$ is a *refining function* in case there exist finitely many partial orders $(X_1, \sqsubseteq_1), \ldots, (X_n, \sqsubseteq_n)$, each of which refines the partial order $(X, \sqsubseteq)$, such that $\Psi \colon \mathcal{D}_{\mathcal{L}^*}(X, \sqsubseteq) \to \mathcal{D}_{\mathcal{L}^*}(X_1, \sqsubseteq_1) \cup \ldots \cup \mathcal{D}_{\mathcal{L}^*}(X_n, \sqsubseteq_n)$.

A function $\Psi \colon \mathcal{D}_{\mathcal{L}^*}^*(X, \sqsubseteq) \to \mathcal{D}_{\mathcal{L}^*}(X_1, \sqsubseteq_1) \cup \ldots \cup \mathcal{D}_{\mathcal{L}^*}(X_n, \sqsubseteq_n)$ is *labeling-invariant* iff

$$\forall F_1, F_2 \in \mathcal{D}_{\mathcal{L}^*}(X, \sqsubseteq). \, F_1 \approx F_2 \Rightarrow \Psi(F_1) \approx^* \Psi(F_2).$$

Definition 1.8. A function $\Psi \colon \mathcal{D}_{\mathcal{L}^*}(X, \sqsubseteq) \to \mathcal{F}$ is *random structure preserving* (RS-preserving) iff there exist finitely many partial orders $(X_1, \sqsubseteq_1), \ldots, (X_n, \sqsubseteq_n)$ of $(X, \sqsubseteq)$ such that $\Psi \colon \mathcal{D}_{\mathcal{L}}(X, \sqsubseteq) \to \mathcal{D}_{\mathcal{L}}(X_1, \sqsubseteq_1) \cup \ldots \cup \mathcal{D}_{\mathcal{L}}(X_n, \sqsubseteq_n)$ and the following holds:

1. Ψ is refining.
2. Ψ is labeling-invariant.
3. If the input data-labelings, after identification up to labeling-isomorphism form a random structure $R = \mathcal{R}_{\mathcal{L}}(X, \sqsubseteq)$, where $\mathcal{L} \subseteq \mathcal{L}^*$ and $|\mathcal{L}| = |X|$, then the *bag* of data-labelings produced from R by application of Ψ yields, after identification up to labeling-isomorphism, a random bag R' of the form

$$R' = \{(\mathcal{R}_{\mathcal{L}_1}(X_1, \sqsubseteq_1), K_1), \ldots, (\mathcal{R}_{\mathcal{L}_n}(X_n, \sqsubseteq_n), K_n)\},$$

where $\forall i \in \{1, \ldots, n\}. \, \mathcal{L}_i \subseteq \mathcal{L}^*$ and $|\mathcal{L}_i| = |X_i|$.

If Ψ is random structure preserving as above, then we denote this by:

$$\Psi \colon R \longmapsto R'.$$

Remark 1.2. Note that condition 3) of Definition 1.8 implies that the random bag R' is strict, which suffices for our present purposes. In chapter 4 this condition will be relaxed to general random bags.

Lemma 1.1. *If* $\Psi \colon \mathcal{D}_{\mathcal{L}}(X, \sqsubseteq) \to \mathcal{D}_{\mathcal{L}}(X_1, \sqsubseteq_1) \cup \ldots \cup \mathcal{D}_{\mathcal{L}}(X_n, \sqsubseteq_n)$ *and* $\Psi \colon R \longmapsto R'$ *then the bag consisting of the images of* Ψ *over the elements of* $\mathcal{D}_{\mathcal{L}}(X, \sqsubseteq)$ *yields, after identification up to labeling-isomorphism, the random bag* R'.

Proof. Note that $\mathcal{D}_{\mathcal{L}}(X, \sqsubseteq) = \cup \mathcal{D}_{\mathcal{L}'}(X, \sqsubseteq)$, where this disjoint union ranges over the subsets $\mathcal{L}'$ of $\mathcal{L}$ which have the same cardinality as $|X|$. The result follows from the fact that Ψ is labeling-invariant and $\Psi \colon R \longmapsto R'$.

Remark 1.3. Random structure preserving functions can be defined over several data structures as opposed to over a single data structure, simply by requiring the function to be random structure preserving over each data structure. Hence in practice we will refer to this more general interpretation as *random bag preserving* (*RB-preserving*) functions Ψ which transform a random *bag* R into a random bag R', denoted by $\Psi: R \longmapsto R'$.

For our present purposes it will suffice to work with a sufficient condition which ensures random bag preservation as outlined in Section 1.7.

It is important to point out that random bag preservation does not necessarily hold in practice. The reader may safely omit the following counter example on first reading and revisit at a later stage. It is included to illustrate the necessity of guaranteeing random bag preservation.

1.6 The Necessity of Guaranteeing Random Bag Preservation

To illustrate the need of guaranteeing random bag preservation, we consider the example of traditional Heapsort, which involves a non-randomness preserving "selection" part. The reader may, prior to reading this section, benefit from a brief look at the traditional Heapsort algorithm discussed in [AHU87, Knu73] or from the definition of this algorithm in Chapter 2. Heapsort consists of a Heapify phase and a Selection phase. The Heapify phase forms a heap out of any given list as specified in [Knu73]. The Selection phase essentially amounts to a "delete"-style operation, even though elements are not actually removed, only ignored during the computation. The Selection phase proceeds as follows: it swaps a label at a specific leaf of the heap with the root label. It subsequently ignores the new leaf label, which is the maximum label, in the remainder of the program execution. The rest of the tree may no longer form a heap due to the swap operation. Hence Heapify is called again to create a heap out of the remaining tree and the Selection process is repeated over the newly created heap.

Counter-Example 1.1 (Heapsort)
Consider lists of size 4 where we assume that list elements are pairwise distinct. After the Heapify part, viewed over all twenty-four input states of size 4, a total of 3 non-label-isomorphic heap states are created which arise with equal probability of $\frac{1}{3}$. We display these heaps of size 4, which we denote, as in the states obtained for Example 1.2, by $H_4[1]$, $H_4[2]$ and $H_4[3]$, for labels $1, 2, 3, 4$:

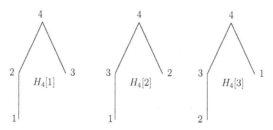

However, this uniform distribution is violated by the Selection phase, which swaps the root label, i.e. the maximum label, with the left-most leaf label. After this phase, the algorithm focuses on the newly created heaps of size 3, obtained by ignoring the left-most leaf. Since the resulting heaps are of size 3, consisting of a root and two leafs, there are 2 possible states. We display these states for labels $1, 2, 3$ in the figure below, where the state displayed first is referred to as $H_3[1]$ and the state displayed below is referred to as $H_3[2]$. It is clearly impossible that these 2 states are created from the 3 states of size 4 with equal probability. Hence the random structure consisting of the two states, which represents uniform distribution, is not an adequate representation of the true distribution. With the notion of random structure at our disposal, we remark that the states produced during this phase of the computation do not correspond to the two states of the underlying partial order. The two necessary states are produced, but an extra copy of one of these states is also produced. Hence the resulting bag of states does not form a random structure, nor of course a random bag. In fact, one can verify that $H_4[1]$ and $H_4[3]$ both are transformed to $H_3[2]$, while $H_4[2]$ is transformed to $H_3[1]$ during the execution of Heapsort, as displayed in the picture below.

$$H_4[2] \longrightarrow \quad \underset{1 \qquad 2}{\overset{3}{\bigwedge}}$$

$$H_3[1]$$

$$\begin{aligned} H_4[1] &\longrightarrow \\ H_4[3] &\longrightarrow \end{aligned} \quad \underset{2 \qquad 1}{\overset{3}{\bigwedge}}$$

$$H_3[2]$$

The argument to show that Heapsort does not preserve the uniform distribution of its data is based on an example discussed in [Ede96], which makes an attempt to solve the open problem of designing a "randomness preserving" version of Heapsort. Edelkamp observes in this context that: "*Diese Betrachtung hat eine exakte average-case Analyse von allen Heapsort-Varianten bis dato unmöglich gemacht*".[7]

To clarify the problem further, and minimizing formality, we remark that in order to obtain a compositional derivation of the average-time of Heapsort for arbitrary size n, one needs in particular to express this time for the case of size 4 as:

(1) the average-time over all 4! list states of size 4
    (used by the Heapify procedure to create the heaps of size 4) +

---

[7] "This fact (i.e. the non-preservation of the uniform distribution for size 4) has made an exact average-case analysis of all Heapsort-variants impossible to date." [Ede96] did not resolve the problem of producing a randomness preserving version of Heapsort. Such a version, called Percolating Heapsort, has been obtained in [SHB04].

(2) the average-time over the 3 heap states of size 4
   (used by the first call to the Selection phase) +
(3) the average time over the 2 hat-shaped heap states of size 3
   (used by an iterated call to the Heapify and Selection phase).

It is part (3) which can not be used in practice to compute the average-time of the iterated call to the Heapify and Selection phase. In the standard average-case time approach of [Knu73], the Selection phase operates on heaps and its average-case time needs to be computed over the possibly states of the heaps of a given size, where heaps are assumed to occur equally likely in any of the two given states.

We recall that the the two states produced for the hat-shaped partial order are *not* equally distributed. The first state $H_3[1]$ occurs once, while the second state $H_3[2]$ occurs twice, indicating that heaps are twice more likely to occur in the second state than in the first. Hence we can no longer express the average-time of the Selection phase in terms of the states of the heaps under consideration and one effectively loses the capacity to track the distribution of the data in question.

This prevents the generation of a recurrence equation (in terms of size) which expresses the average-case time. It is clear that the average-case analysis of Heapsort is notoriously hard due to the fact that Heapsort's Selection process does not preserve randomness (cf. [Knu73], [SS93], [LV93] and [Ede96]) and similar problems arise for deletions and insertions in binary search trees. The lack of "randomness preservation" is also cited in [FSZ91] as preventing an automated average-case analysis of Heapsort. As pointed out by Knuth in [Knu73], regarding the analysis of Heapsort: "But the selection phase is another story, which yet remains to be written!" The optimality of Heapsort's average comparison time was demonstrated relatively recently by Schaffer and Sedgewick [SS93] via an argument by contradiction (cf. also [LV93]). This does not lend itself for static average-case analysis. The exact average comparison time for the (selection phase of this) algorithm and for any of its current variants, remained unknown [Ede96]. The problematic nature of determining Heapsort's average-case time has also been pointed out in [FSZ91]. In [SHB04] a new variant of Heapsort is presented, Percolating Heapsort, which *does* preserve randomness. This new algorithm allows for an elegant and straightforward analysis of its exact average-case time; which constitutes a radical simplification, in comparison with prior average-case analysis methods for Heapsort and its variants, as discussed in Chapter 9.

We remark that the analysis of Percolating Heapsort is achieved via a backward analysis a la Knuth [Knu73], which is based on a combination of a compositionality argument with a constant-time argument as presented in Chapter 9, Section 9.4. This still does not give a fully automated derivation of the algorithm's average-case time, but does resolve the open problem on the exact average-case analysis. Other algorithms will be considered in Chapter 8, such as Treapsort, for which a fully-automated derivation is achievable.

1.7 A Sufficient Condition for Random Bag Preservation

We now return to a sufficient condition for random bag preservation and an illustration of such an operation via the traditional *Split* operation.

We formulate the notion of a separative function.

Definition 1.9. Consider a collection of data-labelings $\mathcal{D}_{\mathcal{L}^*}(X, \sqsubseteq)$ and a function $\Psi: \mathcal{D}_{\mathcal{L}^*}(X, \sqsubseteq) \to \mathcal{F}$. Then Ψ is *separative* iff there exist finitely many partial orders $(X_1, \sqsubseteq_1), \ldots, (X_n, \sqsubseteq_n)$ such that $\Psi: \mathcal{D}_{\mathcal{L}^*}(X, \sqsubseteq) \to \mathcal{D}_{\mathcal{L}^*}(X_1, \sqsubseteq_1) \cup \ldots \cup \mathcal{D}_{\mathcal{L}^*}(X_n, \sqsubseteq_n)$ and:

1. Ψ is refining.
2. Ψ is labeling-invariant.
3. $\Psi \upharpoonright \mathcal{R}_{\mathcal{L}}(X, \sqsubseteq): \mathcal{R}_{\mathcal{L}}(X, \sqsubseteq) \to \mathcal{R}_{\mathcal{L}_1}(X_1, \sqsubseteq_1) \cup \ldots \cup \mathcal{R}_{\mathcal{L}_n}(X_n, \sqsubseteq_n)$ is a bijection.

Remark 1.4. Separative functions can be defined over several data structures as opposed to over a single data structure, simply by requiring the function to be separative over each data structure.

Finally, we remark that if a function Ψ is separative over $\mathcal{D}_{\mathcal{L}^*}(X, \sqsubseteq)$, then Ψ is guaranteed to give rise to a bag of output data-labelings which correspond to a finite collection of random structures $R(X_1, \sqsubseteq_1), \ldots, R_n(X, \sqsubseteq_n)$. This determines a strict random bag $\{(R(X_1, \sqsubseteq_1), 1) \ldots ((R_n(X, \sqsubseteq_n), 1)\}$, in which each random structure has multiplicity one. In the present context, for random bag preserving functions, we perform an extra identification, i.e. the output random bag is subjected to identification up to labeling-isomorphism, which includes an identification up to *order*-isomorphism.

Hence, for separative functions, the random bag which has multiplicities constant one, gives rise to a random bag $\{(R(X_{i_1}, \sqsubseteq_{i_1}), K_1) \ldots ((R_{i_k}(X, \sqsubseteq_{i_k}), K_k)\}$, where of course $\sum_{j=1}^{k} K_{i_j} = n$ and where multiplicities are not necessarily one.

Hence we have the following result.

Proposition 1.1. *Separative functions are random bag preserving.*

We illustrate this via the *Split* example below. Note that all operations are stored in a $\mathcal{MOQA}$ library, joint with information on the data structures (i.e. partial orders) they produce (for arbitrary size n) as well as with the multiplicities in question, which for each operation have been determined in terms of n in advance. This information is then used by Distri-Track to extract the average-case information statically.

Note that not all random bag preserving functions are separative. For instance the product operation as defined in Chapter 5 is RB-preserving, yet the function is only "locally" one-to-one.

We give sufficient conditions for random bag preserving functions to be separative.

Proposition 1.2. *A random bag preserving function* Ψ *with domain* $\mathcal{D}_{\mathcal{L}}(X, \sqsubseteq)$ *and corresponding random structure* R *is separative in case the bag of images of* Ψ *over* R *is a set. Equivalently, a random bag preserving function is separative in case* $\Psi \upharpoonright R$ *is a bijection.*

1.7.1 Split: *an Illustration of Random Bag Preservation*

S-distributions arise naturally, even if one starts with uniformly distributed data at the outset. One well-known operation which illustrates this effect is the Split operation used in algorithms such as Quicksort and Quickselect.

Rather than developing this in general, i.e. for lists of arbitrary size n, we first show that Split is random bag preserving for lists of size 3 and 4. The general case is treated in Section 1.7.2. We consider a simple version of the Split operation. Other versions of *Split*, such as those using two pointers starting at beginning and end of a list [AHU87], result in a similar random bag. We use the simpler version to reduce the technicalities. The pivot for *Split* is chosen to be the first element of the list. This particular choice is irrelevant, since other choices will result in similar random bags with minor technical modifications.

Split proceeds on a list of size n by comparing, in left to right order and starting at the second element, each label of the i-th element, $i \in \{2, \ldots, n\}$, with the pivot label. In case the label of the i-th element is greater than the pivot label, this element and its label is placed above the pivot. Otherwise it is placed below the pivot.

Example 1.3. We illustrate the effect of executing *Split* on lists of size 3 in the illustration at the top of the following page.

It is clear from this illustration that when *Split* is executed on the random structure over the discrete partial order of size 3, i.e. $R(\Delta_3)$, where *Split* is executed over the $3! = 6$ random lists, the result is a random bag consisting of three new random structures. The first random structure is the random structure over the 3 element V-shaped partial order, denoted in the following by $\vee_3$. The second random structure and the third random structure are both the random structure over the linear order of size 3, denoted by S_3. Though the elements of the two linear orders displayed above differ, we will identify these orders in our analysis up to order isomorphism. This means that we have 2 copies of the random structure over S_3 in the random bag. Finally, we obtain the random structure over the 3 element wedge-shaped partial order, denoted by $\wedge_3$. In conclusion, *Split* transforms data-labelings over Δ_3 into a data-labeling over $\vee_3$, S_3 or $\wedge_3$. Moreover, it is clear from our example above that the inputs have 6 states corresponding to $R(\Delta_3)$, while the output data-labelings correspond exactly to the 6 states in the random bag $\{(R(\vee_3), 1), (R(S_3), 2), (R(\wedge_3), 1)\}$. We remark that the function corresponding to *Split* is labeling-invariant and refining. Moreover, this function is a bijection between the random structure Δ_3 and the set

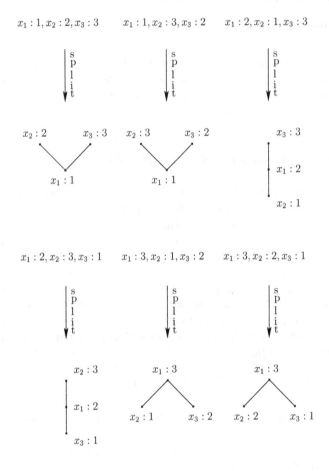

$R(\vee_3) \cup R(S_3) \cup R(S_3') \cup R(\wedge_3)$, where S_3 and S_3' denote the two distinct linear orders displayed in Example 1.3 above. Hence the *Split* operation is separative and thus determines a random bag preserving operation over the random structure $R(\Delta_3)$.

We remark at this stage that there is a clear visual nature to the partial orders associated with the random bag. Indeed, "star"-like objects are being created, with a center element, the pivot, and with in each case a collection of elements above the pivot and below the pivot.

For the case of $\vee_3$ there are two elements above the pivot and zero below the pivot. For the case of S_3 there is one element above the pivot and one element below the pivot. For the case of $\wedge_3$ there are zero elements above the pivot and 2 elements below. This can be generalized to n elements as follows. The partial order $P[i, j]$ over $i + j + 1$ elements is defined to be the order which has one central pivot element, i elements below the pivot and j elements above the pivot, as illustrated below.

The partial order $P[i, j]$

j elements

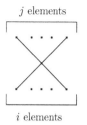

i elements

In general, the partial orders created by the *Split* operation, after identification up to order-isomorphism, are given by: $P[0, n-1], P[1, n-2], P[2, n-3], \ldots, P[n-3, 2], P[n-2, 1], P[n-1, 0]$ as displayed below.

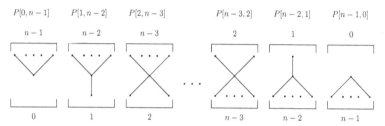

Hence for lists of size 3 it is clear that *Split* transforms the random structure $R(\Delta_3)$ into the random bag $\{(R[P[0, 2], 1), (R(P[1, 1]), 2), (R(P[2, 0], 1)\}$.

Example 1.4. We illustrate that a similar result arises when *Split* is executed on lists of size 4. We record the effect of executing *Split* on the $6! = 24$ states of size 4. First we remark that for the 6 states which have the pivot labeled with 1, *Split* will transform these 6 states exactly in to the 6 states of the partial order $P[0, 3]$ displayed below.

Secondly we remark that the 6 states which have the pivot labeled with 4, *Split* will transform these 6 states exactly in the 6 states of the partial order $P[3, 0]$ displayed below.

Hence it remains to look in the situation where the pivot is labeled with 2 or 3. The results for the pivot labeled with 2 are displayed below.

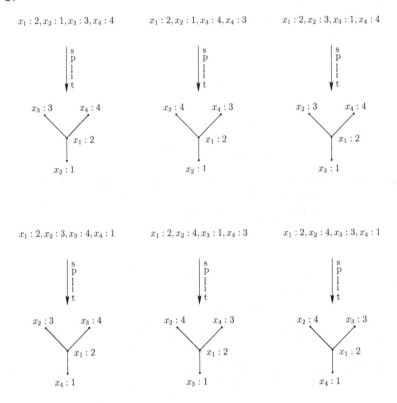

$x_1 : 2, x_2 : 1, x_3 : 3, x_4 : 4$ $x_1 : 2, x_2 : 1, x_3 : 4, x_4 : 3$ $x_1 : 2, x_2 : 3, x_3 : 1, x_4 : 4$

$x_1 : 2, x_2 : 3, x_3 : 4, x_4 : 1$ $x_1 : 2, x_2 : 4, x_3 : 1, x_4 : 3$ $x_1 : 2, x_2 : 4, x_3 : 3, x_4 : 1$

We remark that the first two states in the top row form a random structure. The same holds for the third state in the top row and the second state in the bottom row. Finally, the first and third state in the bottom row form again a random structure.

Clearly the partial orders of these three random structures are order-isomorphic. Hence we obtain three copies of the random structure over the partial order $P[1,2]$ displayed below.

The result for the pivot labeled with 3 are displayed below.

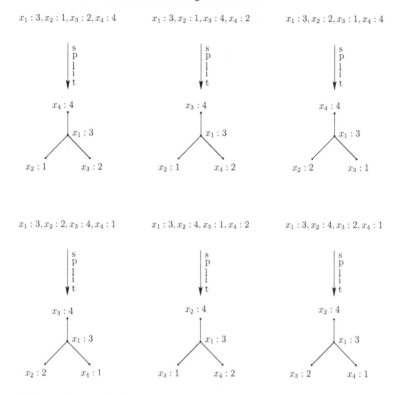

We remark that the first and the third state in the top row together with the underlying partial order form a random structure. The same holds for the second state in the top row and the first state in the bottom row. Finally, the second and third state in the bottom row form again a random structure.

Clearly the partial orders of these three random structures are order-isomorphic. Hence we obtain three copies of the random structure over the partial order $P[2,1]$ displayed below.

Hence *Split* transforms $R(L_4)$ in the random bag

$$\{(R(P[0,3]),1),(R(P[1,2]),3),(R(P[2,1]),3),(R(P[3,0]),1)\}.$$

Again, we remark that *Split* is a separative function from $R(L_4)$ to the random structures over the 8 different partial orders as displayed above.

The multiplicities for *Split* can be directly computed in terms of input size n as outlined below.

1.7.2 Split: *the General Case*

The random split of a discrete partial order

To determine the multiplicities one needs to simply remark that the general split operation, for input lists of size n, will produce, *after identification up to order isomorphism*, the partial orders $P[0, n-1], P[1, n-2], P[2, n-3], \ldots, P[n-3, 2], P[n-2, 1], P[n-1, 0]$.

Prior to identification up to order isomorphism, one can easily determine that the number of partial orders which are (non-identically) order isomorphic to $P[i, j]$, where $i, j \in \{0, 1, \ldots, n-1\}$ and $i + j = n - 1$, is $K_i = \binom{n-1}{i} = \binom{n-1}{j}$. For instance, consider Example 5. There are $\binom{3-1}{1} = 2$ copies of the (linear) partial order $P[1, 1]$.

Hence *Split* is a random bag preserving operation which maps the random structure $R(\Delta_n)$ to the random bag $\{(R(P[n-1, 0]), K_{n-1}), \ldots, (R(P[0, n-1], K_0)\}$. I.e. we have the following result.

Lemma 1.2. Split *determines a random bag preserving function, where*

$$Split: R(\Delta_n) \longmapsto \{(R(P[n-1, 0]), K_{n-1}), \ldots, (R(P[0, n-1]), K_0)\},$$

and where $K_i = \binom{n-1}{i}$ for $i \in \{0, \ldots, n-1\}$.

Remark 1.5. The Split operation is an example of an operation, which is *uniformly random bag preserving*, i.e. the cardinality of a random structure in the output random bag multiplied by its multiplicity is a constant. This notion will discussed in Chapter 4. For Split it is easy to verify that:

$$\forall i \in \{0, \ldots, n-1\}.K_i |R(P[i, n-1-i])| = (n-1)!$$

Indeed, note that $K_i |R(P[i, n-1-i])| = \binom{n-1}{i} i!(n-1-i)! = (n-1)!$

This information on the random bag produced by a Split operation will be used in Chapter 9 to derive the average-case time of Quicksort and Quickselect in a compositional way.

1.7.3 Tracking S-Distributions in $\mathcal{MOQA}$

In our programming language $\mathcal{MOQA}$ the tracking of distributions is achieved by keeping track of the finite partial orders[8] underlying the random structures (random bags), where each operation transforms a collection of partial orders (paired with their multiplicities) into a new collection of partial orders (paired with their multiplicities).

---

[8] Via a suitable representation.

Each operation is formally guaranteed to preserve random bags. As a result the partial orders and the multiplicities of the data can be tracked during the entire computation.

This approach means that we do not need to determine the resulting random bags by computing all output states in a computation from all possible input states. It suffices to identify the operation in question and our operation rules supply, from the given partial orders and multiplicities for input data, directly the new partial orders and multiplicities of the output data. This is feasible since $\mathcal{MOQA}$ operations are verified to be random bag preserving, where, for each such operation, a constructive definition is given of the transformation of the partial orders as well as formulas for computing the multiplicities.

Multiplicities are crucial since they enable the book-keeping of output copies during the computation in a modular way; which in turn is directly linked with the capacity to generate recurrence equations expressing the average-case number of basic operations in a compositional way. This last aspect is clarified via the Linear-Compositionality Theorem below. The static analysis tool *Distri-Track*, developed at CEOL, statically extracts the average number of basic operations from $\mathcal{MOQA}$ code, based on this result.

We outline the basic $\mathcal{MOQA}$ operations below.

1.8 $\mathcal{MOQA}$ Operations

1.8.1 An Overview of the Basic $\mathcal{MOQA}$ Operations

We discuss the main random bag preserving basic $\mathcal{MOQA}$ operations below to illustrate the nature of the language. The first two operations, the random product and the random delete, are core operations for creating and destroying data. All $\mathcal{MOQA}$ operations operate over data-labelings. Each of them can be shown to be random bag preserving.

The random product operation: $\otimes$
This operation can play the role of an insertion of a single element into a data structure, in case one of the data structures provided consists of a single element. This operation also plays a crucial role whenever data structures are merged into a larger whole.

Given two data-labelings, the binary product operation places the first data structure below a second, where all elements of the first order are strictly below all elements of the second. The operation proceeds as follows:

- create a new partial order consisting of the union of the elements of the original two orders,
- create all possible directed links from the maximal elements of the first order to the minimal elements of the second order,
- respect the new order by reorganizing labels via traditional Push-Downs and Push-Ups.

A unary version of this operation will be introduced, which, when carried out on two parts of the partial order of a single data-labeling, results in a new data-labeling.

The random delete operation: $\underline{Del}(k)$
This operation plays a crucial role in removing labels from a data-labeling.
    This unary operation removes a label from a data-labeling by:

• redefining it to be the smallest label present,
• pushing down the label to restore order,
• removing the label together with the minimal element to which it has been pushed-down.

The $\mathcal{MOQA}$ language supports other random bag preserving operations which constitute variants and generalizations of the random deletion. The operations also include the *random projection* operation *Proj(I)*, which permits acting locally on part of a data-labeling. In this context, an "isolation" property is verified on the suborder in question to ensure random bag preservation. Another basic $\mathcal{MOQA}$ operation, encountered earlier, is the *random split* operation *Split*. $\mathcal{MOQA}$ incorporates a number of other operations, such as *Top* and *Bot* to determine minimum and maximum labels, all of which are random bag preserving. Other random bag preserving basic operations could be added according to need.

All $\mathcal{MOQA}$ operations can be applied locally to a data structure as determined by the notion of an "isolated suborder". The timing tool *Distri-Track* statically expresses the average-case number of comparisons of $\mathcal{MOQA}$ programs in terms of the average-case number of comparisons of the basic operations, exploiting compositionality.

1.8.2 Conditionals, Loops, Recursion

The $\mathcal{MOQA}$ language is equipped with conditionals, for-loops and a restricted type of recursion (guaranteed to terminate), all of which have been purpose designed to ensure random bag preservation.

Remark 1.6. (Termination of $\mathcal{MOQA}$ programs)
Termination is a typical and necessary requirement in a static timing context due to the halting problem. As will be observed in chapter 7, all $\mathcal{MOQA}$ programs are guaranteed to terminate. Hence, unless stated to the contrary, all results obtained in the following chapters are derived under the assumption that the programs under consideration terminate on all inputs.

1.9 Compositionality

As outlined at the start of the introduction, one may easily be tempted to conclude that average-case time is automatically compositional. This stems from the fact that average-case time satisfies a simple type of compositionality, namely that of IO-compositionality as outlined below. We discuss this first type of compositionality and will return to it in more detail Chapter 3 in relation to various timing measures.

1.9.1 Average-Case Time is IO-Compositional

Theorem 1.2. *The average-time measure $\overline{T}$ is universal IO-compositional, i.e. the following equality holds for any programming language $\mathcal{PL}$ and for any two programs P_1, P_2 of $\mathcal{PL}$, where P_1 operates on an input bag $\mathcal{I}$ and produces the output bag $\mathcal{O}_{P_1}(\mathcal{I})$:*

$$\overline{T}_{P_1;P_2}(\mathcal{I}) = \overline{T}_{P_1}(\mathcal{I}) + \overline{T}_{P_2}(\mathcal{O}_{P_1}(\mathcal{I})).$$

As discussed in Section 1.1.3, it is crucial to have the capacity to track the data distributions in order to fully exploit compositionality, which is the topic of the following section. This will be further clarified in Chapter 3.

1.9.2 Linear-Compositionality Theorem

The Linear-Compositionality Theorem states two facts. First, the average time of the sequential composition of two random bag preserving programs can be expressed as the sum of the average times of the programs. Secondly, the average time of a random bag preserving program on a random bag is a linear combination of the average times over the random structures of the random bag. The linear coefficients correspond to the probabilities involved. For completeness, we include the technical definition and the theorem.

Definition 1.10. A *random bag preserving program* P is a program for which the collection of input data-labelings, after identification up to labeling-isomorphism, forms a random bag. Moreover, the input-output function of the program, denoted by $[\![P]\!]$, is random bag preserving over the input random bag.

Theorem 1.3. (Linear-Compositionality):

1. Consider a random bag preserving program P such that $[\![P]\!] : R \to R'$. Then:

$$\overline{T}_{P;Q}(R) = \overline{T}_P(R) + \overline{T}_Q(R').$$

2. Consider a random bag $R = \{(\vec{R}_p, \vec{K}_p)\}$; then

$$a)\ \overline{T}_P(R) = \sum_{i=1}^{i=p} Prob_i \times \overline{T}_P(R_i),$$

where $Prob_i = Prob[F \in R_i]$ is the S-probability.

For the particular case where $R = \{(R_1, K_1)\}$, the previous equality reduces to:

$$b)\ \overline{T}_P(R) = \overline{T}_P(R_1).$$

The systematic application of this result on the sequential parts of $\mathcal{MOQA}$ code enables one to express the *exact* average-case number of comparisons of the computation over the original random bag in terms of the average-case number of comparisons of more basic parts of the code over new random bags. Ultimately this enables an expression of the average-case time of the code in terms of a linear combination of the average-case times of the basic operations involved in the code. This in turn can give rise to a recurrence in terms input size, when operating over inductive types. Note that such sequential parts are determined not only by sequential composition, but occur of course due to for-loops and (terminating) recursion. We will discuss conditionals at a later stage.

Note that this result enables a determination of the exact average-case time as opposed to only asymptotic information.

The $\mathcal{MOQA}$ approach allows one to statically extract recurrence equations for the average-case time from $\mathcal{MOQA}$ source code in a modular fashion, via the timing tool *Distri-Track* [Hic07]. After this generation, standard approaches can be followed to either completely solve the recurrence equation through generating functions and a mathematical software package such as Maple or Mathematica, or to obtain information on the ACET for inputs within a given size bound through computing the recurrence via dynamic programming in a fast and effective way. Of course one can also derive asymptotic time information from the recurrence equations.

1.10 Related work and advantages of $\mathcal{MOQA}$

We provide a brief non-exhaustive overview of various approaches to automated average-case analysis and a discussion of randomness preservation in the literature.

Automated Average-Case Analysis has undergone active research. The programming language LUO, developed by Flajolet [FSZ91, FV90], enables the automatic derivation of the average-case complexity of large classes of algorithms by establishing a link between recurrence equations and singularities of associated complex functions. The approach involves generating functions as discussed in [GKP94]. The average-case time is obtained through the use of the mathematical software package Maple which has been partly incorporated in the LUO code. A related and generalized approach involves the use of attribute grammars [Mis03]. Yet another type of approach uses a "chromatic plumbing" metaphor to mimic the execution of a program expressed as a flowchart [Ram96, HC88].

Our work, though related in the aim to automate average-case time analysis, differs from prior approaches in that we achieve compositionality for the average time measure based on the notion of random bag preservation, where distributions are tracked throughout the computations.

The first attempt at a study of randomness preservation was made by Knuth. The papers [Knu77, JK78] on Knott's paradox, that is the loss of randomness preservation when deleting and reinserting an element of a random binary search tree, were forerunners of [MR98] and raised the question of the analysis of randomness preservation. Another paper which brings up the notion of randomness conservation is [Lev84], which treats the issue in the non-constructive context of Kolmogorov complexity.

Despite the usefulness of randomness preservation, which allows one to determine the average-case time analysis in a straightforward linear-compositional way, no systematic study is available of randomness preservation in a (constructive) programming language context.

Finally, we remark that randomized algorithms [MR95] regard the design of algorithms that make probabilistic selections on inputs. Hence the expectation depends only on the random choices made by the algorithm and not on any assumptions about the distribution of the input. The running time becomes a random variable and the analysis involves an understanding of the distribution of this random variable. In contrast, we will focus on algorithms that preserve a random bag representation of the data and their distribution.

The $\mathcal{MOQA}$ language incorporates random bag preserving versions of standard data structuring operations, which enables the natural incorporation of standard sorting and searching algorithms. The $\mathcal{MOQA}$ language, in contrast with prior approaches, such as LUO, provides a deletion operation. The lack of such operations in the past complicated the analysis of algorithms such as Heapsort [SHB04]. As pointed out in [Ede96], the exact average-case time of all Heapsort variants is unknown to date. This is directly linked to the fact that standard Heapsort [AHU87] does not "preserve randomness". [SHB04] reports on a new version of Heapsort, Percolating Heapsort, which is faster (both in average number of comparisons and in "real-time" as measured by a Java profiler) than all standard Heapsort variants. The algorithm has been directly designed based on the $\mathcal{MOQA}$ delete operation.

Though the full automation of the Analysis of Heapsort remains elusive, for reasons discussed in Chapters 9, the $\mathcal{MOQA}$ program Percolating Heapsort, does allow for an exact average-case analysis "by hand" as provided in Chapter 9. This solves the long standing open problem on the determination of the exact average-case of Heapsort variants [Knu73, Ede96]. The argument is based on the randomness preservation of Percolating Heapsort, which enables a backwards analysis à la Knuth. An alternative $\mathcal{MOQA}$ sorting algorithm Treapsort, based on manipulation of Heap Ordered Trees via the $\mathcal{MOQA}$ deletion, is also presented in this chapter, where this algorithm allows for a fully automated analysis.

The $\mathcal{MOQA}$ analysis has another distinctive feature: the compositional derivation of recursive algorithms is very similar in nature to standard denotational style derivations of the semantic meaning of recursive programs. The language has been designed with this purpose in mind and implications for bridging Semantics and Complexity are discussed in Section 1.11.1.

Finally, the language is distinct from prior approaches in that it enables the local applications of operations to so-called isolated subsets, where random bag preservation remains guaranteed. Moreover, its series-parallel data structures drastically simplify the computation of the average-case time as illustrated in Chapter 6 and Chapter 9.

In summary, the $\mathcal{MOQA}$ language has the following unique features:

1. (Random bag preservation) The $\mathcal{MOQA}$ programs are guaranteed to be random bag preserving, where the approach incorporates a new formal development of the notion of randomness preservation.
2. (Modularity) The $\mathcal{MOQA}$ language enables distribution tracking, which combined with the use of inductive types, supports a compositional determination of the recurrence equations expressing the average-case time. In particular, the average-case time is reduced to a linear combination of the average-case times of the basic $\mathcal{MOQA}$ operations.
3. (Random substructures) The $\mathcal{MOQA}$ language incorporates a natural notion of an isolated substructure, over which operations can be naturally applied, leading to randomness preserving operations over the entire data structure. Isolated substructures further support modular analysis of $\mathcal{MOQA}$ code.
4. (SP-data structures) The $\mathcal{MOQA}$ series parallel data structures support the efficient computation of average-case time of the basic operations.
5. (Deletion operation) The $\mathcal{MOQA}$ language, unlike previous languages for automated average-case timing, incorporates a randomness preserving deletion.
6. (Semantics-style nature) The $\mathcal{MOQA}$ language incorporates a typical semantic style flavour via the compositional derivation of average-time information, in particular of recursive programs. This opens up possibilities for bridging the areas of Semantics and Complexity.

1.11 Related Areas

We briefly discuss two related areas which regard the design of languages aimed at static timing and which are distinct from the approaches to language design considered in the context of Automated Average-Case Analysis. The first area broadly can be referred to as "Bridging Semantics and Complexity", while the second is the Real-Time Language area. Each has overlapping interests with the general aim of the current work and an overview of the areas as well as some comparisons with the $\mathcal{MOQA}$ approach are given. These sections are introduced for the reader with a background in either of these areas, but can be omitted by other readers since they are largely independent from the other parts of the book.

1.11.1 Bridging Semantics and Complexity

The central areas of Semantics of Programming Languages and of Complexity Theory have traditionally undergone separate development. The division of the Elsevier journal *Theoretical Computer Science* in Volumes A and B, that typically include complexity related research and semantics related research respectively, further illustrates this fact.

The theoretical interest of bridging Semantics and Complexity stems from the difficulty in designing models that can simultaneously reflect computational behaviour and complexity in a compositional way. The problem has practical relevance because of its ramifications for Real-Time Languages [Gur91]. Indeed, the ability to determine the complexity of programs directly from the complexity of their components, i.e. compositionality at a complexity level, is crucial to guarantee precision in time estimates.

The need to achieving a better understanding of the relationships between Semantics and Complexity has been a concern of the two communities. Several conferences have focused of this topic, such as the 1996 DIMACS workshop on *Computation, Complexity and Programming Languages*, the 1998 *Dagstuhl seminar on Programs: Improvements, Complexity, and Meanings* (9823), as well as the 2000 *Second international workshop on Implicit Computational Complexity*, and the IFIP (TCS) conferences. The means by which the fields should be bridged are far from clear, where opinions range from a potentially "orthogonal" situation in which both approaches would only have an insignificantly small overlap, if any, to the hope of establishing a substantial connection.

There is a clear need to unify techniques from Complexity Theory, that allow one to analyse individual algorithms or classes of algorithms, with techniques from the Programming Language area, that allow one to obtain results about *all* programs of a given language. The reported research in this area has led to a variety of approaches, including category theoretic approaches [Gun92, MA], game theoretic approaches [MR95] for which the semantic aspects have been actively explored [AJM02], approaches based on Quantitative Domain Theory [Sch95, Sch03, Sch04], as well as contributions to Implicit Complexity [Hof98, Hof99], Proof Theory and Complexity at Higher Types [BNS, Coo91, IKR01].

The field of Implicit Complexity has led to a typed language for which first order functions capture exactly the polytime computable functions [Hof00], hence providing an example of a language for which the complexity of the programs is controlled.

Some approaches aimed directly at bridging Semantics and Complexity focused on Operational Semantics [Gre94]. Two pioneering attempts to deal with Denotational Semantics in a complexity context are available at this time: the PhD thesis by Douglas Gurr [Gur91] and the author's PhD thesis [Sch95]. In his thesis, Gurr developed a compositional approach for exact running time, based on an extensive Category Theory framework, and pointed out difficulties with worst-case time regarding compositionality. The approach involves the use of monads and has been followed up by Moggi and Archieri [MA]. Our thesis [Sch95] followed a different approach, related to the Dutch style metric semantics school [BR92] and the work on reconciling the metric and order theoretic approach to Semantics [Smy87, Smy91]. This has led to the development of the theory of Complexity Spaces [Sch95, Sch95a], which has been followed up extensively by the Valencia based research group led by Salvador Romaguera and resulted in an in-depth study of the dual complexity space model, introduced in [RS99] as a mathematically more stable approach. Further work in this area is reported in [RS98, Sch99, RS03]. Other types of models which may be suitable for capturing complexity information have been discussed in the context of quantitative domains [Sch03, Sch04].

Game theoretic approaches have undergone extensive development in the context of Semantics [AJM02]. We remark that Game Theory is relevant to the complexity analysis of algorithms [MR95] but the approach thus far did not lead to a bridge between Semantics and Complexity.

Each of these approaches has its own merit, yet there is not sufficient evidence of their applicability to everyday programming practice, nor do these approaches shed sufficient light on the fundamental issues involved in bridging the two fields.

Key problems preventing progress in bridging Semantics & Complexity include the historic division between the fields and the related differences in approach, as well as the deep issues that quickly arise in the area of Complexity Theory. As we will argue below, a main stumbling block to progress in this area, in particular to test the various models proposed in the literature, is the lack of a programming language for which a non-trivial time measure is compositional.

As a first step to a study of the relationships between Semantics and Complexity we will focus on a central property of Denotational Semantics, namely that of *compositionality*. In Semantics this property guarantees that the meaning of a program can be specified in terms of the meaning of its basic components. Similar to a semantics approach, we will regard a complexity measure to be compositional for a given language in case the complexity of programs can be determined from the complexity of their components. The crucial nature of compositionality cannot be over-stressed: in determining the speed of the program to a reasonable degree of precision, it is a computational necessity to determine this speed directly from the accurate speeds of the components. Compositionality remains the main stumbling block to bridging Denotational Semantics and Complexity. We illustrate this with the current state of the research.

The analysis of exact running time is supported in [Gur91] by a compositional categorical framework relying on monads. Compositionality is a straightforward property of this complexity measure but it is clear that exact time analysis, for inputs of arbitrary size, is infeasible in practice. Thus far no alternatives to standard complexity theoretic techniques for average or worst-case analysis have been provided in a Denotational Semantics context. Worst and average-case extensions of the categorical framework have been discussed in [Gur91] but did not yield compositional models. The complexity space approach of [Sch95, Sch95a] allows one to carry out the average-case analysis of the class of Divide & Conquer algorithms. Again, the models are not guaranteed to be compositional for a general language. Nor is this the case for any of the other approaches mentioned above.

It is easy to see, an issue first raised in [Gur91], that worst-case analysis is essentially non-compositional in nature, hence squashing hope of obtaining a general compositional approach based on this measure. One exception is the new, but potentially costly, Real-Time paradigm for worst-case analysis discussed in [BP02] which amounts to a compositional approach to worst-case analysis in a restricted context. The non-compositionality of worst-case time is reflected by the fact that for Real-Time Languages, worst-case time is approached typically in a non-exact way, i.e. by relying on upper bounds [PK93]. One may be tempted to conclude from this fact that the study of compositionality for the average-case time measure holds little promise, in particular since average-case analysis in general is considerably harder to carry out than worst-case analysis. Moreover, no single unifying theory is available to support this type of analysis and hence the standard average-case analysis techniques incorporate a variety of approaches. Algorithms are analyzed typically on a case-by-case basis, with techniques including the so-called "backward analysis" [Knu73], the "incompressibility method" [SS93, LV93], generating functions [FSZ91, GKP94] as well as related work on randomized algorithms [MR95]. Yet, the conclusion that a compositional approach for average-case analysis is hopeless turns out to be non-founded. We will show that, contrary to the worst-case time measure, the average-case time measure satisfies a special type of "Input-Output compositionality". Also, quite a few interesting algorithms in the literature allow for a compositional average-case analysis. Hence the analysis of compositionality for the average-case time measure is a worthwhile goal.

We believe that the lack of compositional models for basic complexity measures is related to the fact that current language operations are not suited to achieving compositionality at a complexity level. We will illustrate this with examples in Section 3. We argue that a first main and necessary step to developing a bridge between Denotational Semantics and Average-Case Complexity is the design of a "randomness-preserving" programming language.

Indeed, it is well-known that the notion of randomness preservation, though not formulated in a precise framework thus far, is a main factor in the determination of the average-case running time of algorithms. It plays for instance a crucial role in the possibility of carrying out so called "backwards analysis of algorithms" [Knu73].

The issue of randomness preservation, despite involving the simple notion of uniform distribution, has led to complicated problems (e.g. [Ede96], [JK78] and [Knu77]). Several well-known algorithms turn out to be non-randomness-preserving in nature; a case in point being Heapsort for which thus far no randomness-preserving version has been obtained [Ede96] and for which the average-case analysis requires a surprising amount of theoretical machinery [Ede96, SS93, LV93] compared to the average-case analysis of comparable size algorithms such as Quicksort [AHU87].

The complications are due to the fact that the preservation of a distribution depends on the type of computational steps that occur. Hence semantics involving transformations of distributions are available in the literature [Koz81], but in practice it is infeasible in general to track the distributions during the transformations.

While examples of randomness-preserving algorithms have been studied [Knu73] and the subject has been explored to some extent in [Knu77], to the authors knowledge no systematic study of this notion has been carried out in a programming language context. Randomized algorithms form a well-studied field [MR95], but the development has been separate from the issue of randomness preservation.

The formalization of the notion of random structure preservation sheds new light on the field of Algorithms, which is one of the most well-established and notoriously intricate areas of Computer Science (e.g. [Knu73]). As we will see, algorithms can be divided in two classes, namely the class of Random Structure preserving algorithms and its complement.

Currently, when one compares algorithms for which the pseudo-code has comparable size, such as e.g. Quicksort and Heapsort, it is unclear why some algorithms, such as Quicksort, allow for a relatively straight forward average-time analysis and other algorithms, such as Heapsort, require much more complicated techniques such as the incompressibility method ([LV93]). Yet such algorithms are typically indistinguishable by their code, i.e. they use exactly the same type of operations: comparisons, swaps, assignments, loops, etc. A formalization of random structure preservation allows one to distinguish between algorithms in a novel way and inspires new designs of classical algorithms leading to a considerably simplified time analysis.

The $\mathcal{MOQA}$ language presented in his work has the property that its programs are guaranteed to preserve random bags. In this context the computations induce a natural order on the random bags via the notion of a "refinement". The semantics oriented reader may benefit from a glance at the $\mathcal{MOQA}$ pseudo-code for well-known algorithms based on series/parallel recursion in Chapter 8. The corresponding derivations of the average-case time are distinctly semantic style in nature, where the reasoning remains close in spirit to traditional functional fixed point derivations of denotational meanings of programs. A case in point is the analysis of the Treapsort algorithm. It is our view that this approach can give rise to novel semantic models capturing both input-output behaviour of programs and information on average-case complexity. One of the aims of the current presentation is to provide a foundation which may serve as a bridge between Semantics and Complexity. Existing models, discussed at the outset of this section, including game theoretic approaches, monads and quantitative domains, could be explored in this context.

1.11.2 Implications for Real-Time Languages

A central parameter in the design and implementation of real-time applications is the determination of (a bound on) the execution time of the tasks involved. Estimates of the execution time are used to determine the required hardware resources, to plan the timing of interactions between tasks and to allocate tasks to processing units. Real-Time systems are referred to as either `hard` or `soft`.

In hard real-time systems one or more activities must never miss their deadline. An example is the flight control system of an aircraft. In soft real-time systems, the meeting of deadlines is preferable, but the occasional miss of a deadline is tolerated without serious consequences. Examples are the cruise-control application in a car, multimedia and video [Erm03]. Current real-time languages rely on the arguably crude measure of estimating worst-case execution time (WCET). WCET has been extensively studied (e.g. [PK93, Erm03]) and is particularly relevant in a hard real time context (e.g. [KS97, PK93]).

Average case execution time (ACET) can provide useful additional information complementing WCET. Indeed, it has been argued in [MP97], that real-time systems ought to focus on algorithms that minimise the difference between worst and average-case asymptotic behaviour. Using worst-case estimates loses precision and can lead to a waste of resources when one budgets resource allocation based on this measure. Consider for instance the case where a program on average performs much better than in the worst-case. In this situation, worst-case estimates could result in budgeting for an excessive resource allocation. We quote the following from [Ram96] which also illustrates this point: *"We mentioned earlier that the variance between the worst-case computational needs and actual needs must not be very large. We can see why. Since the schedulability analysis is done with respect to worst-case needs, if the variance is large, many transactions that may be doable in the average-case will be considered infeasible in the worst-case"*.

We remark ACET analysis also has relevance for soft real time languages since the average time provides an indication on how well a deadline is respected in general. Yet real-time languages typically do not incorporate ACET analysis. An evaluation of resource allocation based on average and worst-case time is currently out of range since a general average-case analysis tool is not available in a real-time language context.

In contrast, the language that we propose can allow for worst-case analysis, via an adaptation of traditional real-time language techniques (e.g. [PK93]), but also allows for exact average-case analysis in a compositional way. Hence one can take into account the difference between worst-case and average-case time which could potentially allow for a better judgement on whether resources have been allocated in a frugal way. The design of $\mathcal{MOQA}$ may open up the way for novel investigations on ACET analysis for real-time languages. An interesting direction in WCET research is the development of programming language paradigms specifically *designed* for WCET analysis [BP02, Pus03]. This may not be so surprising from a semantics point of view, but from a real-time language point of view the approach can be considered to be a more radical one. Traditionally, existing languages have been adapted to allow for real-time analysis by restricting loops to bounded loops, for instance by restricting recursion to for-loops since such loops have a definite bound and hence it becomes feasible to derive the worst-case time. In [BP02] the proposition is made to significantly *alter* language constructs in order to facilitate the worst-case analysis. This results in a stronger focus on language design than was traditionally the case. The new approach has been strongly motivated by the shortcomings of traditional approaches [BP02]. As remarked above, one can interpret the approach of [BP02] as the design of a restricted language that is compositional with respect to the worst-case execution time. $\mathcal{MOQA}$'s language constructs are directly aimed at facilitating the average case analysis of $\mathcal{MOQA}$ programs and hence the approach complements current real-time language research on new paradigms for worst-case analysis ([BP02]).

Finally, we remark that recent work on Compositional Timing in a Real-Time context focuses for instance on the development of Compositional Real-Time Scheduling Frameworks [SL04]. However this regards combining the time of components which are *not* functionally dependent. In other words, the components are fully independent of one another: a component does not wait for/depend on outputs of another component. Our context is different since "functional dependency" (input-output dependency) is very much at the heart of $\mathcal{MOQA}$. Hence this work also provides a first step towards introducing functional dependencies in a Real-Time context.

We will focus however in the book on presenting $\mathcal{MOQA}$ as an alternative new approach to average-case analysis and will leave Real-Time considerations as a separate matter, with the exception of Chapter 10.

Chapter 2
Introductory Notions

We denote the set of real numbers by $\mathcal{R}$ and the natural numbers by $\mathcal{N}$.

We use the following notation for the combinatorial choice of k integers out of l, without repetitions: $\binom{l}{k}$. We denote the number of choices of k_1 integers out of l, followed by k_2 integers out of $l - k_1, \ldots$, followed by k_n integers out of $l - \sum_{i=1}^{n-1} k_i$ by $\binom{l}{k_1, \ldots, k_n}$, where

$$\binom{l}{k_1, \ldots, k_n} = \binom{l}{k_1}\binom{l - k_1}{k_2} \cdots \binom{l - \sum_{i=1}^{n-1} k_i}{k_n}.$$

The cardinality of a set X is denoted by $|X|$. The *range* of a function $f : X \to Y$ is the set $\{f(x) \mid x \in X\}$, denoted by $Ra(f)$. The result of restricting a function to a subset A of X is denoted by $f \restriction A$. Similarly, the restriction of a partial order $(X, \sqsubseteq)$ to a subset A of X is denoted by $(A, \sqsubseteq \restriction A)$ or often, when no confusion can arise, by $(A, \sqsubseteq)$.

For any finite collection of sets, these sets are said to be *pairwise disjoint* in case any two distinct sets in the collection are disjoint, i.e. a collection of sets $A_1, \ldots, A_n$ is pairwise disjoint in case $\forall i, j \in \{1, \ldots, n\} . i \neq j \Rightarrow A_i \cap A_j = \emptyset$.

The result of concatenating two sequences, say $A = (a_1, \ldots, a_m)$ and $B = (b_1, \ldots, b_n)$ is the sequence $Conc(A, B) = (a_1, \ldots, a_m, b_1, \ldots, b_n)$. Concatenation of more than two sequences, $Conc(A_1, \ldots, A_n)$, is defined in a similar way.

An *affine combination* of a sequence of real-valued functions $f_1, \ldots, f_n$ is an expression of the form $\alpha_1 f_1 + \ldots + \alpha_n f_n$ where $\alpha_1, \ldots, \alpha_n$ are real numbers and $\sum_{i=1}^{n} \alpha_i = 1$.

2.1 Partial Orders & Hasse Diagrams

A *partial order* is a pair $(X, \sqsubseteq)$ consisting of a set X and a binary relation $\sqsubseteq$ between elements of X such that the relation is:

1) Reflexive: $x \sqsubseteq x$
2) Transitive: $x \sqsubseteq y, y \sqsubseteq z \Rightarrow x \sqsubseteq z$.
3) Anti-symmetric: $x \sqsubseteq y, y \sqsubseteq x \Rightarrow x = y$.

Unless stated otherwise, we will only consider finite partial orders in the following. For $x \in X$, we let $x{\downarrow} = \{y \mid y \in X \text{ and } y \sqsubseteq x\}$ and $x{\uparrow} = \{y \mid y \in X \text{ and } x \sqsubseteq y\}$. If $A \subseteq X$ then $A{\uparrow} = \cup_{x \in A} x{\uparrow}$ and $A{\downarrow} = \cup_{x \in A} x{\downarrow}$.

If $(X_1, \sqsubseteq_1)$ and $(X_2, \sqsubseteq_2)$ are partial orders then a function $f : X_1 \to X_2$ is *increasing* iff $\forall x, y \in X_1 . x \sqsubseteq_1 y \Rightarrow f(x) \sqsubseteq_2 f(y)$. In case the function f is an increasing bijection and f^{-1} is increasing, we refer to f as an *order-isomorphism* between the given partial orders.

If $(X, \sqsubseteq)$ is a partial order then $x \sqsubset y \Leftrightarrow (x \sqsubseteq y \text{ and } x \neq y)$. The binary relation $\sqsubset_1$ is defined to be the set of all pairs (x, y) such that $x \sqsubset y$ and $\nexists z . x \sqsubset z \sqsubset y$.

We assume that the reader is familiar with Hasse diagrams [DP90] which will be used to represent partial orders in the examples. The transitive reduction of a partial order $(X, \sqsubseteq)$ is obtained by omitting from $\sqsubseteq$ all its reflexive pairs and pairs that can be inferred by transitivity. The Hasse diagram of a partial order is a digraph representation of its transitive reduction, where one requires that in the representation, related elements x, y where $x \sqsubseteq y$ are displayed such that x is below y in the Hasse diagram. In other words, Hasse diagrams represent directed acyclic graphs for which the transitive reflexive closure is the given partial order. In Hasse diagrams one only displays the relation $\sqsubset_1$. When specifying a finite partial order we typically list a set of pairs specifying the Hasse diagram for the partial order.

A *linear order* $(X, \sqsubseteq)$ is a partial order such that every pair of elements $x, y \in X$ is related with respect to this order, i.e. $\forall x, y \in X . x \sqsubseteq y$ or $y \sqsubseteq x$. For any set X, the *discrete partial order* on X is the partial order consisting only of the reflexive pairs $\{(x, x) \mid x \in X\}$.

For any subset Y of a partial order $(X, \sqsubseteq)$ we say that Y is a *discrete subset* of the partial order in case the restriction of the order $\sqsubseteq$ to Y is the discrete order.

An element x of a partial order $(X, \sqsubseteq)$ is *maximal (minimal)* iff $\nexists y \in X . x \sqsubset y$ $(y \sqsubset x)$. An *extremal element* of a partial order is an element which is maximal or minimal. A *maximum (minimum)* of a partial order $(X, \sqsubseteq)$ is an element $x \in X$ such that $\forall y \in X . y \sqsubseteq x$ $(x \sqsubseteq y)$.

For any two points $x, y \in X$, a sequence $(x_1, \ldots, x_n)$ is a *path* from x to y when $x_1, \ldots, x_n \in X, x_1 = x, x_n = y$ and $\forall i \in \{1, \ldots n - 1\} . x_i \sqsubseteq x_{i+1}$ or $x_i \sqsupseteq x_{i+1}$. A *connected partial order* $(X, \sqsubseteq)$ is a partial order such that for every two points x, y of X there exists a path from x to y. A *component of a partial order* is a non-empty connected subset of maximal size. Any partial order can be partitioned (as a graph) into a set of components. The *length of a path* of a finite partial order is the number of elements on the path. A *chain in a partial order* $(X, \sqsubseteq)$ is a path which forms a linear order under the restriction of $\sqsubseteq$.

2.2 Series-Parallel Orders

We recall some main results regarding series-parallel partial orders [VTL79, Gra81, Gis88, Fin03].

Definition 2.1. Given two disjoint partial orders $(P, \sqsubseteq_1)$ and $(Q, \sqsubseteq_2)$. The *sequential composition*, denoted via a semi-column ";" is the partial order $P; Q$ on $P \cup Q$ such that $x \sqsubseteq y$ in $P; Q \Leftrightarrow$

$$[x, y \in P \text{ and } x \sqsubseteq_1 y] \text{ or } [x, y \in Q \text{ and } x \sqsubseteq_2 y], \text{ or } [x \in P \text{ and } y \in Q].$$

The *parallel composition* $||$ is the partial order $P || Q$ on $P \cup Q$ such that $x \sqsubseteq y$ in $P || Q \Leftrightarrow$

$$[x, y \in P \text{ and } x \sqsubseteq_1 y] \text{ or } [x, y \in Q \text{ and } x \sqsubseteq_2 y].$$

A *series-parallel partial order (SP-order)* is a partial order that can be recursively constructed by applying the operations of sequential and parallel composition starting with a single point [Stan99].

Note that trees form an example of SP-orders as illustrated in Example 2.1 below.

Remark 2.1. For reasons which will become apparent later on, we will refer in the remainder of this work to the sequential composition as the *product operation*. Hence we will use the notation $\otimes$ for sequential composition in the following. The parallel composition of two partial orders in our context will amount to a reference to *components* of partial orders.

From the definition of an SP-order it is clear that each SP-order over a finite set, say $\{x_1, \ldots, x_n\}$, can be represented through a formula from the following inductively defined collection $\mathcal{SP}$, where $\mathcal{SP} = \cup_{n \geq 0} \mathcal{SP}_n$ and:

$$\mathcal{SP}_0 = \{x_1, \ldots, x_n\}$$
$$\forall n \geq 1. \mathcal{SP}_n = \{[y \otimes z] \mid y, z \in \mathcal{SP}_n\} \cup \{[y || z] \mid y, z \in \mathcal{SP}_n\}.$$

Example 2.1. Consider the following SP-order, which corresponds to the formula $[x_1 \otimes [x_2 || [x_3 \otimes [x_4 || x_5]]]]$.

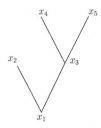

Remark 2.2. Note that in the above approach, there is a unique parsing of each SP formula from $\mathcal{SP}$. However, through associativity, one can drop brackets and focus on the "parallel components" and the "series components" as discussed below.

An SP-order $(P, \sqsubseteq)$, after removing unnecessary brackets, is of one of the following forms:

1) $P = P_1 || \ldots || P_n$ *or*

2) $P = P_1 \otimes \ldots \otimes P_n$.

Definition 2.2. We refer to an SP-order in Remark 2.2 of the first kind as a *parallel SP-order* and to an SP-order of the second kind as a *product SP-order*. Moreover, we refer to the suborders $P_1, \ldots, P_n$ of the parallel SP-order $P = P_1 || \ldots || P_n$ as *parallel components* and to the suborders $P_1, \ldots, P_n$ of $P = P_1 \otimes \ldots \otimes P_n$ as *product components*.

Remark 2.3. It is clear that, by removing unnecessary brackets, we can express a parallel SP-order as an SP-order for which all parallel components are product SP-orders. Similarly we can express a product SP-order as an SP-order for which all product components are parallel SP-orders. We refer to such expressions as *canonical representations* of the SP-order in question.

Example 2.2. Consider the product SP-order $[[x \otimes [y || z]] \otimes [z || [u || v]]$, which can be expressed as the product of parallel components $x \otimes [y || z] \otimes [z || u || v]$.

We discuss the following interesting characterization of SP orders as so-called N-free orders.

Definition 2.3. A partial order is *N-free* if there is no quadruple of elements $\{x, y, u, v\}$ whose non-trivial relations are given by $x \sqsubset u, y \sqsubset u, y \sqsubset v$, i.e. there is no suborder determined by a Hasse diagram corresponding to an "N-shape":

The following proposition provides a characterization of SP-orders as N-free partial orders.

Proposition 2.1. [Fin03, Gis88, Gra81, VTL79] *For finite partial orders, the notions of SP and N-free are equivalent.*

2.3 Trees & Heaps

A tree is a partial order with a maximum element, referred to as the *root* of a tree, for which the Hasse diagram representation has no cycles [HJ99, AHU87]. The elements of this order are referred to as the *nodes* of the tree. We follow here the Computer Science convention in considering the root as the largest element in the tree, rather than the standard mathematical approach of defining the root as the least element. The *leaves* are the minimal nodes, *internal nodes* are nodes that are not leaves, a *child of a node*, provided the given node has elements strictly below it, is a node immediately below the given node in the ordering. Similarly, a *parent of a node*, provided the given node has a node strictly above it, is a node immediately above the given node in the ordering [AHU87]. The *depth of a node* in a tree is the number of nodes (not including the given node) on the unique path from the node to the root. The *size of a finite tree* is the number of nodes in the tree.

A *binary tree* is a tree in which every node has at most two children. A *full binary tree* is a binary tree in which every internal node has two children. A *complete binary tree* is a full binary tree in which all leaves occur at the same depth.

In the following we will only consider *finite binary trees* and will simply refer to these as *tree*.

A *near-heap* is obtained from a complete binary tree as follows:

1) Some leaves are allowed to be omitted in right to left order.
2) All nodes of the tree obtained via 1) are labeled with a natural number such that each parent which is not the root has a label which is greater than those of its children.

A *heap* is a near-heap for which the root has a label which is larger than the labels of its children. The set of all heaps of size n, identified up to labeling-isomorphism, is denoted by $\mathcal{H}_n$ and the cardinality of this set is denoted by $h(n)$.

We display the recurrence for the number $h(n)$ of heaps of size n with labelings from a fixed set of n distinct labels [Ede96], where H_1 and H_2 are the two heaps obtained by removing the root of the original heap of size n:

$$h(n) = \binom{n-1}{|H_1|} \times h(|H_1|) \times h(|H_2|).$$

Remark 2.4. For future reference we remark that: $h(1) = h(2) = 1, h(3) = 2, h(4)$ $= 3, h(5) = 8$ and $h(6) = 20$ and thus $h(3)$ does not divide $h(4)$, $h(4)$ does not divide $h(5)$ and $h(5)$ does not divide $h(6)$.

Treaps were introduced independently by several authors [Vui80, SA96], where the first introduction of these structures is due to [Vui80], which used the terminology of *Cartesian Trees* .

A *key* is a value stored at a node x of a tree, denoted by $x.key$. Keys stem from a totally ordered universe and are pairwise distinct. A *Binary Search Tree* consists of a binary tree with a set X of n items stored at the nodes: some item $y \in X$ is chosen to be stored at the root of the tree, and the left and the right children of the root are binary search trees for the sets $X_< = \{x \in X \,|\, x.key < y.key\}$ and $X_> = \{x \in X \,|\, y.key > x.key\}$. Binary Search trees satisfy the *in-order* property. This means that for any node x in the tree $y.key < x.key$ for all y in the left subtree of x and $x.keq < y.key$ for all y in the right subtree of x. Let X be a set of items each of which has an associated *key* and a *priority*. The priorities, as are the keys, are drawn from a totally ordered universe and are assumed to be pairwise distinct. The two ordered universes need not be the same. A *treap* for X is a binary tree with node set X that is arranged in in-order with respect to the keys and in heap-order with respect to the priorities. Pairwise distinctness of keys and of priorities guarantees that there is a unique treap for X [SA96].

2.4 Basic Sorting Algorithms

We give details of the pseudo-code for several algorithms of which the average-case time will be discussed. For further information we refer the reader to [AHU87] and [Knu73].

We will discuss two standard variants of Heapsort in the work, William's version and Floyd's version. We recall some basic background material, to formulate the Heapsort variants, and for simplicity consider heaps labeled with natural numbers.

The traditional Heapsort algorithm relies on a procedure "Push-Down", which transforms a near-heap to a heap. Two versions of Push-Down are available: Williams' original version [Wil64] which we refer to as "*W-Push-Down*" and the more economic version used by Floyd [Flo64], which we refer to as "*F-Push-Down*". We sketch these alternative versions below. For a precise formulation we refer the reader to [AHU87], [Wil64],[Flo64] and [LV93]. In the description given below, "larger" ("smaller") refers to the order $\geq$ ($\leq$), while "strictly larger" ("strictly smaller") refers to the order $>$ ($<$).

W-Push-Down

Given a near-heap of size n, say with root label l, then *W-Push-Down* proceeds as follows:

Start at the root of the near-heap and compare the labels of the two children. If m is the larger label of these two, then compare the root label l with m. If $m < l$, then the algorithm halts since the near-heap is a heap. Otherwise these labels are swapped. Consider the sub near-heap which has as root the child which was originally labeled with m. Recursively repeat this procedure on this sub near-heap until the children of the root under consideration have labels which are both less than the root label or a leaf is reached.

F-Push-Down

Given a near-heap of size n, say with root label l, then *F-Push-Down* proceeds as follows:

Keep track separately of the root label l. Start at the root of the near-heap and compare the labels of the two children. Select the child which has the larger of the two labels. Repeat the procedure on the sub near-heap which has this child as root until a leaf is reached. This determines a chain from the root of the near-heap to the leaf. Move systematically up the chain (if necessary) until a particular node N is found which has a label greater than the root label l.

At that point, assign the label of this particular node N and of each of its ancestor nodes on the chain, to each of their respective parent nodes. That is, move the labels of each node one node upwards along this chain. Finally, change the label of N to the original root label l.

The main difference, regarding comparisons, is the following: *W-Push-Down* proceeds from the root down the near-heap, making two comparisons per step. *F-Push-Down* proceeds from the root down the near-heap to a leaf, making one comparison per step. Then it backtracks upwards along the chain to the root, making one extra comparison per step until a particular node is reached for which the label is larger than the label of the root.

We recall the Heapify procedure which uses Push-Down (where either of the above versions of Push-Down can be selected) to create a heap from a given list. Push-Down(i, j), where $i \leq j$, comes equipped with two parameters which indicate the boundaries i and j of the sub-list being operated on. I.e. i indicates the index of the label to be "pushed down" and j indicates that we only operate on labels of elements with indices ranging from i up to and including j.

A list $(L[1], \ldots, L[n])$ is interpreted by Heapify as a binary tree, with root node labeled with $L[1]$ and such that each node labeled with $L[j]$, with $j \leq \lceil \frac{n}{2} \rceil$ has either two children labeled with $L[2j], L[2j + 1]$, when $2j + 1 \leq n$, or one child labeled with $L[2j]$ when $2j = n$ [AHU87]. Push-Down is called recursively in the Heapify procedure defined below. Since Push-Down will initially be called on a binary tree with at most 3 elements, this binary tree is automatically a near-heap and hence the recursive calls to Push-Down are well defined.

Heapify
For i = $\lfloor \frac{n}{2} \rfloor$ **downto** 1 **do** Push-Down(i,n);

The Heapsort algorithm relies on a Selection process, in which the largest label of the heap, i.e. the label at the root, is swapped with the label of the rightmost leaf, after which Push-Down is called once more on the newly created near-heap and the process is repeated.

The pseudo-code for Selection is given by:

Selection
For i = n **downto** 2 **do**
  swap(L[1],L[i]);
  Push-Down(1,i-1)

Finally, traditional Heapsort can be formulated as follows, again using either version of the procedure Push-Down:

Heapsort
Heapify; Selection

We recall the pseudo-code of the version of Bubblesort discussed in [AHU87], which we refer to as "Bubblesort-I".

Bubblesort-I
For i = n-1 **downto** 1 **do**
  For j = 1 **to** i **do**
      if L[j] > L[j+1] **then** swap(L[j],L[j+1])

The inner for-loop of Bubblesort-I is denoted by J_i^I where $i \in \{1, \ldots, n-1\}$.

We recall the pseudo-code of the Bubblesort version from [Knu73], which we refer to as Bubblesort-II"". This version keeps track of the number of swaps performed during a run of the inner for-loop; i.e. of the number of comparisons for which $L[j] > L[j+1]$ is true. In case no swaps occur during this run, the sublist under consideration is sorted and the algorithm terminates.

Bubblesort-II
For i = n-1 **downto** 1 **do**
  k := 0;
  For j = 1 **to** i **do**
      if L[j] > L[j+1] **then** k := k+1; **swap**(L[j],L[j+1]);

If k=0 **then return** L

The inner for-loop of Bubblesort-II is denoted by J_i^{II} where $i \in \{1, \ldots, n-1\}$ and $n = |L|$.

2.5 Uniform Distribution and Bags

A *bag*[1] is a finite set-like object in which order is ignored but multiplicity is explicitly significant. Thus, contrary to sets, bags allow for the repetition of elements. Therefore, bags $\{1, 2, 3\}$ and $\{3, 1, 2\}$ are considered to be equivalent, but $\{1, 2, 2, 3\}$ and $\{1, 2, 3\}$ differ. We refer to the number of times an element occurs in a bag as the *multiplicity* of the element. The *cardinality of a bag* is the sum of the multiplicities of its elements. Each bag A of n elements has an *associated set* $B = \{b_1, \ldots, b_k\}$ such that $\cup A = \cup B$ and where each element b_i of B is repeated K_i times where $1 \leq K_i \leq n$ and $\sum_{i=1}^{k} K_i = n$. It is clear that a bag A can be represented in this way as a - set of pairs $\{(b_1, K_1), \ldots, (b_k, K_k)\}$.

In fact it will be convenient to adopt a slight generalization of this type of representation as our formal definition of a bag in the following. I.e. a bag is formally defined in this context as a finite set of pairs $\{(b_1, K_1), \ldots, (b_k, K_k)\}$, where each K_i is a natural number, referred to as the multiplicity of the element b_i and where we do *not* require that the elements b_i are pairwise disjoint. In case $(*)$ $\forall i, j. b_i \neq b_j$, we refer to the finite set of pairs $\{(b_1, K_1), \ldots, (b_k, K_k)\}$ as a *strict* bag. We allow a more flexible approach in which we do not require $(*)$ to hold since in practice some repetitions of an element b may occur in different contexts, e.g. as K repetitions in one context and L in another, in which case we chose to keep track of these repetitions separately as pairs (b, K) and (b, L) in the same bag rather than as a single pair $(b, K + L)$ in the bag.

To keep track of the number of times that a particular output is produced, we will represent the range of the input-output function of a program as a bag. $\mathcal{MOQA}$-programs are guaranteed to terminate, so there are no undefined outputs to be taken into account.

Notation 2.1 (Input and Output Bag)
For any program P we indicate the bag of its inputs by $\mathcal{I}_P$, referred to as the "input bag". The bag of inputs of size n is denoted by $\mathcal{I}_P(n)$. A *bag of inputs* $\mathcal{I}$ for a program P is a sub bag of the input bag $\mathcal{I}_P$. Typically we will require that $\mathcal{I} \subseteq \mathcal{I}_P(n)$ for some n.

$\mathcal{O}_P(\mathcal{I})$ denotes the bag of outputs, referred to as "the output bag", of the computations of a program P on a bag of inputs $\mathcal{I}$.

---

[1] Also referred to as multi-set in the literature.

If $\mathcal{I}_P(n) = \mathcal{I}_n$ for a particular data structure under consideration then we denote the output bag $\mathcal{O}_P(\mathcal{I}_n)$ by $\mathcal{O}_P(n)$.

We recall (cf. Remark 1.6) that all programs under consideration are assumed to terminate. Hence it is clear that in case $\mathcal{I}$ is an input bag for a program P, the bags $\mathcal{I}$ and $\mathcal{O}_P(\mathcal{I})$ have the same cardinality where the input-output relation forms the corresponding bijection.

Example 2.3. 1) Consider a sorting algorithm P. The bag of outputs $\mathcal{O}_P(\mathcal{A}_n)$ is $\{(\mathcal{S}_n, n!)\}$, consisting of $n!$ copies of the sorted list $\mathcal{S}_n$.

2) Consider Bubblesort-I of Section 2.2 and its inner for-loop J_{n-1}^I for $n = 3$, i.e. J_2^I.
Let $\mathcal{A}_3 = \{(1,2,3),(1,3,2),(2,1,3),(2,3,1),(3,1,2),(3,2,1)\}$. The bag of outputs is $\mathcal{O}_{J_2^I}(\mathcal{A}_3) = \{((1,2,3),4), ((2,1,3),2)\}$.

Bags are useful to represent sets of data that are uniformly distributed. A bag $A = \{(b_1, K_1), \ldots, (b_k, K_k)\}$ is called *uniformly distributed* iff $\forall i, j \in \{1, \ldots, n\}. K_i = K_j$. It is clear that if $A = \{(b_1, K_1), \ldots, (b_k, K_k)\}$ is a uniform bag then we can simply use the simplified notation $A = \{(B, K)\}$, which indicates that the bag A consists of K copies of the set B. In particular: $|A| = K|B|$. Each element of a uniform bag $\mathcal{A}$ with associated set B arises with equal probability of $\frac{K}{|A|} = \frac{1}{|B|}$.

Example 2.4. Note that Example 2.3, 1) yields a uniform bag, while this is not the case for Example 2.3, 2).

We recall the main rules for computing probabilities for statements involving $\wedge$, $\vee$ and $\neg$. These will be applied to determine the probabilities of boolean expressions occuring in $\mathcal{MOQA}$ programs.

$$Prob[\neg A] = 1 - Prob[A].$$

For pairwise disjoint event sets $A_1, \ldots, A_n$:

$$Prob[\cup_{i=1}^n A_i] = \sum_{i=1}^n Prob[A_i].$$

The Modularity Law for probabilities two event sets A_1 and A_2:

$$Prob[A_1 \cup A_2] = Prob[A_1] + Prob[A_2] - Prob[A_1 \cap A_2],$$

The Modularity Law for three event sets A_1, A_2 and A_3 :

$$Prob[A_1 \cup A_2 \cup A_3] = Prob[A_1] + Prob[A_2] + Prob[A_3] - Prob[A_1 \cap A_2] - Prob[A_1 \cap A_3] - Prob[A_2 \cap A_3] + Prob[A_1 \cap A_2 \cap A_3].$$

The General Modularity Law for event sets $A_1, \ldots, A_n$ $(n \geq 2)$:

$$Prob[\cup_{i=1}^{n} A_i] = \sum_{i=1}^{n} Prob[A_i] - \sum_{i<j} Prob[A_i \cap A_j] + \ldots + (-1)^{n-1} Prob[\cap_{i=1}^{n} A_i].$$

2.6 Timing Measures

We recall the standard definitions of comparison-based algorithms and of worst-case time and average-case time for comparison-based algorithms. We recall from Chapter 1 that a comparison-based algorithm is an algorithm for which every action during the code execution is determined by a comparison between two elements of the input data structure (e.g. [AHU87]). In particular, every assignment and every swap during the execution of the code is a direct consequence of a comparison between two elements. Most sorting and search algorithms fall into this class and traditional lower bound estimates apply in this context.

As indicated in Chapter 1, static timing in our context regards the counting of comparisons during the execution of comparison-based algorithms.

For a comparison-based algorithm P we define the *exact time* $T_P(I)$ on an input I to be the number of comparisons made by the program P during the computation of the output $P(I)$. The notation $T_P(n)$ indicates the restriction of the function T_P to the set $\mathcal{I}_n$. We will consider subsets $\mathcal{I}$ of $\mathcal{I}_n$ and consider the following time measures with respect to $\mathcal{I}$:

The *total time* of P for inputs from $\mathcal{I}$, denoted by $T_P^t(\mathcal{I})$ is defined by:

$$T_P^t(\mathcal{I}) = \sum_{I \in \mathcal{I}} T_P(I).$$

The *worst-case time* of P for inputs from $\mathcal{I}$, denoted by $T_P^W(\mathcal{I})$ is defined by:

$$T_P^W(\mathcal{I}) = max\{T_P(I) | I \in \mathcal{I}\}.$$

The *best-case time* of P for inputs from $\mathcal{I}$, denoted by $T_P^B(\mathcal{I})$ is defined by:

$$T_P^B(\mathcal{I}) = min\{T_P(I) | I \in \mathcal{I}\}.$$

The *average-case time* of P for inputs from $\mathcal{I}$, denoted by $\overline{T}_P(\mathcal{I})$ is defined by:

$$\overline{T}_P(\mathcal{I}) = \frac{T^t(\mathcal{I})}{|\mathcal{I}|} = \frac{\sum_{I \in \mathcal{I}} T_P(I)}{|\mathcal{I}|}.$$

In order to denote an arbitrary measure, which can include any of the above, we use the notation $\mathcal{T}_P$ and the usual corresponding notations $\mathcal{T}_P(\mathcal{I})$ and $\mathcal{T}_P(n)$.

We observe that:

$$\forall \mathcal{I}. T_P^B(\mathcal{I}) \leq \overline{T}_P(\mathcal{I}) \leq T_P^W(\mathcal{I}).$$

If the exact time of P is a constant C on the inputs from $\mathcal{I}$ then:

$$\overline{T}_P(\mathcal{I}) = T_P^B(\mathcal{I}) = T_P^W(\mathcal{I}) = C.$$

For a given data structure, we let the finite set $\mathcal{I}_n$ denote the set of input states of size n for this particular data structure.

Of course, in case $\mathcal{I} = \mathcal{I}_n$, we will for the total, worst-case, best-case and average-case time respectively use the following standard notation based on size indication only: $T_P^t(n), T_P^W(n), T_P^B(n)$ and $\overline{T}_P(n)$.

We assume familiarity with the asymptotic classification of running times and the notion of a decision tree (e.g. [AHU87]). Given two functions $f, g \colon \mathcal{N} \to \mathcal{R}^+$. Then

$$f \in O(g) \Longleftrightarrow \exists c > 0 \, \exists n_0 \, \forall n \geq n_0. \, f(n) \leq cg(n).$$

$$f \in \Omega(g) \Longleftrightarrow \exists c > 0 \, \exists n_0 \, \forall n \geq n_0. \, f(n) \geq cg(n).$$

For comparison-based algorithms one can show that in the asymptotic hierarchy (e.g. [CLR96]) the worst-case time and the average-case time satisfy the following lower bound: $T_P^W(n) \in \Omega(log(N_n))$ and $\overline{T}_P(n) \in \Omega(log(N_n))$ where N_n is the number of leaves in the decision tree of the algorithm P for inputs of size n.

Chapter 3
Compositionality

The aim is to design a novel type of language $\mathcal{MOQA}$ for which programs induce recurrence equations for the average-case time *in a compositional way* and based on the notion of randomness preservation. The capacity to generate recurrences is particularly important for the average-case time measure since, in general, the direct determination of the average-case time via the formula $\overline{T}_P(n) = \frac{\sum_{I \in \mathcal{I}_n} T_P(I)}{|\mathcal{I}_n|}$ is not feasible. For instance, for the case of sorting algorithms where $|\mathcal{I}_n| = n!$, a direct computation of $\frac{\sum_{I \in \mathcal{I}_n} T_P(I)}{|n!|}$ would require an excessive time in order to add the $n!$ comparison times $T_P(I)$ for the inputs I of size n. This is clear by Stirling's approximation $n! \approx \sqrt{2\pi n}(\frac{n}{e})^n$. The computation time would be too great, even for the relatively small input size of $n = 20$. If on the other hand one has a recurrence expressing the average-case time, this time can be determined for very large values of n. The problem does not arise in the same way for the worst-case time measure since for this measure only a single worst-case input needs to be found.

The usefulness of compositionality for static timing has been indicated in Chapter 1. We discuss compositionality for various practical timing measures in the following.

3.1 Compositionality as a Key to Software Timing

We recall (cf. Remark 1.6) that all programs under consideration are assumed to terminate on all inputs.

We illustrate how compositionality can facilitate timing via the basic time measure of exact time. It is easy to see that the Exact Time T_P is (trivially) compositional, i.e. for any two programs P_1 and P_2, where the output of P_1 on input I is denoted by $P_1(I)$, we have the following *Exact Time Compositionality*:

$$T_{P_1;P_2}(I) = T_{P_1}(I) + T_{P_2}(P_1(I)),$$

where, as usual, we let P_1; P_2 indicate the sequential execution of program P_1 followed by the program P_2.

Compositionality of this nature guarantees that for any given input I the exact time T_P of for-loops

$$P = [\text{For } i = 1 \text{ to } k \text{ do } Q]$$

can be specified via a recurrence equation of the type:

$$T_P(I) = \sum_{i=1}^{k} T_Q(I^{i-1}),$$

where $I^0 = I$ and $\forall i \in \{1, \ldots, k-1\}$. $I^i = [Q; \ldots; Q](I)$, where the program Q is composed i times in the expression $[Q; \ldots; Q]$.

Hence it is clear that compositionality can simplify the time determination of programs by reducing the time of the original program P to a summation in terms of the times of the basic for-loop component Q. This straightforward treatment of for-loops is of particular interest for real-time language design since, in order to enable timing, real-time languages are typically restricted to for-loops or for-loops together with bounded while-loops.

However, the exact time determination for inputs of arbitrary size is infeasible in practice. In the following we focus on the main measures used in practice, namely worst-case time, best-case time and average-case time, and we introduce the novel notion of IO-compositionality as a complexity theoretic interpretation of the classical semantic notion of compositionality for these time measures.

3.2 IO-Compositionality

The compositional treatment for time measures that are defined with respect to sets of inputs of a given size, needs a more refined type of bookkeeping via *output multi-sets*. This is captured by the notion of "IO-compositionality".

Definition 3.1. Given a time measure $\mathcal{T}$. Let $\mathcal{PL}$ denote a programming language for which programs are guaranteed to terminate on inputs. Let P_1, P_2 denote arbitrary programs of the language $\mathcal{PL}$ and let $\mathcal{I}$ denote an input multi-set for P_1. We say that:

$\mathcal{T}$ is *lower IO-compositional w.r.t.* $\mathcal{PL}$ iff $\forall P_1, P_2 \in \mathcal{PL} \ \forall \mathcal{I}$.

$$T_{P_1;P_2}(\mathcal{I}) \leq T_{P_1}(\mathcal{I}) + T_{P_2}(\mathcal{O}_{P_1}(\mathcal{I})).$$

$\mathcal{T}$ is *upper IO-compositional w.r.t.* $\mathcal{PL}$ iff $\forall P_1, P_2 \in \mathcal{PL} \ \forall \mathcal{I}$.

$$T_{P_1;P_2}(\mathcal{I}) \geq T_{P_1}(\mathcal{I}) + T_{P_2}(\mathcal{O}_{P_1}(\mathcal{I})).$$

$\mathcal{T}$ is *semi IO-compositional w.r.t.* $\mathcal{PL}$ iff

$\qquad\qquad$ $\mathcal{T}$ is lower or upper IO-compositional w.r.t. $\mathcal{PL}$.

$\mathcal{T}$ is *IO-compositional w.r.t.* $\mathcal{PL}$ iff

$\qquad\qquad$ $\mathcal{T}$ is lower and upper IO-compositional w.r.t. $\mathcal{PL}$, *i.e.*:

$$\forall P_1, P_2 \in \mathcal{PL} \; \forall \mathcal{I}. \, \mathcal{T}_{P_1;P_2}(\mathcal{I}) = \mathcal{T}_{P_1}(\mathcal{I}) + \mathcal{T}_{P_2}(\mathcal{O}_{P_1}(\mathcal{I})).$$

Finally, in case one of these properties V holds for a given time measure $\mathcal{T}$ with respect to *any* programming language, we say that $\mathcal{T}$ is *universal V*, as e.g. "universal IO-compositional".

Lemma 3.1. *The Total Time T_P^t is universal IO-compositional. The worst-case time T_P^W and the best-case time T_P^B are respectively universal lower and upper IO-compositional.*

Proof. Consider two programs P_1, P_2 of the language $\mathcal{PL}$ and $\mathcal{I}$ an input multi-set for P_1. We first verify the universal IO-compositionality of the Total Time:

$$
\begin{aligned}
T_{P_1;P_2}^t(\mathcal{I}) &= \sum_{I \in \mathcal{I}} T_{P_1;P_2}(I) \\
&= \sum_{I \in \mathcal{I}} T_{P_1}(I) + \sum_{J \in \mathcal{O}_{P_1}(\mathcal{I})} T_{P_2}(J) \\
&= T_{P_1}^t(\mathcal{I}) + T_{P_2}^t(\mathcal{O}_{P_1}(\mathcal{I})).
\end{aligned}
$$

For the best-case time and the worst-case time, we observe that for any input $I \in \mathcal{I}$ the following holds:

$$T_{P_1}^B(\mathcal{I}) + T_{P_2}^B(\mathcal{O}_{P_1}(\mathcal{I})) \le T_{P_1;P_2}(I) = T_{P_1}(I) + T_{P_2}(P_1(I)) \le T_{P_1}^W(\mathcal{I}) + T_{P_2}^W(\mathcal{O}_{P_1}(\mathcal{I})),$$

from which the universal lower and upper IO-compositionality for worst-case and best-case time follows.

Remark 3.1. The right hand-side of the lower IO-compositionality inequality for the worst-case time, $T_{P_1}^W(\mathcal{I}) + T_{P_2}^W(\mathcal{O}_{P_1}(\mathcal{I}))$, is typically used in real-time languages as an upper bound approximation for the worst-case time of a sequential composition $T_{P_1;P_2}^W(\mathcal{I})$. This provides an example of how compositionality, even in this weak form, aids Software Timing.

We will show that the worst-case time T_P^W and the best-case Time T_P^B are in general *not* universal IO-compositional, i.e. the semi IO-compositionality inequalities can be strict in general. Secondly, we will verify that the average-case time $\overline{\overline{T}}_P$ *is* universal IO-compositional.

3.3 Strict Semi IO-Compositionality for Worst-Case and Best-Case Time

We show that IO-compositionality for worst-case time and best-case time can not be achieved in general, i.e. their semi IO-compositionality inequalities are strict in general. Hence the worst-case bounds in a Real-Time context are not exact in general. This is illustrated by the counter-example given below. A similar example can be constructed for the best-case time.

The counter-example is clearly an artificial one. Yet it illustrates nicely the lack of control one has in guaranteeing IO-compositionality for the worst-case time and (via a similar example) for the best-case time. It is easy to see that this problem arises in many cases, where no apparent pattern seems available to obtain some compositional subclass of sufficient generality.

Counter-Example 3.1 (Worst-case time)

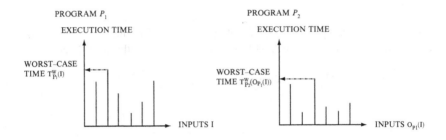

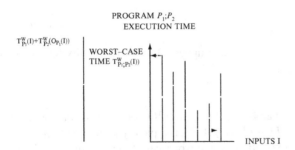

Recent work by Burns-Puschner [BP02] does explore a "compositional"[1] approach to worst-case time in a real-time context by forcing conditional statements to execute both branches which in turn forces the time to be constant. Hence they essentially describe a restricted real-time language with respect to which the worst-

---

[1] [BP02] does not use this terminology, but the underlying concept is the same.

case time *is* IO-compositional. We refer to this language in the following as $\mathcal{BP}^2$. However, as the authors of [BP02] point out, their approach can lead to a drastic increase in the execution time of $\mathcal{BP}$-programs.

The counter-example illustrates that in this case strict semi IO-compositionality holds, i.e. $T^W_{P_1;P_2}(\mathcal{I}) < T^W_{P_1}(\mathcal{I}) + T^W_{P_2}(\mathcal{O}_{P_1}(\mathcal{I}))$. The problem is that in order to guarantee IO-compositionality, a worst-case input I of P_1 needs to give rise to an output $P_1(I)$ which constitutes a worst-case input for P_2. Clearly, this will not be guaranteed in general.

We provide a simple toy-program which illustrates that the above counter-example can arise in practice. Consider the "Conditional Frog-Leap" algorithm. It systematically compares two consecutive elements of a list L and, in case the first is smaller than the second, "frog-leaps" the first element over the others, where it lands in final position.

The operation Frog-Leap (FL), has the following pseudo-code:

FL
```
[L:=Append(Tail(L),Head(L))]
```

In the pseudo-code, Head(L) denotes the list containing the first element of L, while Tail(L) denotes the list obtained from L by removing the first element of this list.

Note that the operation FL implicitly involves re-indexing of the elements. For example if $L[1]$ is frog-leaped to the end of the list $L = (L[1], L[2], \ldots, L[n])$ then the resulting list, which would be $L' = (L[2], \ldots, L[n], L[1])$, is assumed to be re-indexed to $L' = (L'[1], \ldots, L'[n])$.

The pseudo-code for Conditional-Frog-Leap (CFL) is:

CFL
while (L[1] < L[2]) **do** FL(L)

Consider the algorithm CFL* obtained from CFL by inverting the < sign to the > sign. We display the execution of CFL;CFL* on all inputs of size 3, where each arrow indicates a comparison carried out in the while-loops of CFL and CFL*.

$123 \to_{CFL} 231 \to_{CFL} 312 \to_{CFL} 312 \to_{CFL*} 123 \to_{CFL*} 123$
$132 \to_{CFL} 321 \to_{CFL} 321 \to_{CFL*} 213 \to_{CFL*} 132 \to_{CFL*} 132$
$213 \to_{CFL} 213 \to_{CFL*} 132 \to_{CFL*} 132$
$231 \to_{CFL} 312 \to_{CFL} 312 \to_{CFL*} 123 \to_{CFL*} 123$
$312 \to_{CFL} 312 \to_{CFL*} 123 \to_{CFL*} 123$
$321 \to_{CFL} 321 \to_{CFL*} 213 \to_{CFL*} 132 \to_{CFL*} 132$

---

[2] Burns-Puschner.

Clearly $T^W_{CFL;CFL^*}(3) = 5$, while $T^W_{CFL}(3) = 3$. Note that $\mathcal{O}_{CFL}(\mathcal{A}_3) =$ $\{(3,1,2),(3,2,1),$
$(2,1,3)\}$. From the above displayed execution, it is clear that: $T^W_{CFL^*}(\mathcal{O}_{CFL}(\mathcal{A}_3)) =$ 3 and hence

$$T^W_{CFL;CFL^*}(3) = 5 < T^W_{CFL}(3) + T^W_{CFL^*}(\mathcal{O}_{CFL}(\mathcal{A}_3)) = 6.$$

3.4 Average-Case Time *is* IO-Compositional

Proposition 3.1. *The average-time measure is universal IO-compositional. Consider a language* $\mathcal{PL}$ *for which programs terminate on all inputs and two programs* P_1, P_2 *of* $\mathcal{PL}$*, where* P_1 *operates on an input multi-set* $\mathcal{I}$ *and produces the output multi-set* $\mathcal{O}_{P_1}(\mathcal{I})$*. Then the following equality holds:*

$$\overline{T}_{P_1;P_2}(\mathcal{I}) = \overline{T}_{P_1}(\mathcal{I}) + \overline{T}_{P_2}(\mathcal{O}_{P_1}(\mathcal{I})).$$

Proof:

$$
\begin{aligned}
\overline{T}_{P_1;P_2}(\mathcal{I}) &= \frac{\sum_{I \in \mathcal{I}} T_{P_1;P_2}(I)}{|\mathcal{I}|} \\
&= \frac{\sum_{I \in \mathcal{I}} T_{P_1}(I) + \sum_{J \in \mathcal{O}_{P_1}(\mathcal{I})} T_{P_2}(J)}{|\mathcal{I}|} \\
&= \overline{T}_{P_1}(\mathcal{I}) + \overline{T}_{P_2}(\mathcal{O}_{P_1}(\mathcal{I})),
\end{aligned}
$$

where the last equality follows from the fact that $|\mathcal{I}| = |\mathcal{O}_{P_1}(\mathcal{I})|$.

Remark 3.2. (Average-Case Time Paradox)
The IO-compositionality of average-case time is rather surprising since it is well known that average-case time analysis is much harder to determine in practice than worst-case time due to the fact that the first measure needs to take into account the computation times for *all* inputs, while for the second measure it suffices to focus on determining the time for a specific extreme input-case. On the other hand, the IO-compositionality of the average-case time, as opposed to the worst-case time, opens the way to a compositional, and hence simplified, determination of average-time recurrences. We will return to the reasons for this apparent paradox in the next section.

3.5 From IO-Compositionality to Linear-Compositionality

Our aim is to treat the average-case time measure in a "linear-compositional" way. :

Informally stated, we aim to specify the average time of programs as a linear combination of the average times of their basic building blocks. We will from now on, informally, refer to a time measure $\mathcal{T}$, which satisfies the above property with respect to a given programming language $\mathcal{PL}$, as a linearly-compositional *time measure with respect to $\mathcal{PL}$. Again, if this property holds with respect to any programming language, we refer to it as "universal linear-compositionality".*

Remark 3.3. Note that for the particular case of linear-compositionality for the average-case time measure, we do not insist that the average-case time is expressed in terms of size. Instead, for the case of random bag preserving programs, the average-case time of a program is expressed over the input random bag. In other words, linear-compositionality guarantees the expression of the average-case time of a random bag preserving program in terms of the average-case times of its basic building blocks, where these average-case times in turn are expressed over simpler random bags. As we, will see for recursive algorithms this type of linear-compositionality typically yields recurrences in terms of size.

Counter-Example 3.1 shows that the worst-case time measure is not universal IO-compositional. We recall that in [BP02] it is shown that the worst-case time measure is IO-compositional with respect to a restricted real-time language $\mathcal{BP}$. As we will see, the average-case time measure is not universal linearly-compositional. However, we will introduce a natural data structuring language $\mathcal{MOQA}$ with respect to which the average-case time measure *is* linearly-compositional *and* which is expressive enough to include the standard data structure manipulations.

In the following we will analyze to what extent IO-compositionality is sufficient to reach linear-compositionality for the average-case time measure.

As mentioned above, IO-compositionality paves the way for simplifications of the determination of recurrences for average-case time analysis. We illustrate this on the following example.

Consider the sorting algorithms Quicksort and Mergesort, denoted by Q and M. We consider a version of Quicksort for which the worst-case time is $O(n^2)$ for input lists of size n and occurs on the sorted input list. It is well-known that: $\overline{T}_Q(n) \in O(n \log n)$ and $\overline{T}_M(n) \in O(n \log n)$.

For $\mathcal{A}_n$, the lists of size n, and $\mathcal{S}_n$, the single sorted list of size n, we observe that by IO-compositionality:

$$(*) \; \overline{T}_{M;Q}(\mathcal{A}_n) = \overline{T}_M(\mathcal{A}_n) + \overline{T}_Q(\mathcal{O}_M(\mathcal{A}_n)).$$

Hence:

$$(**) \; \overline{T}_{M;Q}(\mathcal{A}_n) = \overline{T}_M(\mathcal{A}_n) + \overline{T}_Q(\{(\mathcal{S}_n, n!)\}).$$

Continuing this computation, we obtain:

$$\overline{T}_Q(\{(\mathcal{S}_n, n!)\}) = \frac{\sum_{i=1}^{n!} T_Q(\mathcal{S}_n)}{n!}$$

$$= T_Q(\mathcal{S}_n) = T_Q^W(\mathcal{S}_n) \in O(n^2).$$

So (∗∗) yields the equality:

$$\overline{T}_{M;Q}(\mathcal{A}_n) = O(nlogn) + O(n^2).$$

Hence:

$$\overline{T}_{M;Q}(\mathcal{A}_n) \in O(n^2).$$

This argument illustrates how the use of output multi-sets, based on IO-compositionality simplifies the determination of the average-case time.

Moreover, IO-compositionality, enables one to express the average-case time of the composition $M; Q$ in terms of the basic components M and Q. Indeed, it is easy to see that since the average time over an output multi-set containing a single list $\mathcal{S}_n$ is of course simply the time on this list, i.e. $\overline{T}_Q(\mathcal{S}_n) = T_Q(\mathcal{S}_n)$, the above argument yields that:

$$\overline{T}_Q(\{(\mathcal{S}_n, n!)\}) = \overline{T}_Q(\mathcal{S}_n).$$

Hence we obtain the compositional expression of $\overline{T}_{M;Q}(\mathcal{A}_n)$ as a *linear combination* of $\overline{T}_M(\mathcal{A}_n)$ and $\overline{T}_Q(\mathcal{S}_n)$:

$$\overline{T}_{M;Q}(\mathcal{A}_n) = \overline{T}_M(\mathcal{A}_n) + \overline{T}_Q(\mathcal{S}_n).$$

Of course the linear combination is a rather trivial one in this case, since the two scalars involved are 1, yielding an ordinary summation. This will be the case in general for the composition of two $\mathcal{MOQA}$ programs, $P_1; P_2$. Indeed, Theorem 1.3 implies that for any program P_1 that transforms a random structure R_1 to a random bag R_2 and for any program P_2 that operates on R_2, the average-case time of the composition of two programs $P_1; P_2$ is given by the following linear combination:

$$\overline{T}_{P_1;P_2}(R_1) = \overline{T}_{P_1}(R_1) + \overline{T}_{P_2}(R_2).$$

Of course, in general, non-trivial linear combinations will be produced for $\mathcal{MOQA}$ programs (cf. Theorem 1.3, 2).

We remark at this stage that, for the above example of the composition of Mergesort with Quicksort, the fact that a single structure $\mathcal{S}_n$ is produced, and hence a fixed number of copies of $\mathcal{S}_n$ is obtained, is a crucial aspect of the argument. Guaranteeing this in general, i.e. achieving a general control over the number of copies of structures produced in the output multi-set, is a non-trivial problem.

In order to achieve this goal, we introduce the notion of a random structure and we require that programs will be *"random structure preserving"*. Random structure preserving programs will in general transform a random structure to a new collection of random structures each of which is copied a given number of times.

The number of copies produced will be computable in practice due to our choice to define a random structure as a collection of states fully determined by a given finite partial order. We will illustrate the basic principles involved regarding the control over the number of copies produced during a computation on another simple example below.

First we clarify the notion of random structure preservation in relation to the previous example. We remark that this example relies heavily on priorly established information. Namely the knowledge of the average times of both Quicksort and Mergesort as well as the fact that sorting algorithms always produce the sorted list as output and the fact that our version of Quicksort has this sorted list as worst-case input. In general, we can not rely on priorly established information and in order for arguments of the above type to succeed, we need to guarantee that a "random structure preserving property" holds for *every* program construct under consideration. In fact, as is clear from the discussion in Chapter 1, we will require the more general condition of random bag preservation. Hence we will require that the property of random bag preservation holds for every basic building block of the programs we consider.

As we will see, not all algorithms are random bag preserving. This fact lies at the root of deep problems with average-case time analysis and divides algorithms in two distinct classes: the class $\mathcal{RB}$ of algorithms that are random bag preserving, i.e. for which each part of the code is random bag preserving, and the complement of this class, $\mathcal{RB}^c$ which contains the algorithms for which some part of the code is not random structure preserving.

We continue to illustrate informally on some basic examples that the preservation of random structures is crucial for average-case time analysis. We first present an example of a toy program "PROJ" which we refer to as "the projection program" and which nicely illustrates how control over the number of copies of random structures produced in the output multi-set is crucial in average-case time analysis. Its pseudo-code is described as follows: $PROJ$ takes lists of size 3 and returns the tail of the input list, i.e. the input list without the first element, as output. One aim of the work is to interpret $\mathcal{MOQA}$ programs as transformation from random bags to random bags, where random structures are interpreted as strict random bags of size 1. $PROJ$ illustrates a transformation of this nature.

For the input-output relation for $PROJ$, displayed on the previous page, x_1, x_2, x_3 represent the elements of the input list of size 3 and x_2, x_3 are the elements of the output list of size 2.

It is clear that the program $PROJ$ transforms the random structure $\mathcal{A}_3$ to three copies of the random structure $\mathcal{A}_2$, after identification up to order-isomorphism. Indeed, the first two output lists form the set $\{(2, 3), (3, 2)\}$, the second two output lists form the set $\{(1, 3), (3, 1)\}$ and the final two form the set $\{(1, 2), (2, 1)\}$. Hence after identification up to order-isomorphism we obtain 3 copies of the random structure $\mathcal{A}_2$.

Identification up to order-isomorphism is typically required to make the average-case time analysis feasible. To ensure that this identification is possible, we need to guarantee that the resulting output multi-set once again amounts to a random bag, in which each random structure is copied a finite number of times. The multiplicity

x_1	x_2	x_3		x_2	x_3
.	.	.		.	.
1	2	3		2	3
.	.	.		.	.
1	3	2		3	2
.	.	.		.	.
2	1	3		1	3
.	.	.		.	.
2	3	1		3	1
.	.	.		.	.
3	1	2		1	2
.	.	.		.	.
3	2	1		2	1
.	.	.		.	.

$$\mathcal{A}_3 \longrightarrow (\mathcal{A}_2, 3)$$

of the random structure plays a crucial role in carrying out the average-case time analysis. We illustrate this on our example PROJ under the assumption that PROJ is composed with another program, say P. Through IO-compositionality *combined* with the fact that PROJ is random structure preserving, the average time of $PROJ; P$ can be specified via the linear combination:

$$\overline{T}_{PROJ;P}(\mathcal{A}_3) = \overline{T}_{PROJ}(\mathcal{A}_3) + \overline{T}_P(\mathcal{A}_2).$$

Indeed, by IO-compositionality and the fact that PROJ is random structure preserving we know that:

$$\overline{T}_{PROJ;P}(\mathcal{A}_3) = \overline{T}_{PROJ}(\mathcal{A}_3) + \overline{T}_P(\mathcal{O}_{PROJ}(\mathcal{A}_3))$$
$$= \overline{T}_{PROJ}(\mathcal{A}_3) + \overline{T}_P(\{(\mathcal{A}_2, 3)\})$$

However

$$\overline{T}_P(\{(\mathcal{A}_2, 3)\}) = \frac{\sum_{I \in \{(\mathcal{A}_2, 3)\}} T_P(I)}{|\{(\mathcal{A}_2, 3)\}|}$$
$$= \frac{3 \sum_{I \in \mathcal{A}_2} T_P(I)}{3 \times 2}$$
$$= \overline{T}_P(\mathcal{A}_2).$$

Of course, this result could be derived directly via Theorem 1.3, 2 b). Hence we obtain the linear expression: $\overline{T}_{PROJ;P}(\mathcal{A}_3) = \overline{T}_{PROJ}(\mathcal{A}_3) + \overline{T}_P(\mathcal{A}_2)$.

So it is clear that, for the case of the above given basic examples, IO-compositionality and random structure preservation implies linear-compositionality. Since IO-compositionality is guaranteed to hold for the average-case time measure, we can state more concisely, for the case of the above examples, that *random structure preservation implies linear-compositionality.*

We will illustrate in Counter-Example 3.2 and by revisiting Counter-Example 1.1 that for well known algorithms, such as Bubblesort and Heapsort, the property of random structure preservation is not guaranteed and that as a result it is not possible to express their average-case time in a linearly-compositional way.

The fact that the class $\mathcal{RB}^c$ is non empty, motivates the need to guarantee random bag preservation in order to achieve a linearly-compositional average-case time analysis. This explains the apparent Average-Case Time Paradox mentioned in Remark 3.2: IO-compositionality in itself is *not* sufficient to simplify the average-case time analysis.

We will illustrate that the violation of random bag preservation can make the analysis hard or even impossible for well-known algorithms. We aim to provide a suitable framework in which random bag preservation is guaranteed.

We verify below that Bubblesort (versions I and II) and Heapsort (including Williams' and Floyd's version), as discussed in Section 2, are not random structure preserving. We will illustrate that the lack of random structure preservation is a fundamental stumbling block in achieving linear-compositionality for the average-case time. In particular, we will show that Heapsort does not allow one to remedy the situation via an equation such as the one of type $(**)$.

Counter-Example 3.2 (Bubblesort)
We will consider the compositionality of the individual passes of the outer for-loop of the Bubblesort algorithm. We assume as usual in the analysis [AHU87] that lists have pairwise distinct elements. Consider the 3! lists of size 3. Both versions of Bubblesort will run in the same way during the first pass of their outer for-loop. After the first pass of the loop, where $i = |L| - 1 = 2$, the 6 resulting lists all have the element 3 "bubbled up" to the final position. It is easy to verify that these 6 lists consist of 4 copies of the list $(1, 2, 3)$ and 2 copies of the list $(2, 1, 3)$. The outcomes are displayed below:

$$(1,2,3) \to (1,2,3) \qquad (2,3,1) \to (2,1,3)$$
$$(1,3,2) \to (1,2,3) \qquad (3,1,2) \to (1,2,3)$$
$$(2,1,3) \to (1,2,3) \qquad (3,2,1) \to (2,1,3)$$

Bubblesort-I will continue on the initial segments of size 2, i.e. 4 copies of $(1, 2)$ and 2 copies of $(2, 1)$ which is no longer uniformly distributed. In other words, the algorithm is not random structure preserving. Bubblesort-II will at that stage ignore the initial segment $(1, 2)$ of the original sorted input list $(1, 2, 3)$ and will hence only be executed on the limited selection consisting of 3 copies of the list $(1, 2)$ and 2 copies of the list $(2, 1)$. This is once again not a uniform distribution.

We remark that for every fixed input size, the comparison time of Bubblesort-I is constant on lists of this size. Hence, it is still possible to determine the average-case

time of Bubblesort-I. Indeed, for every list L of size n we have $T_{B\text{-}I}(L) = \frac{(n-1)n}{2}$.
Hence its average time is $\overline{T}_{B\text{-}I}(\mathcal{A}_n) = \frac{(n-1)n}{2}$.

Bubblesort-I illustrates the existence of *non*-random structure preserving algorithms for which the average-case time still can be determined in a straightforward way due to constant-time behaviour. In general however, algorithms which do not have the constant-time property and which do not preserve randomness will be problematic to analyze and a linearly compositional derivation of the time is not guaranteed. As observed by Knuth, the average-case analysis of the comparison time for Bubblesort-II, which is not randomness preserving nor exhibits constant time behaviour, is *hard* to handle and involves the number of inversion tables [Knu73]. The situation grows worse for Heapsort. We illustrate for this algorithm that the lack of random structure preservation implies that the average-case time measure is not compositional and discuss the deep implications for its average-case time analysis.

Counter-Example 1.1 (Revisited) *(Heapsort)*
We recall that the argument to show that Heapsort does not preserve the uniform distribution of its data is based on a counter-example discussed in [Ede96], which makes an attempt to solve the open problem of designing a "randomness preserving" version of Heapsort. Consider lists of size 4 where we assume that list elements are pairwise distinct. After the heapification phase, viewed over all twenty-four input lists of size 4, a total of 3 non-label-isomorphic heaps are created which arise with equal probability of $\frac{1}{3}$. We display these heaps of size 4, which we denote by $H_4[1], H_4[2]$ and $H_4[3]$, below for labels $1, 2, 3, 4$:

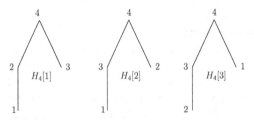

However, this uniform distribution is violated by the selection of the maximal root element which is stored in position 4 for a heap of size 4. After this phase, the algorithm focuses on the heaps obtained by pruning the 4-th element, in this case the leaf of greatest depth, from the heap. Since the resulting heaps are of size 3, we know there are 2 non-label-isomorphic versions of this size. We display these heaps for labels $1, 2, 3$ in the figure below, where the heap of size 3 displayed first is referred to as $H_3[1]$ and the heap of size 3 displayed below this heap is referred to as $H_3[2]$. It is clearly impossible that these 2 heaps are created from the 3 heaps of size 4 with equal probability. In fact, one can verify that $H_4[1]$ and $H_4[3]$ both are transformed to $H_3[2]$, while $H_4[2]$ is transformed to $H_3[1]$, as displayed in the picture below.

$H_4[2] \longrightarrow$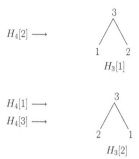

Edelkamp observes in this context: "*Diese Betrachtung hat eine exakte average-case Analyse von allen Heapsort-Varianten bis dato unmöglich gemacht*".[3] The lack of "randomness preservation" is also cited in [FSZ91] as preventing an automated average-case analysis of Heapsort.

We remark that it is truly the break-down of linear-compositionality which prevents a standard average-case analysis. This break-down however only becomes apparent as of size 6, since constant-time behaviour for parts of the algorithm will cause a linear-compositional behaviour despite the absence of random structure preservation.

To illustrate this we focus on the moment at which random structures are no longer preserved, i.e. immediately after the application of the Heapify procedure followed by a single run of the Selection phase consisting of a single swap and Push-Down. We indicate this single run by $Select[1]$ and the remainder of the Selection process by $Select[R]$. Hence

$$Heapsort = Heapify;Select[1];Select[R].$$

As shown above, the uniform distribution will break down in the Selection phase for heaps of size 4. Via a similar argument and using Remark 2.4, we show that, for inputs of at sizes 4, 5 and 6 the uniform distribution must break down following the execution of *Heapify;Select*[1]. Indeed, following Remark 2.4, there are $h(5) = 8$ heaps of size 5 and $h(6) = 20$ heaps of size 6. The Selection phase transforms heaps of size 5 to size 4, where $h(4) = 3$ does not divide $h(5) = 8$. Similarly, the Selection phase transforms heaps of size 6 to size 5, where $h(5) = 8$ does not divide $h(6) = 20$. Hence uniform distribution can not be preserved. As it happens, for heaps of size 4, and similarly for heaps of size 5, the number of comparisons made by the Selection phase is constant (2 and 3 comparisons respectively). This occurs since the heaps produced by *Heapify;Select[1]*, from lists of size 4 and 5, are of size 3 and 4 respectively, for which it is easy to check that the *Select[R]* procedure takes constant time. However this is no longer the case as of size 6 and we obtain[4] that $\overline{T}_{Heapsort}(\mathcal{A}_6) = \frac{10896}{6!}$, while $\overline{T}_{Heapify;Select[1]}(\mathcal{A}_6) = \frac{6864}{6!}$ and $\overline{T}_{Select[R]}(\mathcal{H}_5) = \frac{46}{8}$. Hence:

---

[3] "This fact (i.e. the non-preservation of the uniform distribution for size 4) has made an exact average-case analysis of all Heapsort-variants impossible to date."

[4] Using a program to calculate the number of comparisons for the 6! input lists.

$$\overline{T}_{Heapsort}(\mathcal{A}_6) \neq \overline{T}_{Heapify;Select[1]}(\mathcal{A}_6) + \overline{T}_{Select[R]}(\mathcal{H}_5).$$

The problem is that the swaps in the Selection phase destroy random structure preservation which when combined with the non-constant time behaviour as of size 6 causes the linear-compositionality to fail. As a result, the average-case analysis of Heapsort requires a surprising amount of theoretical machinery compared to the average-case analysis of comparable sized algorithms such as Quicksort ([Ede96], [SS93], [LV93]). One approach involves a Kolmogorov complexity analysis of the Heapsort algorithm using the incompressibility method [LV93], extending Sedgewick's and Schaffer's original approach [SS93]. The determination of a randomness-preserving version of Heapsort is an open problem discussed at length in [Ede96].

It is clear that the absence of randomness preservation can form a main stumbling block in carrying out the average-case time analysis of algorithms.

As remarked above, the lack of random structure preservation can be the cause of non-linear-compositionality, though it is not a sufficient condition. A main theme of this work will be to establish the following central result (Theorem 7.8) for the average-case time measure, which can be informally stated as:

RANDOM BAG PRESERVATION $\Rightarrow$ LINEAR-COMPOSITIONALITY

Chapter 4
Random Bag Preservation and Isolated Subsets

4.1 Random Structures

We revisit the notion of a random structure, which has been defined Definition 1.4 as a quotient consisting of data-labelings (Definition 1.1). Relationships with pomsets are discussed. We recall that the partial orders underlying random structures allow one to incorporate well-known data structures (cf. Example 4.1). One example, from Chapter 1, regards the data structure of lists, determined by the discrete partial order. For lists of size n the identification of data-labelings up to labeling-isomorphism yields as usual the $n!$ permutations over n elements. These can be incorporated as a random structure $\mathcal{A}_n$ over the *discrete* partial order which, when labeled in all possible ways from a finite set of labels, say from the set $\{1, \ldots, n\}$, results in the $n!$ permutations.

Other examples of data structures can be incorporated such as Heap-Ordered-Trees [FS95] and Heaps [AHU87]. A trivial and degenerate example of a random structure is the random structure over the linear order which allows for a single state. This is interpreted as a data structure consisting of the sorted list. We revisit such random structures in detail in Example 4.1 below.

The chapter also introduces the State Theorem (Theorem A.1, Section 4.4). This theorem enables one to interpret states of a random structure as a "generalized permutation". To motivate this, we return to the basic example of the $n!$ permutations over a set $\mathcal{L}$ of n natural numbers. This collection possesses a fundamental "*Randomness Property*":

If one selects an arbitrary permutation from the $n!$ possible permutations over a set of size n then the entire collection of permutations can be generated from the given permutation by carrying out all possible swaps on pairs of elements of the chosen permutation.

As remarked above, we can interpret the collection of permutations as the random structure $\mathcal{A}_n$ over the discrete n-element partial order and hence the randomness property holds for this particular random structure.

The State Theorem provides a generalization of the randomness property of permutations to the context of arbitrary Random Structures. Since, in general, random structures are defined over a non discrete partial order, the notion of a swap on pairs of elements needs to be carefully defined. We introduce the notion of *"free pairs of labels"* for a state from a given random structure, as pairs of labels a and b of incomparable elements x and y for which a swap on the labels a and b will be consistent with the underlying partial order (Definition 4.4), in other words, the newly obtained function is guaranteed to form a new state of the underlying partial order. The State Theorem states that all states of a random structure can be obtained from any arbitrary chosen state of the random structure by carrying out all possible sequences of swaps on free pairs of labels of the chosen state.

Hence we interpret states in random structures as "generalized permutations" for which a "generalized randomness property" holds. We remark that the State Theorem is not a new result and corresponds to the well-known result that the "graph of linear extensions" is connected [Naa00]. We will present a proof which is quite different from standard proofs of this result in Appendix A.

We proceed with formal definitions. We recall the concept of a state, which has been introduced in Chapter 1 as a representative for the equivalence classes obtained by identifying data-labelings by equivalence up to relative order.

We consider a linearly ordered countable collection of labels, say $(\mathcal{L}, <_{\mathcal{L}})$, where in the examples we typically consider $\mathcal{L}$ to be a subset of the natural numbers $\mathcal{N}$.

Definition 4.1. A *state* of a finite partial order $(X, \sqsubseteq)$ *from a set of labels* $\mathcal{L}$, where $|X| = |\mathcal{L}|$, is an increasing injection $F: X \to \mathcal{L}$.

Of course, it follows from the above definition that states are bijections.

Omitting the order in the following notations consists of a slight abuse of notation, which will not cause ambiguities in the work. Let $(X, \sqsubseteq)$ be a finite partial order. We let $m(Y)$ denote the set of minimal elements of $(Y, \sqsubseteq)$ and $M(Y)$ denote the set of maximal elements of $(Y, \sqsubseteq)$. Let F be a data-labeling of this partial order. We let $m(F)$ denote the labels for F of minimal elements of $(X, \sqsubseteq)$, i.e. $F(m(X))$, and we let $M(F)$ denote the labels for F of maximal elements of $(X, \sqsubseteq)$, i.e. $F(M(X))$. For any subset $\mathcal{L}'$ of the set of labels $\mathcal{L}$, we let $m(\mathcal{L}')$ denote the labels in $\mathcal{L}'$ of minimal elements of $(F^{-1}(\mathcal{L}'), \sqsubseteq)$, i.e. $F(m(F^{-1}(\mathcal{L}')))$, and we let $M(\mathcal{L}')$ denote the labels for F of maximal elements of $(F^{-1}(\mathcal{L}'), \sqsubseteq)$, i.e. $F(M(F^{-1}(\mathcal{L}')))$.

Finally we use the following notation: $\vee \mathcal{L}'$ denotes the maximum label of the set $\mathcal{L}'$ while $\wedge \mathcal{L}'$ denotes the minimum label of $\mathcal{L}'$.

Remark 4.1. It is quite evident that the greatest (least) label must occur at a maximal (minimal) element.

Random structures have been defined in Definition 1.4 as a quotient. Here we define such structures directly as collections of states, where we continue to work on representatives.

Definition 4.2. The *random structure* on a finite partial order $(X, \sqsubseteq)$, with respect to a set of labels $\mathcal{L}$ where $|X| = |\mathcal{L}|$, is the set of all states from $\mathcal{L}$ of the partial order. We denote this random structure by: $\mathcal{R}_{\mathcal{L}}(X, \sqsubseteq)$.

Remark 4.2. It is obvious that the cardinality of random structures over partial orders with n elements lies between 1 and $n!$ included, determined by the extreme cases of the linear partial order and the discrete partial order.

Notation: We frequently denote a random structure $\mathcal{R}_{\mathcal{L}}(X, \sqsubseteq)$ by R and in that case refer to the underlying set X and set of labels $\mathcal{L}$ as X_R and $\mathcal{L}_R$.

We remark that the definition of a random structure does *not* require the underlying partial order to be connected.

Remark 4.3. Random structures, $\mathcal{R}_{\mathcal{L}_1}(X, \sqsubseteq)$ and $\mathcal{R}_{\mathcal{L}_2}(X, \sqsubseteq)$, of a given partial order $(X, \sqsubseteq)$ and obtained for two different sets of labels, $\mathcal{L}_1$ and $\mathcal{L}_2$, can easily be seen to be *labeling-isomorphic*, i.e. there exists an order preserving bijection $\Psi_{(\mathcal{L}_1, \mathcal{L}_2)}$ from the linear order $(\mathcal{L}_1, \leq_1)$ to the linear order $(\mathcal{L}_2, \leq_2)$, such that $\mathcal{R}_{\mathcal{L}_2}(X, \sqsubseteq) = \{\Psi_{(\mathcal{L}_1, \mathcal{L}_2)} \circ F \mid F \in \mathcal{R}_{\mathcal{L}_1}(X, \sqsubseteq)\}$. Clearly, if $\mathcal{L}_1 = \{a_1, \ldots, a_n\}$ and $\mathcal{L}_2 = \{b_1, \ldots, b_n\}$ where $\forall i \in \{1, \ldots, n-1\}. a_i <_1 a_{i+1}$ and $b_i <_2 b_{i+1}$ then $\forall i \in \{1, \ldots, n\}. \Psi_{(\mathcal{L}_1, \mathcal{L}_2)}(a_i) = b_i$. We refer to the unique equivalence class for the equivalence relation "labeling-isomorphic" as *the* random structure $\mathcal{R}(X, \sqsubseteq)$ of a partial order $(X, \sqsubseteq)$, which motivated Definition 4.2.

Random structures and pomsets

The reader familiar with "pomsets" may notice that a random structure forms a special type of a pomset. Since pomsets are extensively used in Computer Science, and concurrency in particular, we explain the relation as well as difference with random structures below. We also motivate why we chose not to use the terminology of pomsets in the present work.

Partially ordered bags or pomsets have been used in the context of concurrency ([Pra86]). A *pomset* is defined as the equivalence class of a partial order $(X, \sqsubseteq)$ equipped with an alphabet Σ and labeled via a function $\mu \colon X \to \Sigma$. Two pomsets $(X_1, \sqsubseteq_1, \Sigma_1, \mu_1)$ and $(X_2, \sqsubseteq_2, \Sigma_2, \mu_2)$ are equivalent iff there exists an order preserving bijection $\Psi \colon X_1 \to X_2$ which preserves labels, i.e. $\forall x, y \in X_1. x \sqsubseteq_1 y \Rightarrow \Psi(x_1) \sqsubseteq_2 \Psi(x_2)$ and $\forall x \in X_1. \mu_1(x) = \mu_2(\Psi(x))$.

The data structures of our language will be special types of pomsets since we require the alphabet Σ to be equipped with a linear order and we require the labeling function $\mu \colon X \to \Sigma$ to be order-preserving with respect to the given orders.

Moreover, for the purpose of time analysis, we will focus on data structures, referred to as random structures, for which the labels *are* pairwise distinct. We chose not to use the terminology of partial order *bag* (pomset) since "bag" in this context refers to the fact that labels can be repeated. Hence, to be consistent, for the case where we require labels to be pairwise distinct we should refer to partial order *sets* (posets). The terminology "poset" is standard however for partially ordered sets.

Moreover we will use bags in a different way in our setting and a double use of the terminology would lead to confusion.

As remarked earlier, random structures allow one to incorporate traditional labeled data structures, including heaps, unordered lists, sorted lists, ... , as long as the labelings respect the underlying order. We illustrate this in the next example.

Example 4.1. In each part of the example, we display the Hasse diagram of the given partial order on the left and the states on the right. In each case the underlying set consists of elements $\{x_1, \ldots, x_n\}$, while the labels are the set of indices $\{1, \ldots, n\}$. Parts c), d) and f) illustrate that random structures can incorporate examples such as unordered lists, the sorted list and heaps, in a natural way.

a)

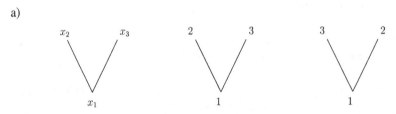

The random structure $\mathcal{R}_{\mathcal{L}}(X, \sqsubseteq)$, where $X = \{x_1, x_2, x_3, x_4\}$, consists of the states F_1 and F_2, where:
$F_1 = \{(x_1, 1), (x_2, 2), (x_3, 3)\}$ and $F_2 = \{(x_1, 1), (x_2, 3), (x_3, 2)\}$.

b)

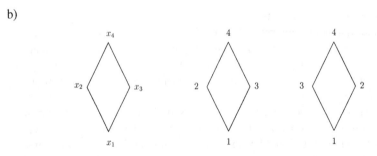

The random structure $\mathcal{R}_{\mathcal{L}}(X, \sqsubseteq)$, where $X = \{x_1, x_2, x_3, x_4\}$, consists of the states F_1 and F_2, where:
$F_1 = \{(x_1, 1), (x_2, 2), (x_3, 3), (x_4, 4)\}$ and $F_2 = \{(x_1, 1), (x_2, 3), (x_3, 2), (x_4, 4)\}$.

c) Consider the partial order $(X, \sqsubseteq)$, where $X = \{x_1, x_2, \ldots, x_n\}$, equipped with the discrete order. The random structure $\mathcal{R}_{\mathcal{L}}(X, \sqsubseteq)$ consists of all $n!$ permutations of labels on the elements of X and can be interpreted as the set of lists of size n. We will denote in the following such a random structure by $\mathcal{A}_n$ where $\mathcal{A}$ stands for "Atomic".

$$x_1 \quad x_2 \quad x_3 \quad \cdots \quad x_{n-1} \quad x_n$$

d) Consider the partial order $(X, \sqsubseteq)$, where $X = \{x_1, x_2, \ldots, x_n\}$, equipped with a linear order. The random structure $\mathcal{R}_\mathcal{L}(X, \sqsubseteq)$ consists of a single state, denoted by $\mathcal{S}_n$, which can be interpreted as the *sorted list*.

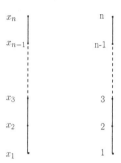

e) We denote the following four-element random structure by $\mathcal{N}$.

The random structure $\mathcal{N}$ consists of the states $F_1, \ldots, F_5$, where

$$F_1 = \{(x_1, 1), (x_2, 2), (x_3, 3), (x_4, 4)\},$$
$$F_2 = \{(x_1, 1), (x_2, 2), (x_3, 4), (x_4, 3)\},$$
$$F_3 = \{(x_1, 2), (x_2, 1), (x_3, 3), (x_4, 4)\},$$
$$F_4 = \{(x_1, 2), (x_2, 1), (x_3, 4), (x_4, 3)\},$$
$$F_5 = \{(x_1, 3), (x_2, 1), (x_3, 4), (x_4, 2)\}.$$

f) Finally, we remark that heaps over a fixed tree structure can be represented as random structures over a partial order which has a tree as Hasse diagram. Heaps of size n are denoted by $\mathcal{H}_n$. For instance, the random structure $\mathcal{H}_3$ determined by the following Hasse diagram and label set $\{1, 2, 3, 4\}$ consists exactly of the states $H_4[1]$, $H_4[2]$ and $H_4[3]$ displayed in Counter-Example 1.1.

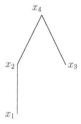

Similarly, Heap Ordered Trees in general can be represented in this way.

4.2 Floor and Ceiling Functions

We introduce "floor" and "ceiling" functions for elements of partial orders. For a partial order $(X, \sqsubseteq)$ and an element $x \in X$, we define $\lceil x \rceil$ to be the set of all elements immediately and strictly above x, i.e.

$$\lceil x \rceil = \{ y \mid y \sqsupset_1 x \}.$$

Similarly, we define:

$$\lfloor x \rfloor = \{ y \mid y \sqsubset_1 x \}.$$

For a discrete subset Y of X, we define:

$$\lceil Y \rceil = \cup_{y \in Y} \lceil y \rceil$$

$$\lfloor Y \rfloor = \cup_{y \in Y} \lfloor y \rfloor.$$

Given a data-labeling F with range $\mathcal{L}$, the floor and ceiling of a label $a \in \mathcal{L}$ is defined as follows:

$$\lceil a \rceil = F(\lceil F^{-1}(a) \rceil)$$

$$\lfloor a \rfloor = F(\lfloor F^{-1}(a) \rfloor).$$

For a subset $\mathcal{A}$ of $\mathcal{L}$ we define:

$$\lceil \mathcal{A} \rceil = F(\lceil F^{-1}(\mathcal{A}) \rceil)$$

$$\lfloor \mathcal{A} \rfloor = F(\lfloor F^{-1}(\mathcal{A}) \rfloor).$$

Of course, we have:

$$a \in \lceil b \rceil \Rightarrow a > b$$

$$a \in \lfloor b \rfloor \Rightarrow a < b.$$

Example 4.2. For the data-labelings displayed in the example, we have that:
$\lceil 2 \rceil = \{3, 5\}$, $\lfloor 2 \rfloor = \{1\}$, $\lceil 4 \rceil = \{5\}$, $\lfloor 4 \rfloor = \{1\}$, $\lceil 5 \rceil = \emptyset$ and $\lfloor 5 \rfloor = \{2, 4\}$.

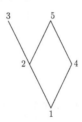

4.3 Free Sets of Labels

We introduce the notion of free sets of labels for a data-labeling F. Intuitively two labels are free if they can be interchanged ("swapped") in the given data-labeling without violating the fact that the data-labeling is increasing. We define a swap operation on pairs of labels.

Definition 4.3. Given a set of labels $\mathcal{L}$ and a pair of labels (a, b) from $\mathcal{L}$, we define $\sigma_{a,b}$ as the permutation of $\mathcal{L}$ which swaps a and b and acts as the identity on all other labels. We define $Swap(a, b)(F) = \sigma_{a,b} \circ F$ for all functions F whose range is included in $\mathcal{L}$.

Remark 4.4. The operation $Swap(a, b)$ can be applied to any data-labeling F with range in $\mathcal{L}$ but this does not necessarily yield a new data-labeling.

Definition 4.4. A pair (a, b) of labels of $\mathcal{L}$ is *free* for a data-labeling $F \in \mathcal{R}_{\mathcal{L}}(X, \sqsubseteq)$ in case $Swap(a, b)(F) \in \mathcal{R}_{\mathcal{L}}(X, \sqsubseteq)$, or in other words, when $Swap(a, b)(F)$ is still a data-labeling. In this case we refer to the application of $Swap(a, b)$ to F as a "free swap". A subset $\mathcal{A}$ of $\mathcal{L}$ is free for F in case its elements are pairwise free for F.

We leave the verification of the following lemma to the reader.

Lemma 4.1. *If $\mathcal{A} \subseteq \mathcal{L}$ is free for F, where $F \in \mathcal{R}_{\mathcal{L}}(X, \sqsubseteq)$ then $F^{-1}(\mathcal{A})$ is a discrete subset of $(X, \sqsubseteq)$.*

Proposition 4.1. *If $\mathcal{A} \subseteq \mathcal{L}$, where $|\mathcal{L}| \geq 2$ and $F \in \mathcal{R}_{\mathcal{L}}(X, \sqsubseteq)$ then the following are equivalent:*

1) $\mathcal{A}$ is free for F

2) i) if $\lceil \mathcal{A} \rceil \neq \emptyset$ then $\vee \mathcal{A} < \wedge \lceil \mathcal{A} \rceil$
  ii) if $\lfloor \mathcal{A} \rfloor \neq \emptyset$ then $\wedge \mathcal{A} > \vee \lfloor \mathcal{A} \rfloor$

Proof. Let $a = \wedge \mathcal{A}$, $b = \vee \mathcal{A}$ and $Y = F^{-1}(\mathcal{A})$.

We show that 1) $\Rightarrow$ 2). We prove (i). The proof of (ii) is similar. Suppose that $\vee \mathcal{A} = b \not< \wedge \lceil \mathcal{A} \rceil$. Then there exist $z \in Y$ and $z' \in \lceil Y \rceil$ such that $z \sqsubset_1 z'$ and (*) $F(z') \leq b$. Let $c = F(z)$. By hypothesis (b, c) is free for F and thus $F' = Swap(b, c)(F)$ is a data-labeling. It follows that $F'(z) < F'(z')$. Now, $F'(z) = b$ by definition of F'. Furthermore $F'(z') = F(z')$. Thus we have $b = F'(z) < F'(z') = F(z') \leq b$, by (*), which is a contradiction.

We show that 2) $\Rightarrow$ 1). We suppose that $\vee \lfloor \mathcal{A} \rfloor < a < b < \wedge \lceil \mathcal{A} \rceil$.

First we note that the hypothesis implies that Y is discrete. Indeed, if $x, y \in Y$ and $x \sqsubset y$ then there is $x' \in \lceil Y \rceil$ such that $x \sqsubset_1 x' \sqsubseteq y$. Thus $a \leq F(x) < F(x') \leq F(y) \leq b$ and thus $b \not< \wedge \lceil \mathcal{A} \rceil$; a contradiction.

We note that since $\lfloor \mathcal{A} \rfloor = F(\lfloor Y \rfloor)$ and $\lceil \mathcal{A} \rceil = F(\lceil Y \rceil)$ and since F is a data-labeling, we have (by definition of a and b) that:

$(*)$ $\forall x \in (Y\!\downarrow - Y).\, F(x) < a.$
$(**)$ $\forall x \in (Y\!\uparrow - Y).\, F(x) > b.$

Let $c, d \in \mathcal{A}$ and $F' = Swap(c, d)(F)$. Let $u = F^{-1}(c)$ and $v = F^{-1}(d)$, where $u, v \in Y$. Suppose now that $x, y \in X$ and $x \sqsubset y$. Since F is a data-labeling and F' coincides with F outside of $\{u, v\}$, we necessarily have that $F'(x) < F'(y)$ if $x, y \notin \{u, v\}$. Otherwise,

If $x \in \{u, v\} \subseteq Y$ then $y \in Y\!\uparrow - Y$ since Y is discrete and thus, using $(**)$, we have: $F'(y) = F(y) > b$. Since $F'(x) \in \{c, d\}$ we have $F'(x) < F'(y)$ as required. Similarly: if $y \in \{u, v\} \subseteq Y$ then $x \in Y\!\downarrow - Y$ since Y is discrete and thus, using $(*)$, we have: $F'(x) = F(x) < a$. Since $F'(y) \in \{c, d\}$ we have $F'(x) < F'(y)$.

Corollary 4.1. *If $a < b$ then*
$\mathcal{A} = \{a, b\}$ *is a free pair of labels for $F \iff$*

1) if $\lceil a \rceil \neq \emptyset$ then $b < \wedge \lceil a \rceil$
2) if $\lfloor b \rfloor \neq \emptyset$ then $a > \vee \lfloor b \rfloor$

Example 4.3. We illustrate free pairs of labels for the following data-labelings.

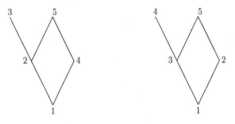

The data-labelings in the above example, displayed in left to right order, are referred to as F_1 and F_2 respectively. F_1 only has one free pair of labels, namely $\{3, 4\}$. Data-Labeling F_1 illustrates that it is not sufficient for two labels to label incomparable elements in order for the labels to form a free pair. Indeed, this is for instance the case for the pairs $\{3, 5\}$ and $\{2, 4\}$. The data-labeling F_2 has two free pairs of labels, namely $\{4, 5\}$ and $\{2, 3\}$.

Comment: We remark that a swap on a free pair of labels preserves the data-labeling property but does not guarantee that the new data-labeling has the same pairs of elements labeled with free labels, as the following counter-example shows.

Counter-Example 4.1 We reconsider the data-labelings F_1 and F_2 of Example 4.3. For F_1 displayed on the left below, we note that the free pairs of labels are $\{2,3\},\{3,4\}$ and $\{4,5\}$. After a swap on the free pair $\{2,3\}$, we obtain the data-labeling F_2 displayed on the right hand side. F_2 still has $\{2,3\}$ and $\{4,5\}$ as free pairs of labels, but $\{2,4\}$ is no longer a free pair for the elements originally labeled with 3 and 4.

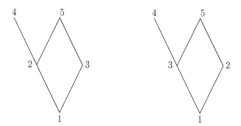

4.4 Free Swaps on Random Structures

We discuss the State Theorem which establishes that states in random structures can be interpreted as generalized permutations. The proof of the State Theorem is of a technical nature, requiring concepts which are not used elsewhere in the monograph. Hence we include this proof as an appendix (Section A).

In order to derive the State Theorem of Chapter A, we will show the following result (Corollary A.4):

For every pair of states F_1, F_2 over a connected partial order there exists a sequence of permutations $\sigma_1, \ldots, \sigma_n$ on free pairs of labels such that $F_2 = \sigma_n \circ \sigma_{n-1} \circ \ldots \sigma_2 \circ \sigma_1 \circ F_1$.

We illustrate Corollary A.4 with the following example.

Example 4.4. We verify for two given states F_1, F_2 that the first can be transformed into the second.

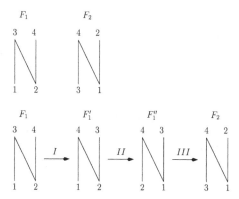

We remark that the sets of free pairs are given by: $FP(F_1) = FP(F_1') = \{\{3, 4\}, \{1, 2\}\}$, $FP(F_1'') = \{\{3, 4\}, \{1, 2\}, \{2, 3\}\}$, $FP(F_2) = \{\{2, 3\}\}$.

Remark 4.5. Each permutation of a free pair in a given state, may cause other pairs to change their status: some pairs which originally were not free may become free after a given swap, while some free pairs may cease to be free after a swap on a given free pair. This fact is illustrated in Example 4.4 by steps II and III respectively.

From the above corollary, we will obtain the following immediate State Theorem, Theorem A.1:

Each random structure on a finite connected partial order can be generated from any given state, by exhaustively carrying out all possible swap sequences on free pairs of labels, where a sequence terminates when a state is repeated.

Example 4.5. Consider the state F_1 of the previous example. Transforming F_1 to F_2 generates four of the five possible states, simply by carrying out the following swap sequences: (I), (I,II) and (I,II,III) . To generate the fifth state one can for instance make a swap on the labels 1 and 2 of F_1.

4.5 Random Bag Preserving Functions

We will define operations for $\mathcal{MOQA}$ that transform a random structure R into a bag of random structures

$$\{(\mathcal{R}_{\mathcal{L}_1}(X_1, \sqsubseteq_1), K_1), \ldots, (\mathcal{R}_{\mathcal{L}_n}(X_n, \sqsubseteq_n), K_n)\}.$$

The notion of random structure preserving function and more generally, random bag preserving function, has been defined in Chapter 1. In Chapter 1, the resulting random bags were strict, as an identification up to labeling-isomorphism was carried out. Here, we loosen the requirement on the output bag, such that general random bags can be considered. This essentially amounts to relaxing the requirement of a complete identification up to labeling-isomorphism in condition 3 of Definition 1.8.

In Chapter 1, general data-labelings were considered in defining random structure/bag preserving functions. We will still consider operations which transform data-labelings to data-labelings, but, to simplify the presentation, we will define RB-preservation in the present chapter directly on random bags. The implicit assumption is made that this approach suffices due to labeling-invariance of the operations. The adaptations to definitions of RB-preservation for general data-labelings are of a technical nature and would needlessly complicate the presentation.

We recall the notion of a *refinement* from Chapter 1. Operations "refine" the original partial order in that the newly created partial orders of the resulting bag have underlying sets X_i that are subsets of the original set X and have orders $\sqsubseteq_i$ that are finer than, i.e. include, the restriction of the original partial order $\sqsubseteq$ to the new set X_i under consideration. The sets X_i can be strict subsets of the original set X since the operations of $\mathcal{MOQA}$ include for instance a deletion operation which removes an element and its labels. We further formalize the notion of refinement below.

Definition 4.5. Let $R = \mathcal{R}_\mathcal{L}(X, \sqsubseteq)$ and $\forall i \in \{1, \ldots, n\}$. $R_i = \mathcal{R}_{\mathcal{L}_i}(X_i, \sqsubseteq_i)$, where $\forall i \in \{1, \ldots, n\}$. $\mathcal{L}_i \subseteq \mathcal{L}$ and $\forall i \in \{1, \ldots, n\}$. $X_i \subseteq X$ and $\forall x, y \in X_i. x \sqsubseteq y \Rightarrow x \sqsubseteq_i y$. We call a bag of random structures $\{R_1, \ldots, R_n\}$ satisfying this condition *a refinement* of the random structure R. We also refer to $\mathcal{L}_i$ as a refinement of the label set $\mathcal{L}$ and to each $(X_i, \sqsubseteq_i)$ as a refinement of the partial order $(X, \sqsubseteq)$.

Definition 4.6. A function $\phi \colon R \to \mathcal{F}$ is *refining* on R if there exists a refinement $\{R_1, \ldots, R_n\}$ of R such that $\phi \colon R \to R_1 \cup \ldots \cup R_n$ is surjective.

Definition 4.7. In case we have determined a refinement $\{R_1, \ldots, R_n\}$ of R, based on which we can establish that the function ϕ is refining on R, then we refer to ϕ in combination with this particular selection of a refinement as a *representation for* ϕ. Such a representation is denoted as follows: $\phi \colon R \longmapsto \{R_1, \ldots, R_n\}$.

The following definition formalizes the notion of random structure preservation, in such a way that the range is allowed to be a general random bag as opposed to a strict random bag. This is achieved through the notion of a partition, which allows for the incorporation of output random bags which may contain two identical random structures. Of course, one could always guarantee that the random bag $\{R_1, \ldots, R_n\}$ is such that the underlying partial orders are pairwise distinct by identifying random structures with the same, i.e. order-isomorphic, underlying partial orders and by adjusting the multiplicities accordingly. We prefer to keep the more general version of RS-preservation at this time, since identification of order-isomorphic partial orders in practice may be costly. For instance, it is clear from Example 5.13, that the random delete operation Del^m introduced in Section 5.3, when called more than once on a given random structure, can produce several copies of the same random structure. These copies are typically not grouped together in the random bag in order to avoid the costly identification of identical copies. This reproduction of identical copies, without necessarily identifying them in the random bag, necessitates a slightly more technical definition of RS-preservation as given in Definition 4.8, as opposed to the simplified definition of Remark 4.6 2), where this last simplification corresponds to the definition considered in Chapter 1 for which the output random bag was assumed to be strict. We revisit the simplification in Remark 5.10, where the potential to make $\mathcal{MOQA}$ operations separative is considered.

Definition 4.8. A function $\mu \colon \mathcal{F} \to \mathcal{F}$ is *random structure preserving on a random structure* R (RS-preserving on a random structure R) iff there exists a partition $\mathcal{F}_1, \ldots, \mathcal{F}_n$ of R, a refinement $\{R_1, \ldots, R_n\}$ of R and non-zero natural numbers $K_1, \ldots, K_n$ such that

$$\forall F \in R_i. |\mu^{-1}(F) \cap \mathcal{F}_i| = K_i.$$

The function μ is called *strongly RS-preserving* if and only if $n = 1$.

Remark 4.6. 1) Note that since multiplicities are required to be non-zero, we obtain, following the notation of Definition 4.8, that: $\forall i \in \{1, \dots, n\}. \mu(\mathcal{F}_i) = R_i$.
2) The definition of RS-preservation is more general than the informal use of randomness preservation in the literature. The informal use of randomness preservation only regards the preservation of the uniform distribution, where a random structure is mapped to a single random structure, as is the case for the Backwards Analysis of [Knu73] and for the cases discussed in [Ede96], and no non-trivial multiplicity is involved (i.e. $K = 1$). This is captured in our context by the notion of a strongly RS-preserving function with multiplicity 1. RS-preserving functions in our context, map a random structure to a *bag* of random structures.

Remark 4.7. It is clear that the definition of RS-preservation could be simplified in case the random structures $R_1, \dots, R_n$ have pairwise distinct underlying partial orders. In that case the definition is equivalent to the following:

$$\forall F \in R_i. |\mu^{-1}(F)| = K_i.$$

The generalization of the intuitive notion of randomness preservation in the literature, i.e. the generalization of the notion of strong RS-preservation with multiplicity 1, to RS-preservation on a random structure (and later on to RB-preservation on a random bag) is important since it allows one to lift the applications from rather straightforward reasonings on preservation of uniform distribution in the context of strong random structure preservation, to more intricate applications of a wider scope.

Definition 4.9. In case we have determined a refinement $\{R_1, \dots, R_n\}$ of R with multiplicities $K_1, \dots, K_n$ with respect to some partition $\mathcal{F}_1, \dots, \mathcal{F}_n$, based on which we can establish that the function μ is RS-preserving on R, then we refer to μ in combination with this particular selection of a refinement, partition and multiplicities as an *RS-representation for* μ. Such an RS-representation for μ is denoted as follows:

$$\mu_{\{\mathcal{F}_1, \dots, \mathcal{F}_n\}} \colon R \longmapsto \{(R_1, K_1), \dots, (R_n, K_n)\}.$$

We remark that the same operation can have two representations. One example is again the Del^m operation, which when composed with itself as in $Del^m \circ Del^m$, can yield multiple copies of a random structure in the output random bag. This allows for two representations: one representation in which the copies are not identified, i.e. occur with multiplicity one in the random bag, and one representation for which the random structures in the random bag are identified and displayed only once, paired with a multiplicity which is greater than one.

Definition 4.10. A partition $\{\mathcal{F}_1, \ldots, \mathcal{F}_n\}$ is *uniform* iff all members of the partition have the same cardinality, i.e. $|\mathcal{F}_1| = |\mathcal{F}_2| = \ldots = |\mathcal{F}_n|$. The function μ is called *uniformly RS-preserving* iff it has an RS-presentation

$$\mu_{\{\mathcal{F}_1, \ldots, \mathcal{F}_n\}} \colon R \longmapsto \{(R_1, K_1), \ldots, (R_n, K_n)\}$$

for which the partition $\{\mathcal{F}_1, \ldots, \mathcal{F}_n\}$ is uniform.

Remark 4.8. Strongly RS-preserving functions are (trivially) uniformly RS-preserving since their representations have partitions of cardinality one.

Notation 4.2 Typically, and with some abuse of notation, we will not mention the partition involved for RS-representations:

$$\mu \colon R \longmapsto \{(R_1, K_1), \ldots, (R_n, K_n)\}.$$

The motivation behind this shorter notation is that once our choice for the refining bag, the partition and the corresponding multiplicities have been determined, we only need the resulting random bag in order to determine the average-case time.

Definition 4.11. A random bag is a finite bag of pairs, $\{(R_1, K_1), \ldots, (R_n, K_n)\}$, each of which consists of a random structure R paired with a multiplicity K.

We extend RS-preserving functions from random structures to random bags as follows:

Definition 4.12. (RB-preservation on a random bag)
If $\{(R_1, K_1), \ldots, (R_n, K_n)\}$ is a random bag and μ is RB-preserving on each of the random structures $R_1, \ldots, R_n$, where

$$\forall i \in \{1, \ldots, n\}.\, \mu \colon R_i \longmapsto \{(R_i^1, K_i^1), \ldots, (R_i^{n_i}, K_i^{n_i})\},$$

then we denote this by:

$$\mu \colon \{(R_1, K_1), \ldots, (R_n, K_n)\} \longmapsto$$
$$\{(R_1^1, K_1^1 \times K_1), \ldots, (R_1^{n_1}, K_1^{n_1} \times K_1), \ldots, (R_n^1, K_n^1 \times K_n), \ldots, (R_n^{n_n}, K_n^{n_n} \times K_n)\}.$$

We say in that case that:

μ is *RB-preserving* on *the random bag* $\{(R_1, K_1), \ldots, (R_n, K_n)\}$.

Remark 4.9. Note that the notion of RS-representation of Definition 4.9 can be generalized to that of RB-representation in the obvious way.

We omit the straightforward verification of the following two results.

Proposition 4.2. *If* μ: $\{(R_1, K_1), \ldots, (R_n, K_n)\} \longmapsto$
$\{(R_1^1, K_1^1 \times K_1), \ldots, (R_1^{n_1}, K_1^{n_1} \times K_1), \ldots, (R_n^1, K_n^1 \times K_n), \ldots, (R_n^{n_n}, K_n^{n_n} \times K_n)\}$ *then:*

$$\sum_{i=1}^{n} K_i \times |R_i| = \sum_{i=1}^{n} \sum_{j=1}^{n_i} K_i \times K_i^j \times |R_i^j|.$$

Lemma 4.2. *The composition of RB-preserving functions on random bags is RB-preserving.*

For strongly RB-preserving functions, Proposition 4.2 yields the following immediate corollary.

Corollary 4.2. *If* μ: $R_1 \longmapsto R_2$ *is a strongly RB-preserving function then* $|R_2|$ *divides* $|R_1|$.

Remark 4.10. Note that no zero-value problem arises, in case one caries out the above division, since for every random structure R one has $|R| \geq 1$. Indeed, if R is the random structure over the empty set, then $|R| = 1$ where R consists of the "empty function".

Definition 4.13. Random bags (random structures) that are the image of some discrete random structure $\mathcal{A}_k$ for a RB-preserving function are called $\mathcal{A}$-*constructible* (Atomic-constructible) random bags (random structures).

Remark 4.11. We state the following open questions in decreasing generality:

[1] "Characterise the existence of RB-preserving functions between random bags."

[2] "Characterise the existence of strongly RB-preserving functions between random structures."

[3] "Characterize the random bags that are $\mathcal{A}$-constructible."

We leave these questions to future research since their exploration would go beyond the scope of the present work. Note that, by Proposition 4.2, a necessary condition for a random bag $[(R_1, K_1), \ldots, (R_n, K_n)]$ to be $\mathcal{A}$-constructible from some discrete random structure $\mathcal{A}_k$ is that $\sum_{i=1}^{n} K_i \times |R_i| = k!$.

Example 4.6. To illustrate a basic application of Corollary 4.2, we remark that the random structure $\mathcal{N}$ of Example 4.1, part (e), is *not* $\mathcal{A}$-constructible. Indeed, the cardinality of $\mathcal{N}$ is 5 which does not divide the cardinality 24 of the discrete four-element random structure.

We remark that a partial solution for the question, related to open question [3], on the constructibility of $\mathcal{MOQA}$ *data structures* from the discrete random structure, is obtained in Section 5.9.

4.6 Isolated Subsets

We introduce the notion of an isolated subset of a partial order. Isolated subsets have the following important property:

For any random structure $\mathcal{R}(X, \sqsubseteq)$, the bag consisting of the restriction of the states of this random structure to an isolated subset I of X forms, after identification up to label-isomorphism, a number of copies of the random structure $\mathcal{R}(I, \sqsubseteq)$.

We continue to use the notation in the above property and remark that the notion of an isolated subset will be useful in the following two contexts:

Defining the projection operation
It is clear from the above key property of isolated sets that isolated subsets enable the definition a notion of projection of a given random structure $\mathcal{R}(X, \sqsubseteq)$ on the random structure $\mathcal{R}(I, \sqsubseteq)$. This is the subject of Section 5.4.

Extending the $\mathcal{MOQA}$ operations
Isolated subsets allow, under appropriate conditions, the extension of the definition of an operation on the random structure $\mathcal{R}(I, \sqsubseteq)$ to the entire random structure $\mathcal{R}(X, \sqsubseteq)$. This extension of $\mathcal{MOQA}$ operations is discussed in Section 4.6.3.

An informal definition of an isolated subset I of X, for a given random structure $\mathcal{R}(X, \sqsubseteq)$, is that the extremal[1] elements of I are the only "exit and entrance points" of the set I to and from "related points" in the complement $X - I$. This motivates the choice of the adjective *isolated* and is captured by condition 1 of Definition 4.14. Moreover, we require that every point of $X - I$ that is immediately below a minimal element of I must be immediately below *every* minimal element of I, which is captured by condition 2 of Definition 4.14. Similarly, we require that every point of $X - I$ that is immediately above a maximal element of I must be immediately above *every* maximal element of I, which is captured by condition 3 of Definition 4.14.

---

[1] Extremal with respect to the restriction of the order $\sqsubseteq$ to the set I.

Definition 4.14. Given a finite partial order $(X, \sqsubseteq)$. A subset I of X is *isolated* iff it satisfies the following three conditions:

1) $\lfloor I - m(I) \rfloor \subseteq I$ and $\lceil I - M(I) \rceil \subseteq I$
2) $\forall x, y \in m(I). \lfloor x \rfloor = \lfloor y \rfloor$
3) $\forall x, y \in M(I). \lceil x \rceil = \lceil y \rceil$

An *atomic isolated subset*, or $\mathcal{A}$-*isolated subset*, is an isolated subset of a partial order for which the restriction of the order to the isolated subset is the discrete order.

An isolated subset is *trivially isolated* in case $\lfloor m(I) \rfloor = \lceil M(I) \rceil = \emptyset$. In that case conditions 2) and 3) are trivially satisfied.

Example 4.7. a) The empty set is trivially isolated.
b) The union of components of a partial order is trivially isolated.
c) Consider a partial order with Hasse diagram as displayed below. The subset I, determined by the elements contained in the ellipse on the diagram, is isolated.

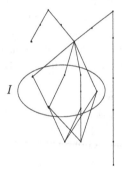

Exercise 4.1. Show that the relation "isolated subset" is transitive. I.e. if I is an isolated subset of the partial order $(X, \sqsubseteq)$ and J is an isolated subset of the restricted partial order $(I, \sqsubseteq)$ then J is an isolated subset of the partial order $(X, \sqsubseteq)$.

Example 4.8. The Hasse diagram below provides an example where the set $\{x_3, x_4\}$ does not form an atomic isolated set, while $\{x_4, x_5\}$ forms an atomic isolated set.

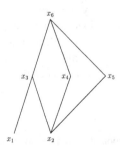

The first part of the following lemma generalizes the observation in Example 4.7 b). The proof of the lemma is left as an exercise.

Lemma 4.3. *1) If I is an isolated subset of $(X, \sqsubseteq)$ then the union of finitely many components of I is also an isolated subset of $(X, \sqsubseteq)$.*
2) Every trivially isolated subset I of $(X, \sqsubseteq)$ is a finite union of components of X.
3) Every isolated subset I of $(X, \sqsubseteq)$ which is not trivially isolated is a subset of a component of X, where this component is denoted by C(I).

Example 4.9. We illustrate Lemma 4.3 1) via Example 4.7, where the set I consists of three isolated components displayed below. For this example it is clear that every union of a finite selection of these components forms again an isolated subset of the original set.

We define the useful notion of a pair of perfectly connected subsets of a partial order and proceed to give an alternative characterization of an isolated subset.

Definition 4.15. Given a partial order $(X, \sqsubseteq)$ and a pair of non-empty subsets A and B of X. The set A is said to be *perfectly below* B and B is said to be *perfectly above* A iff
$$\{(x,y) \mid x \in A, y \in B, x \in \lfloor y \rfloor\} = A \times B.$$

Two non-empty sets A and B are said to be *perfectly connected* $\Leftrightarrow A$ is perfectly below B or A is perfectly above B.

The following lemma shows that perfectly connected sets are always disjoint *discrete* subsets.

Lemma 4.4. *1) If A is perfectly below B then $A \cap B = \emptyset$.*
2) If A and B are non empty subsets and A is perfectly below B then A and B determine discrete suborders.

Proof. 1) Assume by way of contradiction that A is perfectly below B and that $A \cap B \neq \emptyset$, where say $x \in A \cap B$. Note that $(x,x) \in A \times B$ but $(x,x) \notin \{(x,y) \mid x \in A, y \in B, x \in \lfloor y \rfloor\}$. Hence we obtain a contradiction.

2) Consider two non empty subsets A and B such that $\{(x,y) \mid x \in A, y \in B, x \in \lfloor y \rfloor\} = A \times B$. Assume, by way of contradiction, that the restricted order on A or on B is not discrete. Say the order restricted to B is not discrete. The proof for the case where the order restricted to A is non discrete is similar. In case the restricted

order on B is not discrete, we must have that $|B| \geq 2$, hence there exist $x, y \in B$ such that $x \sqsubset y$. Since A is not empty, consider $z \in A$. Since $A \times B = \{(x, y) \mid x \in A, y \in B, x \in \lfloor y \rfloor\}$ and since $(z, x) \in A \times B$, we obtain that $z \in \lfloor x \rfloor$. Hence, since $x \sqsubset y$, we have $z \notin \lfloor y \rfloor$. This contradicts the fact that $(z, y) \in A \times B$.

Example 4.10. We consider the isolated subset I of Example 4.7 c). Note that the sets $A = M(I)$ and $B = \lceil M(I) \rceil$ are perfectly connected. Also note that the sets $C = \lfloor m(I) \rfloor$ and $D = m(I)$ are perfectly connected. The sets A, B, C and D are discrete non empty subsets, where A and B are disjoint and where C and D are disjoint.

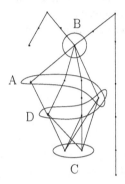

Lemma 4.5. *Given a finite partial order $(X, \sqsubseteq)$. A subset I of X is isolated iff it satisfies the following three conditions:*

1) $\lfloor I - m(I) \rfloor \subseteq I$ and $\lceil I - M(I) \rceil \subseteq I$
2) if $\lfloor m(I) \rfloor \neq \emptyset$ then $\lfloor m(I) \rfloor$ is perfectly below $m(I)$
3) if $\lceil M(I) \rceil \neq \emptyset$ then $M(I)$ is perfectly below $\lceil M(I) \rceil$.

Proof. Exercise.

4.6.1 Strictly Isolated Subsets

We define the notion of a strictly isolated subset of a partial order. This notion will be useful in extending so-called "contractive operations" defined on a random structure determined by a (strictly) isolated subset of a given random structure, to the entire random structure. Contractive operations are operations which reduce the size of the partial orders, where typical examples of such operations are deletions and projections. Contractive operations are discussed in Section 4.6.3.

The notion of a strictly isolated subset relies on the technical concept of a seam.

Definition 4.16. A *seam* of a subset C of a partial order $(X, \sqsubseteq)$ is a pair (A, B) of subsets A, B of C such that:

a) A is perfectly below B
b) $(A{\downarrow}) \cup (B{\uparrow}) = C$

Example 4.11. In the example below the pair (A, B) forms a seam of the given partial order.

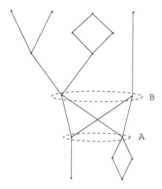

We leave the proofs of Lemma 4.6, Lemma 4.7 and Corollary 4.3 as an exercise.

Lemma 4.6. *If (A, B) is a seam of a component C of $(X, \sqsubseteq)$ then for all collections of labels $\mathcal{L}$ where $|\mathcal{L}| = |C|$ and for all states $F \in \mathcal{R}_{\mathcal{L}}(C, \sqsubseteq)$, the label sets $F(A{\downarrow})$ and $F(B{\uparrow})$ do not vary with F. In other words:*

$$\forall F_1, F_2 \in \mathcal{R}_{\mathcal{L}}(C, \sqsubseteq). F_1(A{\downarrow}) = F_2(A{\downarrow}) \text{ and } F_1(B{\uparrow}) = F_2(B{\uparrow}).$$

Lemma 4.6 ensures that the following notation is sound.

Notation 4.3 If (A, B) is a seam of a component C of $(X, \sqsubseteq)$ and $F \in \mathcal{R}_{\mathcal{L}}(C, \sqsubseteq)$ then $\mathcal{L}_A = F(A{\downarrow})$ and $\mathcal{L}_B = F(B{\uparrow})$.

Lemma 4.7. *If (A, B) is a seam of the component C of $(X, \sqsubseteq)$ then $\mathcal{R}_{\mathcal{L}}(C, \sqsubseteq) = \{F_1 \cup F_2 | F_1 \in \mathcal{R}_{\mathcal{L}_A}(A{\downarrow}, \sqsubseteq), F_2 \in \mathcal{R}_{\mathcal{L}_B}(B{\uparrow}, \sqsubseteq)\}.$*

Corollary 4.3. *If (A, B) is a seam of a component C of $(X, \sqsubseteq)$ then $|\mathcal{R}_{\mathcal{L}}(C, \sqsubseteq)| = |\mathcal{R}_{\mathcal{L}_A}(A{\downarrow}, \sqsubseteq)| \times |\mathcal{R}_{\mathcal{L}_B}(B{\uparrow}, \sqsubseteq)|.$*

Definition 4.17. A *strictly isolated subset* J of a partial order $(X, \sqsubseteq)$ is an isolated subset of X which:

a) is trivially isolated or

b) satisfies the following conditions, using the notation of Lemma 4.3 3):

$$\lfloor m(J) \rfloor \neq \emptyset \Rightarrow (\lfloor m(J) \rfloor, m(J)) \text{ forms a seam of } C(J).$$
$$\lceil M(J) \rceil \neq \emptyset \Rightarrow (M(J), \lceil M(J) \rceil) \text{ forms a seam of } C(J).$$

An *atomic strictly isolated subset* of a partial order is a strictly isolated subset for which the restriction of the order to this subset is the discrete order.

A strictly isolated subset is *trivially strictly isolated* in case it is trivially isolated.

Notation 4.4 If $(X, \sqsubseteq)$ is a partial order and $A \subseteq X$ then

$$\overline{A} = \lceil M(A) \rceil \uparrow \text{ and } \underline{A} = \lfloor m(A) \rfloor \downarrow .$$

Lemma 4.8. *Every strictly isolated subset of a partial order is isolated.*

Proof. Consider a partial order $(X, \sqsubseteq)$ and a strictly isolated subset I of this partial order. If I is trivially isolated then it is isolated. Otherwise, following the notation of Lemma 4.3 3), consider the component $C(I)$ containing I. Note that since $C(I)$ is a component of X, by transitivity (Exercise 4.1), it suffices to verify that I is an isolated subset of $C(I)$. By the definition of a seam, we have $C(I) - I = \overline{I} \cup \underline{I}$. The result follows by an application of Lemma 4.5. Condition 1) of Lemma 4.5 is satisfied since $C(I) - I = \overline{I} \cup \underline{I}$. Conditions 2) and 3) of Lemma 4.5 follow from condition b) of Definition 4.17.

Example 4.12. The empty set $\emptyset$, the set X, and unions of components of X are strictly isolated since each such set is trivially isolated.

Example 4.13. Consider the partial order displayed below. We remark that the subset $I = \{x_1, x_2, x_3, x_4\}$ is a strictly isolated subset, where the relations of the restriction of the partial order to I are indicated via dotted lines.

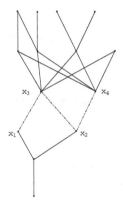

Definition 4.18. Given a partial order $(X, \sqsubseteq)$, we define the following sets:

$\mathcal{I}(X, \sqsubseteq) = \{I \mid I \text{ is an isolated subset of } (X, \sqsubseteq)\}$
$\mathcal{I}^*(X, \sqsubseteq) = \{I \mid I \text{ is a non-trivially isolated subset of } (X, \sqsubseteq)\}$
$\mathcal{AI}(X, \sqsubseteq) = \{I \mid I \text{ is an atomic isolated subset of } (X, \sqsubseteq)\}$

$\mathcal{SI}(X, \sqsubseteq) = \{I \mid I \text{ is a strictly isolated subset of } (X, \sqsubseteq)\}$
$\mathcal{SI}^*(X, \sqsubseteq) = \{I \mid I \text{ is a non-trivially strictly isolated subset of } (X, \sqsubseteq)\}$
$\mathcal{ASI}(X, \sqsubseteq) = \{I \mid I \text{ is an atomic strictly isolated subset of } (X, \sqsubseteq)\}$

Clearly we have that

$$\mathcal{SI}(X, \sqsubseteq) \subseteq \mathcal{I}(X, \sqsubseteq)$$

$$\mathcal{AI}(X, \sqsubseteq) \subseteq \mathcal{I}(X, \sqsubseteq)$$

$$\mathcal{ASI}(X, \sqsubseteq) = \mathcal{SI}(X, \sqsubseteq) \cap \mathcal{AI}(X, \sqsubseteq).$$

Moreover, the notions of trivially isolated and trivially strictly isolated coincide:

$$\mathcal{I}(X, \sqsubseteq) - \mathcal{I}^*(X, \sqsubseteq) = \mathcal{SI}(X, \sqsubseteq) - \mathcal{SI}^*(X, \sqsubseteq).$$

As mentioned in the introduction to this section, isolated subsets possess an important property: the bag consisting of the restriction of all states of a random structure to an isolated subset, after identification up to label-isomorphism, forms multiple copies of the random structure over this isolated subset. This is captured by Proposition 4.3 below. We first need the following technical lemmas.

Lemma 4.9. *We recall that every component C of a partial order $(X, \sqsubseteq)$ is a (trivially) isolated subset. If X consists of the pairwise distinct components $C_1, \ldots, C_n$ then the bag obtained by the restriction of all states from $\mathcal{R}(X, \sqsubseteq)$ to C_k consists of K copies of $\mathcal{R}(C, \sqsubseteq)$, where $K = \binom{|X|}{|C_1| \ldots |C_n|} \prod_{i \neq k}^{n} |R(C_i)|$.*

Lemma 4.10. *In case I is an isolated subset of X we have that:*

1) $\mathcal{R}_{\mathcal{L}}(X, \sqsubseteq) = \cup_{F \in \mathcal{R}_{\mathcal{L}}(X, \sqsubseteq)} \{F \restriction (X - I) \cup G \mid G \in \mathcal{R}_{\mathcal{L} - F(X-I)}(I, \sqsubseteq)\}$ and
2) $|\mathcal{R}_{\mathcal{L}}(X, \sqsubseteq)| = |\{F \restriction (X - I) \mid F \in \mathcal{R}_{\mathcal{L}}(X, \sqsubseteq)\}| \times |R(I, \sqsubseteq)|$

In case I is non-trivially strictly isolated [2] we also have that:

3) $|\mathcal{R}_{\mathcal{L}}(C(I), \sqsubseteq)| = |\mathcal{R}(\lceil M(I) \rceil \uparrow, \sqsubseteq)| \times |\mathcal{R}(I, \sqsubseteq)\}| \times |\mathcal{R}(\lfloor m(I) \rfloor \downarrow, \sqsubseteq)|$

---

[2] The trivially strictly isolated case can be dealt with via a slight generalization of Lemma 4.9.

Proof. We leave 1) and 3) as an exercise and sketch the proof for 2). To show 2), we consider the set consisting of the restrictions of the states of $\mathcal{R}_{\mathcal{L}}(X, \sqsubseteq)$ to the set $X - I$, i.e. the set $\{F \upharpoonright (X - I) | F \in \mathcal{R}(X, \sqsubseteq)\}$. We refer to a data-labeling G in this set as an "outer labeling". We define an equivalence relation on the set of states $\mathcal{R}_{\mathcal{L}}(X, \sqsubseteq)$ as follows: two states are equivalent iff they give rise to the same outer data-labelings. Clearly two states are equivalent iff they differ only on I. Using 1), we obtain that the resulting quotient consists of equivalence classes of size $K_I = |\mathcal{R}(I, \sqsubseteq)|$. In other words, $|\mathcal{R}_{\mathcal{L}}(X, \sqsubseteq)| = M \times K_I$, where M is the cardinality of the quotient, i.e. $M = |\{F \upharpoonright (X - I) | F \in \mathcal{R}(X, \sqsubseteq)\}|$.

Notation 4.5 Consider a random structure $R = \mathcal{R}_{\mathcal{L}}(X, \sqsubseteq)$ and $Y \subseteq X$. We use the following notation: $(R \upharpoonright Y)^{bag}$ is the bag consisting of all restrictions of states from R to the subset Y, in other words: $(R \upharpoonright Y)^{bag} = \{(F \upharpoonright Y, k) | k = \mathrm{Card}(\{G \in R | G \upharpoonright Y = F \upharpoonright Y\})\}$.

We continue to use the notation $\approx$ for the equivalence up to label-isomorphism.

Proposition 4.3. *(Multiplicities for (strictly) isolated sets)*
Let $R = \mathcal{R}(X, \sqsubseteq), Y \subseteq X$ *and* $K = \frac{|\mathcal{R}(X, \sqsubseteq)|}{|\mathcal{R}(Y, \sqsubseteq)|}$.

1) $Y \in \mathcal{I}(X, \sqsubseteq) \Rightarrow (R \upharpoonright Y)^{bag} \approx (\mathcal{R}(Y, \sqsubseteq), K)$.

We discuss the case of a non-trivially strictly isolated subset[3].

2) $Y \in \mathcal{SI}^*(X, \sqsubseteq) \Rightarrow (R \upharpoonright Y)^{bag} \approx (\mathcal{R}(Y, \sqsubseteq), L)$.

To compute L, *let* $L^* = \frac{|\mathcal{R}(C(Y), \sqsubseteq)|}{|\mathcal{R}(Y, \sqsubseteq)|}$.

We have:
$$L^* = |\mathcal{R}(\lceil M(Y) \rceil \uparrow, \sqsubseteq)| \times |\mathcal{R}(\lfloor m(Y) \rfloor \downarrow, \sqsubseteq)|$$

and
$$L = L^* \binom{|X|}{|C(Y)|} \binom{|X| - |C(Y)|}{|C_2| \dots |C_n|} \prod_{i=2}^{n} |R(C_i)|,$$

where $C_2, \dots, C_n$ *are the components of* X *other than* $C(Y)$.

Proof. 1) and 2) follow from Lemma 4.10 2) and 3).

Remark 4.12. The multiplicities in Proposition 4.3 are particularly easy to determine for the case of SP-orders, through the formulas for cardinalities of SP-orders as given in Lemma 5.5.

We illustrate these results on some basic examples below.

---

[3] Again, the case of trivially strictly isolated subsets can be addressed relying on Lemma 4.9.

Example 4.14. The isolated subset Y in the four element binary tree underlying the three states displayed below, consists of the right-most leaf of the tree, indicated via the ellipse. We refer to the underlying partial order as $(X, \sqsubseteq)$.

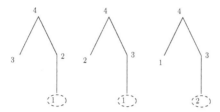

The restriction of the above three states to the right-most leaf yields the following labels for the leaf: 1, 1 and 2. The restriction to the isolated subset consisting of this leaf yields $K = 3$ copies of the random structure A_1. Note that $|R(X, \sqsubseteq)| = 3$ and $|R(Y, \sqsubseteq)| = 1$ and $K = \frac{3}{1}$, consistent with Proposition 4.3 1).

In the following example the non-trivially strictly isolated subset is indicated by the two elements contained in the ellipse.

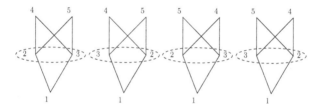

The restriction of the above states to the strictly isolated subset indicated by the ellipse, consists of $K = 2$ copies of the random structure A_2. Note that $|R(X, \sqsubseteq)| = 4$ and $|R(Y, \sqsubseteq)| = 2$ and $K = \frac{4}{2}$, i.e. $K = 2$, consistent with Proposition 4.3 1). Alternatively, via an application of Proposition 4.3 2), we have $L = L^* = |R(\lceil M(Y) \rceil \uparrow, \sqsubseteq)| \times |R(\lfloor m(Y) \rfloor \downarrow, \sqsubseteq)| = 2 \times 1$.

Finally, we present an example of a non-isolated subset Y of which the elements again are contained in the ellipse below. The restriction of the states to this subset do *not* form a number of copies of a random structure. Indeed, the restriction of the final state to Y, with labels 4 and 2 on Y, only represents one state of the newly created restricted discrete two-element partial order $(Y, \sqsubseteq)$, while the second state of $(Y, \sqsubseteq)$, with the labels 2 and 4, assigned to the elements of Y in left to right order on the Hasse diagram below, is missing.

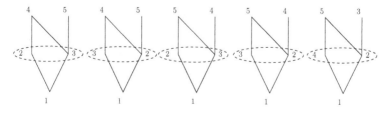

Remark 4.13. To compute a number of states of a finite partial order or in other words the cardinality of a random structure, e.g. in order to determine the number K of Proposition 4.3, state counting results are available from the literature. Relatively fast state counting algorithms have been developed at CEOL, e.g. [Don04]. Counting states is also referred to in the literature as counting the linear extensions of a partial order, for which there exists an extensive literature (e.g. [BPS96]).

The notion of an atomic isolated subset introduced in Definition 4.14 will be useful in defining the $\mathcal{MOQA}$ operation "random split".

An atomic isolated subset intuitively forms a discrete subset in a random structure for which any state, when restricted to this set, forms a set of pairwise free labels. i.e. the labels simply can be permuted on this set without violating the data-labeling condition. The following Lemma captures this idea. The proof of the Lemma is a trivial exercise. One can show that the two conditions stated in Lemma 4.11 are equivalent. The verifications are of a technical nature and we omit them at this stage since we will only avail of the implication in Lemma 4.11.

In fact, Lemma 4.11 is a consequence of a Theorem of Reconstruction presented by T. Vallee and J. Manning [VM07]. We state the Theorem below.

Theorem 4.6. *(T. Vallee, J. Manning) Let $(X, \sqsubseteq)$ be a partially ordered set and $\mathcal{L}$ a set of labels. Then $\forall x, y \in X. x \sqsubset y \Leftrightarrow \forall F \in \mathcal{R}_{\mathcal{L}}(X, \sqsubseteq). F(x) < F(y)$.*

The following Equivalence Theorem is a corollary.

Corollary 4.4. *(T. Vallee, J. Manning) For any set of labels $\mathcal{L}$ and partial orders $\sqsubseteq_1$ and $\sqsubseteq_2$: $\sqsubseteq_1 = \sqsubseteq_2 \Leftrightarrow \mathcal{R}_{\mathcal{L}}(X, \sqsubseteq_1) = \mathcal{R}_{\mathcal{L}}(X, \sqsubseteq_2)$.*

Lemma 4.11. *Given a random structure $\mathcal{R}(X, \sqsubseteq)$. If I is an atomic isolated subset I of X then $\forall F \in \mathcal{R}(X, \sqsubseteq). F(I)$ is a free set of labels for F.*

Remark 4.14. This fact enables one to easily determine, for two given elements of an isolated atomic set, what the probability is that the label of the first element is smaller than the label of the second element. Indeed, it is easy to see that these events are independent and that the probability is $\frac{1}{2}$. For atomic strictly isolated subsets I of a given random structure $\mathcal{R}(X, \sqsubseteq)$, the probability that an element x has a given label a is again easy to determine. The probability that an element x has a given label a is $\frac{1}{|I|}$ whenever $a \in \cup\{F(I)| F \in \mathcal{R}(X, \sqsubseteq)\}$ and 0 otherwise. Such results are of use in the time verification of conditional statements.

The following proposition states that if I is a non-trivially strictly isolated subset, then so are $\underline{I}$ and $\overline{I}$.

Proposition 4.4. *(Characterization of non-trivially strictly isolated set)*
1) $I \in SI^*(X, \sqsubseteq) \Leftrightarrow [\underline{I} \in SI^*(X, \sqsubseteq) \text{ and } \overline{I} \in SI^*(X, \sqsubseteq) \text{ and } C(I) - I = \underline{I} \cup \overline{I}]$.
2) $\underline{I} = \emptyset \text{ or } \overline{I} = \emptyset \Rightarrow [I \in SI^*(X, \sqsubseteq) \Leftrightarrow (C(I) - I) \in SI^*(X, \sqsubseteq)]$.

Proof. To verify 1), we show that in case I is strictly isolated, both $\underline{I}$ and $\overline{I}$ are strictly isolated. The converse is left as an exercise.

Assume that I is strictly isolated. Then:

a) $\lfloor m(I) \rfloor \neq \emptyset \Rightarrow (\lfloor m(I) \rfloor, m(I))$ forms a seam.
b) $\lceil M(I) \rceil \neq \emptyset \Rightarrow (M(I), \lceil M(I) \rceil)$ forms a seam.

If $\lfloor m(I) \rfloor = \emptyset$ then we know that $\underline{I} = (\lfloor m(I) \rfloor = \emptyset)\!\downarrow = \emptyset$ and hence $\underline{I}$ is strictly isolated. Similarly $\overline{I}$ is strictly isolated in case $\lceil M(I) \rceil = \emptyset$. Thus we can assume that $\lfloor m(I) \rfloor \neq \emptyset$ and $\lceil M(I) \rceil \neq \emptyset$. We remark that in particular $(*)$ $I \neq \emptyset$.

By a) and b) we obtain that: $(\lfloor m(I) \rfloor, m(I))$ and $(M(I), \lceil M(I) \rceil)$ each form a seam.

We verify that $\overline{I}$ is strictly isolated. The proof for $\underline{I}$ is similar.

Note $\lceil M(\overline{I}) \rceil = \lceil M(\lceil M(I) \rceil \!\uparrow) \rceil = \lceil M(X) \rceil = \emptyset$.

However $\lfloor m(\overline{I}) \rfloor = \lfloor m(\lceil M(I) \rceil \!\uparrow) \rfloor = \lfloor \lceil M(I) \rceil \rfloor = M(I)$ where the last two equalities follow from the fact that $(M(I), \lceil M(I) \rceil)$ forms a seam.

Since by $(*)$ we know that $I \neq \emptyset$, we obtain that $M(I) \neq \emptyset$ and hence $\lfloor m(\overline{I}) \rfloor \neq \emptyset$.

Hence, in order to verify that $\overline{I}$ is strictly isolated, it suffices to verify that $(\lfloor m(\overline{I}) \rfloor, m(\overline{I}))$ forms a seam. But this follows since we have verified above that $\lfloor m(\overline{I}) \rfloor = M(I)$ and $m(\overline{I}) = \lceil M(I) \rceil$ and since $(M(I), \lceil M(I) \rceil)$ is a seam.

We proceed to verify 2) under the assumption that I is a subset which satisfies $\overline{I} = \emptyset$. The case where $\underline{I} = \emptyset$ is similar.

We show that I strictly isolated implies that $X - I$ is strictly isolated. The converse is shown in a similar way.

Since $\overline{I} = \emptyset$, we obtain that $\lceil M(I) \rceil \!\uparrow = \emptyset$ and hence, since I is strictly isolated, we know that $X - I = \underline{I}$. By 1) we know that $\underline{I}$ is strictly isolated and hence $X - I$ is strictly isolated.

Finally we state the following Lemma, leaving the proof as an exercise, which sheds some light on the relations between the notions of a seam, an isolated subset and a strictly isolated subset.

Lemma 4.12. *Consider a component C of a partial order $(X, \sqsubseteq)$. The following statements are equivalent:*

1) $(C, \sqsubseteq)$ has a seam.

2) $\exists I. \emptyset \subset I \subset C, \overline{I} = \emptyset$ and I is strictly isolated.

3) $\exists I. \emptyset \subset I \subset C, \underline{I} = \emptyset$ and I is strictly isolated.

4) $\exists I. \emptyset \subset I \subset C, I$ and $C - I$ are isolated.

4.6.2 Simplified Definitions for SP-Orders

The theory of random structure preservation and the notions of isolated and strictly isolated subsets have been developed for general partial orders. Some of the structures considered earlier were not SP-orders. E.g. the partial order of Example 4.13 is not an SP-order since it contains an N-shape in the upper left corner (cf. Proposition 2.1). We will see however in Chapter 2.2 that $\mathcal{MOQA}$ data structures can be assumed to be SP-orders. This will entail useful simplifications in the average-case analysis of basic operations (Chapter 6).

Moreover, the definitions of an isolated subset and a strictly isolated subset can be simplified for SP-orders, as illustrated in the following.

Using the terminology of Chapter 2, we remark that the product components of a product SP-order correspond to strictly isolated subsets of this order. Similarly, the parallel components of a parallel SP-order correspond to strictly isolated subsets of the order.

Proposition 4.5. *(Characterizations for the case of SP-orders)*
Consider an SP-order α. We regard product SP-orders in the definition below as parallel SP-orders with a single parallel component. This enables the use of canonical representations for SP-orders α as a parallel SP-order, where $\alpha = \alpha_1 || \ldots || \alpha_n$ and where each of the parallel components α_i is a product SP-order.

μ is an isolated subset of α iff one of the following holds inductively:

1) μ is trivially isolated, i.e. μ is a union of parallel components of α or
2) μ is an isolated subset of a product component of some α_i in the canonical representation of α, where $\alpha = \alpha_1 || \ldots || \alpha_n$.

μ is a strictly isolated subset of α iff one of the following holds:

1) μ is trivially isolated, i.e. μ is a union of parallel components of α or
2) μ is a product component of some α_i in the canonical representation of α, where $\alpha = \alpha_1 || \ldots || \alpha_n$.

4.6.3 Extension Theorem

We will distinguish two types of RB-representations for RB-preserving functions on a random structure. These are the contractive RB-preserving functions on a random structure R which reduce the underlying set of the random structure R to a strict subset of this set, and the non-contractive ones, which leave the underlying set of the random structure unchanged.

Definition 4.19. An RB-representation

$$\mu \colon \mathcal{R}_{\mathcal{L}}(X, \sqsubseteq) \longmapsto \{(\mathcal{R}_{\mathcal{L}_1}(X_1, \sqsubseteq_1), K_1), \ldots, (\mathcal{R}_{\mathcal{L}_n}(X_n, \sqsubseteq_n), K_n)\}$$

is *contractive* iff $\exists i \in \{1, \ldots, n\}. X_i \subset X$ and is *non-contractive* otherwise.

The Extension Theorem states that it suffices to define non-contractive RB-representations on an isolated subset of the partial order of a given random structure and subsequently to extend these to RB-representations on the entire random structure, where multiplicities are not affected. For contractive RB-representations the Extension Theorem holds on condition that the extension occurs on a *strictly* isolated subset.

The reader may wish to postpone reading this part and continue with Section 5 which introduces the RB-representations for the $\mathcal{MOQA}$ operations and return to the Extension Theorem at that stage.

The Extension Theorem will be used to extend the definitions of the basic $\mathcal{MOQA}$ operations in case these are applied locally to an isolated subset.

As usual, with some abuse of notation, we will denote the restriction of the partial order $\sqsubseteq$ to a subset A of X by the partial order $(A, \sqsubseteq)$. We will refer to the notion of labeling-isomorphism in the following and use the corresponding notation introduced in Remark 4.3.

Notation 4.7 $Ref(\mathcal{R}_{\mathcal{L}}(X, \sqsubseteq)) = \{\phi | \phi \text{ is a refining function on } \mathcal{R}_{\mathcal{L}}(X, \sqsubseteq)\}$.

The following definition extends the labeling-isomorphism $\Psi_{\mathcal{L}, \mathcal{L}'} \colon \mathcal{L} \to \mathcal{L}'$, introduced in Remark 4.3 for random structures, to an operation on refining functions.

Definition 4.20. Given $\mathcal{L}, \mathcal{L}'$ and $(X, \sqsubseteq)$ such that $|X| = |\mathcal{L}| = |\mathcal{L}'|$. We define a relabeling operator $\hat{\Psi}_{\mathcal{L}\mathcal{L}'} \colon Ref(\mathcal{R}_{\mathcal{L}}(X, \sqsubseteq)) \to Ref(\mathcal{R}_{\mathcal{L}'}(X, \sqsubseteq))$ as follows:
$\forall \phi \in Ref(\mathcal{R}_{\mathcal{L}}(X, \sqsubseteq)), \forall F' \in \mathcal{R}_{\mathcal{L}'}(X, \sqsubseteq)$.

$$\hat{\Psi}_{\mathcal{L}\mathcal{L}'}(\phi)(F') = \Psi_{\mathcal{L}\mathcal{L}'} \circ [\phi(\Psi_{\mathcal{L}'\mathcal{L}} \circ F')].$$

Lemma 4.13. *Definition 4.20 is sound, i.e., using the notation of Definition 4.20, $\Psi_{\mathcal{L}\mathcal{L}'}$ is composable with $\phi(\Psi_{\mathcal{L}'\mathcal{L}} \circ F')$ and $\hat{\Psi}_{\mathcal{L}\mathcal{L}'}(\phi) \in Ref(\mathcal{R}_{\mathcal{L}'}(X, \sqsubseteq))$.*

Proof. Let $\phi \in Ref(\mathcal{R}_{\mathcal{L}}(X, \sqsubseteq))$ and consider a representation

$$\phi \colon \mathcal{R}_{\mathcal{L}}(X, \sqsubseteq) \longmapsto \{\mathcal{R}_{\mathcal{L}_1}(X_1, \sqsubseteq_1), \ldots, \mathcal{R}_{\mathcal{L}_n}(X_n, \sqsubseteq_n)\}.$$

We remark that since refining functions are surjective, $\forall F' \in \mathcal{R}_{\mathcal{L}'}(X, \sqsubseteq) \exists i \in \{1, \ldots, n\}$ such that $\phi(\Psi_{\mathcal{L}'\mathcal{L}} \circ F') \in \mathcal{R}_{\mathcal{L}_i}(X_i, \sqsubseteq_i)$. Thus the composition $\Psi_{\mathcal{L}\mathcal{L}'} \circ [\phi(\Psi_{\mathcal{L}'\mathcal{L}} \circ F')]$ is defined since ϕ is refining and hence $\mathcal{L}_i \subseteq \mathcal{L}$.

To show that $\hat{\Psi}_{\mathcal{L}\mathcal{L}'}(\phi) \in Ref(\mathcal{R}_{\mathcal{L}'}(X, \sqsubseteq))$, we remark that

$$\hat{\Psi}_{\mathcal{L}\mathcal{L}'}(\phi) \colon \mathcal{R}_{\mathcal{L}'}(X, \sqsubseteq) \longmapsto \{\mathcal{R}_{\mathcal{L}'_1}(X_1, \sqsubseteq_1), \ldots, \mathcal{R}_{\mathcal{L}'_n}(X_n, \sqsubseteq_n)\},$$

where $\forall i \in \{1, \ldots, n\}. \mathcal{L}'_i = \Psi_{\mathcal{LL}'}(\mathcal{L}_i)$. Since $\Psi_{\mathcal{LL}'}$ is a labeling-isomorphism we have $\mathcal{L}_i \subseteq \mathcal{L} \Rightarrow \mathcal{L}'_i = \Psi_{\mathcal{LL}'}(\mathcal{L}_i) \subseteq \Psi_{\mathcal{LL}'}(\mathcal{L}) = \mathcal{L}'$. We leave the verification that $\hat{\Psi}_{\mathcal{LL}'}(\phi)$ is surjective as an exercise.

The following lemma, which uses the notation of Definition 4.20, illustrates that the relabeling operator $\hat{\Psi}$ preserves RB-representations.

Lemma 4.14. *If*

$$\mu_{\{\mathcal{F}_1, \ldots, \mathcal{F}_n\}} \colon \mathcal{R}_{\mathcal{L}}(X, \sqsubseteq) \longmapsto \{(\mathcal{R}_{\mathcal{L}_1}(X_1, \sqsubseteq_1), K_1), \ldots, (\mathcal{R}_{\mathcal{L}_n}(X_n, \sqsubseteq_n), K_n)\}$$

then $[\hat{\Psi}_{\mathcal{LL}'}(\mu)]_{(\mathcal{F}'_1, \ldots, \mathcal{F}'_n)} \colon \mathcal{R}_{\mathcal{L}'}(X, \sqsubseteq) \longmapsto \{(\mathcal{R}_{\mathcal{L}'_1}(X_1, \sqsubseteq_1), K_1), \ldots, (\mathcal{R}_{\mathcal{L}'_n}(X_n, \sqsubseteq_n), K_n)\}$, *where* $\mathcal{F}'_i = \Psi_{\mathcal{LL}'}(\mathcal{F}_i)$ *and* $\forall i \in \{1, \ldots, n\}. \mathcal{L}'_i = \Psi_{\mathcal{LL}'}(\mathcal{L}_i)$.

Proof. Let

$$\mu_{\{\mathcal{F}_1, \ldots, \mathcal{F}_n\}} \colon \mathcal{R}_{\mathcal{L}}(X, \sqsubseteq) \longmapsto \{(\mathcal{R}_{\mathcal{L}_1}(X_1, \sqsubseteq_1), K_1), \ldots, (\mathcal{R}_{\mathcal{L}_n}(X_n, \sqsubseteq_n), K_n)\}.$$

The partition $\mathcal{F}_1, \ldots, \mathcal{F}_n$ of $\mathcal{R}_{\mathcal{L}}(X, \sqsubseteq)$ is such that $\forall i \in \{1, \ldots, n\}. \mu(\mathcal{F}_i) = \mathcal{R}_i$ and $\forall F \in \mathcal{R}_i. |\mu^{-1}(F) \cap \mathcal{F}_i| = K_i$. In order to show that:

$$\hat{\Psi}_{\mathcal{LL}'}(\mu) \colon \mathcal{R}_{\mathcal{L}}(X, \sqsubseteq) \longmapsto \{(\mathcal{R}_{\mathcal{L}'_1}(X_1, \sqsubseteq_1), K_1), \ldots, (\mathcal{R}_{\mathcal{L}'_n}(X_n, \sqsubseteq_n), K_n)\},$$

it suffices to remark that since $\Psi_{\mathcal{LL}'}$ is a labeling-isomorphism and since for each $i \in \{1, \ldots, n\}$, $\mathcal{F}'_i = \Psi_{\mathcal{LL}'}(\mathcal{F}_i)$, we immediately obtain that $\mathcal{F}'_1, \ldots, \mathcal{F}'_n$ forms a partition of $\mathcal{R}_{\mathcal{L}'}(X, \sqsubseteq)$.

It is easy to verify that $\forall F' \in \mathcal{R}_{\mathcal{L}'_i}(X_i, \sqsubseteq_i). |(\hat{\Psi}_{\mathcal{LL}'}(\mu))^{-1}(F') \cap \mathcal{F}'_i| = K_i$.

We now introduce an Extension Operator which extends a refining function defined on a random structure S, determined by an isolated subset of a given random structure R, to the entire random structure R.

Definition 4.21. Suppose that I is an isolated subset of $(X, \sqsubseteq)$ and $G \in \mathcal{R}_{\mathcal{L}}(X, \sqsubseteq)$. The Extension Operator $Ext(G, I) \colon Ref(\mathcal{R}_{G(I)}(I, \sqsubseteq \restriction I)) \to Ref(\mathcal{R}_{\mathcal{L}}(X, \sqsubseteq))$ is defined as follows: $\forall \phi \in Ref(\mathcal{R}_{G(I)}(I, \sqsubseteq \restriction I)), \forall F \in \mathcal{R}_{\mathcal{L}}(X, \sqsubseteq)$.

$$Ext(G, I)(\phi)(F) = F \restriction (X - I) \cup [\hat{\Psi}_{G(I), F(I)}(\phi)(F \restriction I)].$$

The following lemma shows that Definition 4.21 is sound.

Lemma 4.15. *Let* $G \in \mathcal{R}_{\mathcal{L}}(X, \sqsubseteq)$ *and* $\phi \in Ref(\mathcal{R}_{G(I)}(I, \sqsubseteq \restriction I))$ *and consider a representation of* ϕ:

$$\phi \colon \mathcal{R}_{G(I)}(I, \sqsubseteq \restriction I) \longmapsto \{\mathcal{R}_{\mathcal{M}_1}(I_1, \sqsubseteq_1), \ldots, \mathcal{R}_{\mathcal{M}_n}(I_n, \sqsubseteq_n)\}.$$

We show that $Ext(G, I)(\phi)$ *is refining.*

If:
$\mathcal{L}_i$ *is the set:* $\{F \restriction (X - I) \cup [\hat{\Psi}_{G(I), F(I)}(\phi)(F \restriction I)](I_i) | F \in \mathcal{R}_{\mathcal{L}}(X, \sqsubseteq),$
$\qquad \phi(\Psi_{F(I)G(I)}(F \restriction I)) \in \mathcal{R}_{\mathcal{M}_i}(I_i, \sqsubseteq_i)\}$

X_i is the set:

$$(X - I) \cup I_i$$

$\sqsubseteq_i^*$ is the least partial order containing the following sets of pairs: $[\sqsubseteq \upharpoonright (X - I_i)]$, $\sqsubseteq_i, \{(a, b) | a \in M(I_i), b \in \lceil M(I) \rceil\}$, $\{(a, b) | a \in \lfloor m(I) \rfloor, b \in m(I_i)\}$. Then: $\forall i \in \{1, \ldots, n\}$.

$$\mathcal{R}_{\mathcal{L}_i}(X_i, \sqsubseteq_i^*) =$$
$$\{F \upharpoonright (X - I) \cup [\hat{\Psi}_{G(I), F(I)}(\phi)(F \upharpoonright I)] \,|\, \phi(\Psi_{F(I)G(I)}(F \upharpoonright I)) \in \mathcal{R}_{\mathcal{M}_i}(I_i, \sqsubseteq_i)\}$$

and $Ext(G, I)(\phi)$ is refining with representation:

$$Ext(G, I)(\phi) \colon \mathcal{R}_{\mathcal{L}}(X, \sqsubseteq) \longmapsto \{\mathcal{R}_{\mathcal{L}_1}(X_1, \sqsubseteq_1^*), \ldots, \mathcal{R}_{\mathcal{L}_n}(X_n, \sqsubseteq_n^*)\}.$$

Proof. We show that $\forall i \in \{1, \ldots, n\}$.

$$\mathcal{R}_{\mathcal{L}_i}(X_i, \sqsubseteq_i^*) =$$
$$\{F \upharpoonright (X - I) \cup [\hat{\Psi}_{G(I), F(I)}(\phi)(F \upharpoonright I)] \,|\, \phi(\Psi_{F(I)G(I)}(F \upharpoonright I)) \in \mathcal{R}_{\mathcal{M}_i}(I_i, \sqsubseteq_i)\}.$$

Note that I_i is an isolated subset of $(X, \sqsubseteq)$ and hence, by the definition of X_i and $\sqsubseteq_i^*$, I_i is also an isolated subset of $(X_i, \sqsubseteq_i^*)$. Hence, by Lemma 4.10 1), we know that:

$$\mathcal{R}_{\mathcal{L}_i}(X_i, \sqsubseteq_i^*) =$$
$$\{H \upharpoonright (X_i - I_i) \cup H' \,|\, H \in \mathcal{R}_{\mathcal{L}_i}(X_i, \sqsubseteq_i^*) \text{ and } H' \in \mathcal{R}_{\mathcal{L}_i - H(X_i - I_i)}(I_i, \sqsubseteq_i^*)\}.$$

We remark that $\{F \upharpoonright (X - I) \cup [\hat{\Psi}_{G(I), F(I)}(\phi)(F \upharpoonright I)] \,|\, \phi(\Psi_{F(I)G(I)}(F \upharpoonright I)) \in \mathcal{R}_{\mathcal{M}_i}(I_i, \sqsubseteq_i)\} = \{H \upharpoonright (X_i - I_i) \cup H' \,|\, H \in \mathcal{R}_{\mathcal{L}_i}(X_i, \sqsubseteq_i) \text{ and } H' \in \mathcal{R}_{H(I_i)}(I_i, \sqsubseteq_i)\}$ since $X - I = X_i - I_i$ and since $\{[\hat{\Psi}_{G(I), F(I)}(\phi)(F \upharpoonright I)] \,|\, \phi(\Psi_{F(I)G(I)}(F \upharpoonright I)) \in \mathcal{R}_{\mathcal{M}_i}(I_i, \sqsubseteq_i)\} = \{H' \,|\, H \in \mathcal{R}_{\mathcal{L}_i}(X_i, \sqsubseteq_i) \text{ and } H' \in \mathcal{R}_{H(I_i)}(I_i, \sqsubseteq_i)\}$, by the surjectivity of ϕ and by the definition of a labeling-isomorphism.

We verify that the function $Ext(G, I)(\phi)$ is refining. Note that $\mathcal{L}_i \subseteq \mathcal{L}$, $X_i \subseteq X$ and the $\forall x, y \in X_i. x \sqsubseteq y \Rightarrow x \sqsubseteq_i^* y$. The last claim follows from the fact that $\sqsubseteq_i$ refines $\sqsubseteq$ and from the definition of $\sqsubseteq_i^*$. We leave the fact that $Ext(G, I)(\phi) \colon \mathcal{R}_{\mathcal{L}}(X, \sqsubseteq) \to \mathcal{R}_{\mathcal{L}_1}(X_1, \sqsubseteq_1^*) \cup \ldots \cup \mathcal{R}_{\mathcal{L}_n}(X_n, \sqsubseteq_n^*)$ is surjective, as an exercise.

We use the notations of Definition 4.21 and of Lemma 4.15 in Theorem 4.8.

Theorem 4.8. (Extension Theorem) *Consider a random structure $\mathcal{R}_{\mathcal{L}}(X, \sqsubseteq)$ and an isolated subset I of X and $G \in \mathcal{R}_{\mathcal{L}}(X, \sqsubseteq)$. Consider a refining function*

$$\mu \colon \mathcal{R}_{G(I)}(I, \sqsubseteq I) \longmapsto \{\mathcal{R}_{\mathcal{M}_1}(I_1, \sqsubseteq_1), \ldots, \mathcal{R}_{\mathcal{M}_n}(I_n, \sqsubseteq_n)\}.$$

If a) μ is non-contractive or b) (μ is contractive and I is strictly isolated) and if

$$\mu \colon \mathcal{R}_{G(I)}(I, \sqsubseteq \restriction I) \longmapsto \{(\mathcal{R}_{\mathcal{M}_1}(I_1, \sqsubseteq_1), K_1) \ldots, (\mathcal{R}_{\mathcal{M}_n}(I_n, \sqsubseteq_n), K_n)\}$$

is RB-preserving then

$$Ext(G, I)(\mu) \colon \mathcal{R}_{\mathcal{L}}(X, \sqsubseteq) \longmapsto \{(\mathcal{R}_{\mathcal{L}_1}(X_1, \sqsubseteq_1^*), K_1), \ldots, (\mathcal{R}_{\mathcal{L}_n}(X_n, \sqsubseteq_n^*), K_n)\}$$

is RB-preserving.

Chapter 5
Basic $\mathcal{MOQA}$ Operations

The present chapter introduces the basic $\mathcal{MOQA}$ operations, including the Random Product, the Random Deletion and Percolation, the Random Projection, the Random Split and the Top and Bot operations. These are sufficient to implement many well-known algorithms as illustrated in Chapter 8. We recall that the operations $\mathcal{MOQA}$ product operation and the $\mathcal{MOQA}$ deletion operation have been described in an informal way in Section 1.8.1, while the $\mathcal{MOQA}$split operation has been described in Section 1.7.1.

Each of the $\mathcal{MOQA}$ operations is shown to be random bag preserving. Deletion operations typically are not included in the context of automated average-case analysis, since the analysis of deletions with respect to average-case time is well-known to be problematic, even in the context of traditional average-case analysis. Hence the Random Deletion opens up the way for the inclusion of novel algorithms, such as Percolating Heapsort and Treapsort, which are analyzed in Chapter 9. The Extension Theorem of Chapter 4 is applied to extend these operations from local applications on isolated subsets to applications over the entire random structure. Uniformly random bag preserving operations are singled out as of particular interest, since this type of operations enables simplifications of probability computations in later chapters. The $\mathcal{MOQA}$ operations are shown to preserve series-parallel data structures which yields a characterization of the so-called $\mathcal{MOQA}$ atomic-constructible data structures as series-parallel orders. Finally, some simplifications for the series-parallel case are obtained in the context of the computation of cardinalities of random structures. Such simplifications for series-parallel orders will also be useful in the context of Chapter 6, which regards the average-case analysis of the basic $\mathcal{MOQA}$ operations. Finally, separative functions as a sufficient condition for random bag preservation are discussed in relation to the basic $\mathcal{MOQA}$ operations.

5.1 The Fundamental Data Structuring Problem

Most results on worst and average-case analysis have been obtained for the general class of data structure manipulation algorithms [Knu73, MR95], which include of course sorting and searching algorithms. Hence we initiated our exploration of modular static average-case timing in the data structuring context. This has to a great extent influenced the design of the prototype language $\mathcal{MOQA}$ to which we return below. We remark in this context that the $\mathcal{MOQA}$ basic operations incorporate the main operations listed in the basic data structuring problem discussed in [MR95]. For the fundamental data structuring problem one is required to maintain a collection of sets of items so as to efficiently support certain types of queries and operations. These operations include the capacity to insert an element in a data structure, delete an element from a data structure, merge data structures into a larger whole, split a data structure according to data being larger or smaller than a given value and find a value in a data structure. Such operations are included in $\mathcal{MOQA}$ as follows: inserting an element is achieved by applications of the $\mathcal{MOQA}$ product operation to two components of a data structure, one of which consists of a single element. Deletion is incorporated via the $\mathcal{MOQA}$ deletion operation. Merging of data structures again is achieved via the $\mathcal{MOQA}$ product. A $\mathcal{MOQA}$ split operation is included and some search capacity is incorporated via the $\mathcal{MOQA}$ implementation of Quickselect. In contrast with [MR95], $\mathcal{MOQA}$ operations operate over general partial order data structures as opposed to trees and $\mathcal{MOQA}$ operations are guaranteed to be random bag preserving, facilitating modular static average-case analysis.

Comment: The operations introduced below can be extended to take more arguments than specified in their definition. The details are of a technical nature and have been omitted. We will restrict the definitions to the minimum number of arguments in each case.

Remark 5.1. We will typically first define the operations on partial orders, then define the operation on data-labelings and finally define the operation on a random structure. To generalize the operations we will use two extension results. We will use the Extension Theorem (Theorem 4.8) to allow the operations to be applied to isolated subsets of the partial order corresponding to a random structure. Finally, though we will not state this explicitly for each operation, we define the randomness-preserving extension of each operation, from random structures to random bags, via Definition 4.12.

5.2 The Random Product

In order to define the random product, we first define the product of two finite partial orders. The definition is similar to the one given in [DP90]. Then we define the product of two data-labelings. Finally, we define the random product on a random structure as a unary operation, which performs an operation on two sub structures of the given random structure and reproduces a new random structure. A high level description of general product type operations is provided in [FV90]. We provide a random bag preserving product operation for the $\mathcal{MOQA}$ language.

5.2.1 The Product of two Finite Partial Orders

Definition 5.1. Given two finite *disjoint* partial orders $(X_1, \sqsubseteq_1)$ and $(X_2, \sqsubseteq_2)$, i.e. partial orders for which $X_1 \cap X_2 = \emptyset$.

The set $X_1 \otimes X_2$ is defined to be the union of the disjoint sets X_1 and X_2. The relation $\sqsubseteq_1 \otimes \sqsubseteq_2$ is defined to be the least partial order on $X_1 \otimes X_2$ containing $\sqsubseteq_1$ and $\sqsubseteq_2$ and $X_1 \times X_2$.

It is easy to verify that the partial order $\sqsubseteq_1 \otimes \sqsubseteq_2$ is the transitive closure of the binary relations $\sqsubseteq_1, \sqsubseteq_2$ and the set of pairs $\{(M, m) | M$ is a maximal element of $(X_1, \sqsubseteq_1)$, m is a minimal element of $(X_2, \sqsubseteq_2)$.

Example 5.1. If we consider the sets $X_1 = \{x_1, x_2, x_3\}$ and $X_2 = \{x_4, x_5, x_6, x_7\}$ then $X_1 \otimes X_2 = \{x_1, x_2, x_3, x_4, x_5, x_6, x_7\}$. We indicate the new pairs added in the Hasse diagram via the operation $\otimes$ via dashed lines.

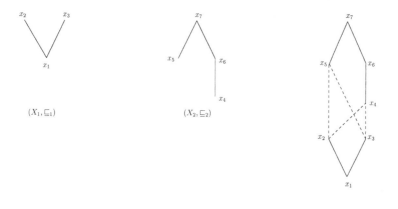

$$(X_1 \otimes X_2, \sqsubseteq_1 \otimes \sqsubseteq_2)$$

Note that the sets X_1 and X_2 form a pair of completely connected subsets (cf. Definition 4.15) of the product partial order $(X_1 \otimes X_2, \sqsubseteq_1 \otimes \sqsubseteq_2)$.

We define the product of two data-labelings as a first step towards the definition of the random product of two random structures.

5.2.2 The Product of Two Data-Labelings

Let F_1, F_2 be data-labelings on finite partial orders $(X_1, \sqsubseteq_1)$ and $(X_2, \sqsubseteq_2)$ respectively. We call F_1 and F_2 *disjoint* when their domains X_1 and X_2 are disjoint and their ranges $F_1(X_1)$ and $F_2(X_2)$ are disjoint.

Pseudo-code for the product $\otimes$ on data-labelings
Let F_1, F_2 be disjoint data-labelings which are provided as inputs.

We define the product of the two data-labelings. To avoid technicalities, we assume in the following pseudo-code that the data-labelings F_1 and F_2 of which the product is taken are (implicitly) processed first to retrieve a new function F, consisting of the union of the data-labelings F_1 and F_2. The creation of F will be indicated in the pseudo-code for the random product by the initial code line: $F = F_1 \cup F_2$, where we consider the graph union of these functions.

We will also assume the implicit generation of the restrictions of this function F, i.e. $F \upharpoonright X_1$ and $F \upharpoonright X_2$, to the sets X_1 and X_2 respectively and hence won't specify the detailed implementation of these restrictions in the pseudo code. The function F and its restrictions $F \upharpoonright X_1$ and $F \upharpoonright X_2$ will freely be referred to in the pseudo-code.

The pseudo-code to generate a data-labeling from $F = F_1 \cup F_2$ is based on a generalization of the procedures Push-Down in the pseudo-code of the Heapsort Algorithm in Section 2 and the related Push-Up operation. We will provide pseudo-code for Williams versions of the Push operations and remark that it is straightforward to specify Floyd versions of these procedures. We omit the details but will refer to these generalizations as F-Push-Down and F-Push-Up in the following. We provide pseudo-code for generalized versions of Williams' Push operations:

W-Push-Down(b, F)
while $\lfloor b \rfloor \neq \emptyset$ **and** $b < \vee \lfloor b \rfloor$
        swap$(b, \vee \lfloor b \rfloor, F)$

W-Push-Up(a, F)
while $\lceil a \rceil \neq \emptyset$ **and** $a > \wedge \lceil a \rceil$
        swap$(a, \wedge \lceil a \rceil, F)$

As before, we will use Push-Down and Push-Up freely in the pseudo-code, without specifying which version we use since this is a matter of choice of implementation.

We will define the operations on isolated subsets of a given random structure and use the Extension Theorem (Theorem 4.8) to extend the operation to the entire random structure.

We provide the pseudo-code for the Data-Labeling-Product Algorithm where the inputs for the algorithm are the disjoint data-labelings F_1 and F_2. We denote the function F returned by the Data-Labeling-Product algorithm by $F_1 \otimes F_2$.

Pseudo-code for the Data-Labeling-Product Algorithm

$F := F_1 \cup F_2$;
while $\vee M(F \upharpoonright X_1) > \wedge m(F \upharpoonright X_2)$ **do**
  $a := \vee M(F \upharpoonright X_1); b := \wedge m(F \upharpoonright X_2)$;
  swap (a, b, F);
  Push-Down(b, F);
  Push-Up(a, F)
Return F

This proof of the following lemma follows via straightforward technical verifications from the pseudo-code of the random product algorithm. We omit the details.

Lemma 5.1. *If F_1 and F_2 are disjoint data-labelings then $F_1 \bigotimes F_2$ is a data-labeling.*

Example 5.2. In the example given below, we consider two data-labelings F_1 and F_2 for the partial orders displayed below and illustrate the steps involved in executing the Data-Labeling-Product Algorithm.

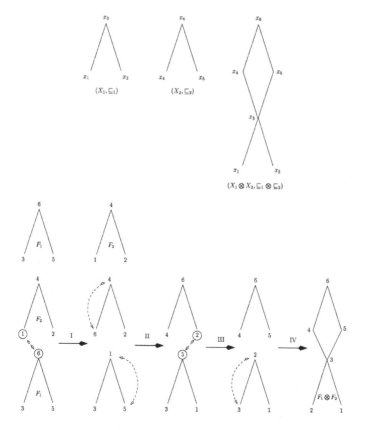

We indicate the selection of labels of extremal elements on the previous picture by full circles, where these elements are swapped in the next phase of the picture. For each while loop execution, initiated by a first swap of labels of two extremal elements, the other pairs of labels to be swapped are linked in the picture via a double arrow (in dashed line display). These labels are swapped in the next phase of the picture. The final illustration displays the end result of the computation, namely the data-labeling $F_1 \otimes F_2$.

Definition 5.2. Let $\mathcal{L}_1$ and $\mathcal{L}_2$ be disjoint sets of labels. The *data-labeling-product function*

$$\bigotimes: \mathcal{R}_{\mathcal{L}_1}(X_1, \sqsubseteq_1) \times \mathcal{R}_{\mathcal{L}_2}(X_2, \sqsubseteq_2) \to \mathcal{R}_{\mathcal{L}_1 \cup \mathcal{L}_2}(X_1 \otimes X_2, \sqsubseteq_1 \otimes \sqsubseteq_2)$$

is defined by: $\bigotimes(F_1, F_2) = F_1 \otimes F_2$.

The following result is important to obtain that the random product is a RB-preserving operation.

Theorem 5.1. *The data-labeling-product function is a bijection.*

Proof. Consider two disjoint partial orders $(X_1, \sqsubseteq_1)$ and $(X_2, \sqsubseteq_2)$.

We present a proof for Williams's versions of the Push operations. The proof for Floyd's version is similar.

We view the execution of the data-labeling product algorithm as a series of swaps along chains of $X_1 \otimes X_2$. For a given pair of disjoint labelings, F_1 and F_2, each such chain is determined by a single run of the two push operations in the code of the random product. We recall that at the start of the while loops, labels a and b are involved in the swaps, where in terms of the pseudo-code, $a = \vee M(F \upharpoonright X_1)$ and $b = \wedge m(F \upharpoonright X_2)$. We refer to these labels as the *extremal labels*. The label b is swapped downwards along a unique chain in the partial order $(X_1, \sqsubseteq_1)$ labeled by F_1 and a is swapped upwards along a unique chain in the partial order $(X_2, \sqsubseteq_2)$ labeled by F_2. The result of appending these two paths forms a chain in the product partial order $(X_1 \otimes X_2, \sqsubseteq_1 \otimes \sqsubseteq_2)$. We will show that each such swap sequence along such a unique chain is injective. It follows that the data-labeling-product function $\bigotimes$ is injective.

In order to show the result, we assume that we have two data-labelings F_1, F_1' of the partial order $(X_1, \sqsubseteq_1)$ and two data-labelings F_2, F_2' of the partial order $(X_2, \sqsubseteq_2)$ such that F_1 and F_2 are disjoint, F_1' and F_2' are disjoint and $F_1 \otimes F_2 = F_1' \otimes F_2'$. We show that $F_1 = F_1'$ and $F_2 = F_2'$.

We will display the labels on the chain determined by the swap sequence arising from the call to $F_1 \otimes F_2$, by:

$$[a_1, a_2, \ldots, a_m], [b_1, b_2, \ldots, b_k],$$

where (a, b) is the first pair which is swapped by the algorithm, $a_m = a, b_1 = b$.

The sequence $[a_1, a_2, \ldots, a_m]$ consists of the labels in the labeled partial order $(X_1, \sqsubseteq_1, F_1)$ which are respectively swapped with b and the sequence $[b_1, b_2, \ldots, b_k]$ consists of the labels in the labeled partial order $(X_2, \sqsubseteq_2, F_2)$ which are respectively swapped with a.

In the above, we allow the case where $m = 0$ and $k = 0$, i.e. no swap occurs.

Similarly,we display the labels on the chain determined by the swap sequence arising from the call to $F_1' \otimes F_2'$, by:

$$[a_1', a_2', \ldots, a_n'], [b_1', b_2', \ldots, b_l'],$$

where (a', b') is the first pair which is swapped by the algorithm, $a_n' = a'$, $b_1' = b'$, the sequence $[a_1', a_2', \ldots, a_m']$ consists of the labels in the labeled partial order $(X_1, \sqsubseteq_1, F_1')$ which are respectively swapped with b' and the sequence $[b_1', b_2', \ldots, b_k']$ consists of the labels in the labeled partial order $(X_2, \sqsubseteq_2, F_2')$ which are respectively swapped with a'.

In the above, we again allow the case were $n = 0$ and $l = 0$, i.e. no swap occurs.

We remark that $Ra(F_1) = Ra(F_1') = \mathcal{L}_1$ and that $Ra(F_2) = Ra(F_2') = \mathcal{L}_2$. This implies that $a = a'$ and $b = b'$.

We show that $a = a'$. The case $b = b'$ is similar. The algorithm selects the maximal label a at depth 0 in the labeled partial order $(X_1, \sqsubseteq_1, F_1)$ and the maximal label a' in the labeled partial order $(X_1, \sqsubseteq_1, F_1')$. Since $Ra(F_1) = Ra(F_1') = \mathcal{L}_1$ and data-labelings are increasing, we know that the maximum label of $\mathcal{L}_1$ must occur as a label of a maximal element and thus $a = a' = maximum(\mathcal{L}_1)$.

We remark that this fact does not alter, even after the first two push operations in the algorithm have been run through a number of times. Inductively one can show that $Ra(F_1) = Ra(F_1')$ remains true. Indeed, in case $a < b$ no swaps will occur and the result holds trivially. Otherwise, after the first series of swaps has happened for the first two while loops, we obtain that in $Ra(F_1)$, the label a simply has been replaced by the label b and in F_1' the same has taken place. Hence we preserve the fact that the ranges of the respective data-labelings coincide, which suffices to yield the desired property.

It follows by the fact that $a = a'$ and $b = b'$ at the start of each swap sequence, the number of non-trivial swap sequences induced by $F_1 \otimes F_2$ is identical to the number of non-trivial swap sequences induced by $F_1' \otimes F_2'$.

Hence we can focus on the *last* swap sequences induced by $F_1 \otimes F_2$ and $F_1' \otimes F_2'$ respectively and assume that both swap sequences, by the above, must start with a swap on the same pair of elements, a and b. Since the data-labelings of course have changed during the previous swap sequences, we denote the data-labelings at the start of the final swap sequences by G_1, G_2 and G_1', G_2' respectively.

Consider these final chains along which the labels are swapped, i.e. the chain

$$[G_1^{-1}(a_1), G_1^{-1}(a_2), \ldots, G_1^{-1}(a_m)], [G_2^{-1}(b_1), G_2^{-1}(b_2), \ldots, G_2^{-1}(b_k)]$$

and the chain

$$[(G_1')^{-1}(a_1'), (G_1')^{-1}(a_2'), \ldots, (G_1')^{-1}(a_n')],$$
$$[(G_2')^{-1}(b_1'), (G_2')^{-1}(b_2'), \ldots, (G_2')^{-1}(b_l')].$$

To show injectivity for the final swap sequences, it suffices that these chains must be identical.

Indeed, assume that these paths are the same, say a path denoted by P. Since $F_1 \otimes F_2 = F_1' \otimes F_2'$ and the swap sequence on P does of course not affect labels of $X_1 - P$, the data-labelings G_1 and G_1' must coincide on the set $X_1 - P$. Moreover, since the net result of the Push-Down operation is to move the label of the maximal element of P to the element originally labeled with b in F_2 and to move every other label of an element of P to the element immediately above it on P, we obtain that G_1 must be identical to G_1'.

We claim that it is always the case that the swap sequences corresponding to b must be the same for G_1 and G_1' and hence, by the above, the final swap operations form an injective operation.

We recall that since $F_1 \otimes F_2 = F_1' \otimes F_2'$, we must have that at the end of both Push-Down operations the label b is a label of the same element in the partial order.

We assume by way of contradiction that the paths are not identical and hence diverge at one point. Because b must end up at the end of the final swap sequences in the same position, we know there is a first time, after the sequences diverge, that the label b ends up as a label of the same element z of X. Say that prior to these swaps we had: $H_1^{-1}(x) = b$ and $H_1'^{-1}(y) = b$ where $x \neq y$ and where H_1 and H_1' are the data-labelings obtained from G_1 and G_1' by carrying out the swaps on G_1 and G_1' up to the point prior to the first convergence of the paths.

We clarify the situation for both data-labelings H_1 and H_1' in the following figure. In H_1 the label b will be swapped with a label α while in H_1' the label b will be swapped with a label β.

Since after these swaps the labels of x and y will not be changed again, the labels as displayed in the figure below, are the only ones possible in order to guarantee that the final results of the Push-Down calls are identical.

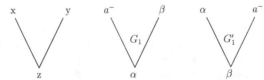

We now obtain a contradiction since from data-labeling H_1 it is clear that $\alpha < \beta$ while from data-labeling H_1' we obtain that $\beta < \alpha$.

Hence we cannot have divergence of the path and the result follows.

Since the same argument holds for a, we obtain that both swap paths must be identical.

The proof can now be concluded by an inductive argument remarking that the same must hold for every pair of swap sequences, when run through in reverse order of their occurrence. Since on elements outside the swap paths, no labels are ever swapped, we obtain that $F_1 = F_1'$ and $F_2 = F_2'$.

Finally we need to verify that the data-labeling-product function is surjective. It suffices to verify that $|\mathcal{R}_{\mathcal{L}_1}(X_1, \sqsubseteq_1)| \times |\mathcal{R}_{\mathcal{L}_2}(X_2, \sqsubseteq_2)| = |\mathcal{R}_{\mathcal{L}_1 \cup \mathcal{L}_2}(X_1 \otimes X_2, \sqsubseteq_1 \otimes \sqsubseteq_2)|$.

We remark that $|\mathcal{R}_{\mathcal{L}_1 \cup \mathcal{L}_2}(X_1 \otimes X_2, \sqsubseteq_1 \otimes \sqsubseteq_2)| = |\mathcal{R}_{\mathcal{L}_1'}(X_1, \sqsubseteq_1)| \times |\mathcal{R}_{\mathcal{L}_2'}(X_2, \sqsubseteq_2)|$, where $\mathcal{L}_1'$ consists of the first $|X_1|$ elements in the sorted version of $\mathcal{L}$ while $\mathcal{L}_2'$ consists of the last $|X_2|$ elements in the sorted version of $\mathcal{L}$. This follows by the fact that the sets X_1 and X_2 are completely connected in the partial order $(X_1 \otimes X_2, \sqsubseteq_1 \otimes \sqsubseteq_2)$. Since we can identify data-labelings up to labeling-isomorphism, it is clear that $|\mathcal{R}_{\mathcal{L}_1}(X_1, \sqsubseteq_1)| = |\mathcal{R}_{\mathcal{L}_1'}(X_1, \sqsubseteq_1)|$ and that $|\mathcal{R}_{\mathcal{L}_2}(X_2, \sqsubseteq_2)| = |\mathcal{R}_{\mathcal{L}_2'}(X_2, \sqsubseteq_2)|$. Hence the result follows.

We obtain the following immediate corollary, which motivates the choice of terminology random "product".

Corollary 5.1. *It $\mathcal{L}_1$ and $\mathcal{L}_2$ form a partition of the set of labels $\mathcal{L}$ then*

$$|\mathcal{R}_{\mathcal{L}}(X_1 \otimes X_2, \sqsubseteq_1 \otimes \sqsubseteq_2)| = |\mathcal{R}_{\mathcal{L}_1}(X_1, \sqsubseteq_1)| \times |\mathcal{R}_{\mathcal{L}_2}(X_2, \sqsubseteq_2).|$$

In the example given below, we illustrate that the random product is an injective process.

Example 5.3. We do not display all cases, but restrict our attention to the case of a fixed set of labels which can be used on the first partial order, say $\{1, 2, 3, 4\}$, and a fixed set of labels which can be used on the second partial order, say $\{5, 6, 7\}$.

It is easy to verify that the number of possible combinations of data-labelings for the given partial orders from the set of labels $\{1, 2, 3, 4, 5, 6, 7\}$ is $\binom{7}{4} \times 5 \times 2 = 350$, preventing a complete illustration of all cases.

The first five combinations of pairs of data-labelings are displayed at the top of the following page, followed by the computation steps involved in the random product.

The next five combinations are displayed again on the next page, followed by the computation steps involved in the random product.

Following this example, we define the binary random product below, which may be a product which comes to mind first. We indicate some problems with this approach, motivate a restricted use of the operation and introduce the unary random product, which is the one that will be used in the applications.

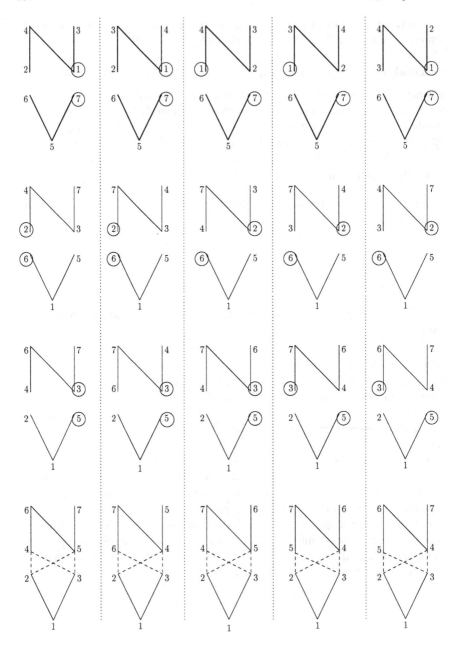

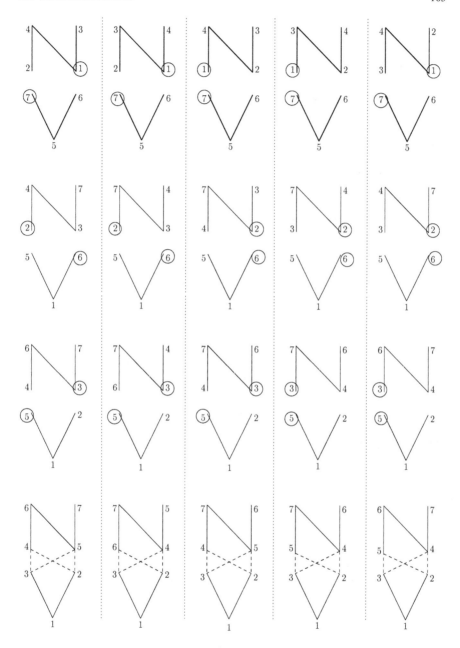

5.2.3 The Binary Random Product

Definition 5.3. Let $\mathcal{R}_{\mathcal{L}_1}(X_1, \sqsubseteq_1)$ and $\mathcal{R}_{\mathcal{L}_2}(X_2, \sqsubseteq_2)$ be two disjoint random structures. We define *the binary random product*, $\mathcal{R}_{\mathcal{L}_1}(X_1, \sqsubseteq_1) \bigotimes \mathcal{R}_{\mathcal{L}_2}(X_2, \sqsubseteq_2)$, by $\mathcal{R}_{\mathcal{L}_1 \cup \mathcal{L}_2}(X_1 \bigotimes X_2, \sqsubseteq_1 \bigotimes \sqsubseteq_2)$.

Lemma 5.2. *The binary random product is RS-preserving.*

Proof. This follows from Theorem 5.1.

Remark 5.2. The binary random product leads to complications regarding the determination of average-time. Indeed, the binary random product has an average time which is a function of the label sets $\mathcal{L}_1$ and $\mathcal{L}_2$. Consider the case where the largest label of the set $\mathcal{L}_1$ happens to be less than the least label of $\mathcal{L}_2$. In this case the binary random product will require no Push-Downs nor Push-Ups. At the other extreme, consider label sets $\mathcal{L}_1'$ and $\mathcal{L}_2'$ for which the labels of $\mathcal{L}_2'$ all are less than the least label of $\mathcal{L}_1'$. In that case clearly the binary random product $\mathcal{R}_{\mathcal{L}_1'}(X_1, \sqsubseteq_1) \bigotimes \mathcal{R}_{\mathcal{L}_2'}(X_2, \sqsubseteq_2)$ will require a large amount of Push-Down and Push-Up operations. Hence its average time will be strictly greater in general than the average time of $\mathcal{R}_{\mathcal{L}_1}(X_1, \sqsubseteq_1) \bigotimes \mathcal{R}_{\mathcal{L}_2}(X_2, \sqsubseteq_2)$. The dependency of the binary product operation on the label sets involved leads to complications regarding the determination of its average time.

The $\mathcal{MOQA}$ language operations include the unary random product, defined below. This avoids the above problem with determining the average-time of the general binary random product, where formulas have been derived expressing the average-case time of the unary random product.

5.2.4 The Unary Random Product

Definition 5.4. Consider a random structure $\mathcal{R}(X, \sqsubseteq)$ and distinct components I_1 and I_2 of an isolated subset I of X. We define *the unary random product* of the partial order $(X, \sqsubseteq)$ with respect to I_1, I_2 and I to be the partial order $(X, \sqsubseteq_{I_1 \bigotimes I_2})$ where $\sqsubseteq_{I_1 \bigotimes I_2}$ is the least partial order containing $\sqsubseteq \cup ((\sqsubseteq \restriction I_1) \bigotimes (\sqsubseteq \restriction I_2))$.

We define the unary random product to be the function:

$$\mu_{I_1 \bigotimes I_2}(X, I) \colon \mathcal{R}(X, \sqsubseteq) \to \mathcal{R}(X, \sqsubseteq_{I_1 \bigotimes I_2})$$

where $\forall F \in \mathcal{R}(X, \sqsubseteq). \, \mu_{I_1 \bigotimes I_2}(X, I)(F) \restriction (I_1 \bigotimes I_2) = (F \restriction I_1) \bigotimes (F \restriction I_2)$ and
$$\mu(F) \restriction (X - (I_1 \cup I_2)) = F \restriction (X - (I_1 \cup I_2)).$$

Theorem 5.2. *Consider a random structure $\mathcal{R}(X, \sqsubseteq)$ and distinct components I_1 and I_2 of an isolated subset I of X. The unary random product $\mu_{I_1} \bigotimes_{I_2}(X, I)$ is RB-preserving with multiplicity $\binom{|I_1|+|I_2|}{|I_1|}$.*

Proof. By the Extension Theorem it suffices to verify that the random product $\mu_{I_1} \bigotimes_{I_2}(I_1 \cup I_2, I_1 \cup I_2)$ is RB-preserving. Let $\mathcal{L}$ be a set of labels for $I_1 \cup I_2$. From Corollary 5.1 we obtain that for any partition $(\mathcal{L}_1, \mathcal{L}_2)$ of $\mathcal{L}$: $|\mathcal{R}_{\mathcal{L}}(I_1 \bigotimes I_2, \sqsubseteq_1 \bigotimes \sqsubseteq_2)| = |\mathcal{R}_{\mathcal{L}_1}(I_1, \sqsubseteq_1)| \times |\mathcal{R}_{\mathcal{L}_2}(I_2, \sqsubseteq_2)|$. The result follows from Theorem 5.1 and from the observation that there are $\binom{|I_1|+|I_2|}{|I_1|}$ such partitions.

We provide an example of the unary random product.

Example 5.4. Consider the Hasse diagram of the following tree:

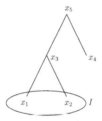

We display the eight states of the tree, where we selected the two leaves at the deepest level, i.e. x_1 and x_2, to form the atomic isolated subset I and labels for this set have been indicated as below.

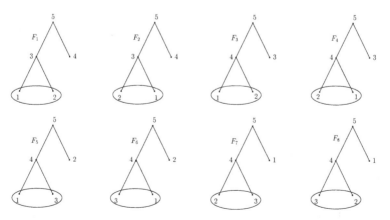

We apply the unary random product to the isolated subset $I = \{x_1, x_2\}$ and we use the components $I_1 = \{x_1\}$ and $I_2 = \{x_2\}$. The result is displayed below. The multiplicity involved is $\binom{|I_1+I_2|}{|I_1|} = \binom{2}{1} = 2$. Two copies of a random structure are obtained, a first copy consisting of the data-labelings marked by (I), i.e. the data-labelings F_i' with odd indices i, and a second copy consisting of the data-labelings marked by (II), i.e. the data-labelings F_i' with even indices i.

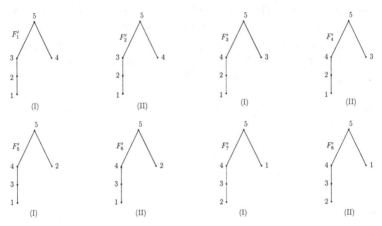

5.3 Random Deletion and Percolation

In this subsection we introduce two important data structure operations $\overline{Del}$, $\underline{Del}$ of deleting a label from a random structure. These operations allow one to incorporate a Heapsort style algorithms, which as we will see removes a main obstacle in the determination of average-case time of this type of algorithms. They are generalizations of two operations Del^M and Del^m which are introduced below.

Remark 5.3. We chose to implement the Deletion operations such that the element and its label a, to be deleted, will be returned by the operation. The element x labeled by a is removed from the partial order under consideration. It is easy to see that the operations could be defined in an alternative way such that the element x is actually kept after deletion as an extremal element of the partial order, where a is kept as the label of this new extremal element, which now becomes a minimum or a maximum. These variants are captured via the Percolation operations.

5.3.1 Deleting an Extremal Label

Definition 5.5. Consider $(X, \sqsubseteq)$ a finite partial order. For any extremal element e of the partial order, we define $(X, \sqsubseteq) - \{e\} = (X - \{e\}, \sqsubseteq_e)$, where $\sqsubseteq_e$ is obtained from the binary relation $\sqsubseteq$ by removing all pairs of $\sqsubseteq$ which contain the element e.

We leave the straightforward proof of the following lemma to the reader.

Lemma 5.3. *Let* $(X, \sqsubseteq)$ *be a finite partial order and let e be an extremal element of the partial order.* $(X, \sqsubseteq) - \{e\} = (X - \{e\}, \sqsubseteq_e)$ *is a partial order which we refer to as the result of deleting the extremal element e from the given partial order* $(X, \sqsubseteq)$.

We define the Random Deletion operations on a partial order.

Definition 5.6. Given a finite partial order $(X, \sqsubseteq)$. $\underline{Del}(X, \sqsubseteq)$ is defined to be the sequence of partial orders $(X - \{x\}, \sqsubseteq_x)_{x \in m(X)}$ while $\overline{Del}(X, \sqsubseteq)$ is defined to be the sequence of partial orders $(X - \{x\}, \sqsubseteq_x)_{x \in M(X)}$.

We recall that the greatest (least) label must occur at a maximal (minimal) element (cf. Remark 4.1).

Definition 5.7. We define the operation of deleting the largest label a from a given data-labeling F as follows: $Del^M(F) = F \restriction (X - x)$ where x is the element labeled with a. We define the operation of deleting the largest label a from a given random structure R to be the result of applying this operation to each state of R, i.e. $Del^M(R) = \{Del^M(F) | F \in R\}$. We will informally refer to $Del^M(R)$ as the result of deleting the maximum element of the random structure $\mathcal{R}_{\mathcal{L}}(X, \sqsubseteq)$. In a similar way one can define Del^m in two stages, first as an operation on data-labelings and subsequently as an operation on random structures.

We state the following RB-preservation result for the operation Del^M which returns a bag of random structures, each of which has multiplicity 1. Similar results hold for the operation Del^m.

Proposition 5.1. *If* $\mathcal{R}_{\mathcal{L}}(X, \sqsubseteq)$ *is a random structure and a the largest label of* $\mathcal{L}$ *then:*

1) $\mathcal{R}_{\mathcal{L} - a}(X - x, \sqsubseteq_x) = \{F \restriction (X - x) | F \in \mathcal{R}(X, \sqsubseteq), F(x) = a\}$.

2) $Del^M(\mathcal{R}_{\mathcal{L}}(X, \sqsubseteq)) = \{(\mathcal{R}_{\mathcal{L} - \{a\}}(X - \{x\}, \sqsubseteq_x), 1)\}_{x \in M(X)}$

Proof. Exercise.

We illustrate the deletion of the minimum label via Del^m on the following example.

Example 5.5. We circle the label 1 to be deleted.

The effect of deleting the label 1 is given by:

Hence we obtain two random structures, consisting of the states from the label set $\{2, 3, 4\}$ of a connected V-shaped partial order and of a partial order consisting of a two element linear component and a single element component.

A straightforward deletion of a label which is not a label of an extremal element on the other hand does *not* necessarily yield a random bag. For instance, a direct deletion of the label 2 from each of the five states, would result in the following set of data-labelings, which do not form a random bag:

The problem is resolved in Section 5.3.2 via a generalized deletion.

In the $\mathcal{MOQA}$ language the operations of deleting an extremal label will take as inputs the data-labelings corresponding to states from a random structure, where these data-labelings are stored in a variable X. Hence the operations will be denoted as: $Del^M(X)$ and $Del^m(X)$ for the deletion of a maximum label and a minimum label respectively.

5.3.2 Percolation and Deletion of Arbitrary Labels

We consider here the case of labels for elements which are not necessarily extremal. It is clear that the deletion of an internal label cannot simply occur by removing a label from all possible data-labelings where connections with other elements are deleted in a similar way as for the deletion of an extremal label. The same problem arises as for the deletion of the label 2 in Example 5.5.

In order to delete an arbitrary label a from a random structure, for a given data-labeling F, we proceed as follows in two steps. First we *percolate* an internal label to a position where it becomes a label of an extremal element. Then we carry out the deletion of the newly created extremal label as described in the previous section.

In the following we will assume that the label a to be deleted actually occurs as a label in the random structure.

Percolation
Percolation of a label a is carried out as follows:

We sketch two methods to remove the label, via downwards or upwards percolation, each of which can be applied in $\mathcal{MOQA}$.

We describe the process of percolating a label downwards.

Perc

Here we replace the value of a by a value less than any label from the data-labeling F under consideration. This value is only a technical aid and is indicated by a^-. The label a^-, which will become a part of the given data-labeling, is then pushed down in the usual way, i.e. the process is exactly the opposite as in the definition of $\otimes$ where we insert one element into a random structure.

The label a^- is systematically swapped with the largest label among the elements which are immediately below the element labeled with a^-, in case there are at least two elements immediately below the given element, or with the label of the single element immediately below the element labeled with a^- (depending on which is the case) until label a^- becomes the label of a minimal element. Of course, in case a^- was already a label of a minimal element, no swaps are necessary.

Remark 5.4. The above distinction between more than one element and a single element immediately below a given element means that in practice the algorithm will need $n - 1$ comparisons in case there are $n \geq 2$ children below the node under consideration (in order to determine the maximum label of the children) and, at first glance, it would appear that no comparisons need to be made in case of a single child below the node under consideration. Indeed, in case of a single child, we can immediately perform a swap since the parent node is labeled with a^- which by definition is smaller than the label of the unique child. However, in practice one also needs to determine whether a parent has one or more children, which inherently involves a comparison. In order to obtain a better representation of cost, we will assume in the following that heaps are full binary trees, i.e. every parent has exactly two children, some of which may be the empty tree. A leaf then is a node for which both children are empty. In case of a single child, one comparison will be counted to determine this situation. We will return to this issue in the analysis of Percolating Heapsort.

Next we describe the process of percolating a label upwards.

$\overline{\text{Perc}}$

Here we replace the label of a by a value which is larger than all labels from F, denoted by a^+ and push up the label in a similar way.

Two related operations can be derived from this process, in a similar spirit as the approach to Del^M and Del^m, which are referred to as $\underline{Perc}^M$ and $\overline{Perc}^m$ and which re-insert the "percolated" element and its label in the correct order determined by the label value. We sketch the definition of the $\underline{Perc}^M$ operation. $\underline{Perc}^M$, similar to the $\underline{Del}$ operation, pushes down a label from a data-labeling to a minimal element position, after which it is deleted and subsequently the element (and its label) are re-introduced as a maximum element with the given label. Of course, a similar $\overline{Perc}^m$ operation, creating a minimum element, can be defined. $\underline{Perc}^M$ will proceed in two steps. First it consists of an execution of the <u>Perc</u> operation called on the greatest label a of the original data-labeling. Following the Push-Down of the relabeled element a^-, the operation will remove the corresponding minimal element labeled with a^- and re-introduce this element as the maximum of the partial order. Moreover, it will relabel the resulting maximum element with a. It is easy to verify that the result is a new data-labeling. The effect of $\underline{Perc}^M$ is to reset the input data-labeling to this new data-labeling restricted to the elements excluding the new maximum element. For a given data-labeling stored in a variable X, this restriction is indicated by $\underline{X}$; i.e. $\underline{X}$ is the data-labeling stored in X, restricted to the part below its maximum element.

We leave it to the reader to verify that the $\underline{Perc}^M$ operation is RB-preserving, yielding a similar Random Bag as for the delete operation (with appropriate maximum elements created by $\underline{Perc}^M$) for which the random structures have multiplicities one.

Example 5.6. We illustrate the effect of $\underline{Perc}^M$ on the following data-labeling:

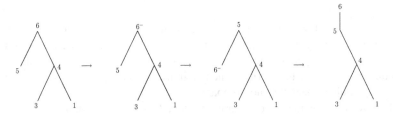

Theorem 5.3. *The operations $\underline{Perc}^M$ and $\overline{Perc}^m$ are RB-preserving. $\underline{Perc}^M$ has the same average-case comparison time as the $\underline{Del}$ operation executed on the largest label and $\overline{Perc}^m$ has the same average-case comparison time as the $\overline{Del}$ operation executed on the least label.*

Deletions of arbitrary labels

Finally, the operations $\underline{Del}$ and $\overline{Del}$ are again first defined on data-labelings and then extended to random structures. To define the operations on data-labelings, we consider two inputs: an index k and a data-labeling F. We define the deletion of an arbitrary label of a given data-labeling, which generalizes the deletion of extremal labels.

$\underline{Del}(\mathbf{k}, \mathbf{F})$ is defined to be the operation of percolating the k-th smallest label a downwards as a label a^- followed by the deletion of the extremal element labeled by a^-. The output returned is the deleted label and the random structure is updated to be the newly obtained random bag, i.e. a bag of partial orders all labeled from the same set of labels to form the random structures. The definition of $\overline{Del}(\mathbf{k}, \mathbf{F})$ is similar.

We note that in contrast with the deletion operation which generates a random bag, the percolation operation only generates a single random structure. The Delete operations return the deleted element and label and updates the random structure to a new random bag as described above.

We illustrate both deletion processes in the following example.

Example 5.7. Consider the partial order $(X, \sqsubseteq)$ given by the Hasse diagram:

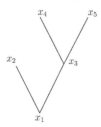

For a given set of labels $\mathcal{L} = \{1, 2, 3, 4, 5\}$ we obtain the following states:

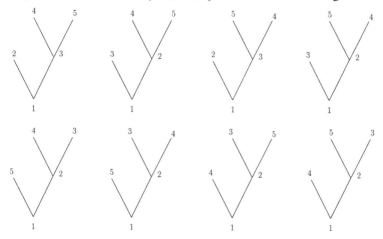

We illustrate removing the label 2 via the <u>*Del*</u> method:

We only illustrate the end result which involves a partial order with a singleton component and a three element V-shaped component.

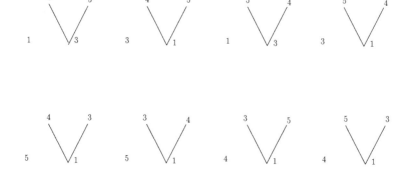

Full details are given for the $\overline{Del}$ method which is illustrated next.

We illustrate the result of removing the second smallest label, which for the case of the example is the label 2, from the above random structure via the $\overline{Del}$ method and display the change of the label 2 to 2^+, the subsequent end result of calling Push-Up on this new label and finally we display the resulting sequence of random structures.

We first illustrate the effect of removing the second smallest label via the $\overline{Del}$ method on the first four states.

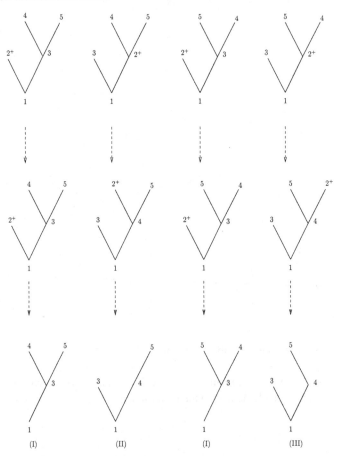

(I)   (II)   (I)   (III)

We illustrate the effect on the next four states.

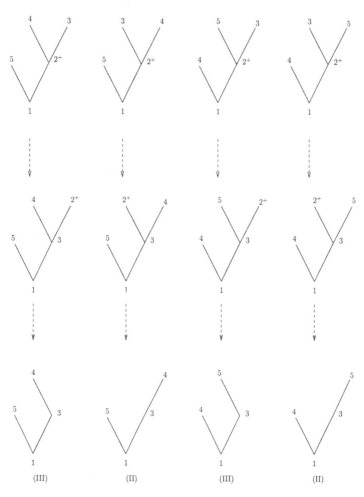

Hence we obtain a sequence of three new random structures, identified by (I),(II) and (III), each of which is labeled from the set of labels $\{1, 3, 4, 5\}$. Of course, one can see that (II) and (III) are identical. Hence they can be identified during an analysis of the deletion process. Since however the copies created in this way depend on the structure of the original partial order, we will not identify the copies at this stage and treat each as a new random structure. The problem is that the verification of identical copies for arbitrary partial orders would require too much time in general. Later on, in a complexity analysis of an algorithm involving a deletion process, if needed, we can make the necessary identifications during the set up of the recurrence equations depending on the partial order under consideration. The need for such an identification can be eliminated via an elegant representation of partial orders introduced in [Hic08].

The following result states that the Deletion operation is RB-preserving.

Theorem 5.4. *Let $R = \mathcal{R}_{\mathcal{L}}(X, \sqsubseteq))$ be a random structure and $k \in \{1, \ldots, |X|\}$. The operation $\underline{Del}(k)$ is a bijection over R, where $\underline{Del}(k)\colon R \to \{\mathcal{R}_{\mathcal{L}-\{a\}}(X - \{x\}, \sqsubseteq_x)\}_{x \in m(X)}$ and where a is the k-th smallest label of $\mathcal{L}$.*

Proof. Consider the random structure R. We will show that the $\underline{Del}(k)$ function is injective on R. Consider the partial order $(X, \sqsubseteq)$ of R and the label set $\mathcal{L}$, where $a \in \mathcal{L}$ is the k-th smallest label. In order to show the result, we assume that we have two states F, F' of the partial order $(X, \sqsubseteq)$ from the same set of labels $\mathcal{L}$ such that $\underline{Del}(k, F) = \underline{Del}(k, F')$. We show that $F = F'$.

Note that the label a will be replaced by the label a^-, following the notation of the pseudo-code. We view the execution of the delete algorithm for a given state F as a chain of swaps involving the element a^- along the partial order $(X, \sqsubseteq)$. For a state F such a swap-chain is determined by a single run of the Push-Down operation in the code of the delete. The label a^- is swapped downwards along a unique chain in the partial order $(X, \sqsubseteq)$.

We will display the labels on the chain determined by the swap sequence arising from the call to $\underline{Del}(k, F)$ by $[a_1, a_2, \ldots, a_m]$, where $a_1 = a^-$ and the sequence $[a_2, \ldots, a_m]$ consists of the labels in the labeled partial order $(X, \sqsubseteq, F)$ which are respectively swapped with a^-. We allow the case where $m = 1$, i.e. no swap occur.

Similarly, we display the labels on the chain determined by the swap sequence arising from the call to $\underline{Del}(k, F')$, by $[a'_1, a'_2, \ldots, a'_n]$ where $a'_1 = a^-$ and the sequence $[a'_2, \ldots, a'_m]$ consists of the labels in the labeled partial order $(X, \sqsubseteq, F')$ which are respectively swapped with a^-. We again allow the case were $n = 1$, i.e. no swap occurs.

Consider the two chains along which the label a^- is swapped, i.e. the chain

$$[F^{-1}(a_1), F^{-1}(a_2), \ldots, F^{-1}(a_m)]$$

and the chain

$$[(F')^{-1}(a'_1), (F')^{-1}(a'_2), \ldots, (F')^{-1}(a'_n)].$$

To show injectivity for the swap sequences, it suffices to show that these chains must be identical. Indeed, assume that these paths are the same, say a path denoted by P. Since $\underline{Del}(k, F) = \underline{Del}(k, F')$ and the swap sequence on P does of course not affect labels of $X - P$, the states F and F' must coincide on the set $X - P$. Moreover, since the net result of the Push-Down operation is to move the label a^- of a given fixed element in P to a minimal element of the partial order (the same minimal element for both states F and F' since the swap chain is assumed to be the same for both) and to move every other label of an element of P to the element immediately above it on P, we obtain that F must be identical to F'. The fact that the final position of a^- is a minimal element is clear since a^- by definition is the smallest element of the label set $\mathcal{L}' = (\mathcal{L} - \{a\}) \cup \{a^-\}$.

We claim that, under the assumption that $\underline{Del}(k, F) = \underline{Del}(k, F')$, it is always the case that the swap sequences corresponding to a^- must be the same for F

and F' and hence, by the above, we obtain that $F = F'$. We recall that since $\underline{\text{Del}}(k, F) = \underline{\text{Del}}(k, F')$ we must have that at the end of both Push-Down operations the label a^- is a label of the same (minimal) element in the partial order. We assume by way of contradiction that the paths are not identical and hence diverge at one point. The argument is similar to the one presented in the proof of Theorem 5.1. Because a^- must end up at the end of the final swap sequences in the same position, we know there is a first time, after the sequences diverge, that the label a^- ends up as a label of the same element z of X. Say that prior to these swaps we had: $G^{-1}(x) = a^-$ and $G'^{-1}(y) = a^-$ where $x \neq y$ and where G and G' are the states obtained from F and F' by carrying out the swaps on F and F' up to the point prior to the first convergence of the paths. We display the situation for both data-labelings G and G' in the following figure. In G the label a^- will be swapped with a label α while in G' the label a^- will be swapped with a label β. Since after these swaps the labels of x and y will not be changed again, the labels as displayed in the figure below, are the only ones possible in order to guarantee that the final results of the Push-Down calls are identical.

We now obtain a contradiction since from data-labeling G it is clear that $\alpha < \beta$ while from data-labeling G' we obtain that $\beta < \alpha$. Hence we cannot have divergence of the path and the result follows.

Finally we need to verify that the $\underline{\text{Del}}$ function is bijective. For this it suffices to note that the domain of this function and its range have same cardinality. Indeed, note that for every minimal element $m_i \in \mathcal{M}(X)$, where say $i \in \{1, \ldots, k\}$, the following holds: $|\mathcal{R}_{\mathcal{L}-\{a\}}(X - \{m_i\}, \sqsubseteq)| = |\mathcal{R}_{\mathcal{L}'}(X, \sqsubseteq) \restriction \{F | F \in \mathcal{R}_{\mathcal{L}'}(X, \sqsubseteq)$ and $F(m_i) = a^-\}|$, where $\mathcal{L}' = (\mathcal{L} - \{a\}) \cup \{a^-\}$.

Theorem 5.5. *Let $R = \mathcal{R}_{\mathcal{L}}(X, \sqsubseteq))$ be a random structure and $k \in \{1, \ldots, |X|\}$. The operation $\underline{\text{Del}}(k, R)$ is RB-preserving,*

$$\underline{\text{Del}}(k) \colon R \longmapsto \{(\mathcal{R}_{\mathcal{L}-\{a\}}(X - \{x\}, \sqsubseteq_x), 1)\}_{x \in m(X)},$$

where a is the k-th smallest label of $\mathcal{L}$. A similar result holds for $\overline{\text{Del}}(k)$. Both operations lead to random bags for which the multiplicities are constant 1.

Remark 5.5. We remark that both deletion operations transform the empty Random Structure $\emptyset$ to $\emptyset$.

As for the previous operations, all versions of the random deletion can be extended via the Extension Theorem (Theorem 4.8) on strictly isolated subsets and finally extended to arbitrary random bags via Definition 4.12.

5.4 The Random Projection

We first define a contractive version of the random projection, referred to as *the strong random projection* which takes data-labelings from a given partial order and an isolated subset of this order as arguments and restricts the data-labelings to this isolated subset, destroying the complement of this isolated subset in the process.

Definition 5.8. Let $(X, \sqsubseteq)$ be a partial order with an isolated subset I. The strong random projection $SProj((X, \sqsubseteq), I)$ of $(X, \sqsubseteq)$ on I is defined to be the restricted partial order $(I, \sqsubseteq)$.

Rather than

Definition 5.9. *The strong random projection on an isolated subset* I *of the order of a data-labeling* F *is defined to be the restriction* $F{\upharpoonright}I$. *The strong random projection on an isolated subset* I *of a random structure* $R = \mathcal{R}_{\mathcal{L}}(X, \sqsubseteq)$ *is defined as follows:* $SProj(I, R)$ *is the bag* $R{\upharpoonright}I$ *resulting from the restriction of all states of* $\mathcal{R}_{\mathcal{L}}(X, \sqsubseteq)$ *to the subset* I.

Next we consider the random projection which produces *a copy* of the restriction of a data-labeling to an isolated subset.

Definition 5.10. Let $(X, \sqsubseteq)$ be a partial order with an isolated subset I. The random projection $Proj((X, \sqsubseteq), I)$ of $(X, \sqsubseteq)$ on I obtained as follows: let J be a newly created set, disjoint from X and such that J is equipped with a partial order $\sqsubseteq_J$ where $(J, \sqsubseteq_J)$ is order-isomorphic to the restricted partial order $(I, \sqsubseteq)$.

Definition 5.11. *The random projection on an isolated subset* I *of a data-labeling* F *is defined as follows: consider the random projection* $(J, \sqsubseteq_J)$ *of the partial order* $(X, \sqsubseteq)$ *with respect to* I *and* $\Psi \colon (I, \sqsubseteq) \to (J, \sqsubseteq_J)$ *an order-isomorphism.* $Proj(I, F)$ *is the data-labeling* F_J *resulting from the transposition of* F *to the subset* J *as follows:* $\forall j \in J. F_J(j) = F(\Psi^{-1}(j))$.

The random projection on an isolated subset I *of a random structure* $R = \mathcal{R}_{\mathcal{L}}(X, \sqsubseteq)$ *is defined as follows: consider the random projection* $(J, \sqsubseteq_J)$ *of the partial order* $(X, \sqsubseteq)$ *with respect to* I *and* $\Psi \colon (I, \sqsubseteq) \to (J, \sqsubseteq_J)$ *an order-isomorphism.* $Proj(I, R)$ *is the bag* $\{F_J | F \in R\}$ *resulting from the transposition of all states from* R *to the subset* J *as follows:* $\forall F \in R \ \forall j \in J. F_J(j) = F(\Psi^{-1}(j))$.

Theorem 5.6. *Consider an isolated subset* I *of a random structure* $R = \mathcal{R}(X, \sqsubseteq)$.
a) The strong random projection is RB-preserving, where

$$SProj(I, R) \colon \mathcal{R}(X, \sqsubseteq) \to \{(\mathcal{R}(I, \sqsubseteq), K)\} \text{ and } K = \frac{|\mathcal{R}(X, \sqsubseteq)|}{|\mathcal{R}(I, \sqsubseteq)|}.$$

In case I is strictly isolated, we have: $K = |\mathcal{R}(\lceil M(I) \rceil \uparrow, \sqsubseteq)| \times |\mathcal{R}(\lfloor m(I) \rfloor \downarrow, \sqsubseteq)|.$

b) The random projection is RB-preserving, where

$$Proj(I, R): \mathcal{R}(X, \sqsubseteq) \to \{(\mathcal{R}(J, \sqsubseteq_J), K)\} \text{ and } K = \frac{|\mathcal{R}(X, \sqsubseteq)|}{|\mathcal{R}(J, \sqsubseteq_J)|}.$$

The above includes a slight abuse of notation in that the resulting random structure is produced in addition to the original random structure, which is unchanged and which is not displayed in the above notation.
In case I is strictly isolated, we have: $K = |\mathcal{R}(\lceil M(I) \rceil \uparrow, \sqsubseteq)| \times |\mathcal{R}(\lfloor m(I) \rfloor \downarrow, \sqsubseteq)|.$

Proof. These results follow from Proposition 4.3.

We consider the example of a strong random projection on an isolated subset of the random structure $\mathcal{A}_3$.

Example 5.8. We illustrate the effect of a strong random projection on the atomic random structure $\mathcal{A}_3 = \mathcal{R}_{\{1,2,3\}}(\{x_1, x_2, x_3\}, \sqsubseteq)$. In the picture below, the first column indicates the possible labels for x_1, the second column indicates the labels for x_2, while the third column indicates the labels for x_3. Let $I = \{x_1, x_3\}$. We display the result of $Proj(I, \mathcal{R}(X, \sqsubseteq))$, which results in $K = \frac{3!}{2!} - 3$ copies of $\mathcal{A}_2$. Indeed, we obtain a copy consisting of the data-labelings $\{(1, 3), (3, 1)\}$, indicated by (I) on the picture, a copy consisting of the data-labelings $\{(1, 2), (2, 1)\}$, indicated by (II) on the picture, and a copy consisting of the data-labelings $\{(2, 3), (3, 2)\}$, indicated by (III) on the picture.

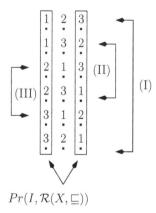

$$Pr(I, \mathcal{R}(X, \sqsubseteq))$$

The $\mathcal{MOQA}$ language implementation currently comes equipped with the random projection, as opposed to a strong random projection, but could of course be extended to include both types of projections.

5.5 The Random Split

We define the random split operation first on an atomic random structure $\mathcal{A}_n$ and then use the Extension Theorem (Theorem 4.8) to allow applications of the random split operation to atomic isolated subsets. Note that the random split already has been defined in Chapter 1. We discuss in the current section the split operation as it is typically defined, e.g. [AHU87], where two pointers are kept, one moving from the start of the list to the right, a second one moving from the end of the list to the left. The material illustrates, as pointed out in Chapter 1, that for the case of this more traditional split version, the same type of random bag is created. The reader may wish to omit this material on first reading and proceed with other basic operations first. Contrary to the split operation presented in Chapter 1, we will not explicitly track the element indices in the output data-labeling produced in the split operation from a given input data-labeling, though the material below could be extended to do so. Instead, we will take a more abstract view and focus on identifying the random bag which will be created after identifying the partial orders of the produced data-labelings up to order isomorphism, in order to demonstrate RB-preservation.

5.5.1 The Random Split of a Discrete Partial Order

Definition 5.12. We define the random split operation on a discrete partial order $(X, \sqsubseteq)$ where say $X = \{x_1, \ldots, x_n\}$. The enumeration of the elements of X is irrelevant. Different enumerations will yield order- and label-isomorphic end results for the split operation.

For every $m \in \{1, \ldots, n\}$ we define Ξ_{x_m} to be the partial order obtained on X via the transitive reflexive closure of the relation $\underline{X}_{x_m} \cup \overline{X}_{x_m}$, where $\underline{X}_{x_m} = \{(x_k, x_m) \mid 1 \le k < m\}$, $\overline{X}_{x_m} = \{(x_m, x_l) \mid m < l \le n\}$ and where the first set is defined to be empty in case $m = 1$ and the second set is defined to be empty in case $m = n$.

The *random split of the discrete partial order* $(X, \sqsubseteq)$ is defined to be the sequence

$$((X, \Xi_{x_1}), \ldots, (X, \Xi_{x_n})).$$

The partial order Ξ_{x_m} is illustrated via the following diagram:

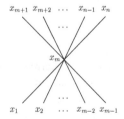

Example 5.9. We illustrate the resulting sequence of partial orders obtained via a random split on the discrete four-element partial order $(X, \sqsubseteq)$, where say $X = \{x_1, x_2, x_3, x_4\}$.

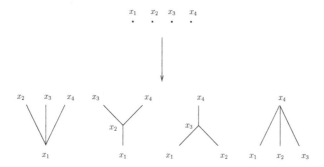

5.5.2 Random Split of a Random Structure

Since a split involves an operation on an atomic isolated subset, we first discuss the result of carrying out a split operation on an atomic random structure, $\mathcal{A}_n = \mathcal{R}_\mathcal{L}(X, \sqsubseteq)$.

The first part of the definition involves the random split operation on a single state of an atomic random structure $\mathcal{A}_n = \mathcal{R}_\mathcal{L}(X, \sqsubseteq)$ and then define the random split of $\mathcal{A}_n$ to be the result of applying this operation to each state of $\mathcal{A}_n$. Let $\{x_1, \ldots, x_n\}$ be an enumeration of X and let $x \in X$. The reader will remark that the pseudo-code for the random split is similar to the one used in traditional Quicksort [AHU87]. Indeed, Quicksort is an example of an algorithm which uses a partitioning of elements based on a random split operation. The "pivot" around which the elements are partitioned is indicated by "x" in the pseudo-code below.

Pseudo-code for random split $Split_x(F)$ **on a state F of $\mathcal{A}_n$**
$u := 1; v := n; a := F[x]$;
while $u < v$ **do**
    while $F[x_u] < a$ **do** $u := u + 1$;
    while $F[x_v] > a$ **do** $v := v - 1$;
    if $u < v$ then **swap**$(F[x_u], F[x_v], F)$

Remark 5.6. Let $\mathcal{L}' = (a_1, \ldots, a_n)$ be the sorted list obtained from the set of labels $\mathcal{L}$. If m is the position of the label $F(x)$ in the sorted list $\mathcal{L}'$, i.e. $F(x) = a_m$, then $Split_x(F)(x_m) = a_m$. Moreover the labels to the left of a_m form the set of labels smaller than a_m, i.e. $\{a_1, \ldots, a_{m-1}\}$, and the labels to the right of a_m form the set of labels larger than a_m, i.e $\{a_{m+1}, \ldots, a_n\}$.

We define $Split_x(\mathcal{A}_n)$ to be the set of functions obtained by applying the preceding algorithm to each of the $n!$ states F of $\mathcal{A}_n$.

In the following we will identify (for each $m \in \{1, \ldots, n\}$);

- data-labelings G from (X, Ξ_{x_m}), and
- data-labelings G from $Split_x(\mathcal{A}_n)$, where $G = Split_x(F)$ for some $F \in \mathcal{A}_n$, which

satisfy:

$$G(x_k) < G(x_m) \text{ if } k < m, G(x_m) = a_m \text{ and } G(x_l) > G(x_m) \text{ if } l > m.$$

It is easy to verify that any choice of x will produce the same set of functions, i.e. $\forall x, x' \in X. Split_x(\mathcal{A}_n) = Split_{x'}(\mathcal{A}_n)$. Hence the choice of x does not need to be specified in this context, but of course will be specified in particular $\mathcal{MOQA}$ programs that are based on the Split Operation since the choice of x will affect the way subsequent computations proceed.

For every choice of $x \in X$, we let $\mathcal{A}_n{}^{x,m}$ denote the set of states of $\mathcal{A}_n$ for which the label $F(x)$ is the m-th element, i.e. a_m, in the sorted list $\mathcal{L}'$. We let $Split_x(\mathcal{A}_n{}^{x,m})$ denote the set of functions obtained by applying random split to all states F of $\mathcal{A}_n{}^{x,m}$.

Remark 5.7. We remark that $|\mathcal{A}_n{}^{x,m}| = (n-1)!$ and $|\mathcal{R}_{\mathcal{L}}(X, \Xi_m)| = (m-1)!(n-m)!$

Lemma 5.4. *For all $\mathcal{L}, X, x \in X, m \leq |X| = |\mathcal{L}| = n$, we have:*

1) $\forall m \in \{1, \ldots, n\}. Split_x(\mathcal{A}_n^{x,m}) = \mathcal{R}_{\mathcal{L}}(X, \Xi_m)$.

2) $|Split_x^{-1}(G) \cap \mathcal{A}_n^{x,m}|$ is independent of G, when $G \in \mathcal{R}_{\mathcal{L}}(X, \Xi_m)$.

Proof. To show 1), we remark that the inclusion from left to right follows from the definition of the pseudo-code of the Split operation. To show the converse, let $G \in R = \mathcal{R}_{\mathcal{L}}(X, \Xi_m)$, then, still from the definition of the pseudo-code, it is clear that $G = Split_x(F)$, when $F \in \mathcal{A}_n$ is obtained from G by swapping only the labels $G(x)$ and $G(x_m)$ of x and x_m respectively. Hence we obtain the local surjectivity of $Split_x$ with respect to $\mathcal{A}_n^{x,m}$, i.e. $Split_x(\mathcal{A}_n^{x,m}) = \mathcal{R}_{\mathcal{L}}(X, \Xi_m)$.

To show 2), we remark that for every $G, G' \in \mathcal{R}_{\mathcal{L}}(X, \Xi_m)$, we have $G(x) = G'(x)$. Let $a = G(x)$. Because of the structure of the partial order (X, Ξ_m), it is clear that there is a permutation σ of the labels of G which satisfies $\sigma(a) = a, \forall b. b < a \Rightarrow \sigma(b) < a$ and $b > a \Rightarrow \sigma(b) > a$ and which is such that $G' = \sigma \circ G$. But then, it is clear that for any $F \in \mathcal{A}_n^{x,m}$ we have: $Split_x(F) = G \Leftrightarrow Split_x(\sigma \circ F) = \sigma \circ G$, from which 2) follows immediately.

Proposition 5.2. *For all $\mathcal{L}, X, x \in X, m \leq |X| = |\mathcal{L}| = n$, we have:*

$$Split_x \colon \mathcal{A}_n \longmapsto \{(\mathcal{R}_\mathcal{L}(X, \Xi_1), K_1), \ldots, (\mathcal{R}_\mathcal{L}(X, \Xi_n), K_n)\},$$

$$\text{where } \forall m \in \{1, \ldots, n\}. \, K_m = \binom{n-1}{m-1}.$$

Proof. We remark that $\mathcal{A}_n^{x,m}$ forms a partition of $\mathcal{A}_n$. Combining 1) and 2) of Lemma 5.4, we obtain that $|Split_x^{-1}(G) \cap \mathcal{A}_n^{x,m}| = K_m$ for some non-zero constant K_m. Finally, we remark that $\forall m \in \{1, \ldots, n\}. \, K_m = \binom{n-1}{m-1}$ by Remark 5.7.

From Proposition 5.2 and the Extension Theorem (Theorem 4.8), we obtain (using the notation of Theorem 4.8):

Theorem 5.7. *Let $R = \mathcal{R}_\mathcal{L}(X, \sqsubseteq)$ be a random structure and let I be an atomic isolated subset of $(X, \sqsubseteq)$. Then, using the notion related to Theorem 4.8,*

$$Ext(I)(Split_x) \colon R \longmapsto \{(\mathcal{R}_\mathcal{L}(X, \sqsubseteq_1^*), K_1), \ldots, (\mathcal{R}_\mathcal{L}(X, \sqsubseteq_n^*), K_n)\},$$

$$\text{where } \forall i \in \{1, \ldots, n\}. \, K_m = \binom{n-1}{m-1}.$$

The following example illustrates the effect of a split on an atomic strictly isolated subset I. This subset has no degree of freedom on the labels for the set $X - I$. Indeed, $X - I$ consists of the maximum and the minimum of the underlying partial order and hence there is a unique label assigned to each of these elements. For such an atomic strictly isolated subset, the effect of a split is essentially the same as the effect of a split on atomic random structures $\mathcal{A}_n$ as discussed in Lemma 5.4. The example nevertheless provides a good illustration of the type of random structures generated via a split operation. Example 5.11 illustrates how a split operates on a more general type of atomic isolated subset I.

Example 5.10. We illustrate the effect of a split on the following partial order $(X, \sqsubseteq)$ for which the elements of a strictly isolated subset I have been indicated via the ellipse:

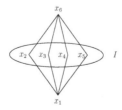

After performing the split on $I = \{x_2, \ldots, x_5\}$, we obtain the bag:

$$\{(X, \sqsubseteq_{x_2}), \ldots, (X, \sqsubseteq_{x_5})\}$$

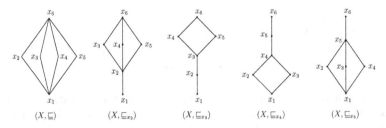

We continue the example and consider the set of labels $\mathcal{L} = \{1, 2, 3, 4, 5, 6\}$, where the number of possible states for the partial order $(X, \sqsubseteq)$ is 24. We consider the atomic strictly isolated subset I of $\mathcal{R}_{\mathcal{L}}(X, \sqsubseteq)$ determined by the four element subset $\{x_2, x_3, x_4, x_5\}$. We consider the set of states $\mathcal{F}$, consisting of the six states that label the element x_4, with the label 4 as displayed in the following picture.

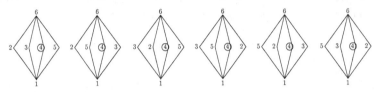

The split of the partial order $(X, \sqsubseteq)$ results in the partial order with Hasse diagram:

Finally, we display the result of the operation $Ext(I)(Split)(\mathcal{R}_{\mathcal{L}}(X, \sqsubseteq))$ on the subset of states $\mathcal{F}$.

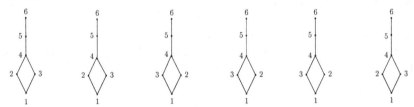

Clearly $n = 4$ and $m = 3$. Thus $\binom{n-1}{m-1} = \binom{3}{2} = 3$ copies of the random structure $\mathcal{R}_{\mathcal{L}}(X, \sqsubseteq_{y_4})$ have been produced.

The following example illustrates the effect of a split on an atomic isolated subset I of a given random structure $\mathcal{R}(X, \sqsubseteq)$ for which the labels on $X - I$ can vary.

We obtain two copies of a random structure indicated by (I) and (II), where the split operation, as defined, does not automatically identify these random structures. Of course this identification can be achieved via a simple adaptation of the definition of the split operation if desired or during the time analysis later if this turns out to be useful.

Example 5.11. We consider the same tree and random structure over this tree as in Example 5.4. After performing a split, $Ext(I)(Split)(R)$ determined by the atomic isolated subset I enumerated by x_1, x_2, and by the Extension Theorem, Theorem 4.8, we obtain a set of data-labelings for a new partial order as displayed below.

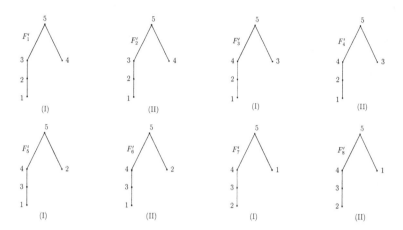

5.6 Top and Bot Operations

The operation Top will be useful to create heap-ordered treaps in $\mathcal{MOQA}$. Since the reader is by now familiar with the notion of an RB-preserving operation and its definition on partial orders and on data-labelings, we sketch Top's definition below and omit the details of the verification of RB-preservation.

A similar operation[1], for the case of lists, is discussed in [FS08] to generate increasing binary trees. The $\mathcal{MOQA}$ Top operation[2], which we denoted by Top, is close in spirit to the Del^M operation. In the last case the element with maximum label is removed, while in the first case the status of the underlying element is changed to that of a maximum. The proofs of the random bag preservation of these operations are similar. In the presence of a strong projection, one can show that the Del^M operation over a random structure can be obtained via the sequential composition of the Top operation with a strong random projection $SProj$, where one projects each random structure in the random bag (obtained by Top) on the strictly isolated part below the maximum.

Definition 5.13. Consider a partial order $(X, \sqsubseteq)$ with say m maximal elements $\mathcal{M}(X) = \{x_{i_1}, \ldots, x_{i_m}\}$. For each $j \in \{1, \ldots, m\}$, we define the partial order $\sqsubseteq_j$ to be the least partial order $(X, \sqsubseteq_j)$ containing $(X, \sqsubseteq)$ and the relation

---

[1] In fact an operation similar to the Bot operation discussed further on.
[2] Introduced by J. Townley.

$\{(x_{i_k}, x_{i_j}) | k \in \{1, \ldots, m\}, k \neq j\}$. In other words this is the partial order obtained from $(X, \sqsubseteq)$ by making the maximal element x_{i_j} the *maximum* element.

The operation Top transforms each data-labeling F from a random structure $\mathcal{R}(X, \sqsubseteq)$ into a new data-labeling F' as follows: Top determines the largest label a among the labels obtained by restricting F to the maximal elements of X (via $m - 1$ comparisons). Say the label a labels the maximal element x_{i_k} for some $k \in \{1, \ldots, m\}$. Then the partial order over which F' is defined is $(X, \sqsubseteq_k)$ and the *function F'* is defined to be the function F over the set X. i.e. the operation Top acts on data-labelings F as the identity function in the sense that each element retains its original label. Of course, the resulting data-labeling F' is different from the original data-labeling F, since the associated partial order has changed as described above. We recall that a data-labeling consists of a pair consisting of the function and the partial order.

Remark 5.8. A similar operation Bot is introduced which determines the least label of a data-labeling among the minimal elements of the partial order and alters the ordering such that the least label labels a minimum.

We leave the verification of the following result to the reader.

Theorem 5.8. *Let $R = \mathcal{R}_{\mathcal{L}}(X, \sqsubseteq)$ where $(X, \sqsubseteq)$ has m maximal elements. The operation Top is RB-preserving on R, where*

$$Top: \mathcal{R}_{\mathcal{L}}(X, \sqsubseteq) \longmapsto \{(\mathcal{R}_{\mathcal{L}}(X, \sqsubseteq_1), 1), \ldots, (\mathcal{R}_{\mathcal{L}}(X, \sqsubseteq_m), 1)\}.$$

This concludes the discussion of the current main $\mathcal{MOQA}$ operations. Obviously the list can be extended further as long as the operations in question are RB-preserving. In Section 5.7 we revisit the basic $\mathcal{MOQA}$ operations which are contractive, since such operations form a special case in the Extension Theorem, Theorem 4.8. In Section 5.8 we classify the basic $\mathcal{MOQA}$ operations which correspond to uniformly RB-preserving functions. Finally, in Section 2.2 we discuss the classification of the data structures which can be generated from the atomic random structure via the basic $\mathcal{MOQA}$ operations. We demonstrate that all such data structures correspond to random bags for which the underlying partial orders are series-parallel[3] and we show that the data structures corresponding to a (number of copies of a) single random structure, correspond exactly to the random structures for which the underlying partial order is series-parallel. Finally, in Section 5.11, we show that the fact that data structures can be assumed to be series-parallel in our context, drastically simplifies various aspects of the $\mathcal{MOQA}$ approach.

---

[3] Chapter 2 introduces the notion of a series-parallel order.

5.7 Contractive Operations Revisited

We provide two counter-examples demonstrating that the Extension Theorem can not be generalized to isolated subsets for the case of contractive operations. As discussed in this theorem, contractive operations can be applied to *strictly* isolated subsets.

Counter-Example 5.9 (Deletion) We illustrate that the deletion operation, when applied to isolated subsets, does not in general allow for an extension as in Theorem 4.8. Consider the partial order given in Example 4.1 f) and the corresponding random structure $\mathcal{H}_4$ of heaps of size 4 displayed in Counter-Example 1.1. We consider the isolated subset $I = \{x_1, x_2\}$ (cf. Example 4.1 f)). If we apply the deletion operation $\underline{Del}$ to data-labelings of the four copies of the random structure $\mathcal{S}_2$ determined by this isolated subset, then we obtain the following heaps, which do *not* form a random structure.

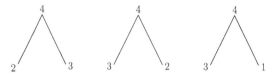

Counter-Example 5.10 (Strong projection) Consider the random structure $\mathcal{H}_4$ discussed in the previous counter-example and the isolated subset $I = \{x_1, x_2\}$. Consider a strong projection on the isolated subset $J = \{x_1\}$ of the set I. The result is displayed below. Once again, we do not obtain a random structure.

5.8 Uniformly RB-preserving Functions Revisited

Uniformly RB-preserving functions have been introduced in Definition 4.10. By Remark 4.8 and the fact that the random product and the random projection are strongly RB-Preserving, it follows that these operations are uniformly RB-preserving. We recall from Chapter 1, Remark 1.5, that the random split is uniformly RB-preserving. However the random deletion is not uniformly RB-preserving. This can be readily verified from Example 5.7. If one applies the random deletion operation Del^M to each of the eight data-labelings displayed in Example 5.7, a partition yielding an RB-representation of this operation necessarily constitutes of three components: one component of cardinality 2 and two components of cardinality 3. This follows from an inspection of the three partial orders corresponding to the random bag which has been obtained as the result of the deletion. By bijectivity of the deletion operation, the partition consists of one part of size 2 and two parts of size 3 and hence the operation is not uniformly RB-preserving. Similarly, the operations $\underline{Perc}^M$ and $\overline{Perc}^m$, Top and Bot are not uniformly RB-preserving. However, when restricted to applications to atomic random structures, these operations are uniformly RB-preserving.

5.9 $\mathcal{MOQA}$-Constructible Random Bags

We recall that Problem [3] of Section 4.5 raises the characterization of $\mathcal{A}$-constructible random bags was raised. In other words, Problem [3] regards the characterization of the random bags that are the image of a random structure preserving function on a discrete random structure. Here we address the related problem of characterizing the random bags that are constructible via $\mathcal{MOQA}$ operations from the discrete random structure.

Definition 5.14. A random bag is $\mathcal{MOQA}$-constructible iff it is produced through a sequential composition of basic $\mathcal{MOQA}$ from a discrete random structure

We address the following restricted problem (cf. also the open problems listed in Section 4.5):

[4] "Characterize the random structures that are $\mathcal{MOQA}$-constructible."

We will show that all random bags, which are produced through basic $\mathcal{MOQA}$ operations from discrete random structures, consist of random structures for which the partial order is a series-parallel partial order (cf. Section 2.2). In this sense, all $\mathcal{MOQA}$ data structures are series-parallel in nature. This opens up possibilities for parallellization of $\mathcal{MOQA}$ constructs, such as the $\mathcal{MOQA}$ parallel recursion introduced in Chapter 7. More speculatively, the SP-nature of $\mathcal{MOQA}$ data structures potentially lends itself to software-hardware co-design for improved quantitative static analysis, in view of the well-known series-parallel graph approach of electrical engineering [Fin03].

Remark 5.9. It is important to recall that $\mathcal{MOQA}$ operations of course perfectly apply to random bags for which the underlying partial orders are general partial orders, as opposed to SP-orders. Moreover, some constructs, in particular first order random conditionals discussed in Chapter 7, if incorporated in $\mathcal{MOQA}$, could create non-SP orders when not properly controlled. At this stage we require that $\mathcal{MOQA}$ programs operate over series-parallel data structures. We recall that in the current context, we require that all data structures are generated by $\mathcal{MOQA}$ programs from input data corresponding to atomic random structures. Due to the fact that SP orders are preserved by $\mathcal{MOQA}$ programs, the data structures are guaranteed to correspond to random bags for which all partial orders are SP. As we will see in Section 5.11, this considerably simplifies various aspects of the $\mathcal{MOQA}$ approach. But again, if needed, $\mathcal{MOQA}$ programs could operate on data structures which are non-SP, e.g.

for inputs of a random structure over a non SP-order, since the crucial property of RB-preservation holds in this more general context.

A solution to Problem [4] will be obtained through the characterization of the $\mathcal{MOQA}$-constructible random structures in Proposition 5.3.

5.10 $\mathcal{MOQA}$-Constructible Random Bags are Series-Parallel

Proposition 5.3. *1) All partial orders underlying the random structures in $\mathcal{MOQA}$-constructible random bags are SP.*
2) The $\mathcal{MOQA}$-constructible random structures are exactly the random structures for which the underlying partial order is series-parallel.

Proof. We sketch the argument. To show 1), note that the discrete partial order is an SP-order and, as is easily verified, all basic $\mathcal{MOQA}$-operations preserve SP-orders.

To show 2), note that by 1) each $\mathcal{MOQA}$-constructible random structure must have an underlying SP-order.

Consider a random structure for which the underlying partial order is SP. We need to show that the SP order is constructible via basic $\mathcal{MOQA}$-operations. For this, it suffices to remark that $\mathcal{MOQA}$ incorporates the two basic construction operators for SP-orders: the sequential composition (random product) and the parallel composition (via components of a partial order). The result follows from the definition of an SP-order as a recursively generated order from single elements through these two fundamental operations introduced in Definition 2.1 of Chapter 2.

Example 5.12. An immediate corollary of Proposition 5.3 and Proposition 2.1, which characterizes SP-orders as N-free orders, is that the random structure $\mathcal{N}$ of Example 4.1, part (e), is not $\mathcal{MOQA}$-$\mathcal{A}$-constructible. This can also be< demonstrated, as in Example 4.6, using a cardinality argument and the fact that $\mathcal{MOQA}$ operations are RB-preserving.

5.11 Simplifications for SP-Orders

The trivial observation of Remark 2.2 has considerable repercussions for the theory of randomness preservation. It opens the way to potential parallellization of the language, facilitates programming in the $\mathcal{MOQA}$ language, as will be apparent from the recursive $\mathcal{MOQA}$ constructs introduced in Chapter 7, and simplifies the computation of the average-case time of basic $\mathcal{MOQA}$ constructs as discussed in Chapter 6.

As a first illustration we remark that labeling-counting is well-known to be a polynomial time operation for partial orders over an SP-order. The cardinality of the random structure over an SP-order can be determined as follows by induction:

Lemma 5.5. *a) For any atomic discrete SP-order D, $|R(D)| = |D|!$*

b) For any parallel SP-order $P = P_1|| \ldots ||P_n$ and $i, j \in \{1, \ldots, n\}$.

$$|R(P)| = \binom{|P|}{|P_1| \ldots |P_n|} \times \prod_{i=1}^{n} |R(P_i)|$$

c) For any product SP-order $P = P_1 \otimes \ldots \otimes P_n$ and $i, j \in \{1, \ldots, n\}$.

$$|R(P))| = \prod_{i=1}^{n} |R(P_i)|$$

5.12 Partitions and separative functions

We recall that Chapter 4 introduced a more general notion of random bag preservation, which enables the inclusion of operations which transform random structures to random bags which are not necessarily strict. Example 5.13 below illustrates that $\mathcal{MOQA}$ operations in general can give rise to non-strict random bags.

Example 5.13. Consider the three heaps of Counter-Example 1.1. Applying the deletion operation Del^m twice to the three heaps in this random structure, yields a non-strict random bag containing three copies of a linear partial order of size 2, with labels 3 and 4.

Remark 5.10. (Separative functions revisited) In case of separative random functions the creation of non-strict random bags does not arise. For instance for the Split operation discussed in Chapter 1, the tracking of indices during the computation makes sure that all partial orders created are distinct. If this property is guaranteed at all times, one would obtain a strict random bag in Example 5.13, where the three linear orders of size 2 would be distinct from one another, since the elements involved would have distinct indices. It is interesting to note that the non-contractive $\mathcal{MOQA}$ operations in general will yield separative functions. This is clear for operations other than the product operation. To make the product operation correspond to a separative function, one could insist that each swap of the operation on labels also involves a swap on the indices of the elements at which these labels reside. One can verify that the product operation, carried out over an atomic random structure and adapted to incorporate swaps on indices, will yield data-labelings for which all partial orders are distinct. I.e. the corresponding function is separative. Following this approach, as in Chapter 1, it is clear that an identification up to order-isomorphism can be carried out which will introduce multiplicities which are not necessarily constant 1.

The approach of tracking indices in addition to labels during a computation is not novel and is well-understood from history based approaches in Computer Science as well as decision tree reasoning. Its incorporation in this context could lead to an approach involving separative functions which would simplify the notion of random bag preservation from Definition 4.8 to the definition given in Remark 4.7, with the additional overhead of tracking indices. We remark that, viewing $\mathcal{MOQA}$ operations as computations starting from atomic random structures, the above approach amounts to simply keep the index i of each element x_i, in the original discrete partial order of the atomic random structure, paired with the label a originally assigned to the element x_i. I.e. at each point in the computation, the original input data-labeling (permutation), giving rise to this computation would be known.

Chapter 6

Average-Case Time of Basic $\mathcal{MOQA}$ Operations
Joint with D. Early

In this chapter, we outline formulas for computing the average running time of basic $\mathcal{MOQA}$ operations, obtained by D. Early. First, we outline a simplification of the average running time of the product function in terms of a more elementary function. In the second part, we show how this function can be further simplified in the special case of partial orders which can be constructed by series-parallel operations alone. We also show how the average running time for the delete operation can be simplified in these cases. Finally, we show how the simplifications derived in the second part can be applied to certain inductively defined structures.

6.1 Definitions

Let A and B be two disjoint components of a finite partial order, where the partial order has an underlying set consisting of $A \cup B$. Generalizations to applications of the random product to components of an isolated subset of a partial order can be obtained based on the Extension Theorem. The average-case time is typically not affected by such generalizations.

We let $\mathcal{A}$ and $\mathcal{B}$ denote the random structures on A and B respectively, and $|\mathcal{A}|$ and $|\mathcal{B}|$ denote the number of states in $\mathcal{A}$ and $\mathcal{B}$ respectively. We let A_{max} be the set of maximal elements in A, and B_{min} be the set of minimal elements in B.

We let $S(A, B)$ be the set of all valid data-labelings of A and B from a single set of labels $\{a_1, a_2, \cdots, a_{|A|+|B|}\}$ which satisfies $a_i < a_j$ for all $i < j$. It is easy to see that $|S(A, B)| = \binom{|A|+|B|}{|A|}|\mathcal{A}||\mathcal{B}|$.

We let $S_k(A, B)$ be the subset of $S(A, B)$ containing all those data-labelings which have precisely k elements of $\{a_1, a_2, \cdots, a_{|A|}\}$ as labels on the partial order B (or equivalently, precisely k elements of $\{a_{|A|+1}, \cdots, a_{|A|+|B|}\}$ as labels on the partial order A). It is easy to see that $|S_k(A, B)| = \binom{|A|}{k}\binom{|B|}{k}|\mathcal{A}||\mathcal{B}|$.

All references to the "running time" of an operation refer to the number of comparisons made in carrying out that operation. All references to the "average running time" of an operation, unless otherwise stated, refer to the average number of comparisons made when the operation is called on every element of $S(A, B)$.

In particular, we investigate the average running time of the product operation as the average number of comparisons made in performing the product operation $A \otimes B$ on each data-labeling of A and B in $S(A, B)$. We denote this average running time by $\overline{T}[A \otimes B]$.

We refer to the number of elements in a set that a particular element is greater than or equal to as the 'rank' of that element in that set.

Consider the effect of replacing the minimum label in a data-labeling of A with a new label, of rank k in the new set of labels on A. We define $x_k(A)$ to be the average running time of a Push-Up operation on this label, where the average is taken over every state in the random structure $\mathcal{A}$.

Finally, we define $\tau_{up}(A) = \overline{x}(A) = \frac{\sum_{i=1}^{|A|} x_i(A)}{|A|}$. So, $\tau_{up}(A)$ is the average time taken by a Push-Up from the node with minimum label. We define $\tau_{down}(A)$ in an equivalent manner, as the average time taken by a Push-Down operation starting from the node with maximum label.

6.2 Average-Case Time

6.2.1 The While Condition

The condition for the loop of the product operation to execute is

$$\vee M(F|A) > \wedge m(F|B).$$

We know that finding the minimum or maximum element of a set of n independent elements requires $n - 1$ comparisons, and therefore finding the maximum element of $M(F|A)$ and the minimum element of $m(F|B)$ must require $|A_{max}| + |B_{min}| - 2$ comparisons.
Having found the relevant elements, an additional comparison is made to evaluate the '>' boolean, giving a total of $|A_{max}| + |B_{min}| - 1$ comparisons in evaluating the while condition.

Lemma 6.1. *The product operation runs through the while loop an average of* $\frac{|A||B|}{|A|+|B|}$ *times.*

Proof. Firstly, we observe that whenever a label is swapped from A to B, it must be (i) bigger than all of the other labels on A and (ii) bigger than the label that it is swapping with. In other words, it is bigger than at least $|A|$ labels. Similarly, any element being swapped down to A must be smaller than at least $|B|$ labels. Since these two sets form a partition of the full set of labels, we know that swaps can only go in one direction. Further, since the operation does not stop until the smallest label on B is greater than the biggest label on A, it follows that the total number of swaps made in the operation must be exactly the number of labels initially out of place. So the average number of swaps made (and hence the average number of executions of the while loop) must be

$$\sum_{k=1}^{\min(|A|,|B|)} \frac{k|S_k(A,B)|}{|S(A,B)|} = \frac{1}{\binom{|A|+|B|}{|A|}} \sum_{k=1}^{\min(|A|,|B|)} k\binom{|A|}{k}\binom{|B|}{k}.$$

But now, using the combinatorial identity

$$\sum_{k} k\binom{|A|}{k}\binom{|B|}{k} = \frac{(|A|+|B|-1)!}{(|A|-1)!(|B|-1)!}$$

(Lemma 6.4 of Section 6.4.3) this reduces to $\frac{|A||B|}{|A|+|B|}$.

Now since we know that each evaluation of the boolean requires the same number of comparisons, and that the average number of evaluations of the boolean is simply $\frac{|A||B|}{|A|+|B|} + 1$ (once at the start of each loop, and once after the last loop to confirm that the operation is complete), it follows that the average number of comparisons made in evaluating the boolean is:

$$\left(\frac{|A||B|}{|A|+|B|} + 1\right)(|A_{min}| + |B_{max}| - 1)$$

6.2.2 Push-Up and Push-Down

Lemma 6.2. *When the label* a_k *is swapped onto the partial order B by the product operation, it's rank in the set of labels on B is* $k - |B|$.

Proof. The label a_k is greater than or equal to exactly k labels in the set of labels on both A and B. But in order to be swapped up, a_k must be greater than all the other labels previously on A, and greater than the label which was swapped down, and so

a_k is greater than every label then on A. This means that there are exactly $k - |A|$ labels on B which a_k is greater than or equal to, and hence the rank of a_k in the set of labels on B is $k - |A|$.

Lemma 6.3. *Swapping any label with the minimum label in each state of the random structure $\mathcal{A}$ and then calling Push-Up on that label is a bijective random bag preserving operation.*

Proof. This is a direct consequence of the data-labeling product function being a bijection — we simply consider the random product of $\mathcal{A}$ with a partial order with a single element.

Remark 6.1. Because the data-labelings on B initially form $\binom{|A|+|B|}{|A|}|\mathcal{A}|$ copies of the random structure on B, and because of Lemma 6.3, the data-labelings on B after each execution of the while loop must form $\binom{|A|+|B|}{|A|}|\mathcal{A}|$ copies of the random structure on B.

Theorem 6.1. *The average running time of each call to the Push-Up operation on the label a_k is $x_{k-|A|}(B)$.*

Proof. From the previous two lemmas, we know that the set of data-labelings on B always forms some number of copies of the complete random structure on B, and the rank of the label a_k in the set of labels on B is always $k - |A|$, whenever it is swapped up. But since the average running time of a Push-Up operation on a complete random structure is simply $x_r(A)$ where r is the rank of the label being pushed up, the result follows.

Theorem 6.2. *The average running time of the random product operation on the partial orders A and B is*

$$\overline{T}[A \otimes B] =$$
$$\frac{|A||B|}{|A|+|B|}(\tau_{down}(A) + \tau_{up}(B)) + \left(\frac{|A||B|}{|A|+|B|} + 1\right)(|A_{max}| + |B_{min}| - 1).$$

Proof. If we pick a certain label a_m with $m > |A|$, the total number of data-labelings in the set $S(A, B)$ in which that label is on A must be $\binom{|A|+|B|-1}{|B|}|\mathcal{A}||\mathcal{B}|$. The average number of comparisons made in pushing this label up into place when product in called on all of the data-labelings in $S(A, B)$ is $x_{m-|A|}(B)\dfrac{\binom{|A|+|B|-1}{|B|}|\mathcal{A}||\mathcal{B}|}{|S(A,B)|} = x_{m-|A|}(B)\dfrac{|A|}{|A|+|B|}$.

Summing this over all the labels greater than $a_{|A|}$ gives the average total number of comparisons made in pushing up each label, and hence the overall average total number of comparisons made by the Push-Up operation:

$$
\sum_{i=|A|+1}^{|A|+|B|} x_{i-|A|} \frac{|A|}{|A|+|B|} = \frac{|A|}{|A|+|B|} \sum_{i=1}^{|B|} x_i(B)
$$

$$
= \frac{|A||B|}{|A|+|B|} \frac{\sum_{i=1}^{|B|} x_i(B)}{|B|} = \frac{|A||B|}{|A|+|B|} \tau_{up}(B)
$$

By the symmetry of the Push-Up and Push-Down operations, it is easy that a similar result will hold for the average running time of the Push-Down operation — namely, that average will be $\frac{|A||B|}{|A|+|B|} \tau_{down}(A)$.

Combining all three results, we obtain that the average running time of the random product operation on the partial orders A and B is

$$
\overline{T}[A \otimes B] = \frac{|A||B|}{|A|+|B|} (\tau_{down}(A) + \tau_{up}(B)) + \\
\left(\frac{|A||B|}{|A|+|B|} + 1 \right) (|A_{max}| + |B_{min}| - 1).
$$

6.3 Series-Parallel Partial Orders

We recall that an introduction to series-parallel orders (SP-orders) is included in Chapter 2. Series-parallel partial orders are inductively defined in terms of two functions — series ($\mathcal{S}$) and parallel ($\mathcal{P}$). If $\mathcal{L}$ is the set of all partial orders, then both series and parallel map from $\mathcal{L} \times \mathcal{L}$ to $\mathcal{L}$.

$A \otimes B$ is the result of applying the series operation to (A, B), which is the same as the partial order created by applying the product operation to (A, B).

$A \| B$ is the result of applying the parallel function to A and B (the parallel function is commutative). It contains all the elements of the sets A and B, and all of the links of the two partial orders, with no additional links.

Effectively, the series operation puts the partial order B 'above' the partial order A (i.e. after the operation, we have $a \sqsubseteq b \ \forall \ a \in A, b \in B$), whereas the parallel operation puts A 'beside' B (i.e. all of the nodes in A remain independent of the nodes in B).

6.3.1 Series-Parallel Composition Laws for the τ Function

Series-parallel composition enables us to define a large set of partial orders inductively in terms of smaller ones. In a similar way, we show in this section how the value of the τ function for a particular series-parallel partial order can be derived in terms of its value for the constituent parts.

In order to do this, it is necessary to introduce some secondary functions. We define $\sigma_{up}(A) = x_{|A|}(A)$ (that is, the average time taken to push a label from the node with minimum label of A all the way through the partial order). We define $\kappa_{up}(A)$ to be the average (over all data-labelings) over all ranks of the number of labels pushed up as far as a maximal node in A. We define σ_{down} and κ_{down} similarly.

Also, we observe that the trivial composition laws for $|A|$, $|A_{min}|$ and $|A_{max}|$ are as follows:

1. $|(A \otimes B)| = |(A\|B)| = |A| + |B|$
2. $|(A \otimes B)_{min}| = |A_{min}|$
3. $|(A \otimes B)_{max}| = |B_{max}|$
4. $|(A\|B)_{min}| = |A_{min}| + |B_{min}|$
5. $|(A\|B)_{max}| = |A_{max}| + |B_{max}|$

Using only the values of these functions applied to A and B, it is possible to determine each of their values for both $A \otimes B$ and $A\|B$ as follows:

1. $\tau_{up}(A \otimes B) = \dfrac{|A|\tau_{up}(A) + \kappa_{up}(A)|B_{min}| + |B|(\tau_{up}(B) + |B_{min}| + \sigma_{up}(A))}{|A| + |B|}$
2. $\sigma_{up}(A \otimes B) = \sigma_{up}(A) + \sigma_{up}(B) + |B_{min}|$
3. $\kappa_{up}(A \otimes B) = \kappa_{up}(B)$
4. $\tau(A\|B) = \dfrac{|A|\tau(A) + |B|\tau(B)}{|A| + |B|}$
5. $\sigma(A\|B) = \dfrac{|A|\sigma(A) + |B|\sigma(B)}{|A| + |B|}$
6. $\kappa(A\|B) = \kappa(A) + \kappa(B)$

The first three rules are stated only for the 'up' cases, but the 'down' ones are similarly obtained. The last three rules are symmetrical for the 'up' and 'down' versions, and the subscripts have been omitted. In each case, the proof is given only for the 'up' case, but the 'down' can be proven in a similar manner.

Proof. 1. If a label is of rank $r \leq |A|$, then after its Push-Up is complete, it will be on A, and the number of comparisons involved will be exactly the same as if B were not there — i.e. the average number will be $\tau_{up}(A)$. For each of the $\kappa_{up}(A)$ ranks which are pushed up as far as the maximal nodes of A, there will be an additional $|B_{min}|$ comparisons to ensure that the label should not be pushed any further. Therefore, summing over all ranks $r \leq |A|$, and averaging over all valid data-labelings, we get a total number of comparisons of $|A|\tau_{up}(A) + \kappa_{up}(A)|B_{min}|$. For each label of rank $r > |A|$, the label will be on B after its Push-Up. Each such label must therefore pass all the way through A (an average of $\sigma_{up}(A)$ comparisons) and be swapped onto B (which requires $|B_{min}|$ comparisons). But now the label has a rank from 1 to $|B|$ in the set of labels on B, and therefore the average number of comparisons in pushing it up must be $\tau_{up}(B)$. Summing over all ranks and averaging over all valid data-labelings therefore gives a total number of comparisons of $|B|(\sigma_{up}(A) + |B_{min}| + \tau_{up}(B))$.

Adding the two totals and dividing by $|A| + |B|$ to get the average over all ranks gives the desired result, that

$$\tau_{up}(A \otimes B) = \frac{|A|\tau_{up}(A) + \kappa_{up}(A)|B_{min}| + |B|(\tau_{up}(B) + |B_{min}| + \sigma_{up}(A))}{|A| + |B|}.$$

2. Pushing a label up through $A \otimes B$ consists of (i) pushing the label up through A, (ii) swapping it on to B, and (iii) pushing it up through B. But since the data-labelings of A and B are independent of one another, and the number of comparisons in swapping from a maximal node of A to a minimal node of B is $|B_{min}|$ regardless of the data-labeling, the desired average is simply the sum of the averages of the three separate parts:

$$\sigma_{up}(A \otimes B) = \sigma_{up}(A) + |B_{min}| + \sigma_{up}(B).$$

3. Any label with rank $r \leq |A|$ will end up on A, which is mutually exclusive from the set of maximal nodes of $A \otimes B$ (which must be a subset of the nodes in B). Any label with rank $r > |A|$ will be pushed through A and swapped on to B. But now it has a rank between 1 and $|B|$ in the set of labels on B, and so the average number of ranks between 1 and $|A| + |B|$ to get to the top of $A \otimes B$ will be precisely the average number of ranks between 1 and $|B|$ to get to the top of B:

$$\kappa_{up}(A \otimes B) = \kappa_{up}(B).$$

4. For any given simultaneous data-labeling of A and B with labels from the first $|A| + |B|$ positive integers, there is a $\frac{|A|}{|A|+|B|}$ probability that the 1 will be placed on A, and hence that the Push-Up operation used to evaluate the τ function will take place on the partial order A, and a $\frac{|B|}{|A|+|B|}$ probability that it will be placed on B and that the Push-Up operation will take place on B.

We consider a particular data-labeling of A with the first $|A|$ positive integers. The labels on the path followed by a label being pushed up through A, will be some subsequence of the first $|A|$ positive integers. We let a_i be one less than the $i + 1^{th}$ label on the Push-Up path, and b_i be the number of predecessors the node with that label has. Then the average (over all ranks from 1 to $|A|$) number of comparisons made in pushing up a label in this data-labeling is $\frac{\sum (|A|-a_i)b_i}{|A|}$. The average of this over all data-labelings is simply $\tau(A)$.

Now suppose that A and B are simultaneously labelled using the first $|A| + |B|$ natural numbers, and that the 1 is placed on A (so that the label being pushed up is on the partial order A). We consider the average value of the label on the ith node in the Push-Up path when all the labels except one are chosen from the positive integers between 2 and $|A| + |B|$. By the Lemma 6.5 of Section 6.4.3, and since the order of the label relative to the others is fixed by the data-labeling, this average will be the average value of the $(a_i)^{th}$ element in an $|A| - 1$ element subset of the natural numbers in the range $[2, |A| + |B|]$, which will be one more than the same average for a subset of the first $|A| + |B| - 1$ natural numbers, i.e. $1 + \frac{|A|+|B|}{|A|} a_i$. This means that, averaged over all the possible sets of labels, $|A| + |B| - \frac{|A|+|B|}{|A|} a_i$ of the $|A| + |B|$ possible ranks will be pushed up past the ith node.

This gives an average number of comparisons over all $|A| + |B|$ ranks of

$$\frac{\sum \left(|A| + |B| - \frac{|A|+|B|}{|A|} a_i\right) b_i}{|A| + |B|}.$$

But, cancelling above and below, this is simply $\frac{\sum (|A|-a_i) b_i}{|A|}$, the average number of comparisons with the original label set. Averaging this over all data-labelings, we once again get $\tau(A)$ — in other words, the average number of comparisons made in a Push-Up through $A||B$ when the 1 is on A is exactly the same as the number of comparisons made in a push up through A, and hence $\tau(A + B)$ is simply an average weighted by the probabilities of the 1 being on A and B respectively — that is

$$\tau(A||B) = \frac{|A|\tau(A) + |B|\tau(B)}{|A| + |B|}.$$

5. Since the number of comparisons made in pushing up a label which is greater than any of the labels on a given structure depends only on the data-labeling, and not on the label set, the average number of comparisons required to push a label up through $A||B$ is simply $\sigma(A)$ if the element is pushed through A (i.e. if the 1 is on A) and $\sigma(B)$ if it is pushed through B (i.e. if the 1 is on B). As with the τ function, this allows us to write $\sigma(A||B)$ as a simple weighted average of $\sigma(A)$ and $\sigma(B)$:

$$\sigma(A||B) = \frac{|A|\sigma(A) + |B|\sigma(B)}{|A| + |B|}.$$

6. We consider the average value of the largest label in the Push-Up path of A over all data-labelings with the first $|A|$ positive integers, which we shall denote by $\overline{m}(A)$. For any given data-labeling, the number of ranks which are pushed up as far as the maximal node is $|A|+1-t$, where t is the value of the largest label in the Push-Up path. Averaging this over all data-labelings, we get $\kappa(A) = |A| + 1 - \overline{m}(A)$.

Now we consider also the function $\overline{m}(A\backslash(A||B))$, which is the same function, but averaged over all sets of labels including 1 chosen from the first $|A| + |B|$ positive integers (i.e. all possible label sets of $|A|$ from a data-labeling of $A||B$ which place the 1 on A).

For any given data-labeling, let the largest label in the Push-Up path be s. Then the average value of the largest label when each of the different label sets are applied to the same data-labeling will be (by the lemma in 4) $1 + \frac{|A|+|B|}{|A|}(s-1)$.

So $\overline{m}(A\backslash(A||B)) = 1 + \frac{|A|+|B|}{|A|}(\overline{m}(A) - 1)$.

But now, $\overline{m}(A||B)$ is the average value of the largest element in the Push-Up path of $A||B$, which must be the average (weighted by the probability of the 1

being on each structure) of $\overline{m}(A\backslash(A||B))$ and $\overline{m}(B\backslash(A||B))$ — i.e. $\overline{m}(A||B) =$
$$\frac{|A|\overline{m}(A\backslash(A||B)) + |B|\overline{m}(B\backslash(A||B))}{|A| + |B|} = \overline{m}(A) + \overline{m}(B) - 1.$$
So finally, combining all these relationships, we can write:
$$\kappa(A||B) = |A| + |B| + 1 - \overline{m}(A||B)$$
$$= (|A| + 1 - \overline{m}(A)) + (|B| + 1 - \overline{m}(B))$$
$$= \kappa(A) + \kappa(B).$$

Using these rules, it is possible to determine the τ function for a series-parallel partial order using only its series-parallel composition, and the values of the given functions in the base cases, which we can easily observe to be:

1. $\tau_{up}(\bullet) = \tau_{down}(\bullet) = 0$
2. $\sigma_{up}(\bullet) = \sigma_{down}(\bullet) = 0$
3. $\kappa_{up}(\bullet) = \kappa_{down}(\bullet) = 1$
4. $|\bullet| = |\bullet_{min}| = |\bullet_{max}| = 1$

Finally, we observe that, since they have the same initial values and composition rules, we must have $\kappa_{up}(A) = |A_{max}|$ (and similarly $\kappa_{down}(A) = |A_{min}|$) for any series-parallel partial order A.

6.3.2 Series-Parallel Composition Laws for Delete

We consider the average running time of two different delete operations in $\mathcal{MOQA}$; the average time taken to delete a label of a particular rank (i.e. where the average is taken over all data-labelings for a fixed rank) and the average time to delete any given label (i.e. where the average is taken over all ranks and all data-labelings).

Let $\Delta(A, k)$ be the average number of comparisons made when $\underline{Del}$ is called on the kth smallest label in A, averaged over all data-labelings of A. We also define $\Delta(A, k) = 0$ for $k < 0$ and $k > |A|$ (this allows us to dispense with bounds of summation).

Let $\Delta(A)$ be the average number of comparisons per node when $\underline{Del}$ is called on each node of each data-labeling of A (where each call is independent — that is, each node is deleted from the same data-labeling, rather than from the data-labeling left after some previous node or nodes have been deleted). It is easy to see that

$$\Delta(A) = \frac{\sum \Delta(A, k)}{|A|}.$$

Although we do not explicitly consider the case of $\overline{Del}$, it is easy to derive and prove similar results for that operation in the same manner.

The following formulae give the relationship between the running times of delete on two partial orders A and B and the running time on $A \otimes B$ and $A||B$:

1. $\Delta(A \otimes B, k) = \begin{cases} \Delta(A, k) & \text{for } k \le |A| \\ \Delta(B, k - |A|) + |A_{max}| - 1 + \Delta(A, |A|) & \text{for } k > |A| \end{cases}$.

2. $\Delta(A \otimes B) = \dfrac{|A| \Delta(A) + |B|(\Delta(B) + |A_{max}| - 1 + \Delta(A, |A|))}{|A| + |B|}.$

3. $\Delta(A \| B, k) = \dfrac{\sum_i \binom{k-1}{i-1}\binom{|A|+|B|-k}{|A|-i}\Delta(A, i) + \sum_i \binom{k-1}{i-1}\binom{|A|+|B|-k}{|B|-i}\Delta(B, i)}{\binom{|A|+|B|}{|A|}}.$

4. $\Delta(A \| B) = \dfrac{|A| \Delta(A) + |B| \Delta(B)}{|A| + |B|}.$

Proof. 1. Obviously $k < 0$ or $k > |A| + |B|$ gives $\Delta(A \otimes B) = 0$, which is consistent with the definition. But now, we know that all of the labels on B are greater than all of the labels on A, so that a label has rank k in the set of labels on A if and only if it has rank k in the set of labels on both A and B, and similarly and label has rank k in the set of labels on B if and only if it has rank $k + |A|$ in the set of labels on both A and B.

So, to delete the kth smallest label from $A \otimes B$, for $1 \le k \le |A|$, we need only delete the kth smallest label from A, which obviously takes an average of $\Delta(A, k)$ comparisons.

On the other hand, for $|A| + 1 \le k \le |A| + |B|$, we need to delete the $k - |A|$th label from B, then swap the label down to A and push it all the way to a minimal node of A so that it can be deleted. Now, the number of comparisons made in deleting the label through B is independent of the data-labeling of A, so that the average over all data-labelings must be simply $\Delta(B, k - |A|)$. Moreover, the number of comparisons made in swapping the label down to A is always $|A_{max}| - 1$, independent of either data-labeling (note that this is one less than the corresponding number of comparisons for a Push-Down, since in this context, we do not need to compare the largest label on A to the label being deleted, since it will always be smaller). Finally, the average number of comparisons for deleting the label down through A is independent of the data-labeling on B, and so the average over all data-labelings must simply be $\Delta(A, |A|)$ (since we are deleting from the node with maximum label).

So, in each of the two cases, the result is proven.

2. To prove the second result, we use the fact that $\Delta(A \otimes B) = \dfrac{\sum \Delta(A \otimes B, k)}{|A| + |B|}$. Taking account of the zero values for $k \notin [1, |A| + |B|]$ and of the two cases for the values of $\Delta(A \otimes B, k)$, we get

$$\Delta(A \otimes B) = \frac{(\sum \Delta(A, k)) + (\sum \Delta(B, k)) + |B|(|A_{max}| - 1 + \Delta(A, |A|))}{|A| + |B|}$$

$$= \frac{|A| \Delta(A) + |B|(\Delta(B) + |A_{max}| - 1 + \Delta(A, |A|))}{|A| + |B|},$$

exactly as required.

3. For each i between 1 and $|A|$, we consider the number of ways to split the set of labels on A and B such that the kth smallest label in the entire set becomes the ith smallest on A.

For such a split to take place, we must choose $i - 1$ labels from the set of the $k - 1$ smallest labels to put on A, and also $|A| - i$ labels from the set of the $|A| + |B| - k$ largest labels (so that we have $i - 1$ labels smaller than the label of rank k, and the remaining labels larger). Since these choices are independent, there are exactly $\binom{k-1}{i-1} \binom{|A|+|B|-k}{|A|-i}$ different splits of the set of labels in which the kth label in the full set becomes the ith label in the set of labels on A.

Similarly, there are exactly $\binom{k-1}{i-1} \binom{|A|+|B|-k}{|B|-i}$ splits in which the kth label in the full set becomes the ith label in the set of labels on B.

But the average number of comparisons for deleting the ith label on A and B are simply $\Delta(A, i)$ and $\Delta(B, i)$ respectively, so taking an average over all different possible splits of the set of labels, we get an average number of comparisons of

$$\Delta(A\|B, k) = \frac{\sum_i \binom{k-1}{i-1} \binom{|A|+|B|-k}{|A|-i} \Delta(A, i) + \sum_i \binom{k-1}{i-1} \binom{|A|+|B|-k}{|B|-i} \Delta(B, i)}{\binom{|A|+|B|}{|A|}},$$

exactly as required.

4. Again, we prove the second result using the first result and the fact that $\Delta(A\|B) = \frac{\sum \Delta(A\|B,k)}{|A|+|B|}$.

We first simplify the sum $\sum_k \sum_i \binom{k-1}{i-1} \binom{|A|+|B|-k}{|A|-i} \Delta(A, i)$. Reversing the order of summation, we get $\sum_i \Delta(A, i) \left(\sum_k \binom{k-1}{i-1} \binom{|A|+|B|-k}{|A|-i} \right)$. Now we make use of the combinatorial identity $\sum_k \binom{k-1}{i-1} \binom{|A|+|B|-k}{|A|-i} = \binom{|A|+|B|}{|A|}$ (Lemma 6.6 of Section 6.4.3) to get $\sum_k \sum_i \binom{k-1}{i-1} \binom{|A|+|B|-k}{|A|-i} \Delta(A, i) = \binom{|A|+|B|}{|A|} \sum_i \Delta(A, i)$. Now inserting the above derived values of $\Delta(A\|B, k)$ into the equation $\Delta(A\|B) = \frac{\sum \Delta(A\|B,k)}{|A|+|B|}$ and using the above simplification, we get simply

$$\Delta(A\|B) = \frac{\sum_i \Delta(A, i) + \sum_k \Delta(B, k)}{|A| + |B|}$$

$$= \frac{|A|\Delta(A) + |B|\Delta(B)}{|A| + |B|},$$

which is exactly what we wanted.

Remark 6.2. The determination of the k-th smallest/k-th largest label during a deletion operation, in general will involve the determination of this label via a $\mathcal{MOQA}$ search program. For the case of atomic structures, the $\mathcal{MOQA}$ program *Quickselect* can be applied to determine this label, for which the average-case comparison time is determined in Section 8.8.

Remark 6.3. The $\mathcal{MOQA}$ basic operations $\overline{Perc}^m$ and $\underline{Perc}^M$ discussed in Chapter 5, involve the same number of comparisons as the operations $\overline{Del}$ applied to the smallest label and $\underline{Del}$ applied to the largest label respectively. Hence the formulas discussed above for the deletion operation can be applied to determine the average-case time of the operations $\overline{Perc}^m$ and $\underline{Perc}^M$.

Exercise 6.1. Determine the average-case time of the Top and Bot operations (cf. Section 5.6).

6.4 Examples

6.4.1 Calculating the τ Function

As a simple application, we calculate the tau function for the partial order given by $(\bullet||(\bullet \otimes (\bullet||\bullet) \otimes \bullet)) \otimes \bullet$, or by the following Hasse diagram:

The following diagram shows the results of the calculations, where the five numbers in each box are $\tau(A)$, $\sigma(A)$, $|A|$, $|A_{max}|$ and $|A_{min}|$ (in that order), for A the partial order in the box.

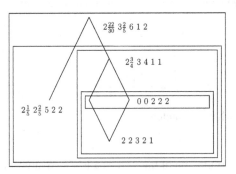

This result for τ can be confirmed by averaging the number of comparisons made in pushing up a label of each rank into each of the ten data-labelings of the partial order:

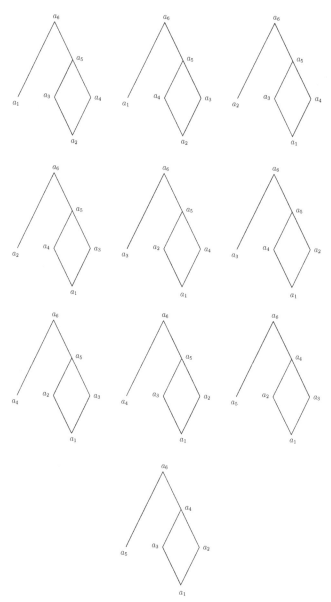

6.4.2 Inductively Defined Structures

Certain types of structures can be defined inductively using only the series and parallel operations — for instance, discrete and linear orders and complete binary trees. If we apply the above-derived composition laws for τ or Δ to these inductive definitions, we get recurrence equations which can often be solved in closed form. We present some examples here.

6.4.2.1 Linear Orders   The linear order of size n, which we denote by Υ_n, can be defined in terms of the series operation as $\Upsilon_n = \bullet \otimes \Upsilon_{n-1}$ for $n > 1$, with the base case $\Upsilon_1 = \bullet$.

Clearly $|\Upsilon_n| = n$, $|\Upsilon_n|_{min} = 1$ and $|\Upsilon_n|_{max} = 1$ for all n, so all that we need to get a recurrence for $\tau_{up}(\Upsilon_n)$ is $\sigma_{up}(\Upsilon_n)$. Applying the series composition law for σ to the definition of Υ_n, we get

$$\sigma_{up}(\Upsilon_n) = \sigma_{up}(\Upsilon_{n-1}) + \sigma_{up}(\bullet) + |\Upsilon_{n-1}|_{min} = \sigma_{up}(\Upsilon_{n-1}) + 1.$$

Combining this with the base case of $\sigma_{up}(\Upsilon_1) = \sigma_{up}(\bullet) = 0$, we get

$$\sigma_{up}(\Upsilon_n) = n - 1.$$

Finally, applying the series composition law for τ to the definition of Υ_n and replacing for the know values of the various functions on Υ_{n-1} and $\bullet$, we get

$$\tau_{up}(\Upsilon_n) = \frac{(n-1)\tau_{up}(\Upsilon_{n-1})}{n} + 1.$$

Letting $f(n) = n\tau_{up}(\Upsilon_n)$, we get $f(n) = f(n-1) + n = \sum_{i=2}^{n} i + f(1)^1 = \frac{n(n+1)}{2} - 1$. Finally, substituting back in for $f(n)$, we get

$$\tau_{up}(\Upsilon_n) = \frac{n+1}{2} - \frac{1}{n}.$$

6.4.2.2 Complete Binary Trees   The complete binary tree of depth n, which we denote by β_n, can be defined in terms of the series and parallel operations as $\beta_n = [\beta_{n-1}\|\beta_{n-1}] \otimes \bullet$ for $n > 1$ and $\beta_1 = \bullet$.

It is easy to see that $|\beta_n| = 2^n - 1$, $|\beta_n|_{min} = 2^{n-1}$ and $|\beta_n|_{max} = 1$ for all n, so that all we need to get a recurrence for $\tau_{up}(\beta_n)$ is $\sigma_{up}(\beta_n)$. Applying the series and parallel composition laws for σ to the definition of β_n (and using the fact that $\sigma_{up}(A\|A) = \sigma_{up}(A)$ for any partial order A), we get

$$\sigma_{up}(\beta_n) = \sigma_{up}(\bullet) + \sigma_{up}(\beta_{n-1}) + |\bullet|_{min} = \sigma_{up}(\beta_{n-1}) + 1.$$

Combining this with the base case of $\sigma_{up}(\beta_1) = \sigma_{up}(\bullet) = 0$, we get

$$\sigma_{up}(\beta_n) = n - 1.$$

---

[1] $f(1) = 1.\tau_{up}(\Upsilon_1) = \tau_{up}(\bullet) = 0.$

Finally, applying the series and parallel composition law for τ to the definition of β_n and replacing for the know values of the various functions on β_{n-1} and $\bullet$, we get

$$\tau_{up}(\beta_n) = \frac{n + 1 + (2^n - 2)\tau_{up}(\beta_{n-1})}{2^n - 1}.$$

Letting $g(n) = (1 - 2^{-n})\tau_{up}(\beta_n)$, we get

$$g(n) = g(n-1) + \frac{n+1}{2^n} = \sum_{i=2}^{n} \frac{i+1}{2^i} + g(1)^2.$$

We can evaluate the given sum[3] to get $g(n) = \frac{2^{n+1} - n - 3}{2^n}$, and hence

$$\tau_{up}(\beta_n) = \frac{2^{n+1} - n - 3}{2^n - 1}.$$

Note that this value tends asymptotically towards two — although the partial order grows to arbitrarily large depths, most of the elements are always clustered towards the bottom, so that on average a label is not pushed up very far.

6.4.3 Combinatorial Identities

We provide the proofs to the combinatorial identities used in this chapter here.

Lemma 6.4. $\displaystyle\sum_k k\binom{|A|}{k}\binom{|B|}{k} = \frac{(|A| + |B| - 1)!}{(|A| - 1)!(|B| - 1)!}$

Proof. First, we note that $k\binom{|A|}{k} = \frac{k.|A|!}{k!(|A|-k)!} = \frac{|A|.(|A|-1)!}{(k-1)!(|A|-k)!} = |A|\binom{|A|-1}{|A|-k}$, so substituting this in and dividing across by $|A|$, we see that it is sufficient to prove that

$$\sum_k \binom{|A|-1}{|A|-k}\binom{|B|}{k} = \frac{(|A| + |B| - 1)!}{|A|!(|B|-1)!} = \binom{|A| + |B| - 1}{|A|}.$$

Suppose that we want to choose an $|A|$ element subset of the first $|A| + |B| - 1$ positive integers, with exactly k elements greater than $|A| - 1$. The total number of ways to do this is $\binom{|A|-1}{|A|-k}\binom{|A|}{k}$.

But now, summing this over all k, we get the total number of ways to choose an $|A|$ element subset of the first $|A| + |B| - 1$ positive integers with $0, 1, 2, \cdots, |B|$ elements greater than $|A| - 1$. But since every $|A|$-element subset must have some

---

[2] $g(1) = \frac{1}{2}\tau_{up}(\beta_1) = \frac{1}{2}\tau_{up}(\bullet) = 0$

[3] $g(n) = 2g(n) - g(n) = \displaystyle\sum_{i=1}^{n-1} \frac{i+2}{2^i} - \sum_{i=2}^{n} \frac{i+1}{2^i} = \frac{3}{2} - \frac{n+1}{2^n} + \sum_{i=2}^{n-1} \frac{1}{2^i} = \frac{3}{2} - \frac{n+1}{2^n} +$

$\frac{1}{2} - \frac{1}{2^{n-1}}.$

number of elements, every subset is counted once (and, clearly, only once), so that the total must be the total number of ways to choose an $|A|$-element subset from a set with $|A| + |B| - 1$ elements, which is simply $\binom{|A|+|B|-1}{|A|}$ as required.

Lemma 6.5. *The average value of the mth smallest element in an r element subset of the first n positive integers is $m\frac{n+1}{r+1}$.*

Proof. The number of sets with i as the mth smallest element is simply $\binom{i-1}{m-1}\binom{n-i}{r-m}$, so since the total number of r element subsets of the first n positive integers is $\binom{n}{r}$, the average value required is $\dfrac{\sum i\binom{i-1}{m-1}\binom{n-i}{r-m}}{\binom{n}{r}} = m\dfrac{\sum \binom{i}{m}\binom{n-i}{r-m}}{\binom{n}{r}}$.

Now consider all $r + 1$ element subsets of the first $n + 1$ positive integers. For each i, there are $\binom{i}{m}\binom{n-i}{r-m}$ of these whose $m + 1^{th}$ element is $i + 1$, and hence the total number is $\binom{n+1}{r+1} = \sum \binom{i}{m}\binom{n-i}{r-m}$.

Using this substitution, the desired average simplifies to $m\dfrac{\binom{n+1}{r+1}}{\binom{n}{r}} = m\dfrac{n+1}{r+1}$.

Lemma 6.6. $\displaystyle\sum_{k} \binom{k-1}{i-1}\binom{|A|+|B|-k}{|A|-i} = \binom{|A|+|B|}{|A|}$

Proof. Suppose that we want to choose an $|A|$ element subset of the first $|A| + |B|$ positive integers, such that the ith element in the set is k. Then we must choose $i - 1$ of the $k - 1$ numbers smaller than k and $|A| - i$ of the $|A| + |B| - k$ numbers bigger than k, along with k itself. The total number of ways to do this is $\binom{k-1}{i-1}\binom{|A|+|B|-k}{|A|-i}$.

But now, summing this over all values of k, we get the total number of ways to choose an $|A|$ element subset whose i^{th} element is $1, 2, 3, \cdots, |A| + |B|$. But since every $|A|$-element subset has some i^{th} element in this range, every such subset is counted once (and, clearly, only once), so that the total must be the total number of ways to choose an $|A|$-element subset from a set with $|A| + |B|$ elements, which is simply $\binom{|A|+|B|}{|A|}$ as required.

Chapter 7
The $\mathcal{MOQA}$ Language

In this chapter we provide the specifications for the $\mathcal{MOQA}$ language. The intention is to sketch in sufficient detail the main concepts of the language as opposed to a strict and exhaustive formal development. The language specifications suffice to develop the examples considered in Chapters 8 and 9.

Note that $\mathcal{MOQA}$ is a domain specific language. It shares its restrictive nature with current languages aimed at automating average-case timing, including [Coh74, Weg 75, Ram96, FSZ89, FSZ91]. $\mathcal{MOQA}$'s distinctive feature is that it enables one to implement algorithms built from randomness preserving operations over abstract data types, which supports its modularity. $\mathcal{MOQA}$ can be interpreted as a suite of purposely designed operations aimed at facilitating average time analysis.

Most languages for automated average-case analysis can not incorporate traditional data structures, such as lists, binary search trees and heaps, in a natural way and hence stay quite removed from traditional programming practice. The $\mathcal{MOQA}$ language, though still restricted in nature, aims at incorporating traditional data structures and provides a new basis to support the development of static average-case analysis tools, where its main distinctive feature is the incorporation of the notion of randomness preserving operations to support compositionality.

In specifying $\mathcal{MOQA}$ we stay close in spirit to the basic imperative languages discussed in semantics text books (e.g. [Gun92]). These languages are kept to a minimum to facilitate subsequent model constructions and can be extended with more syntactic constructs according to need. For our purposes it will suffice to work with a basic language of this nature with recursive call capacity and for-loops, which we refer to as $\mathcal{MOQA}$. Its extension by while-loops will be referred to as $\mathcal{MOQA}^*$. All programs in $\mathcal{MOQA}$ are guaranteed to terminate. Termination is a typical requirement in a static timing context due to the halting problem.

In the context of (real-)time analysis, the termination of programs is typically achieved by requiring that while-loops are restricted in order to guarantee termination or by excluding while-loops entirely. Exclusion of while-loops is the most common approach taken in this context. In this sense, $\mathcal{MOQA}$ can be interpreted, in a very broad sense, as a "real-time variant" of $\mathcal{MOQA}^*$. The language will be used to specify programs for which the average-case time can be determined in a linear-compositional way.

The $\mathcal{MOQA}$ language includes for-loops and two restricted types of recursion. For-loops specify a bound on the number of executions via the for-loop parameters and hence, due to the predictability of number of executions of the for-loop body, are a preferred type of loop in a static timing context.

A restricted use of recursion is allowed. If recursion were not allowed, the pseudo-code for standard algorithms such as Mergesort and Quicksort would be substantially different, e.g. using stacks in order to avoid the recursive function call. As a result, the average-case analysis of non-recursive versions of algorithms would differ substantially from the standard analysis for the typical recursive style pseudo-code of these algorithms provided in most textbooks [AHU87]. In order to include standard algorithms we chose to allow a basic form of recursive calls which is guaranteed to terminate.

7.1 Conventions

We will proceed under the assumption that all data structures of the $\mathcal{MOQA}$ language are constructed from atomic random structures. This is not an essential requirement, but will facilitate the presentation. Clearly, since $\mathcal{MOQA}$ operations are random bag preserving, the programs could be allowed to take inputs which have states belonging to a random bag, without requiring that the data have first been constructed through another $\mathcal{MOQA}$ program from an atomic random structure. Our approach will be however that random bags are not created by the user "out of the blue", but need to be constructed at some stage. Hence the requirement is made that each program operates on data structures which have at one point been constructed from an atomic random structure via a $\mathcal{MOQA}$ program.

The data on which programs operate will be data-labelings. Due to random bag preservation, programs can be interpreted in our context as state transformations. Programs will induce transformations on states, i.e. transformations over states from a random bag. The net effect, viewed over all states of a given random bag, is the transformation of this random bag into a new random bag. This allows one to track the data structures and their distribution throughout the computations. To achieve such tracking, we work in a "typed" context. Typing will remain informal in this work and is used to indicated the scope of so-called "structural variables". Since each random structure is determined by its underlying finite partial order, random bags will simply be tracked as bags of partial orders. Hence $\mathcal{MOQA}$ types are bags of partial orders, occurring in the random bags, where each partial order is paired with a multiplicity. In practice these partial orders will be SP-orders and efficient representations have been worked out for these in the $\mathcal{MOQA}$ implementation as discussed in Chapter 10.

7.2 Variables

Universal variables
Each partial order $(X, \sqsubseteq)$ of a random structure in a random bag has an associated underlying finite set X. To specify such finite sets and following Definition 1.6, we fix a universe consisting of a countable list of variables $\mathcal{U} = \{x_n \mid n \in \mathcal{N}\}$, where these variables store labels. As usual we require the labels to stem from a countable linear ordered set and in particular will assume, w.l.o.g. that our labels distinct (cf. Chapter 1).

Numeric variables
Natural numbers used during a computation can be stored in variables, referred to as $\mathcal{N}$-*variables* (*Numeric variables*) . The collection of $\mathcal{N}$-variables is denoted by $\mathcal{V}$. $\mathcal{N}$-variables are denoted in the following by lower case letters $i, j, k, \ldots$, excluding the letter x which is reserved for universal variables.

Structural variables
In the following, upper case letters U, V, W, X, Y, Z, which can be equipped with indices $i, j, k, \ldots$, to denote *structural variables* or *S-variables*. Structural variables come equipped with a type and store data-labelings over the partial orders of the given type. We let $\mathcal{W}$ denote the countable set of S-variables. Typing will remain informal in this work and will be restricted to indicate the scope of S-variables.

In some cases, an S-variable will, for each given size n, contain only data-labelings on a *single* partial order of this size, such as for the case of lists (the discrete order), sorted lists (the linear order) or heaps (over a single tree order). Hence the type of the S-variable will be a bag of cardinality one, consisting of a single partial order, paired with a multiplicity.

This does not need to be the case in general of course. Consider the result of a RB-preserving operation which is not strongly RB-preserving, such as the random split and the random deletion. In that case, the result is a random bag of at least size 2. The bag of partial orders corresponding to this random bag forms the type of the output data-labelings.

7.3 Types

Again following Definition 1.6, we consider the set of all finite partial orders, denoted by $\mathcal{PO}_{fin}(\mathcal{U})$.

$$\mathcal{PO}_{fin}(\mathcal{U}) = \{(U, \sqsubseteq) \mid U \subseteq \mathcal{U}, U \text{ is finite}, \sqsubseteq \text{ is a partial order over } U\}.$$

The set of finite bags, consisting of elements from $\mathcal{PO}_{fin}(\mathcal{U})$ paired with multiplicities, is denoted by $\mathcal{B}_{fin}(\mathcal{PO}_{fin}(\mathcal{U}))$, will serve as the set of $\mathcal{MOQA}$ types, denoted by $\mathcal{T}$.

To simplify the presentation, we will assume that each $\mathcal{MOQA}$ program P has a *single* input variable, given by an $\mathcal{S}$-variable, which is referred to as the *input $\mathcal{S}$-variable for P*. Similarly, every $\mathcal{MOQA}$ program is assumed to have a single *output $\mathcal{S}$-variable* of some type τ.

Certain types can be naturally equipped with a size. Such types include types for which the partial orders are inductively defined structures (Section 6.4.2) and types involving partial order bags such as the star-shaped structures generated by the split operation. In each such case, it is possible to refer to the type of size n, where the structure of the partial orders in the type can be completely determined once the size is given. In this context, we denote discrete orders and linear orders for a given size n, by Δ_n and Υ_n respectively. If we wish to make the choice of the underlying set, say U_n, explicit, we will use the notation (U_n, Δ_n) and (U_n, Υ_n) respectively.

To guarantee the soundness of the application of certain $\mathcal{MOQA}$ operations, such as the split operation and the projection operation, it is necessary to verify that certain subsets of partial orders are atomic isolated or isolated. The verification that certain subsets of partial orders are isolated or strictly isolated is necessary in the context of an application of the Extension Theorem (Theorem 4.8) in order to generalize $\mathcal{MOQA}$ operations. The properties "isolated subset, atomic isolated subset" and "atomic strictly isolated subset" are *computable*. This is incorporated in the current Java 5.0 implementation of $\mathcal{MOQA}$ at CEOL. In fact, the determination of these properties can be simplified, since, as shown in Chapter 5, the partial orders underlying $\mathcal{MOQA}$ data structures are series-parallel.

In order to determine whether the various isolation-properties hold, it is necessary at each stage of the computation to have knowledge of the partial order underlying a data-labeling. In $\mathcal{MOQA}$ this is resolved by the fact that each data-labeling consists of a function paired with its corresponding partial order. After each step of the computation it is possible to determine the newly created data-labeling *and* its corresponding partial order.

Isolated types, corresponding to isolated subsets of the input partial order(s) play an important role in $\mathcal{MOQA}$. At this stage, we note that for a given program $P[X : \tau]$, structural variables occurring in the program will hold data-labelings of an *isolated subset* of one of the partial orders of τ. We remark that this is automatically guaranteed for the input $\mathcal{S}$-variable X since it has the entire partial order as type. The fact that this holds in general can be formally deduced by induction on the structure of $\mathcal{MOQA}$ programs provided their initial assignments hold data-labelings over isolated subsets, which will be the case in practice. The result follows from the fact that $\mathcal{MOQA}$ programs can be shown to be RB-preserving, combined with the fact that the RB-preserving operations we consider are refining.

In the present context we will focus on the following isolated $\mathcal{MOQA}$-types for $\mathcal{S}$-variables: $[Y : \mathcal{I}(X)]$, $[Y : \mathcal{AI}(X)]$ and $[Y : \mathcal{SI}(X)]$. For example, the notation $[Y : \mathcal{AI}(X)]$ indicates that Y must contain data-labelings over an *atomic* isolated subset of one of the partial orders corresponding to the type of X. I.e., in case there is a single partial order in the type, we require that the data-labelings stored in Y are data-labelings over a fixed atomic isolated subset of the input partial order. In case the type of X is a bag of partial orders, the notation indicates that Y must at all times contain a data-labeling from an atomic isolated subset of one of the input partial orders, where the atomic subset is fixed per choice of input partial order. Some approaches as to how *Distri-Track* deals with representations of such isolated subsets are provided in [Hic08].

Notation 7.1 For S-variables Y, where $[Y \colon \mathcal{AI}(X)]$, we know that Y at all times will store a data-labeling of some atomic isolated subset U of one of the input partial orders corresponding to X. For a given data-labeling F over a partial order $(U, \sqsubseteq)$, we will use the enumeration of the elements of U determined by the fixed enumeration of the universe $\mathcal{U}$. For instance, in case X stores a data-labeling over $(U, \sqsubseteq)$, we know that $Y \colon (\{x_{i_1}, \ldots, x_{i_{|Y|}}\}, \sqsubseteq)$ for some atomic isolated subset $\{x_{i_1}, \ldots, x_{i_{|Y|}}\}$ of U. This allows for a reference to the "j-th element" of an atomic isolated subset Y, indicated by $(X, Y[j])$. I.e., following the above notation, $(X, Y[j])$ corresponds to x_{i_j}. The notation $Y[j]$ is close to common practice, e.g. as in [AHU87] where the j-th element of a list L is denoted by $L[j]$. So, in case the input S-variable is clear from the context, we will simply refer to $Y[j]$. Continuing Notation 7.1, we refer to $Y[1], \ldots, Y[|Y|]$ as the *atomic variables (derived from Y)*.

We remark that we do not allow direct reference to a label $Y[j]$ for the case where Y refers to data-labelings of non-discrete partial orders.

Remark 7.1. In the following we will indicate the semantic meaning of expressions and statements via the double-bracket notations, following the standard notation of [Gun92]. For instance, the semantic meaning of an arithmetical expressions A is denoted by $[\![A]\!]$.

7.4 Arithmetical Expressions

In the next inductive definition, x represents a numeric variable while X is a structural variable.

$$A = |\, \underline{n} \,|\, x \,|\, Size(X) \,|\, [A_1 + A_2] \,|\, [A_1 \times A_2] \,|\, \lfloor \tfrac{A}{2} \rfloor \,|\, \lceil \tfrac{A}{2} \rceil \,|$$

In the following we will represent the size of a structural variable X by $|X|$. The semantic interpretation is that for any data-labeling stored in X, the size of X is the size of the partial order corresponding to the data-labeling stored in X. The notation $Size(X)$ is only used in the previous definition to avoid confusion with the vertical separation bars which form part of the inductive definition.

We consider the collection A^* of closed arithmetical expressions, which is the subset of the previous collection consisting of expressions without numeric variables.

$$A^* = |\, \underline{n} \,|\, [A_1^* + A_2^*] \,|\, [A_1^* \times A_2^*] \,|\, \lfloor \tfrac{A^*}{2} \rfloor \,|\, \lceil \tfrac{A^*}{2} \rceil \,|$$

7.5 Boolean Expressions

Static time analysis is complicated due to branching and while-loops. Both types of statements are complicated to analyze due to their dependence on boolean statements. While-loops are not analyzable in full generality due to non-decidability of termination, i.e. the halting problem. Even when a while-loop is guaranteed to terminate, the problem remains that in order to determine the running time it is necessary to determine *when* the loop exits, which depends on the boolean condition. Similarly, for a conditional statement, it is necessary for average-case analysis to determine the probability of executing the first branch and the probability of executing the second branch, which again is related to the boolean condition involved. Investigations are under way for *Distri-Track* to provide the probability for the boolean condition of a conditional statement as a user-input, e.g. after experimental determination of the probability or following a separate user-analysis of the probability.

Here we are interested in the determination of specific classes of boolean statements for which it can be guaranteed that the probability can be statically derived. Such classes are necessarily restricted in nature. Yet they are of obvious interest since, whenever available, they provide an aid to the (semi-)automatization of average-case analysis.

We introduce a special kind of boolean expression which is referred to as a "structural (boolean) expression", or boolean S-expression. Each boolean S-expression involves one or more structural variables. We distinguish in the following between "first-order" boolean S-expressions and "second-order" boolean S-expressions.

The first type of boolean expression regards comparisons between labels of elements of an isolated subset of the type under consideration. This regards a "first-order" property of labels as opposed to a "second-order" property regarding the entire data-labelings, such as comparisons involving the *size* of a data-labeling. At any given stage of the computation, where a variable X holds data-labelings with states from a random bag R, the first type of boolean expression regards a property on *labels* of a fixed data-labeling with a state from R under consideration in the computation. The second type of expression regards a property on *data-labelings* with a state from the random bag R and as such is a "second-order" statement.

We define the two kinds of boolean expression below. Certain equational boolean S-expressions are singled out as "prime" expressions. We will show that the other boolean S-expressions reduce to these prime cases; a useful technical fact which will aid the determination of probabilities.

We note at this stage that the results for second-order boolean expressions indicate that this type of expression is particularly suited for analysis in our context. As we will see, first-order boolean expressions are more complicated to deal with and require further investigation. We still treat this particular case to illustrate some of the complications involved and to shed some light on potential future approaches which may overcome these issues. Our formulation of the $\mathcal{MOQA}$ language, at this stage, is restricted to second-order boolean expressions.

Notation 7.2 We add some syntactic sugar and will denote the negation of an equality expression $\neg[E_1 = E_2]$ as $[E_1 \neq E_2]$. Size-based expressions, $[|X| = \underline{k}]$ will include an "empty-test" $[|X| = \underline{0}]$, for which we allow the notation: $[X = \emptyset]$.

Convention 7.3 In the following, in case we do not indicate the type of an $\mathcal{S}$-variable, it is assumed that this type forms a bag of isolated subsets of the partial orders in the input-partial order bag. This assumption is consistent with the fact that the orders of input random bags are refined during computations and by the fact that operations are carried out on isolated subsets.

1) First-order boolean S-expressions We recall that it suffices in our context to focus on SP-types, though of course the $\mathcal{MOQA}$ approach holds in the more general context of arbitrary finite partial orders. Since probabilities over atomic types typically allow for a straightforward computation and since SP orders essentially can be viewed as products and parallel composition over discrete partial orders, we choose to express the conditionals in this section in terms of expressions over discrete partial orders. I.e. the types of the structural variables involved will be atomic. Second-order boolean statements will not have this condition and their structural variables can have arbitrary type.

Definition 7.1. Let Y be an $\mathcal{S}$-variable of type Δ_n. We let $m_k(Y)$, where $k \in \{1, \dots, n\}$, denote the k-th smallest label of the data-labeling stored in Y. Similarly, we let $\mathcal{M}_k(Y)$ denote the k-th largest label of the data-labeling stored in Y. These can be computed in $\mathcal{MOQA}$ by Quickselect, which has $O(n)$ average-case time (cf. Section 8.8).

Definition 7.2. A *first-prime boolean S-expression* is a boolean expression of the form:

$$[Y[i] = m_k(Y)| Y : \mathcal{AI}(X)], \text{ where } |Y| = n, i, k \in \{1, \dots, n\}.$$

Definition 7.3. A *first-order boolean S-expression* is a boolean expression which is first-prime or of one of the following forms, where @ represents an inequality from $\{<, \leq, >, \geq\}$:

$[Y[i] @ m_k(Y)| Y : \mathcal{AI}(X)], |Y| = n, i, k \in \{1, \dots, n\}$

$[Y[i] = \mathcal{M}_k(Y)| Y : \mathcal{AI}(X)]$ or $[Y[i] @ \mathcal{M}_k(Y)| Y : \mathcal{AI}(X)], |Y| = n, i, k \in \{1, \dots, n\}$

$[Y[i] = Y[j]| Y : \mathcal{AI}(X)],$ or $[Y[i] @ Y[j]| Y : \mathcal{AI}(X)], |Y| = n, i, j \in \{1, \dots, n\}$ and $i \neq j$.

The collection of first-order boolean S-expressions is denoted by BSE^1.

The intended semantic interpretation of the expressions is indicated by the following examples, where the other cases are similar: $[Y : \mathcal{AI}(X)]$ indicates that the variable Y will store data-labelings over an atomic isolated subset of the type of X, say of size n. The boolean expression $[Y[i] = m_k(Y) | Y : \mathcal{AI}(X)]$ is true when the label of the i-th element of the data-labeling of the atomic random structure $\mathcal{A}_n$ under consideration coincides with the k-th smallest element of the corresponding label set, and false otherwise. Similarly, the boolean expression $[Y[i] = \mathcal{M}_k(Y) | Y : \mathcal{AI}(X)]$ is true when the label of the i-th element of the data-labeling from atomic random structure $\mathcal{A}_n$ under consideration coincides with the k-th largest element of the corresponding label set, and false otherwise. The boolean expression $[Y[i] < Y[j] | Y : \mathcal{AI}(X)]$ is true when the label of the i-th element of the data-labeling from $\mathcal{A}_n$ under consideration is strictly less than the label of the j-th element of this data-labeling and false otherwise.

We remark that during the analysis of $\mathcal{MOQA}$ programs, we assume that data-labelings have pairwise distinct labels. Hence in the analysis expressions of the type $[Y[i] = Y[j]]$ where $i \neq j$ will not come into play. Moreover it is clear that, during the analysis, it suffices to consider the cases where $[Y[i] < Y[j]]$ and $[Y[i] > Y[j]]$ and not the inequalities involving $\leq$ or $\geq$, though these could of course occur as part of a $\mathcal{MOQA}$ program. Finally, it is clear that it suffices to consider expressions of the form $[Y[i] < Y[j]]$ only, since these are, by symmetry, equivalent to expressions of the form $[Y[j] > Y[i]]$.

Notation 7.4 The prime boolean S-expression: $[X[i] = m_k(X) | X : \mathcal{AI}(X)]$ is typically abbreviated to $[X[i] = m_k(X)]$ and similarly for the other boolean S-expressions.

2) Second-order boolean S-expressions
We introduce second-order S-expressions which involve comparisons based on size. Note that, in order to simplify the discussion, we do not allow sizes to occur as part of an arithmetical expression. I.e. sizes will occur on one side of an inequality, without occurring embedded as part of an arithmetic expression. Further generalizations can be obtained to deal with sizes embedded within arithmetical expressions, e.g. not containing numeric variables, in which case sizes could be included as part of the inductive definition of closed arithmetical expressions via the addition of an extra base case $|X|$.

Definition 7.4. A second-prime boolean S-expression is a boolean expression of the form $[Size(Y) = A^*]$, for some S-variable Y and closed arithmetical expression A^*.

Definition 7.5. A second-order boolean S-expression is a boolean expression which is second-prime or an expression of the form $[Size(Y) = A^*]$, $[Size(Y) > A^*]$, $[Size(Y) < A^*]$, $[Size(Y) \leq A^*]$ or $[Size(Y) \geq A^*]$.

The collection of second-order boolean S-expressions is denoted by BSE^2.

Remark 7.2. It is possible to generalize the definitions of the boolean expressions to include arithmetical boolean expressions. However, this would entail the tracking of numeric variables during the course of the computation. Under certain restrictions this will be possible, but the general case defies static analysis. We hence will focus in what follows on the simpler case of boolean expressions for which the only variables are S-variables or closed arithmetical expressions.

Convention 7.5 In the following when we refer to a "boolean statement" it is implicitly assumed to mean either a first-order or a second-order boolean statement. Similarly if we refer to a "(boolean) S-expression, it refers to either a first-order or a second-order (boolean) S-expression.

7.6 Boolean Statements

We define first-order and second-order boolean statements.

Definition 7.6. The collection of first-order boolean statements is defined inductively by:

$$B^1 = \mid BSE^1 \mid [B_1 \text{ or } B_2] \mid [B_1 \text{ and } B_2] \mid \neg B \mid$$

Definition 7.7. The collection of second-order boolean statements is defined inductively by:

$$B^2 = \mid BSE^2 \mid [B_1 \text{ or } B_2] \mid [B_1 \text{ and } B_2] \mid \neg B \mid$$

7.6.1 Probabilities of Boolean Statements

We define the probability of a boolean statement and show how computations of such probabilities, for the case of data-labelings restricted to isolated subsets, can be reduced to computations directly over the isolated subsets.

Definition 7.8. A boolean statement B is said to be a *boolean statement over the S-variable* Y in case B contains at least one occurrence of Y and no variable other than Y. In that case we denote B by $B(Y)$.

Remark 7.3. Note that boolean statements $B(Y)$ are independent from the relative label-order of the data-labeling assigned to Y, i.e. we assume if two data-labelings F_1 and F_2 over Y are label-isomorphic then the truth values of $B(F_1)$ and $B(F_2)$ are the same.

During computations it is useful to determine the probability of boolean statements for the case of data-labelings which have been obtained as restrictions of data-labelings of a given type to an isolated subset. This case arises frequently since $\mathcal{MOQA}$ operations are typically applied on isolated subsets of types. This type of probability is captured by the following definition.

Definition 7.9. We consider the case of a boolean statement B over a structural variable Y, where Y is assigned data-labelings which arise from the restriction of data-labelings stored in an S-variable X of the program. The data-labelings stored in Y are assumed to be obtained as restrictions of data-labelings over X to an isolated subset of the type of X, i.e. $Y \colon \mathcal{I}(X)$. In this case the boolean statement B is indicated by $B(X|Y)$.

Definition 7.10. The *cardinality* $|B(Y)|$ *of a boolean statement* $B(Y)$ is the number of states over the type σ of Y that satisfy B. The *probability of* $B(Y)$, indicated by $Prob(B(Y))$, is defined by:

$$Prob(B(Y)) = \frac{|B(Y)|}{|R(\sigma)|}.$$

Since probabilities only depend on the types involved, we will also on occasion use the notation $B(\sigma)$ instead of $B(Y)$ when $Y \colon \sigma$.

The cardinality $|B(X|Y)|$ of a boolean statement $B(X|Y)$, where Y is an S-variable such that $[Y \colon \mathcal{I}(X)]$ and where say $X \colon \tau$, is defined to be the number of states over the type of X that, when restricted to the type of Y, satisfy $B(X|Y)$. The probability of $B(X|Y)$, indicated by $Prob(B(X|Y))$, is defined by:

$$Prob(B(X|Y)) = \frac{|B(X|Y)|}{|R(\tau)|}.$$

In case Y is identical to X, it is clear that $|B(X|X)| = |B(X)|$. Since probabilities only depend on the types involved, we will also on occasion use the notation $B(\tau|\sigma)$ instead of $B(X|Y)$ when $X \colon \tau, Y \colon \sigma$.

Lemma 7.1. *Consider a boolean statement* $B(X|Y)$. *Assume that* $X \colon \tau$, $Y \colon \mathcal{I}(X)$ *and* $Y \colon \sigma$. *Let* $\alpha = |\{F \restriction (\tau - \sigma)| \, F \in \mathcal{R}_{\mathcal{L}}(\tau)\}|$. *We have that*

$$|B(X|Y)| = \alpha|B(Y)|$$

$$|R(\tau)| = \alpha|R(\sigma)|$$

$$Prob(B(X|Y)) = Prob(B(Y)).$$

Proof. Note that $Y \colon \mathcal{I}(X)$. Let $\alpha = |\{F \restriction (\tau - \sigma)| \, F \in \mathcal{R}_{\mathcal{L}}(\tau)\}|$. Then, by Lemma 4.10 2), we obtain: $|R(\tau)| = \alpha|R(\sigma)|$. Moreover, by Lemma 4.10 1), any data-labeling over τ which when restricted to σ satisfies B, corresponds uniquely to the union of a data-labeling over $\tau - \sigma$ and a data-labeling over σ. Hence the truth of $B(X|Y)$ only depends on whether this second part of the data-labeling, i.e. the data-labeling over σ, satisfies B. It follows that $|B(X|Y)| = \alpha|B(Y)|$. Hence:

$$Prob(B(X|Y)) = \frac{\alpha|B(Y)|}{\alpha|R(\sigma)|} = Prob(B(Y)).$$

By Lemma 7.1, it is clear that when data-labelings are restricted to atomic isolated subsets, it suffices to compute the probabilities over these atomic isolated subsets. These probabilities are computed as below for the first-order S-expressions.

Lemma 7.2. *(Probability of first-order S-expressions)*

$$Prob[Y[i] = m_k(Y)|\, Y: \mathcal{AI}(X)] = Prob[Y[i] = \mathcal{M}_k(Y)|\, Y: \mathcal{AI}(X)] = \tfrac{1}{n}.$$

$$Prob[Y[i] > Y[j]|\, Y: \mathcal{AI}(X)] = \tfrac{1}{2}.$$

Proof. It is easy to verify that if X is an $\mathcal{S}$-variable which takes data-labelings with states from $\mathcal{A}_n$ then:

$$Prob[X[i] = m_k(X)] = Prob[X[i] = \mathcal{M}_k(X)] = \tfrac{1}{n}.$$

$$Prob[X[i] > X[j]] = \tfrac{1}{2}.$$

The general result now follows by a straightforward application of Lemma 7.1 applied to a boolean expression over a single structural variable Y.

In general when boolean S-expressions occur combined in boolean statements, the determination of probabilities becomes more involved. In particular in the "mixed case" where one element is compared to several others, e.g. as in $[Y[1] < Y[2]] \wedge [Y[2] < Y[3]]$.

In the following we will illustrate how to compute probabilities for general boolean statements through a reduction of the statement to Disjunctive Normal Form. For short statements, typically, a DNF is easy to obtain. In general, the computation time to reach a DNF can grow drastically.

7.6.2 Computing Probabilities of Boolean Statements

We assume that the reader has some familiarity with the notion of a Disjunctive Normal Form (DNF) and the fact that every propositional statement is equivalent to a DNF [Ham88]. We recall the definition of some relevant concepts.

Definition 7.11. A *literal* is a propositional variable or the negation thereof. In the first case, a literal is referred to as a *positive literal*, in the second case as a *negative literal* . A *positive conjunction* is a conjunction in which each literal is positive.

A *Disjunctive Normal Form* is a disjunction $C_1 \vee \ldots \vee C_n$, where each C_i is a conjunction of literals.

Definition 7.12. A DNF is *first-prime/second-prime* iff its boolean expressions are first-prime/second-prime and it does not contain negative literals. A DNF is a *prime DNF* in case it is first-prime or second-prime. A *first-prime/second-prime conjunction* is a conjunction of first-prime/second-prime boolean S-expressions. A boolean expression is a *prime boolean S-expression* in case it is first-prime or second-prime boolean S-expression. In case the prime DNF/prime conjunction is a boolean statement over a structural variable Y, we refer to this prime DNF/prime conjunction as a *prime DNF/prime conjunction over Y*.

We discuss how to determine the probability for arbitrary boolean statements. We will show in the Section 7.6.3 that each first-order boolean statement can be transformed to an equivalent first-prime DNF, i.e. a DNF $C_1 \vee \ldots \vee C_k$, where each C_i, $i \in \{1, \ldots, k\}$, is a first-prime conjunction. Similarly, we will show that each second-order boolean statement can be transformed to an equivalent second-prime DNF.

The probability of a prime DNF can be computed via the General Modularity Law of Section 2.5. Clearly, after applying the General Modularity Law to $Prob(C_1 \vee \ldots \vee C_k)$, the resulting expression only requires the determination of probabilities of boolean expressions which are prime conjunctions, each over a finite collection of structural variables. We discuss in the Section 7.6.4 the determination of probabilities of prime conjunctions.

7.6.3 Reduction to Prime DNF's

We show how every first-order boolean statement can be replaced by an equivalent first-prime DNF. Since all boolean statements can be reduced to equivalent DNF's, it suffices to show how negative literals can be eliminated.

Lemma 7.3. *Every first-order boolean statement over a collection of structural variables is equivalent to a first-prime DNF over this collection of structural variables.*

Proof. We show that two of the non-first-prime boolean expressions are definable in terms of first-prime boolean expressions only. The other cases are treated in a similar way. We remark that for $i, k \in \{1, \ldots, n\}$:

$$[Y[i] = \mathcal{M}_k(Y) | Y \colon \mathcal{AI}(X)] \Leftrightarrow [Y[i] = m_{n-k+1}(Y) | Y \colon \mathcal{AI}(X)].$$

Moreover, note that:

$$[Y[i] < Y[j] | Y \colon \mathcal{AI}(X)] \Leftrightarrow$$
$$[Y[i] = m_1(Y) | Y \colon \mathcal{AI}(X)] \vee$$

$$[[Y[i] = m_2(Y)|Y : \mathcal{AI}(X)] \wedge [Y[j] \neq m_1(Y)|Y : \mathcal{AI}(X)]] \vee$$
$$[[Y[i] = m_3(Y)|Y : \mathcal{AI}(X)] \wedge [Y[j] \neq m_1(Y)|Y : \mathcal{AI}(X)] \wedge$$
$$[Y[j] \neq m_2(Y)|Y : \mathcal{AI}(X)]] \vee$$
$$\dots$$
$$[[Y[i] = m_{n-1}(Y)|Y : \mathcal{AI}(X)] \wedge [Y[j] \neq m_1(Y)|Y : \mathcal{AI}(X)] \wedge \dots$$
$$\wedge [Y[j] \neq m_{n-2}(Y)|Y : \mathcal{AI}(X)]].$$

The negations of the boolean S-expressions, i.e.:

$$[Y[j] \neq m_k(Y)|Y : \mathcal{AI}(X)], [Y[j] \neq \mathcal{M}_k(Y)|Y : \mathcal{AI}(X)], [Y[i] \not< Y[j]|Y : \mathcal{AI}(X)],$$

can also be defined solely in terms of first-prime boolean expressions. We illustrate this for the case of $[Y[j] \neq m_k(Y)|Y : \mathcal{AI}(X)]$. The other cases are similar.

$$[Y[j] \neq m_k(Y)|Y : \mathcal{AI}(X)] \Leftrightarrow$$

$$[[Y[j] = m_1(Y)|Y : \mathcal{AI}(X)] \vee [Y[j] = m_2(Y)|Y : \mathcal{AI}(X)] \vee \dots \vee$$
$$[Y[j] = m_{k-1}(Y)|Y : \mathcal{AI}(X)] \vee [Y[j] = m_{k+1}(Y)|Y : \mathcal{AI}(X)] \vee \dots \vee$$
$$[Y[j] = m_n(Y)|Y : \mathcal{AI}(X)]].$$

Next, we observe that every second-order boolean statement can be replaced by a second-prime DNF.

Lemma 7.4. *Every second-order boolean statement over a collection of structural variables with pairwise disjoint types is equivalent to a second-prime DNF over this collection of structural variables.*

Proof. Similar reasoning as in the proof of Lemma 7.3.

7.6.4 Probabilities for Prime Conjunctions

From Lemmas 7.3 and 7.4 it follows that for boolean statements we can focus on determining the probabilities of their prime DNF's.

The probability of a prime DNF can be computed via the General Modularity Law of Section 2.5. Clearly, after applying the General Modularity Law to $Prob(C_1 \vee \dots \vee C_k)$, the resulting expression only requires the determination of probabilities of boolean expressions which are prime conjunctions. Lemmas 7.6 and 7.7 regard the computation of probabilities of prime conjunctions.

Probabilities of first-prime conjunctions
As usual, in the context of average-case analysis, we consider labels which are pairwise distinct. This enables one to filter out "inconsistent" pairs of expressions which have probability zero.

Definition 7.13. A first-prime conjunction is *consistent* iff

1) It does not contain two expressions of the form:

$$[Y[i] = m_k(Y)|\, Y: \mathcal{AI}(X)] \text{ and } [Y[j] = m_k(Y)|\, Y: \mathcal{AI}(X)], \text{ where } i \neq j.$$

2) It does not contain two expressions of the form:

$$[Y[i] = m_k(Y)|\, Y: \mathcal{AI}(X)] \text{ and } [Y[i] = m_l(Y)|\, Y: \mathcal{AI}(X)], \text{ where } k \neq l.$$

We refer to any such pair of expressions occurring in one of the first-prime conjunctions of a first-prime DNF, identified in 1) and 2), as an *inconsistent pair of the DNF*.

For the sake of illustration, in the examples of first-prime DNF's we will not refer to the k-th smallest element of a data-labeling, but will assume that for an underlying set of size n, we consider labels which take values in $\{1, \ldots, n\}$ and we will assume that the k-th smallest element has been determined in the collection of labels, e.g. through Quickselect. For the particular set of labels $\{1, \ldots, n\}$ the k-th smallest element is represented as $\underline{k}$.

Example 7.1. Consider the following first-prime Disjunctive Normal Form:

$$[X[2] = \underline{3}] \vee \{[X[4] = \underline{3}] \wedge [X[1] = \underline{1}]\} \vee \{[X[1] = \underline{3}] \wedge \{[X[2] = \underline{1}]\} \vee \{[X[1] = \underline{3}] \wedge [X[3] = \underline{1}] \wedge [X[2] = \underline{3}]\}.$$

The last conjunction, $\{[X[1] = \underline{3}] \wedge [X[3] = \underline{1}] \wedge [X[2] = \underline{3}]\}$ is inconsistent since it contains the inconsistent pair $[X[1] = \underline{3}]$ and $[X[2] = \underline{3}]$ which violates condition 1) of Definition 7.13.

Lemma 7.5. *If C is an inconsistent first-prime conjunction then $Prob(C) = 0$.*

Proof. Note that no data-labeling will satisfy an inconsistent pair.

By Lemma 7.5 we can eliminate all inconsistent first-prime conjunctions from the first-prime DNF of a boolean expression, without changing the probability. Hence we focus in the following Lemma on first-prime DNF's which only have consistent first-prime conjunctions.

Lemma 7.6. *Consider a consistent first-prime conjunction C over Y, where $Y: AI(X)$ and where C occurs in the first-prime DNF of a boolean statement. Then $Prob(C) = \frac{(n-l)!}{n!}$ where l is the number of conjuncts of the consistent first-prime conjunction C.*

Proof. It suffices to remark that every component $[Y[i] = m_k(Y)| Y: \mathcal{AI}(X)]$ of a consistent first-prime conjunction reduces the degree of freedom of the data-labelings satisfying this conjunction by one, i.e. the label of the element $Y[i]$ is fixed to have value $m_k(Y)$. Moreover, by consistency, each pair of components, say $[Y[i] = m_k(Y)| Y: \mathcal{AI}(X)]$ and $[Y[j] = m_l(Y)| Y: \mathcal{AI}(X)]$ is such that i, j and k, l are pairwise distinct. So each component of the conjunction determines a genuine, i.e. non-duplicate, reduction in the degree of freedom of the original data-labelings and hence the result follows.

Example 7.2. Consider the first-prime DNF of Example 7.1, i.e. $[X[2] = \underline{3}] \vee \{[X[4] = \underline{3}] \wedge [X[1] = \underline{1}]\} \vee \{[X[1] = \underline{3}] \wedge \{[X[2] = \underline{1}]\}.$ *The states of* $\mathcal{A}_4$ *satisfying the conjunction* $C = [X[4] = \underline{3}] \wedge [X[1] = \underline{1}]$ *are:* $(1, 2, 4, 3)$ *and* $(1, 4, 2, 3)$. *Among the 24 states of* $\mathcal{A}_4$ *this subset has probability* $\frac{2}{24}$, *which corresponds indeed to* $Prob(C) = \frac{(4-2)!}{4!} = \frac{2}{24}$.

Probabilities of second-prime conjunctions
Second-order boolean statements are useful since they can achieve a selection of random structures from a given random bag, as discussed below.

We discuss how to determine the probability of $[\|Y\| = \underline{k}]$ for a program with $\mathcal{S}$-variable Y where $[Y: \mathcal{I}(X)]$ for the input $\mathcal{S}$-variable X.

Definition 7.14. Consider a program with input $\mathcal{S}$-variable X where $[Y: \mathcal{I}(X)]$. Assume that $[Y: \tau]$ where τ is the bag $\{(\alpha_1, K_1), \ldots, (\alpha_n, K_n)\}$ and where Y stores data-labelings with states from the random bag corresponding to τ, say $R = \{(R_1, K_1), \ldots,$
$(R_n, K_n)\}$, where for each $i \in \{1, \ldots, n\}$, $R_i = R(\alpha_i)$. Let $\{\alpha_{i_1}, \ldots, \alpha_{i_m}\}$ be the, possibly empty, bag of partial orders which have size k.
  In case the bag is empty, we conclude that $Prob[\|Y\| = \underline{k}] = 0$.
  Otherwise, we remark that the condition $[\|Y\| = \underline{k}]$, for each data-labeling F will return true in case $F \in R_{i_1} \cup \ldots \cup R_{i_m}$ and false otherwise. In other words, the condition when applied to all data-labelings with states from R will determine the collection $R_{i_1} \cup \ldots \cup R_{i_m}$ and hence amounts to an RB-preserving operation.
  We refer to the random bag $\{(R_{i_1}, K_{i_1}), \ldots, (R_{i_k}, K_{i_m})\}$ as the *selection determined by* $[\|Y\| = \underline{k}]$, indicated by $Selection([\|Y\| = \underline{k}], R)$.
  The *selection determined by a second-order boolean statement* B is defined in the obvious way through appropriate intersections and unions corresponding to the logical connections $\wedge$ and $\vee$ in B.

We obtain the following immediate result.

Lemma 7.7. *Using the notion of Definition 7.14, we note that*

$$Prob[\|Y\| = \underline{k}] = \frac{\sum_{j=1}^{m} K_{i_j} |R_{i_j}|}{|R|}.$$

In case $(*) \forall j, l \in \{1, \dots, m\}$. $K_{i_j}|R_{i_j}| = K_{i_l}|R_{i_l}|$, *the probability simplifies:*

$$Prob[|Y| = \underline{k}] = \frac{\sum_{j=1}^{m} K_{i_j}|R_{i_j}|}{|R|} = \frac{mK_{i_1}|R_{i_1}|}{n|R_{i_1}|} = \frac{m}{n}.$$

Remark 7.4. We will show that $\mathcal{MOQA}$ programs correspond to RB-preserving functions. It is easy to see in this context that $\mathcal{MOQA}$ programs only involving product, split and projection operations correspond to uniformly RB-preserving programs (cf. Definition 4.10). In case the variable Y is an output variable of a program which determines a uniformly RB-preserving function, we obtain that condition $(*)$ holds. Hence the probability of $[|Y| = k]$ is easy to obtain in case Y is the output variable of a uniformly RB-preserving $\mathcal{MOQA}$ program.

7.7 Random Structure Expressions

In the following we define random structure expressions. Some of the random structure operations are required to operate on data-labelings of atomic isolated subsets. This will be indicated in the definition with a vertical bar separating the operation from the type declaration of its S-variables, as in $[Split_i(X, Y) \,|\, Y : \mathcal{AI}(X)]$. This particular notation indicates that the random split needs to be carried out on a data-labeling restricted to an atomic isolated subset of a partial order in the type of the input S-variable X.

We use $\emptyset$ to indicate the constant, which denotes the empty random structure with a single empty state.

In case of an S-variable X of type τ, where τ involves only a single partial order $(V, \sqsubseteq)$, $\mathcal{C}(X)$ indicates the component set of $(V, \sqsubseteq)$.

We recall from the discussion on the Extension Theorem, that the contractive operations random deletion and the strong random projection require subsets to be strictly isolated (cf. Section 5.7). For our purposes it will be sufficient to consider a version of $\mathcal{MOQA}$ which only provides for the random projection as described in Section 5.4, which produces a *copy* of the restrictions of data-labelings to an isolated subset.

Here we implicitly assume that in creating a partial order for this copy, new variables from $\mathcal{U}$ are introduced which do not occur in the program nor have been introduced by any prior operation of the program.

We define random structure expressions in the following.

$$
\begin{aligned}
RS = \;& |\,\emptyset\,|\,X\,|\,[Y[j]|\,Y : \mathcal{AI}(X)]\,| \\
& [(X, U, Y) \bigotimes (X, U, Z)\,|\,U : \mathcal{I}(X), Y, Z : \mathcal{C}(U), Y \neq Z]\,| \\
& [\mathbf{Del}(A, X, Y)|\,Y : \mathcal{SI}(X)]\,|\,[\overline{\mathbf{Del}}(A, X, Y)|\,Y : \mathcal{SI}(X)]\,| \\
& [\mathbf{Perc}^M(X, Y)|\,Y : \mathcal{I}(X)]\,|\,[\overline{\mathbf{Perc}}^m(X, Y)|\,Y : \mathcal{I}(X)]\,| \\
& [\mathbf{Top}(X, Y)|\,Y : \mathcal{I}(X)]\,|\,[\mathbf{Bot}(X, Y)|\,Y : \mathcal{I}(X)]\,| \\
& [\mathbf{Proj}(X, Y)|\,Y : \mathcal{I}(X)]]\,|\,[\mathbf{Split}_j(X, Y)\,|\,Y : \mathcal{AI}(X)]
\end{aligned}
$$

Remark 7.5. For the deletion $\underline{\textbf{Del}}(A, X, Y)$ we require that the range for the semantic interpretation of A is between 1 and $|Y|$. In case the semantic interpretation of A is 1, we use the notation $\textbf{Del}^m(X, Y)$ and similarly, we denote $\overline{\textbf{Del}}(A, X, Y)$ by $\textbf{Del}^M(X, Y)$ in case A evaluates to $|Y|$.

We will occasionally omit the type notation and the $\mathcal{S}$-variables which are not the input $\mathcal{S}$-variable in the random structure expressions when the context is clear. E.g. in case X and Y coincide.

In order to discuss $\mathcal{MOQA}$ programs, we first consider the case of conditional statements and of recursive calls.

7.8 Random Conditional Statements

Conditional statements in $\mathcal{MOQA}$ are statements of the form [If B then P_1 else P_2].

Regarding the boolean expression B involved in this conditional statement, we remark that second-order boolean expressions allow for a straightforward treatment, while first-order boolean expressions, as we will illustrate, can lead to complications. Hence, we will require in the current specifications of the $\mathcal{MOQA}$ programs, that conditional statements involve second-order boolean conditions only, i.e. B is assumed to be a second-order boolean expression. First-order conditionals will be the subject of future investigation, while some potential approaches to first-order conditionals are indicated in the following.

Note that a random conditional statement will transform a given random bag into two new random bags, the first of which consists of the data-labelings which satisfy the boolean statement and the second random bag consisting of the data-labelings which do not satisfy the boolean statement. For the case of $\mathcal{MOQA}$ conditional statements, data-labelings satisfying a second-order boolean expression automatically form a random bag, as is clear from the definition of the selection procedure corresponding to a second-order boolean expression, Definition 7.14. From this selection, it is also clear that the data-labelings which do not satisfy the boolean statement, again form a random bag. Hence such $\mathcal{MOQA}$ conditional statement is automatically random bag preserving.

This is not the case for conditional statements involving first-order boolean expressions. We illustrate via counter-example 7.6 that the use of conditionals can violate RB-preservation, even for the case where the input $\mathcal{S}$-variable stores data-labelings with states from an atomic random structure.

Counter-Example 7.6 Consider the $\mathcal{S}$-variable X which stores labelings from the atomic random structure $\mathcal{A}_3$ and consider the following pseudo-code:

If $X[1] < X[3]$ **then** $X[1] \bigotimes (X[2], X[3])$ **else skip**.

We display the result of executing this program on $\mathcal{A}_3$ below:

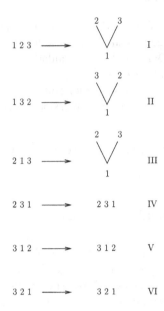

$$123 \longrightarrow \bigvee \quad I$$

$$132 \longrightarrow \bigvee \quad II$$

$$213 \longrightarrow \bigvee \quad III$$

$$231 \longrightarrow 231 \quad IV$$

$$312 \longrightarrow 312 \quad V$$

$$321 \longrightarrow 321 \quad VI$$

It is clear that the program specified by the above pseudo-code when executed on $\mathcal{A}_3$ is not RB-Preserving: the data-labelings I, II, III over the V-shaped partial order do not form (multiple copies of) a random structure and the data-labelings IV,V,VI over the discrete three element partial order again do not form a random structure.

In order to guarantee RB-preservation for conditional statements, one possible approach could be to represent the collection of data-labelings selected as part of the "if"-branch of a statement, as a random bag and similarly for the complement collection of data-labelings, corresponding to the selection made as part of the "else"-branch[1]. This is similar to the approach of the "selection" as already described for second-order boolean statements.

For instance, for the above example, it is clear that the condition $X[1] < X[3]$ is satisfied exactly by the states from the random structure R_1 over the partial order P_1 displayed below. Similarly, the labelings which do not satisfy the condition $X[1] < X[3]$, i.e. the labelings for which $X[1] > X[3]$, correspond exactly to the states from the random structure R_2 over the partial order P_2 displayed below.

$$P_1 \qquad\qquad P_2$$

Clearly, in case we identify a random bag which consists of the data-labelings which satisfy the condition B in a conditional statement [if B then P_1 else P_2], then the problem in counter-example 7.6 will not occur if we insist that the conditions governing the applicability of a product operation are checked in the first place on the random bag determined by the condition B. This would prevent the execution of the random product in conditional of the counter example as it would not satisfy the rules governing the application of the random product. Further investigation is needed in this area, in particular the use of the random bag representing the data-labelings which satisfy B, to guide computations.

As outlined earlier, $\mathcal{MOQA}$ basic operations preserve SP-orders and such structures considerably facilitate computing the average-case time. Hence it is useful in general to aim for the preservation of such structures. Again, conditional statements based on second-order boolean expressions preserve SP-orders since they involve a simple selection process among the given random structures of a random bag. However, for conditionals involving a first-order boolean expression, there is no guarantee that the random bag representing the data-labelings which satisfy the boolean expression, will involve SP-orders only. Moreover, even if these data-labelings happen to form a random bag involving SP-orders only, there is no guarantee that the complement, i.e. the collection of data-labelings not satisfying the boolean expression, will form an SP-order. Aside from negations, disjunctions also can cause problems for first-order conditionals, since overlap can occur between disjunctive parts, which complicates representation as a random bag. This can be resolved by transforming disjunctive statements into equivalent statements involving exclusive or connectives only. This last problem with disjunctive statements, again does not arise for second-order conditionals, which either completely overlap or are mutually exclusive, due to their size-based nature.

7.9 Recursion

We will consider two types of recursion: parallel recursion, executed on inductively defined parallel SP-orders, and product recursion, executed on inductively defined product SP-orders[2]

The Extension Theorem will enable recursive calls on (strictly) isolated subsets of a random bag consisting of a single random structure[3]. We recall that when the recursive call on a subset amounts to the application of a non-contractive operation, the subset is required to be isolated. In case the recursive call on a subset amounts to the application of a contractive operation, the subset is required to be strictly isolated.

---

[2] A more general scheme including both cases and referred to as "series-parallel recursion" is presented in [Hic08]. This generalized version works on inductively defined structures.

[3] General random bags bags are dealt with via a "padding" approach as discussed further on in this section in the context of product recursion.

Recursive calls in each case will occur on strictly isolated subsets.

Note that both types of recursion are guaranteed to terminate since the size of each of the partial orders on which the recursion is called is, in each case, strictly less than the size of the subset on which recursion is originally called.

Parallel Recursion

To store data-labelings over an inductively defined parallel subtype, we consider an S-variable X of this parallel type, say α_n of size n. Moreover, we represent the parallel type of X as follows: $X\colon \alpha_{s_1} \,||\, \ldots \,||\, \alpha_{s_{k_0}}$, for some fixed value $k_0 \leq n$.

In addition to the variable X, we consider k_0 variables, $X_1, \ldots, X_{k_0}$ of types $\alpha_{s_1}, \ldots, \alpha_{s_{k_0}}$ respectively.

A typical example of parallel recursion is the recursion used by Divide and Conquer style algorithms such as Mergesort [AHU87]. Mergesort takes input data-labelings over the discrete partial order of size n and is recursively called on the two halves of the list. I.e. the algorithm is called on lists of size $\lfloor \frac{n}{2} \rfloor$ and $n - \lfloor \frac{n}{2} \rfloor + 1$ respectively. The discrete type of size n will be represented in this case by two parallel components Δ_{s_1} and Δ_{s_2}, as in $\Delta_n = \Delta_{s_1} \,||\, \Delta_{s_2}$ where $s_1 = \lfloor \frac{n}{2} \rfloor$ and $s_2 = n - \lfloor \frac{n}{2} \rfloor + 1$. The types Δ_{s_1} and Δ_{s_2} determine the types which will be involved in the recursive call.

Definition by Parallel Recursion

Consider a program Q of type $(\alpha_n)_n \to (\beta_n)_n$, where each α_n is expressed as a parallel SP-order $\alpha_{s_1} \,||\, \ldots \,||\, \alpha_{s_{k_0}}$. Here k_0, with some abuse of notation, depends on n. The selection of these types can be determined in a computable way. Returning to the Mergesort example, the computation is provided by the "division" boundary $\lfloor \frac{n}{2} \rfloor$. Consider a program $P\colon \beta_{s_1} \,||\, \ldots \,||\, \beta_{s_{k_0}} \to \beta$ where β is a refinement of $\beta_{s_1} \,||\, \ldots \,||\, \beta_{s_{k_0}}$.

The program Q can be defined by parallel recursion as follows:

$$Q(X) = P[Q(X_1) \,||\, \ldots \,||\, Q(X_{k_0})].$$

Here $X_1, \ldots, X_{k_0}$ contain the restrictions of the data-labeling stored in X to the components $\alpha_{s_1}, \ldots, \alpha_{s_{k_0}}$ respectively. The program P takes an input variable Y of type $\beta_{s_1} \,||\, \ldots \,||\, \beta_{s_{k_0}}$, storing the data-labeling (recursively) computed by $Q(X_1) \,||\, \ldots \,||\, Q(X_{k_0})$.

Remark 7.6. Note that even though we use the parallel notation in the definition of the program Q, in practice the computation will proceed sequentially, as in $Q(X_1); \ldots; Q(X_{k_0})$. For instance, the execution of Mergesort when implemented in $\mathcal{MOQA}$ will involve a sequential execution as is traditionally the case. The potential for a truly parallel execution of parallel recursion is present of course and could be exploited.

Product Recursion

We consider an $\mathcal{S}$-variable X of type Δ.

A product-recursive program Q will be defined below. The definition of Q involves a program P which transforms an inductive SP type of size n, say α_n into a type consisting of a random bag with $k(n)$ product SP orders, denoted by $\beta_1, \ldots, \beta_{k(n)}$. Thus

$$P: \alpha_n \to \{(\beta_1, K_1), \ldots, (\beta_{k(n)}, K_{k(n)})\},$$

where, for $i: 1, \ldots, k(n)$, $\beta_i = \alpha_{s_i(1)} \otimes \ldots \otimes \alpha_{s_i(l(i))}$.

A typical example of such an operation is split. Consider for instance the result of executing split on an atomic random structure of size n. The resulting random bag consists of n "star-shaped" product SP-orders. Hence in this particular case $k(n) = n$. Note that the number of product components $l(i)$ in β_i varies with i. For instance, consider the result of the split operation on the discrete four-element partial order $(X, \sqsubseteq)$, where say $X = \{x_1, x_2, x_3, x_4\}$.

Note that this diagram displays the partial orders obtained after identification up to order isomorphism and hence indices no longer reflect the actual tracking of indices during the computation. In this context, indices are simply are used, via an arbitrary assignment, to refer to the elements of the partial orders.

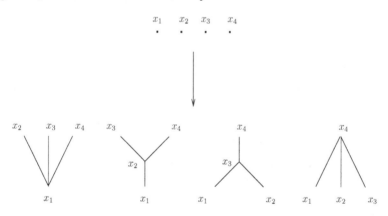

The first and last partial orders, i.e. $(x_1 \otimes (x_2 || x_3 || x_4))$ and $(x_1 || x_2 || x_3) \otimes x_4)$, each have 2 product components, while the second and third partial orders, i.e. $(x_1 \otimes x_2 \otimes (x_3 || x_4))$ and $((x_1 || x_2) \otimes x_3 \otimes x_4)$, each have three product components.

It is clear that one can regard the products as having a constant amount of components through "padding" with the empty set. Indeed, consider again the case of the result of split for $n = 4$. One can obtain the padded result as follows:

$(\emptyset \otimes x_1 \otimes (x_2 || x_3 || x_4))$ and $((x_1 || x_2 || x_3) \otimes x_4 \otimes \emptyset)$, now each have 3 product components, as do $(x_1 \otimes x_2 \otimes (x_3 || x_4))$ and $((x_1 || x_2) \otimes x_3 \otimes x_4)$.

For the sake of simplicity, we assume that padding will be implicitly arranged for in every operation which produces a random bag consisting of product SP-orders. Hence from here on we assume that $l(i)$ is a constant which we denote by l. Thus

$$P: \alpha_n \rightarrow \{(\beta_1, K_1), \dots, (\beta_{k(n)}, K_{k(n)})\},$$

where, for $i \in \{1, \dots, k(n)\}$, $\beta_i = \alpha_{s_i(1)} \otimes \dots \otimes \alpha_{s_i(l)}$.

Finally, in addition to the variable X we introduce $\mathcal{S}$-variables Y_j, where $j \in \{1 \dots l\}$. Each Y_j stores data-labelings with states from the random bag determined by the j-th components of the products $\beta_i = \alpha_{s_i(1)} \otimes \dots \otimes \alpha_{s_i(l)}$, where $i \in \{1, \dots, k(n)\}$. I.e. Y_j stores data-labelings with states from the random bag $\{(\alpha_{s_1(j)}, K_1 \times L_1^j), \dots, (\alpha_{s_{k(n)}(j)}, K_{k(n)} \times L_{k(n)}^j)\}$, where for $i = 1, \dots, k(n)$, $L_i^j = \Pi_{k \neq j} s_i(k)$.

Remark 7.7. Note that, by construction, any two $\mathcal{S}$-variables Y_j and Y_k where $j \neq k$, have partial orders α_j^i and α_k^i which are pairwise disjoint, where $i \in \{1, \dots, k(n)\}$.

Definition by Product Recursion

We will allow recursion on a fixed selection of the variables Y_j, where $j \in \{1, \dots, l\}$. Say this selection is $Y_{j_1}, \dots, Y_{j_s}$, where the selection of indices is required to be pairwise distinct. In that case, Q is recursively defined by product recursion (version I):

$$I) \quad Q(X) = P(X); Q(Y_{j_1}); Q(Y_{j_2}); \dots; Q(Y_{j_s}).$$

Remark 7.8. Note that the recursive calls to Q on the product components could be replaced by several recursive calls on the parallel components of such product components. This approach will be used in the definition of the Treap-gen algorithm of Section 8.6. Also note that sequential execution $Q(Y_{j_1}); Q(Y_{j_2}); \dots; Q(Y_{j_s})$ could be replaced by a parallel execution.

We will discuss below how to make a further selection among the random structures in the random bag, through a second-order conditional.

Second-order selection

Consider a sequence of second-order boolean statements, say $B_1, \dots, B_m$, where for each $j \in \{1, \dots, m\}$, the statement B_j has all variables included in the collection $\{Y_1, \dots, Y_l\}$, such that :

(*) the selections determined by these second-order boolean statements from the random bag $\{(R(\alpha_1), K_1), \dots, (R(\alpha_{k(n)}), K_{k(n)})\}$ are pairwise disjoint.

To define the second-order conditional statement, for every $j \in \{1, \dots, m\}$, a selection of $\mathcal{S}$-variables occurring in B_j is determined, say $Y_{j_1}, \dots, Y_{j_{s(j)}}$. The corresponding second-order conditional statement is defined by:

$$C_j = [\textbf{if } B_j \textbf{ then } Q(Y_{j_1}); Q(Y_{j_2}); \ldots; Q(Y_{j_{s(j)}}) \textbf{ else skip}]$$

We remark that the recursive calls $Q(Y_{j_1}), Q(Y_{j_2}), \ldots, Q(Y_{j_{s(j)}})$ are independent from one another, since the types of the $\mathcal{S}$-variables $Y_1, \ldots, Y_l$ are pairwise disjoint (cf. Remark 7.7).

The program $Q[X : \alpha]$ is defined by product recursion (version II) as follows:

$$II) \ Q(X) = P(X); C_1; \ldots; C_m.$$

We remark that by condition (*) the calls to $C_1, \ldots, C_m$ are independent from one another.

Product recursion version II) generalizes version I) defined above. This is clear when one simply allows the statements C_i to be $Q(Y_{j_i})$ for $m = s$ and $i \in \{1, \ldots, s\}$.

7.10 $\mathcal{MOQA}$ Programs

We include a regular type of for-loop and a "downto"-version. As usual, the first version requires that the loop-parameters A_1 and A_2 are such that A_1 corresponds to a number less than or equal to the number determined by A_2, while the downto-version requires that the number determined by A_1 is greater than or equal to the number determined by A_2.

The $\mathcal{MOQA}$ programs are defined by:

$$
\begin{array}{lll}
P = & \ | \ [X := RS] \ | \ \textbf{skip} \ | & (1) \\
& [P_1; P_2] \ | & (2) \\
& [\textbf{if } B \textbf{ then } P_1 \textbf{ else } P_2] \ | & (3) \\
& [\textbf{ for } i = A_1 \textbf{ to } A_2 \text{ do } P] \ | & (4) \\
& [\textbf{ for } i = A_1 \textbf{ downto } A_2 \text{ do } P] \ | & (5) \\
& [Q(X) = P[Q(X_1) \ || \ \ldots, \ || \ Q(X_{k(0)})]] \ | & (6) \\
& [Q(X) = P(X); C_1; \ldots; C_m] | . & (7)
\end{array}
$$

Remark 7.9. The conditional (3) as well as the program defined by parallel recursion (6) and by product recursion (7) are required to satisfy the conditions outlined in the previous discussions of these particular program constructs. In particular we only consider second-order conditionals in this context.

The $\mathcal{MOQA}^*$ programs are defined by:

$$P = \mid P \in \mathcal{MOQA} \mid [\textbf{while } B \textbf{ do } P] \mid$$

Remark 7.10. We note that we could formulate the conditional and the two types of recursion such that these programs can be applied to isolated subsets. However, one would need to distinguish between contractive and non-contractive applications. This would lead to additional technical overload, which we avoid in the current presentation. The Linear-Compositionality Theorem for $\mathcal{MOQA}$, Theorem 7.8, can be adapted to incorporate these cases via an application of the Extension Theorem (Theorem 4.8).

Since we will show that $\mathcal{MOQA}$ programs are RB-preserving, we will interpret programs as transformations from random bags to random bags. Single element random bags will simply be referred to as "random structures". Hence for the basic operations, such as the random product, when we refer to "a random structure" as an argument, this random structure is regarded as a random bag with a pair consisting of the random structure and the multiplicity one.

7.11 Randomness Preservation

We verify that $\mathcal{MOQA}$ Programs are random bag preserving. This follows by a straightforward induction on the structure of programs.

Theorem 7.7. *The $\mathcal{MOQA}$ programs are RB-preserving. Moreover, $\mathcal{MOQA}$ programs solely constructed from product, split an projection operations are uniformly RB-preserving.*

Proof. We sketch the proof. We have shown that the basic $\mathcal{MOQA}$ operations are RB-preserving and that the composition of RB-preserving functions is RB-preserving. The fact that the basic $\mathcal{MOQA}$ operations are RB-preserving follows from Theorems 5.2, 5.3, 5.5, 5.6, 5.7 and 5.8. It is easy to verify that these results extend inductively on the structure of $\mathcal{MOQA}$ programs to all $\mathcal{MOQA}$ programs. Indeed, we remark that conditional statements are RB-preserving, as is clear from the selection procedure for second-order conditionals in Section 7.6.4. Since for-loops as well as parallel recursion and product recursion are guaranteed to terminate, they amount to finite compositions of RB-preserving programs, which by Lemma 4.2 yields RB-preservation of these loops.

The fact that $\mathcal{MOQA}$ programs solely constructed from product, split and projection operations are uniformly RB-preserving follows by a similar argument and the discussion in Section 5.8.

We recall from Chapter 3 that Heapsort and Bubblesort-I are not RB-preserving, hence these algorithms are not implementable in $\mathcal{MOQA}$. It is useful to illustrate in an informal way at a syntactic level why these algorithms are not implementable in the language.

For the case of Heapsort, one can implement the Heapify procedure, as will be illustrated for Percolating Heapsort. However the Selection phase can not be implemented. Indeed, the subsequent swap between the top element of the heap and the final list element is not permissible in $\mathcal{MOQA}$ since this swap cannot be obtained by performing any of the operations on random structures. Access to the final list element in the heap is invalid since the heap, as a random structure, is an indivisible unit which can only be involved in operations with other (disjoint) random structures or can only be accessed through operations on isolated subsets.

For the case of Bubblesort-I we remark that this algorithm has an input $\mathcal{S}$-variable of type Δ. For size n, there are $n!$ possible states for the input lists. For any fixed data-labeling that corresponds to an input list, the first pass of the outermost while loop compares the labels of the first two elements. To implement Bubblesort-I in $\mathcal{MOQA}$ the next step should be an application of $\otimes$ in order to create a new random structure on $X[1], X[2]$ with as underlying partial order the set $\{(X[1], X[1]), (X[2], X[2]), (X[1], X[2])\}$. Again, to incorporate Bubblesort-I in $\mathcal{MOQA}$, the next step once more should be a call to $\otimes$ on the labels of $X[2]$ and $X[3]$. However at this stage $X[2]$ and $X[3]$ no longer form components of an isolated set of the random structure under consideration, since $X[1]$ is immediately below $X[2]$ but not immediately below $X[3]$.

7.12 Compositional Determination of Average-Case Time

In the following we discuss the compositional average-case time derivation for $\mathcal{MOQA}$ programs. The results remain true for any programs which can be given an interpretation $[\![P]\!]$ which is a RB-preserving function. We recall the Linear-Compositionality Theorem, Theorem 1.3.

Theorem 1.3 (Linear-Compositionality)

1. Consider a random bag preserving program P such that $[\![P]\!] : R \to R'$. Then:

$$\overline{T}_{P;Q}(R) = \overline{T}_P(R) + \overline{T}_Q(R').$$

2. Consider a random bag $R = \{(\overrightarrow{R}_p, \overrightarrow{K}_p)\}$; then

$$a)\ \overline{T}_P(R) = \sum_{i=1}^{i=p} Prob_i \times \overline{T}_P(R_i),$$

where $Prob_i = Prob[F \in R_i] = \frac{K_i |R_i|}{|R|}$, is the S-probability.

For the particular case where $R = \{(R_1, K_1)\}$, the previous equality reduces to:

$$b)\ \overline{T}_P(R) = \overline{T}_P(R_1).$$

The systematic application of this result to the sequential parts of $\mathcal{MOQA}$ code enables one to express the *exact* average-case number of comparisons of the computation over the original random bag in terms of the average-case number of comparisons of more basic parts of the code over new random bags. Ultimately this enables an expression of the average-case time of the code in terms of a linear combination of the average-case times of the basic operations involved in the code. This is captured by Theorem 7.8 below.

7.13 Linear-Compositionality for $\mathcal{MOQA}$ Programs

The following theorem, Theorem 7.8, states that the average-case comparison time of $\mathcal{MOQA}$ programs can be obtained in a linear-compositional way. This involves the reduction of the average-case time of programs in terms of the average-case time of the basic $\mathcal{MOQA}$ operations.

The average-case times of the basic $\mathcal{MOQA}$ operations random product, random deletion and percolation can be computed via the formulas obtained in Chapter 6. The average-case times of the Split operation as well as the Top or Bot operations applied to an atomic random structure of size n is $n - 1$. Though we have not explicitly included these, formulas similar to the one obtained in Chapter 6, can be obtained to express the average-case time of the general version of Top and Bot. The Projection and Skip operation take 0 comparisons on average. The following theorem illustrates how the average-case time of $\mathcal{MOQA}$ statements reduces to the average-case time of basic $\mathcal{MOQA}$ operations.

Theorem 7.8. Linear-Compositionality for $\mathcal{MOQA}$
In the following, R represents a random bag, say $R = \{((R_1, K_1), \ldots, (R_n, K_n))\}$. Random bags $R = (R_1, 1)$ of length one with multiplicity 1 are interpreted as Random Structures R_1. If P is a $\mathcal{MOQA}$ program then we represent the RB-preserving function corresponding to P as usual by $[\![P]\!]$. The average-case comparison time of $\mathcal{MOQA}$ statements can be reduced in the following way:

1) For second-order boolean statements:

  a) If $B = [|Y| = A]$ (or one of its alternative versions with $\leq, \geq, < $ or $>$) then $\overline{T}_B(R) = 1$

  b) If B is build up via logical connectors $\vee, \wedge, \neg$ from the boolean expressions $B_1, \ldots, B_k$ then $\overline{T}_B(R) = \sum_{i=1}^{k} \overline{T}_{B_i}(R)$.

2) $\overline{T}_{[P_1;P_2]}(R) = \overline{T}_{P_1}(R) + \overline{T}_{P_2}(R')$ in case $[\![P]\!] : R \to R'$.

3) $\overline{T}_P(R) = \sum_{i=1}^{n} \alpha_i \overline{T}_P[R_i]$, when $R = \{(R_1, K_1), \ldots, (R_n, K_n)\}$ and

$$\forall i \in \{1, \ldots, n\}. \, \alpha_i = \frac{K_i \times |R_i|}{\sum_{i=1}^{n} K_i \times |R_i|}.$$

4) $\overline{T}_{[\textbf{if } B \textbf{ then } P_1 \textbf{ else } P_2]}(R) =$

$$\overline{T}_B(R) + Prob(B)\overline{T}_{P_1}(R^B) + (1 - Prob(B))\overline{T}_{P_2}(R^{\neg B}),$$

where $R^B = \{F \mid F \in R \text{ and } [\![B]\!](F) = True\}$

and $R^{\neg B} = \{F \mid F \in R \text{ and } [\![B]\!](F) = False\}$

5) $\overline{T}_{[\textbf{for } i = A_1 \textbf{ to } A_2 \textbf{ do } P(i)]}(R) = \sum_{i=1}^{[\![A_2]\!]-[\![A_1]\!]+1} \overline{T}_P([\![P]\!]^{i-1}(R)),$

where $[\![P]\!]^0(R) = R$

and $[\![P]\!]^{i-1} = [\![P([\![A_1]\!] + i - 2)]\!] \circ \ldots \circ [\![P([\![A_1]\!])]\!].$

6) $\overline{T}_{[\textbf{for } i = A_1 \textbf{ downto } A_2 \textbf{ do } P(i)]}(R) = \sum_{i=1}^{[\![A_1]\!]-[\![A_2]\!]+1} \overline{T}_P([\![P]\!]^{i-1}(R)).$

$[\![P]\!]^0(R) = R$

and $[\![P]\!]^{i-1} = [\![P([\![A_1]\!] - i + 2)]\!] \circ \ldots \circ [\![P([\![A_1]\!])]\!].$

7) *To treat the case of parallel recursion, we recall briefly the notation involved in this case. To store data-labelings over an inductively defined parallel subtype, we consider an S-variable X of this type, say α_n of size n. Moreover, we represent the parallel type of X as follows: $X: \alpha_1 \| \ldots \| \alpha_{k_0}$, for some fixed value $k_0 \leq n$. In addition to the variable X, we consider k_0 variables, $X_1, \ldots, X_{k_0}$ of types $\alpha_1, \ldots, \alpha_{k_0}$ respectively.*

Consider a program Q of type $(\alpha_n)_n \to (\beta_n)_n$, where each α_n is expressed as a parallel SP-order $\alpha_1 \| \ldots \| \alpha_{k_0}$, where this selection of types can be determined in a computable way. Consider a program $P: \beta_1 \| \ldots \| \beta_{k_0} \to \beta_m$ where β_m is a refinement of $\beta_1 \| \ldots \| \beta_{k_0}$ and $m \leq n$.

The program Q can be defined by parallel recursion as follows:

$$Q(X) = P[Q(X_1) \| \ldots \| Q(X_{k_0})].$$

Here $X_1, \ldots, X_{k_0}$ contain the restrictions of the data-labeling stored in X to the components $\alpha_1, \ldots, \alpha_{k_0}$ respectively.

The program P takes an input variable Y of type $\beta_1 \| \ldots \| \beta_{k_0}$, where Y stores the data-labeling (recursively) computed by $Q(X_1) \| \ldots \| Q(X_{k_0})$.

$$\overline{T}_{[Q(X)=P[Q(Y_1)\| \ldots \| Q(Y_{k(0)})]]}(\alpha_n) = \sum_{i=1}^{k_0} \overline{T}_Q(R(\alpha_i)) + \overline{T}_P(R(\beta_m))^4.$$

---

[4] Following Remark 7.6, if the execution where truly in parallel as opposed to sequential, the formula obtained in 7) ought to be adjusted accordingly.

8) In the case of product recursion, we deal only with the case which does not involve selections through second-order boolean statements. The case where such selections are involved can easily be dealt with via a generalization using case 4).

We recall that for product recursion, a program Q is defined in terms of a program P which transforms the type inductive type α_n into a type corresponding to a random bag with $k(n)$ product SP orders, denoted by $\beta_1, \ldots, \beta_{k(n)}$. Thus

$$P: \alpha_n \to \{(\beta_1, K_1), \ldots, (\beta_{k(n)}, K_{k(n)})\},$$

where, for $i: 1, \ldots, k(n)$, $\beta_i = \alpha_{s_i(1)} \otimes \ldots \otimes \alpha_{s_i(l)}$. We recall that Q is defined by product recursion via $Q(X) = P(X); Q(Y_{j_1}); Q(y_{j_2}); \ldots; Q(Y_{j_s})$, where Y_j stores data-labelings with states from the random bag

$$\{(R(\alpha_{s_1(j)}), K_1 \times L_1^j), \ldots, (R(\alpha_{s_{k(n)}(j)}), K_{k(n)} \times L_{k(n)}^j)\},$$

where for $i = 1, \ldots, k(n)$, $L_i^j = \Pi_{k \neq j} s_i(k)$. Finally, we determine a fixed selection of the variables Y_j, via $Y_{j_1}, \ldots, Y_{j_s}$, where $\{j_1, \ldots, j_s\} \subseteq \{1, \ldots, l\}$.

$$\overline{T}_{[Q(X)=P(X); Q(Y_{j_1}); \ldots; Q(Y_{j_s})]}(R(\alpha_n)) = \overline{T}_P(R(\alpha_n)) +$$

$$\sum_{m=1}^{s} \overline{T}_Q(\{(R(\alpha_{s_1(j_m)}), K_1 \times L_1^{j_m}), \ldots, (R(\alpha_{s_{k(n)}(j_m)}), K_{k(n)} \times L_{k(n)}^{j_m})\})^5.$$

Proof. Case 1) is immediate. Cases 2) and 3) follow from Theorem 1.3. To show Case 4), we note that for a given conditional statement $[\textbf{if } B \textbf{ then } P_1 \textbf{ else } P_2](R)$, we know (cf. Section 7.5) that the sets of data-labelings $R^B = \{F \mid B(F) = True\}$ and $R^{\neg B} = \{F \mid B(F) = False\}$ will form new random structures.

We remark that $Prob(B) = \frac{|R^B|}{|R|}$ and of course $Prob(\neg B) = \frac{|R^{\neg B}|}{|R|} = 1 - Prob(B)$.

$$\overline{T}_{[\textbf{if } B \textbf{ then } P_1 \textbf{ else } P_2]}(R)$$

$$= \sum_{F \in R} \frac{T_{[\textbf{if } B \textbf{ then } P_1 \textbf{ else } P_2]}(F)}{|R|}$$

$$= \frac{\sum_{F \in R} T_B(F)}{|R|} + \frac{\sum_{F \in R^{True}} T_{P_1}(F)}{|R|} + \frac{\sum_{F \in R^{False}} T_{P_1}(F)}{|R|}$$

$$= \overline{T}_B(R) + \frac{\sum_{F \in R^B} T_{P_1}(F)}{|R^B|} \frac{|R^B|}{|R|} + \frac{\sum_{F \in R^{\neg B}} T_{P_1}(F)}{|R^{\neg B}|} \frac{|R^{\neg B}|}{|R|}$$

$$= \overline{T}_B(R) + Prob(B)\overline{T}_{P_1}(R^B) + (1 - Prob(B))\overline{T}_{P_2}(R^{\neg B}).$$

Finally, cases 5) and 6) follow by Theorem 1.3, while cases 7) and 8) follow from a combination of Theorems 1.3 and 4.8.

---

[5] Following Remark 7.8, if the execution where truly in parallel as opposed to sequential, the formula obtained in 8) ought to be adjusted accordingly.

Remark 7.11. As indicated at the outset of the chapter, the language specifications provided here serve the purpose of providing a basis on which to develop the examples of Chapters 8 and 9. Clearly, to develop the static timing tool *Distri-Track* , further aspects need to be taken into account. One of these is the representation of random bags of arbitrary size n. This is addressed in more detail in Chapter 10, e.g. in relation to the Split operation, and an approach involving inductive data structures is outlined in [Hic08]. Another issue is the automated derivation of the time in the presence of nested for-loops. Theorem 7.8 presents in cases 5) and 6) a method to compute the average time of for-loops. Clearly the treatment of dependent parameters of nested for-loops needs special care. This is a topic beyond the scope of the present book. An approach to deal with nested for-loops is presented in [Hic08]. Finally, it is clear that further extensions of $\mathcal{MOQA}$ could be explored, some of which are discussed in Chapter 11.

Chapter 8
Examples of $\mathcal{MOQA}$ Programs

We provide several examples of well-known algorithms for sorting and searching, programmed in $\mathcal{MOQA}$. Two new sorting algorithms are introduced, Percolating Heapsort and Treapsort, based on the $\mathcal{MOQA}$ deletion operation. Percolating Heapsort provides the first randomness preserving version of Heapsort.

In the following examples X denotes the input $\mathcal{S}$-variable while Z denotes the output $\mathcal{S}$-variable.

We adopt the convention in the presentation that $\mathcal{MOQA}$ algorithms when called on orders of size 0 or 1 act as the identity operation, i.e. will simply return the data-labeling of a partial order of size 0 or 1.

Moreover, when referring to a call to a basic operation on an $\mathcal{S}$-variable X, we assume implicitly that the data-labeling stored in the variable X is reset to the output data-labeling computed by the basic operation. For instance, we will refer to $Top(X)$ as opposed to $[X := Top(X)]$ in the pseudo-code.

8.1 Insertionsort

The $\mathcal{MOQA}$ code for Insertionsort captures the traditional insertion operation, of inserting a single element into a sorted list, via the $\mathcal{MOQA}$ product operation.

Insertionsort$[\text{X}: \Delta]$
```
Z: = X[1]
```
for $\text{i} = \underline{2}$ **to** $|\text{X}|$ **do** $\text{Z}: = \text{Z} \otimes \text{X[i]}$

8.2 Merge

The merge algorithm is a traditional "pop-the-top" style merge operation, where systematically the least element of two sorted lists is removed and stored in a new list to create the sorted list as output.

We consider an input $\mathcal{S}$-variable X of a parallel type, denoted by σ, which consists of the union of two disjoint linear orders, say $[X: (I_1, \Upsilon) \cup (I_2, \Upsilon), I_1 \cap I_2 = \emptyset]$. The merge algorithm is defined by product recursion, where the operation Bot is called on the data-labelings stored in X. The result is a data-labeling over a new partial order with a minimum. We denote the restriction of this data-labeling to partial order with the minimum removed, by $\overline{X}$.

Merge$[X: (I_1, \Upsilon) \cup (I_2, \Upsilon), I_1 \cap I_2 = \emptyset]$
`Merge(X) = Bot(X); Merge(X̄)`

8.3 Mergesort

We define the $\mathcal{MOQA}$ pseudo-code for Mergesort by parallel recursion. We use the following notation for the type Δ: if Δ has underlying set $U = \{x_{i_1}, \ldots, x_{i_n}\}$ then Δ_1 indicates the discrete order with underlying set $U_1 = \{x_{i_1}, \ldots, x_{i_{\lfloor \frac{n}{2} \rfloor}}\}$ and Δ_2 indicates the discrete order with underlying set $U_2 = U - U_1$. In the following pseudo-code we consider three variables, $[Y_1: \Delta_1]$, $[Y_2: \Delta_2]$ and $[Y: (U_1, \Upsilon) \cup (U_2, \Upsilon)]$.

MS$[X: \Delta]$
$[\texttt{MS(X)} = \texttt{Merge(MS(Y}_1\texttt{); MS(Y}_2\texttt{))}].$

8.4 Quicksort

We discuss Quicksort based on the *Split* operation introduced in Chapter 1. The treatment of Quicksort based on the standard *Split* operation defined in Chapter 5 is the same since both *Split* operations require the same average-case number of comparisons.

We recall some notation regarding *Split*. As pointed out in Chapter 1, the *Split* operation when executed on data-labelings over the discrete order of size n, produces a random bag for which each partial order is order-isomorphic to one of the orders $P[0, n-1], P[1, n-2], P[2, n-3], \ldots, P[n-3, 2], P[n-2, 1], P[n-1, 0]$. We recall that each of these orders has a "star-shape" as displayed below.

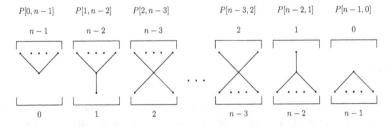

We recall that star-shaped orders are defined to be partial orders which are order-isomorphic to some $P[i, j]$. Star-shaped partial orders have the following form: a central element (the pivot element), an "upper part", I^{UPPER}, which forms a strictly isolated subset consisting of the j elements above the pivot and a "lower part", I^{LOWER}, which forms a strictly isolated subset and consisting of the i elements below the pivot. Note that for the star-shaped orders which are order-isomorphic to $P[0, n-1]$ and $P[n-1, 0]$, I^{LOWER} and I^{UPPER} respectively are empty.

Finally, we recall that, by Lemma 1.2, *Split* determines a random bag preserving function, where

$$Split: A_n \longmapsto \{(R(P[0, n-1]), K_{n-1}), \ldots, (R(P[n-1, 0]), K_0)\},$$

and where $K_i = \binom{n-1}{i}$ for $i \in \{0, \ldots, n-1\}$.

Quicksort is defined by product recursion, case I). Using the notation for product recursion (Section 7.9), we remark that program P in product recursion corresponds to the *Split* operation in this case where we select the first element $X[1]$ of X as pivot.

Quicksort will, following a call to *Split* recursively call itself on the restriction of the data-labelings to the I^{UPPER} and the I^{LOWER} part of the star-shaped partial orders.

This is an example of an application of an operation to data-labelings which are restricted to a strictly isolated subset of the partial order.

The part I^{UPPER}, viewed over the random bag

$$\{(R(P[0, n-1]), K_{n-1}), \ldots, (R(P[n-1, 0]), K_0)\},$$

determines a type $\{(\Delta_{n-1}, K_{n-1}), \ldots, (\Delta_0, K_0)\}$, while the strictly isolated subset I^{LOWER} determines the same type.

We consider, in a manner consistent with the definition of the variables Y_1, Y_2, Y_3 in product recursion (for $l = 3$), a selection of variables $Y_1 \colon \{\Delta_0, \ldots, \Delta_{n-1}\}$ and $Y_3 \colon \{\Delta_{n-1}, \ldots, \Delta_0\}$.

The definition by product recursion for Quicksort in $\mathcal{MOQA}$ is the following:

Qsort[X: Δ]
```
Qsort(X) = Split₁(X, X); Qsort(Y₁); Qsort(Y₃)
```

The previous examples are known to be randomness preserving, in the informal meaning of this concept (e.g. [Knu73]). We consider the Heapsort algorithm which, as shown in Section 3.5, is not RB-preserving.

8.5 Percolating Heapsort

The problem with Heapsort's average-case analysis has been extensively studied in the literature. As an application we re-program Heapsort in $\mathcal{MOQA}$ and obtain the first RB-preserving variant of the algorithm, Percolating Heapsort. First, we present the historic context of the difficulties encountered with Heapsort's average-case analysis.

8.5.1 Historical Background

The average-case analysis of Heapsort is notoriously hard due to the fact that Heapsort's selection process does not preserve randomness (cf. [Knu73], [SS93], [LV93] and [Ede96]). The sorting algorithm Heapsort was introduced by Williams in 1964, motivated by the fact that heaps are ideally suited for large priority queue Applications [Wil64]. An improved version of the algorithm has been discussed by Floyd in [Flo64]. The pseudo-code for both versions is given in Chapter 1. Heapsort's running time for either variant is guaranteed to be of order $nlogn$. Indeed, it is easy to establish that Heapsort is $O(nlogn)$ in the worst case (e.g. [Knu73]) and hence it is also $O(nlogn)$ in the average-case. This last fact however only provides partial information on the average-case, since the constant factor involved remains unknown. Knuth undertook one of the earliest attempts to obtain a more precise average-case analysis of Heapsort [Knu73] and showed that the heap creation phase of the algorithm preserves randomness. In other words, after heapification of all lists of a given size, we obtain a uniform distribution on the resulting heaps of that size (cf. Theorem H, Section 5.2.3 of [Knu73]). The proof of the theorem involves a "backward analysis" argument, which essentially establishes that the number of the lists giving rise to a given heap after heapification, is constant. As discussed in [Knu73]: "... the selection phase is another story, which remains to be written". This remained a crucial stumbling block until an analysis of the average case was obtained in [SS93]. I. Munro suggested a solution involving Kolmogorov complexity and the related incompressibility method, as discussed in [LV93] (Section 6.3). The method proceeds by contradiction and is based on extensive theoretical machinery involving probabilistic as well as recursion-theoretic results. As such, the incompressibility method provides a beautiful but inherently complex solution to the problem. Since the method proceeds by contradiction (as does Sedgewick's and Schaffer's), it results in estimates and does not allow one to provide the *exact* average-case comparison time for the selection phase of Heapsort or of Heapsort variants such as bottom-up-Heapsort [Weg90]. This problem is discussed in [Ede96], where Dutton's weak-Heapsort [Dut92] is analyzed. We recall (cf. Section 2) that the selection phase of Heapsort (or any of its existing variants) does not preserve randomness of heaps (e.g. [Ede96]).

Edelkamp observes in this context: "*Diese Betrachtung hat eine exakte average-case Analyse von allen Heapsort-Varianten bis dato unmöglich gemacht[1]*". A similar

---

[1] "This fact has made an exact average-case analysis of all Heapsort-variants impossible to date."

remark is made in [Weg90], where the average-case for the variant Bottom-Up-Heapsort is analyzed: "... for the heap creation phase exact results are obtained. For the selection phase, we run into the same problems as those encountered in the analysis of the average-case behaviour of Heapsort. Deleting the root of a random heap and applying the heapify procedure (after replacing the root by another heap-element) does not lead to a random heap. The analysis is possible only under certain assumptions. The results are justified by experiments." Because of this problem, straightforward techniques, such as backward analysis, cannot be applied. Edelkamp discusses Dutton's weak-Heapsort [Dut92] which provides an interesting example of a Heapsort variant which almost (!) allows for a backward analysis. Edelkamp shows that a backward analysis is possible *provided* one accepts the use of a model which approximates the true behaviour of weak-Heapsort. One needs to assume that the "weak-heaps" of size n are, during all steps of the selection phase, of uniform distribution. As pointed out in [Ede96], this model does not represent reality, but it can be assumed that for large values of n, a uniform distribution is "approximated". Again, the computations are rather involved.

The problematic nature of determining Heapsort's Average-Case Time has also been pointed out in the context of automatic average-case analysis of algorithms [FSZ91]. The programming Language LUO, developed by P. Flajolet, enables the automatic derivation of the average-case complexity of classes of algorithms by establishing a link between recurrence equations and singularities of associated complex functions. The Average-Case Time is obtained in this way through the use of the mathematical software package Maple which has been partly incorporated in the LUO code. However LUO is limited to so called "static" data structures. As reported in "Automatic Average-Case Analysis of Algorithms", by P. Flajolet, B. Salvy and P. Zimmerman:

"Observe that (for LUO) there are no explicit variable assignments, and in a deep sense, one cannot modify structures nor create new structures. Judging from the entirety of the analyses contained in Knuth's volume on sorting and searching, the only algorithms that we know how to analyse are those whose complexity is equivalent to a parameter of a static structure. No general method is known in order to analyse intrinsically "dynamic" algorithms." As reported on page 64 of [FSZ91]: *"examples that typically leave us helpless are heapsort and balanced trees that modify either an ordered array structure or a tree structure.".*

We present Percolating Heapsort which *does* preserve uniform distribution, as opposed to (current variants of) Heapsort, which leads to a determination of its exact average comparison time. We remark that for technical purposes, we relax the definition of a heap somewhat in that we replace condition 1) in the definition of a near-heap by the weaker condition: "Some leaves are allowed to be omitted". i.e. we no longer require the omissions to take place in right to left order. This is needed in order for Percolating Heapsort to perform deletions in a more flexible way. In essence we will work with Heap-Ordered Binary Trees.

8.5.2 Pseudo-Code for Percolating Heapsort

The formulation and the analysis of the algorithm are surprisingly simple. Hence the worst-case as well as the average-case analysis of Percolating Heapsort can be included as part of standard algorithm courses. This can be contrasted with standard Heapsort and its current variants, for which the average-case analysis typically is postponed to a specialized graduate course (if covered at all), since its precise formulation involves complex arguments such as the incompressibility method [LV93, Weg90].

The new Heapsort variant is easy to implement and is competitive with existing Heapsort variants.

We first show how to implement the Heapify procedure in $\mathcal{MOQA}$. We recall that for a data-labeling stored in X and represented as a binary tree (cf. Section 2) the element with greatest index which has children is the element $X[\lfloor \frac{|X|}{2} \rfloor]$. Moreover, in case this element only has one child, i.e. in case $2\lfloor \frac{|X|}{2} \rfloor = |X|$, then in addition to this child $X[|X|]$, we interpret the "second child" to be the child $X[|X|+1]$, which is defined to be $\emptyset$.

Heapify$[X: \Delta]$
for $j := \lfloor \frac{|X|}{2} \rfloor$ **downto** $\underline{1}$ **do** $X[j] := (X[\underline{2}j], X[\underline{2}j+1]) \bigotimes X[j]$

The $\mathcal{MOQA}$ pseudo-code for Percolating Heapsort is defined below via product recursion. We consider an $\mathcal{S}$-variable X of type Δ. Data-Labelings stored in X are transformed by $\underline{Perc}^M$ into new data-labelings over a partial order with a maximum. The restriction of these data-labelings to the partial order without the maximum is denoted in the following pseudo-code by $\underline{X}$.

PH$[X : \Delta]$
Heapify(X);
$PH(X) = \underline{Perc}^M(X);\ PH(\underline{X})$

We illustrate Percolating Heapsort for lists of size 4. After the heapification phase, three heaps of size 4 are produced (as is the case for traditional versions of Heapsort).

Example 8.1. Percolating Heapsort creates, after the first run of the percolation process, one copy of the random structures R_1 and R_2 on the following page.

Percolating Heapsort's effect on the random heaps of size 4 can be contrasted with traditional Heapsort which does not produce a random structure after the first cycle of the Selection phase (cf. Example 1.1).

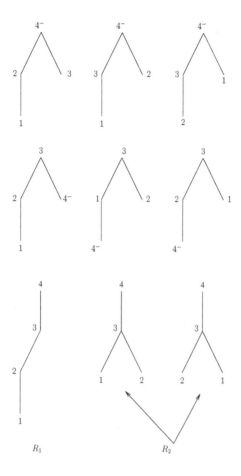

8.6 Treap-gen

8.6.1 Oriented Binary Trees

We follow the approach of [MR95] of considering *endogenous* binary trees, i.e. binary trees for which all key values are stored at internal nodes and all leaf nodes are empty. As remarked in [MR95], this assumption simplifies presentations, but is in general not an essential requirement. Alternative code and technical adaptations in order to ignore leafs labeled with the empty set can be provided if needed.

We recall the inductive data type of an oriented binary tree.

Definition 8.1. An *oriented (endogenous) binary tree* is a tree obtained by the following inductive process:

$T_0 = \emptyset$ (the empty tree) and T_1 is the three-node tree, consisting of a root node and two children labeled with the empty set. Let $\tau_0 = \{T_0\}$ and $\tau_1 = \{T_1\}$. Then we define the collection τ_n of trees by induction as follows: $\forall n \geq 2$ the set τ_n obtained via the construction displayed in the diagram below, where T_i indicates a tree from τ_i and T_{n-1-i} indicates a tree from τ_{n-1-i}.

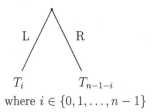

$$\text{where } i \in \{0, 1, \ldots, n-1\}$$

We refer to the trees from the set T_i as the *left-subtrees* and to the trees from the set T_{n-1-i} as the *right-subtrees*.

Remark 8.1. We will follow the convention of counting comparisons for algorithms operating on binary trees as indicated earlier in Remark 5.4. Note that in this convention we will not count testing for a leaf since in practice this test is typically not counted for Heapsort variants. Again, counting such tests can be obtained via technical adaptations if needed.

Rather than labeling the branches with L and R in order to display the orientation we will assume this orientation is implicitly given by the display of the branches on the page, drawn as "directed to the left" and "directed to the right", when emerging from the parent node.

We remark that Oriented (Endogenous) Binary Trees are full trees, a notion defined in Chapter 2. The following is a well-known fact regarding full binary trees.

Lemma 8.1. *A full binary tree of size* $2n - 1$ *has* $n - 1$ *internal nodes and* n *leaves.*

8.6.2 Treaps in $\mathcal{MOQA}$

Oriented binary trees are incorporated via a random structure in $\mathcal{MOQA}$ relying on an encoding of the orientations. This is achieved by the requirement that the indices of the elements of the partial order must be "consistent with the orientation".

Definition 8.2. Given an oriented binary tree determined by a finite partial order over the set $\{x_1, \ldots, x_n\}$. We say that *the ordering is consistent with the orientation* provided the following holds for every parent node x_i in the tree:

a) if x_i has a left child x_j then $i > j$
b) if x_i has a right child x_k then $k > i$.

Definition 8.3. A *Heap-Ordered (Binary) Tree*, is an ordered binary tree which is equipped with a data-labeling. A *Treap* is a Heap-Ordered Binary Tree for which the underlying partial order is consistent with the orientation. If $\mathcal{L}$ is a label set of cardinality n then $\mathcal{TREAP}_{\mathcal{L}}(n)$ denotes the random bag consisting of the random structures with label set $\mathcal{L}$, over the Oriented Binary Trees of size n for which the order is consistent with the orientation.

Note that Heap-Ordered Treaps correspond to treaps as defined in Chapter 2. The labels of a Treap correspond to the priorities, while the indices of the elements in the finite partial order correspond to the keys.

Lemma 8.2. *If the index set is fixed and of size n for a given partial order of size n, then each oriented binary tree has exactly one indexing of the elements for which the partial order is consistent with the orientation.*

Proof. We remark that the partial order consistent with the orientation has an order on indices which is equivalent to the standard binary search tree order and hence there is a unique indexing for each oriented binary tree such that the associated partial order is consistent with the orientation.

We discuss a Heap-Ordered Treap Generation algorithm, Treap-gen, which is guaranteed to produce all Heap-Ordered Treaps of a given size from the states of the discrete random structure of that size. Hence the issue of orientation consistency will not arise explicitly since the algorithm is guaranteed to produce outputs respecting this property (cf. Remark 8.4).

Remark 8.2. In the following lemma we use a Delete operation on a full binary tree which consists of pruning one of the "leaves". We recall that we consider endogenous trees for which a leaf consist of a full binary trees of size 3 which has an internal node and two leafs indicated by $\emptyset$. This type of deletion reflects the outcome of the $\mathcal{MOQA}$-Delete operation at the level of the partial order.

Lemma 8.3. *The Delete operation, introduced in Remark 8.2, when executed in all possible ways at the partial order level, i.e. at all leaves and on all trees from $OBT(2n-1)$, produces $n-1$ copies of $OBT(2(n-1)-1)$.*

Proof. Consider a tree from $OBT(2(n-1)-1)$. If one extends a leaf of such a tree, by removing its designation as $\emptyset$ and replacing it with a full binary tree of size 3 with one internal node (at the original leaf) and two new leaves, each labeled with $\emptyset$, the resulting tree belongs to $OBT(2n-1)$. By Lemma 8.1 each tree from $OBT(2(n-1)-1)$ has $n-1$ leaves, hence this process of extending the leaves can be carried out in $n-1$ different ways. One can verify that conversely, each tree from $OBT(2(n-1)-1)$ is the result of removing a single full binary tree of size 3 of the above kind from exactly $n-1$ trees from $OBT(2n-1)$.

Example 8.2. We illustrate Lemma 8.3 for $n = 4$, $\underline{Del}(OBT(7)) = 3 \times OBT(5)$. This result is obtained via the Delete operation which at the partial order level will result in removing the oriented binary trees of size 3 indicated in "dash-dotted"-form, where the effect of each such pruning on a tree from $OBT(7)$ produces a copy of the tree from $OBT(5)$ indicated in solid lines on the diagram below.

Finally, we conclude with a similar result for Treaps.

Proposition 8.1. *The $\mathcal{MOQA}$ Delete operation when executed on all trees from $\mathcal{TREAP}(n - 1)$ produces $n - 1$ copies of $\mathcal{TREAP}(n - 2)$.*

Proof. We sketch the proof. Note that $OBT(2n - 1)$ after the removal of its nodes labeled with the empty set corresponds to $\mathcal{TREAP}(n - 1)$ and a similar process on $OBT(2(n - 1) - 1)$ yields $\mathcal{TREAP}(n - 2)$. From Theorem 5.4 we know that the $\underline{Del}(k)$ operation is a bijection on Treaps. During the application of the operation, the k-th smallest label a has become the least label a^- of the resulting Treaps and is then removed. Hence the application of the operation is equivalent to the removal, at the partial order level, of the minimal elements of the Treaps produced after the Push-Down operation on a^-. The result is obtained as a corollary of this observation in combination with Lemma 8.3.

The following Proposition is an immediate Corollary of Proposition 8.1 and the fact that $\underline{Perc}^M$ acts in a similar way as the $\underline{Del}$ operation.

Proposition 8.2. *The* $\mathcal{MOQA}$ $\underline{Perc}^M$ *operation when executed on all treaps from* $\mathcal{TREAP}(n-1)$ *returns* $n-1$ *copies of* $\mathcal{TREAP}(n-2)$.

Note that we do not insist for the $\underline{Perc}^M$ operation, when it resets an input data-labeling to a new data-labeling, to preserve an orientation from the root of the new tree to its child, i.e. the operation will create a new root for which the index in general no longer respects the orientation. However, the algorithm to be considered will operate on the data-labeling returned by the $\underline{Perc}^M$ operation, restricted to the partial order without the newly introduced maximum at the root, which is the Treap-part of the new data-labeling.

8.6.3 Treap-Generation

To present the pseudo-code for Treap-gen, defined by product recursion, we introduce some notation. In the following, we focus on the actions of Top on the atomic random structure $\mathcal{A}_n$. If $F \in \mathcal{A}_n$ and if $Top(F) = F'$, then F' is a data-labeling over the following partial order in which one of the originally maximal elements, namely the maximal element x_i labeled with the largest label, has become the maximum element:

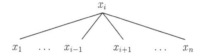

Consider the discrete random structure $\mathcal{A}_n$, with underlying set $\{x_1, \ldots, x_n\}$. For $i \in \{1, \ldots, n\}$, $\mathcal{A}_n[i]$ is defined to be the random structure for which the partial order has a Hasse diagram consisting of the pairs $\{(x_j, x_i)|\, j \in \{1, \ldots, n\}, j \neq i\}$, as displayed above. Moreover, we define the following isolated subsets on the partial order of $\mathcal{A}_n[i]$: for each data-labeling F of $\mathcal{A}_n[i]$: $I_1 = \{x_1, \ldots, x_{i-1}\}$ and $I_2 = \{x_{i+1}, \ldots, x_n\}$.

Whenever X stores a data-labeling F in the pseudo-code below, X_1 stores the restriction of the data-labeling F to I_1 and X_2 stores the restriction of the data-labeling F to I_2.

We present the recursive pseudo-code for the generation of Treaps via Treap-gen.

Treap-gen$[\mathrm{X}\colon \varDelta]$
$[\texttt{Treap-gen}(\mathrm{X}) = [\texttt{Top}(\mathrm{X})]; \texttt{Treap-gen}(\mathrm{X}_1); \texttt{Treap-gen}(\mathrm{X}_2)]$

Remark 8.3. We remark that $Treap\text{-}Gen$ produces a random bag, where each random structure has multiplicity one and forms a collection of treaps over a fixed tree. $Treap\text{-}Gen$ determines a bijection from $\mathcal{A}_n$ to $\mathcal{TREAP}(n)$.

Example 8.3. We illustrate the effect of Treap-gen on two states from $\mathcal{A}_3$ over the label set $\{1, 2, 3\}$.

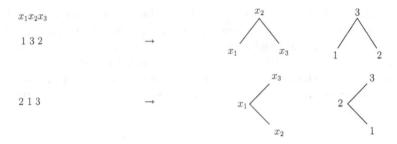

Remark 8.4. It is easy to verify that the Treaps created by Treap-gen from the discrete random structure $\mathcal{A}_n$ satisfy, as required, that the ordering is consistent with the orientation (cf. Definition 8.3).

8.7 Treapsort

Treapsort is a new sorting algorithm which creates Heap Ordered Treaps (Treaps) via the Treap-gen algorithm and systematically uses the root label, i.e. the largest label in the treap, to form a sorted list. In this sense it is similar in spirit to Heapsort variants. Treapsort differs however from traditional Heapsort variants in that its worst-case time, like Quicksort, is $O(n^2)$ while its average-case time is $O(nlogn)$.

Pseudo-code for Treapsort on $\mathcal{TREAP}(n)$:

Treapsort$[X : \Delta]$
$[\texttt{Treap-gen(X)}]$;
$[\texttt{Treapsort(X)} = \underline{\texttt{Perc}}^M(\texttt{X}); \texttt{Treapsort}(\underline{\texttt{X}})]$.

8.8 Quickselect

Finally, we present an example of a search algorithm, Quickselect, which finds the k-th smallest (alternatively the k-th largest) element in a given list. Quickselect is defined by product recursion in $\mathcal{MOQA}$, case II), involving a second-order conditional.

This example will be revisited in Chapter 10 as an illustration of an application of the static average-case timing tool *Distri-Track*. Moreover, an analysis is provided comparing the theoretical prediction of the average-case time obtained for Quickselect by *Distri-Track* with the average-case analysis obtained in the context of the RTSJ through profiling and sample input spaces.

Using the notation for product recursion (Section 7.9), we remark that program P in product recursion corresponds in this case to the *Split* operation, where we select the first element $X[1]$ of X as pivot.

Following the notation of product recursion, we consider variables Y_1, Y_2, Y_3 where for all $j \in \{1, 2, 3\}$ we have $[Y_j : \{I_j^1, \ldots, I_j^n\}]$. Here, following similar notation as for the case of the Quicksort algorithm, Y_1 corresponds to the lower part of the star shaped partial orders $P[i, j]$ and Y_3 corresponds to their upper part, while Y_2 refers to the strictly isolated subset consisting of the middle element.

For $j \in \{1, 2, 3\}$, let $p_j^i = |I_j^i|$. Note that $p_2^i = 1$ and $\forall i \in \{1, \ldots, n\}. p_1^i = n - i$ and $p_3^i = i - 1$.

We provide the pseudo-code for Quickselect via product recursion, case II), i.e. relying on the selection procedure. Note that Quickselect on the base case of size one is the identity function.

Qselect[X: $\Delta, \underline{k}$]
Split$_1$(X,X);
If $|Y_1| \geq \underline{k}$ **then** Qselect($Y_1, \underline{k}$)
    else if $|Y_1| = \underline{k} - \underline{1}$ **then** Qselect($Y_2, \underline{1}$)
        else Qselect($Y_3, \underline{k} - |Y_1| - \underline{1}$)

Chapter 9
Average-Case Analysis of $\mathcal{MOQA}$ programs

We illustrate in this section the determination, in a compositional way, of the average-case time of some $\mathcal{MOQA}$ programs. The examples focus on sorting and search algorithms. Note that some of the resulting average-case times will differ slightly from those presented in the literature. For instance for the case of Insertionsort, some additional comparisons are counted due to the definition of the $\mathcal{MOQA}$ product operation which includes an outer while loop, involving a single comparison. In traditional Insertionsort, a single insertion process is called, based on a Push-Down operation of the i-th label of a list into a priorly sorted list of size $i - 1$. No extra comparison is made to determine whether this process needs to be repeated. Due to the generality of the product operation, included in the pseudo-code of the Insertionsort algorithm presented below, an additional comparison will be made. This could be avoided via fine-tuning of the $\mathcal{MOQA}$ product operation adapted to this special case, which can be done without losing RB-preservation. However, rather than adapting $\mathcal{MOQA}$ operations to specific algorithms, it is acceptable to have a slight increase in running time, using the standard $\mathcal{MOQA}$ operations, since slight time increases are in general accepted to facilitate static timing.

9.1 Insertionsort

We recall the $\mathcal{MOQA}$ code for Insertionsort.

Insertionsort$[\mathrm{X} : \Delta]$
```
Z: = X[1]
for i = 2 to |X| do Z: = Z ⊗ X[i]
```

We let $J(i)$ denote the body $\mathrm{Z} : \; = \mathrm{Z} \bigotimes \mathrm{X}[\mathrm{i}]$ of the for-loop, for $i \in \{2, \ldots, |X|\}$.

The program Insertionsort, which we will denote by I, has an average-case time which by Linear Compositionality (Theorem 7.8 13)) reduces for a given size n to:

$$\overline{T}_I(\mathcal{A}_n) = \sum_{i=2}^{n} \overline{T}_{J(i)}(J^{i-1}(\mathcal{A}_n)),$$

where $J^0(\mathcal{A}_n) = \mathcal{A}_n$ and $\forall i \geq 2.\, J^{i-1} = J(i); \ldots; J(2)$.

Let $|X| = n$, $[X : (U, \Delta)]$, $U = \{u_{j_1}, \ldots, u_{j_n}\}$ and $U_i = \{u_{j_1}, \ldots, u_{j_i}\}$.

Let $\tau_1 = (U, \Delta_n)$, and thus $\mathcal{R}(\tau_1) = \mathcal{A}_n$, and let τ_i for $i \geq 2$ denote the partial order on U consisting of the linear order (U_i, Υ_i) and the discrete order $(U - U_i, \Delta_{n-i})$. Hence $\forall i \geq 2.\, J(i): \tau_{i-1} \to \tau_i$ and $J(i)(\mathcal{R}(\tau_{i-1})) = (\mathcal{R}(\tau_i), K_i)$ where K_i is the multiplicity corresponding to the random product as defined in Theorem 5.2[1]:

$$\overline{T}_I(\mathcal{R}(\tau_1)) = \sum_{i=2}^{n} \overline{T}_{J(i)}(\mathcal{R}(\tau_i), K_i).$$

By Theorem 1.3 2), the multiplicity K_i can be eliminated for the average time for a random bag of size one:

$$(1)\overline{T}_I\,(\mathcal{R}(\tau_1)) = \sum_{i=2}^{n} \overline{T}_{J(i)}\,(\mathcal{R}(\tau_i))$$

But now, $\overline{T}_{J(i)}\,(\mathcal{R}(\tau_i))$ can be evaluated using the formula derived in 6.2 for the average running time of a product. The average time for the product operation $A \otimes B$ is

$$\frac{|A||B|}{|A| + |B|}\,(\tau_{down}(A) + \tau_{up}(B)) + \left(\frac{|A||B|}{|A| + |B|} + 1\right)(|A_{max}| + |B_{min}| - 1).$$

In this context, A is a linear order of size $i - 1$, and B is a singleton element. Inserting the trivial values for B, and the values for A derived in 6.4.2.1, we get

$$\overline{T}_{J(i)}\,(\mathcal{R}(\tau_i)) = \left(\frac{(i-1).1}{(i-1)+1}\right)\tau(\mathcal{L}(i-1)) + \left(\frac{(i-1).1}{(i-1)+1} + 1\right)$$

$$= \left(\frac{i-1}{i}\right)\left(\frac{i}{2} - \frac{1}{i-1}\right) + \frac{i-1}{i} + 1$$

$$= \frac{i+3}{2} - \frac{i}{2}.$$

Inserting this into (1) above, we get the average running time for Insertionsort:

$$\overline{T}_I(n) = \overline{T}_I(\mathcal{R}(\tau_1)) = \sum_{i=2}^{n} \left[\frac{i+3}{2} - \frac{i}{2}\right] = \frac{n^2 + 7n - 8H_n}{4},$$

and hence the algorithm has $O(n^2)$ average-case time as expected.

---

[1] For the sake of completeness we remark that: $K_i = \binom{(i-2)+1}{1} = i - 1$.

9.2 Mergesort

We leave the analysis of the Merge algorithm as an exercise (cf. also Exercise 6.1).

We recall the $\mathcal{MOQA}$ pseudo-code for Mergesort by parallel recursion. We use the following notation for the type Δ: if Δ has underlying set $U = \{x_{i_1}, \ldots, x_{i_n}\}$ then Δ_1 indicates the discrete order with underlying set $U_1 = \{x_{i_1}, \ldots, x_{i_{\lfloor \frac{n}{2} \rfloor}}\}$ and Δ_2 indicates the discrete order with underlying set $U_2 = U - U_1$. In the following pseudo-code we consider three variables, $[Y_1 : \Delta_1]$, $[Y_2 : \Delta_2]$ and $[Y : (U_1, \Upsilon) \cup (U_2, \Upsilon)]$.

MS[x: Δ]
[MS(X) = Merge(MS(Y₁); MS(Y₂))].

By Theorem 7.8 2) and 7), the average time of Mergesort is given by:

$\overline{T}_{MS}(\mathcal{A}_n) = \overline{T}_{MS}(\mathcal{A}_{\lfloor \frac{n}{2} \rfloor}) + \overline{T}_{MS}(\mathcal{A}_{n-\lfloor \frac{n}{2} \rfloor+1}) + \overline{T}_{Merge}(R(\sigma_n))$, where we recall that σ_n consists of two components, i.e. two linearly ordered sets of size $\lfloor \frac{n}{2} \rfloor$ and $n - \lfloor \frac{n}{2} \rfloor + 1$ respectively. When formulated in terms of sizes, this amounts to the standard Mergesort recurrence which can be solved in the classical way:

$$\overline{T}_{MS}(n) = \overline{T}_{MS}(\lfloor \frac{n}{2} \rfloor) + \overline{T}_{MS}(n - \lfloor \frac{n}{2} \rfloor + 1) + \overline{T}_{Merge}(\lfloor \frac{n}{2} \rfloor, n - \lfloor \frac{n}{2} \rfloor + 1).$$

9.3 Quicksort

We recall the pseudo-code by product recursion for Quicksort in $\mathcal{MOQA}$:

Qsort[x: Δ]
Qsort(X) = Split₁(X, X); Qsort(Y₁); Qsort(Y₃)

We recall that, by Lemma 1.2, *Split* determines a random bag preserving function, where

$$Split: \mathcal{A}_n \longmapsto \{(R(P[0, n-1]), K_{n-1}), \ldots, (R(P[n-1, 0]), K_0)\},$$

and where $K_i = \binom{n-1}{i}$ for $i \in \{0, \ldots, n-1\}$. By Theorem 7.8 8), we obtain the equality (*):

$$\overline{T}_{Qsort}(\mathcal{A}_n) = \overline{T}_{\mathbf{Split}_1(X,X)}(\mathcal{A}_n) +$$

$$\overline{T}_{Qsort}(\{(\mathcal{A}_0, K_1 \times L_1^1), \ldots, (\mathcal{A}_{n-1}, K_n \times L_n^1)\}) +$$

$$\overline{T}_{Qsort}(\{(\mathcal{A}_{n-1}, K_1 \times L_1^3), \ldots, (\mathcal{A}_0, K_n \times L_n^3)\}).$$

Where in the notation of Theorem 7.8 8), we note that: $L_i^j = \Pi_{k \neq j} s_i(k)$ and thus: $L_i^1 = (n-i)!$ and $L_i^3 = (i-1)!$

Note that since $\mathcal{A}_0$ corresponds to the random structure over the empty set, the average-time of $Qsort$ in that case is zero and the terms over $\mathcal{A}_0$ can be dropped.

We recall that $\overline{T}_{\mathbf{Split}_1(X,X)}(\mathcal{A}_n) = |X| - 1 = n - 1$. Theorem 7.8 3) then yields:

$$\overline{T}_{Qsort}(\mathcal{A}_n) = n - 1 + \sum_{i=1}^{n-1} \alpha_i^3 \overline{T}_{Qsort}(\mathcal{A}_{i-1}) + \sum_{i=1}^{n-1} \alpha_i^1 \overline{T}_{Qsort}(\mathcal{A}_{n-i}),$$

where

$$\alpha_i^1 = \frac{K_i \times L_i^1 \times |\mathcal{A}_{n-i}|}{\sum_{i=1}^{n} K_i \times L_i^3 \times |\mathcal{A}_{n-i}|} = \frac{K_i \times |R(P[i-1, n-1])|}{\sum_{i=1}^{n} K_i \times |R(P[i-1, n-1])|} = \frac{1}{n}.$$

The last equality is obtained from the fact that the split operation is uniformly RB-preserving, with as fixed partition size $(n-1)!$ (cf. Remark 1.5 and Definition 4.10). Similarly, we obtain that $\alpha_i^3 = \frac{1}{n}$. Hence the standard recurrence equation for Quicksort is obtained, i.e.

$$\overline{T}_{Qsort}(n) = n - 1 + \frac{1}{n}\sum_{i=1}^{n-1} \overline{T}_{Qsort}(n-i) + \frac{1}{n}\sum_{i=1}^{n-1} \overline{T}_{Qsort}(i-1),$$

which can be solved in the usual way [FV90], where the solution is $\overline{T}_Q(n) = 2(n+1)H_n - 4n$, where $H(n) = \sum_{i=1}^{n} \frac{1}{i}$. It is well-known that $H(n) \approx ln(n) + \gamma + \frac{1}{2n} - \frac{1}{12n^2} + O(n^{-4})$ where $\gamma = 0.577216\ldots$ is Euler's constant. Hence $\overline{T}_Q(n) \approx 2(n+1)ln(n) + (2\gamma - 4)n + (1 + 2\gamma) + \frac{5}{6n} - \frac{1}{6n^2}O(n^{-3})$ or $\overline{T}_Q(n) \in O(nln(n))$.

Note that we stayed close in spirit to an automated derivation of the average-case time of this algorithm, but could have simplified the argument by observing that $L_i^1 = L_{n-i+1}^3$, which allows for a simplification of (*) to:

$$\overline{T}_{Qsort}(\mathcal{A}_n) = \overline{T}_{\mathbf{Split}_1(X,X)}(\mathcal{A}_n) +$$

$$2\overline{T}_{Qsort}(\{(\mathcal{A}_0, K_1 \times L_1^1), \ldots, (\mathcal{A}_{n-1}, K_n \times L_n^1)\}).$$

And hence the familiar simplified recurrence is obtained:

$$\overline{T}_{Qsort}(n) = n - 1 + \frac{2}{n}\sum_{i=1}^{n-1} \overline{T}_{Qsort}(n-i).$$

9.4 Percolating Heapsort

We carry out an analysis of the average time of Percolating Heapsort.

Remark 9.1. We recall (cf. Remark 5.4) that we interpreted a node with a single child as a node with two children, where the artificially introduced node is the empty tree. In that case a comparison will be carried out leading to a swap with the correct label, i.e. the label for the non-empty node.

In analysing Percolating Heapsort, it suffices to focus on heaps of size $2^k - 1$, where k is a natural number such that $k \geq 1$. This is standard practice in algorithmic analysis. For a formal justification of this approach we refer the reader to [Lev03].

By Theorem 1.3 we can express the recurrence for Percolating Heapsort's comparison time as follows:

$$\overline{T}_{PH}(\mathcal{A}_n) = \overline{T}_H(\mathcal{A}_n) + \overline{T}_P(\mathcal{H}_n).$$

The average time required for the heapification procedure, implemented in the standard way [AHU87], is of course well-known (e.g. [Knu73],[Weg90] or [Ede96]). For the sake of completeness, we recall (cf. [Ede96]) that for $\alpha_i = \sum_{j=1}^{\infty} \frac{1}{2^{j-1}}$ and $\beta = \sum_{k=2}^{\infty} \frac{1}{2^k(2^k-1)}$, the average comparison time for Williams' version of the Push-Down operation [LV93]is: $(\alpha_1 + \alpha_2 - 2)n + O(logn)$, while the average comparison time for Floyd's bottom up version of the Push-Down operation [LV93] is: $(\frac{9}{2} - \alpha_1 - \alpha_2 - \beta)n + O(logn)$.

We recall the $\mathcal{MOQA}$ pseudo-code for the heapification procedure.

Heapify[X: Δ]
for j $:= \lfloor \frac{|X|}{2} \rfloor$ **downto** $\underline{1}$ **do** $X[j] := (X[\underline{2}j], X[\underline{2}j+1]) \bigotimes X[j]$

We leave the analysis of the $\mathcal{MOQA}$ code for the Heapification case as an exercise. The reader may wish to compare this with the average-case time of the traditional implementation.

We recall the pseudo-code for Percolating Heapsort.

PH[X : Δ]
Heapify(X);
PH(X) = $\underline{Perc}^M$(X); PH($\underline{X}$)

In order to determine the average-time for the percolation phase we will carry out a backwards analysis a la Knuth. This should be contrasted with the situation of the Selection phase for traditional Heapsort, which, due to its non-randomness preservation, does not allow for a backward analysis. Hence the analysis we provide below constitutes progress on the state of the art in Algorithmic Analysis, since as pointed out earlier, the exact average-case analysis of all Heapsort variants remained unknown.

One should take into account in this context that the analysis we provide below can not be automated at this stage. Indeed, the analysis will proceed via a backwards argument, without explicitly setting up the recurrence equation for the average-case time of the algorithm. This is due to the fact that the recursive call on the percolation operation $\underline{Perc}^M$ does not proceed from the collection of Heaps of size n to the collection of heaps of size $n - 1$. Instead, a sub collection of the Heap-Ordered Trees of size $n - 1$ is created.

The algorithm Treapsort, which will be discussed next, as well as the other algorithms outlined in this chapter, do allow for an automated average-case analysis. Note that Treapsort operates over Treaps of size n, which are reduced to Treaps of size $n - 1$, which enables the derivation of the recurrence equation. As we will see, Treapsort does not share Heapsort's typical $O(nlogn)$ average and worst-case time behaviour. Instead, while it has $O(nlogn)$ average time, the worst-case time is $O(n^2)$. Hence it remains an interesting problem to determine a Heapsort variant which shares the typical $O(nlogn)$ average-case and worst-case time of Heapsort and which allows for a fully automated derivation of the average-case time. The algorithm Percolating Heapsort however has excellent average-case time behaviour, which can be derived via a formal analysis, as discussed below.

We recall that the $\mathcal{MOQA}$-deletion is a bijective operation as discussed in Theorem 5.4. Similarly, the percolation operation $\underline{Perc}^M$ establishes a one to one correspondence between inputs and outputs since the computation chains leading from an input to an output are unique. In fact one can reverse both versions of the Push-Down operation via a corresponding "Push-Up" operation. Hence we can "run" Percolate "backwards" starting with all possible outputs; that is the set $\mathcal{H}_n$ of all heaps of size n. We note that at each stage of the reverse unwinding of the Deletion operation, i.e. for i ranging from 1 to n, the i-th largest element is percolated upwards in all heaps of $\mathcal{H}_n$ until it reaches the top.

Viewed over all heaps of $\mathcal{H}_n$, we can see that the comparison time of Percolate is exactly the number of comparisons made in pushing up each individual element of *each individual* heap to the top; in other words the lengths of the chains leading from the root to each node of the heap. Hence the number of a comparisons for Percolate is *constant* per heap. This follows from remark 9.1 above. In fact the constant is exactly the total number of internal path lengths, i.e. the sum of the path-lengths from the root to each node in the tree. It is easy to compute this constant via the formula below. This is verified by induction, e.g. [Par95]:

$$\sum_{i=1}^{k-1} i2^i = (k-1)2^{k+1} - k2^k + 2.$$

Since the comparison time of Percolate is a constant value for all heaps of size $n = 2^k - 1$, we immediately obtain that:

$$\overline{T}_{\underline{\text{Perc}}M}(\mathcal{H}_n) = \sum_{i=1}^{k-1} i2^i.$$

We compute the outcome:

$$\sum_{i=1}^{k-1} i2^i = (k-1)2^{k+1} - k2^k + 2 = k2^k - 2^{k+1} + 2$$

$$= k(2^k - 1) + k - 2^{k+1} + 2 = kn + k - 2(n+1) + 2$$

$$= (k-2)n + k.$$

Remark 9.2. It is easy to verify that the number of swaps coincides with the number of comparisons.

The reader may contrast this with the traditional version of Williams' Push-Down nor Floyd's pushdown [LV93], which would could take as much as twice the number of comparisons (for Williams' version). Percolation is still cheaper than Floyd's version since we proceed from the root to a leaf, carrying out single comparison (at most) per step. Floyd's version would need to proceed from the leaf upwards again to reach the correct position to insert the element involved in the Push-Down. Hence Percolation is faster than the traditional Push-Down versions. This is supported by a more detailed analysis of the various versions of Heapsort made in [SHB04], where it is experimentally shown that Percolating Heapsort is up to 17% faster on average than Floyd's traditional Heapsort version.

So in order to determine the average comparison time for Percolating Heapsort, it suffices to determine $\overline{T}_{\underline{\text{Perc}}M}(n)$. From the above calculations and the fact that the comparison time needed by P is constant over all heaps of size $n = 2^k - 1$, it follows that $\overline{T}_P(n) = (k-2)n + k$. Since $k = \lceil log_2 n \rceil$, we obtain that: $\overline{T}_P(n) = (\lceil log_2 n \rceil - 2)n + \lceil log_2 n \rceil$.

Hence the average time of Percolating Heapsort has been precisely determined, including the constant factors for the terms $n\lceil log_2 n \rceil$ as well as for the linear terms. This may be contrasted with prior average-case analysis of Heapsort, for which the constant factors for the linear terms remain unknown.

Performance of the algorithm

The average-case analysis of Heapsort has been discussed in [SS93] where it was shown that Heapsort's average time, $\overline{T}_H$ satisfies the following bound: $nlgn - nlglgn - 4n \leq \overline{T}_H(n)$. In [LV93] it is shown that the average comparison time of Heapsort, for Williams' and Floyd's version respectively, is given by: $2nlogn - O(n)$ and $nlogn + O(n)$, where the exact value for the linear terms is unknown. As pointed out, experiments made in [SHB04] indicate that in practice Percolating Heapsort beats Floyd's version of standard Heapsort. Since the constants involved for Floyd's version are not known, experimentation is the only way to obtain a sound comparison. We have shown that the same constants are involved for Percolating Heapsort as for Floyd's version of standard Heapsort and have carried out an analysis of the exact comparison time for the selection phase. We obtain in particular that Percolating Heapsort, with the standard Heapify algorithm, beats clever Quicksort in average comparison time, for large values of n (cf. [Weg90]).

9.5 Treap-gen

We recall the pseudo-code for Treap-gen:

Treap-gen[X: Δ]
[Treap-gen(X) = [Top(X)]; Treap-gen(X₁); Treap-gen(X₂)]

The following result is immediate since Top carries out $n-1$ comparisons on any data-labeling with a state from $\mathcal{A}_n$ in order to determine the maximum label.

Lemma 9.1. $\overline{T}_{Top}(\mathcal{A}_n) = n - 1$.

We remark that Treap-gen is defined via a generalized form of product recursion discussed in Remark 7.8. We compute the multiplicities involved in this generalized approach.

Since Top is RB-preserving we obtain, using the notation of Section 8.6.3:

$$Top: \mathcal{A}_n \longmapsto \{(\mathcal{A}_n[1], 1), \ldots, (\mathcal{A}_n[n], 1)\}.$$

We recall from Section 8.6.3 that the variables X_1 and X_2 store restrictions of data-labelings with states from $\mathcal{A}_i[n]$ to the isolated subset $I_1 = \{x_1, \ldots, x_{i-1}\}$ and the isolated subset $I_2 = \{x_{i+1}, \ldots, x_n\}$.

This leads to multiple copies of the random structures $\mathcal{A}_{i-1}$ and $\mathcal{A}_{n-i}$, where we denote these numbers by K_{i-1} and K_{n-i} respectively. We determine K_{i-1} where the determination of K_{n-i} is similar. The multiplicity K_{i-1} is obtained by observing that the restriction to I_1 will single out the first $i-1$ elements of the partial order underlying $\mathcal{A}_n[i]$. The label for the i-th element of this partial order is the maximum label. Hence the labels for the remaining $n-1$ elements of the partial order are obtained by the $(n-1)!$ possible permutations of the remaining labels, i.e. the labels excluding the largest one. Note that when we restrict these states to the first $i-1$ elements of the partial order, there are $\binom{n-1}{i-1}$ choices for a fixed set of labels of cardinality $i-1$. Moreover, each of the states of the first $i-1$ elements obtained in this way, will occur $(n-i)!$ times, i.e. once for each state of the remaining $n-i$ elements of the partial order. Hence $K_{i-1} = \binom{n-1}{i-1} \times (n-i)! = \binom{n-1}{i-1} \times (n-(i-1)-1)!$

Hence an application similar to the one of Theorem 7.8 8) yields:

$$\overline{T}_{Treap\text{-}gen}(\mathcal{A}_n) = \overline{T}_{Top}(n) + \overline{T}_{Treap\text{-}gen}(\{(\mathcal{A}_0, K_0), \ldots, (\mathcal{A}_{n-1}, K_{n-1})\})$$

$$+\overline{T}_{Treap\text{-}gen}(\{(\mathcal{A}_{n-1}, K_{n-1}), \ldots, (\mathcal{A}_0, K_0)\}).$$

Via Lemma 9.1 and Theorem 1.3 we obtain:

$$\overline{T}_{Treap\text{-}gen}(\mathcal{A}_n) = (n-1) + 2 \sum_{i=0}^{n-1} \alpha_i \times \overline{T}_{Treap\text{-}gen}(\mathcal{A}_i),$$

where $\forall i \in \{0, \ldots, n-1\}. \alpha_i = \frac{K_i \times |\mathcal{A}_i|}{|\mathcal{A}_n|}$. Note that $K_i = \binom{n-1}{i} \times (n-i-1)! = \frac{|\mathcal{A}_n|}{n \times |\mathcal{A}_i|}$. Hence $\forall i \in \{0, \ldots, n-1\}. \alpha_i = \frac{1}{n}^2$ and thus, replacing the random structures $\mathcal{A}_i$ by their size i:

$$\overline{T}_{Treap\text{-}gen}(n) = (n-1) + \frac{2}{n} \times \sum_{i=0}^{n-1} \overline{T}_{Treap\text{-}gen}(i).$$

This recurrence equation happens to be identical to the recurrence equation expressing the comparison time for Quicksort and can be solved via traditional means. We sketch the approach: we let $g(n) = \overline{T}_{Treap\text{-}gen}(n)$. Then:

$$g(n) = (n-1) + \frac{2}{n} \sum_{i=0}^{n-1} g(i).$$

To solve this recurrence, one can show that $ng(n) - (n+1)g(n-1) = 2(n-1)$ and, dividing by $n(n+1)$ yields:

$$\frac{g(n)}{n+1} - \frac{g(n-1)}{n} = \frac{2(n-1)}{n(n+1)}.$$

Finally, let $\Psi(n) = \frac{g(n)}{n+1}$. Then

$$\Psi(n) = \Psi(n-1) + \frac{2n-2}{n(n+1)}$$

and thus $\Psi(n) = \sum_{i=1}^{n} \frac{2i-2}{i(i+1)} \approx \sum_{i=1}^{n} \frac{2}{i} \approx 2 \ln n^3$ Hence $g(n) \approx 2(\ln n)(n+1)$, i.e.

$$(*) \quad \overline{T}_{Treap\text{-}gen}(n) \approx 2(n+1)\ln(n).$$

9.6 Treapsort

Pseudo-code for Treapsort on $\mathcal{TREAP}(n)$, where $F \in \mathcal{A}_n$:

---

[2] Which, following Section 5.8, could be obtained through a uniform RB-preservation argument for the special case of the Top operation over the discrete random structure $\mathcal{A}_n$.

[3] Where we use the harmonic numbers approximation: $\sum_{i=1}^{} n\frac{1}{i} \approx \ln n$.

Treapsort$[X : \Delta]$
$[\texttt{Treap-gen(X)}]$;
$[\texttt{Treapsort(X)} = \underline{\texttt{Perc}}^{M}(\texttt{X}); \texttt{Treapsort}(\underline{\texttt{X}})]$.

In the following we let $(\underline{\texttt{Perc}}^{M})^{n}$ denote the n-fold composition of the $\underline{\texttt{Perc}}^{M}$ operation with itself, i.e. $(\underline{\texttt{Perc}}^{M})^{n} = \underline{\texttt{Perc}}^{M} \circ \ldots \circ \underline{\texttt{Perc}}^{M}$, with $\underline{\texttt{Perc}}^{M}$ repeated n times in case $n \geq 1$. In case $n = 0$ we let $(\underline{\texttt{Perc}}^{M})^{0}$ be the identify function on data-labelings.

From the pseudo-code of Treapsort, Remark 8.3, approximation $(*)$ above and the Linear-Compositionality Theorem one obtains:

$$\overline{T}_{Treap\text{-}sort}(\mathcal{A}_n) = \overline{T}_{Treap\text{-}gen}(\mathcal{A}_n) + \sum_{i=1}^{n} \overline{T}_{\underline{\texttt{Perc}}^{M}}((\underline{\texttt{Perc}}^{M})^{i-1}(\mathcal{TREAP}(n))$$

$$\approx 2(n+1)ln(n) + \sum_{i=1}^{n} \overline{T}_{\underline{\texttt{Perc}}^{M}}((\underline{\texttt{Perc}}^{M})^{i-1}(\mathcal{TREAP}(n))$$

Applying Proposition 8.2 we obtain:

$$\sum_{i=1}^{n} \overline{T}_{\underline{\texttt{Perc}}^{M}}((\underline{\texttt{Perc}}^{M})^{i-1}(\mathcal{TREAP}(n)) =$$

$$\overline{T}_{\underline{\texttt{Perc}}^{M}}(\mathcal{TREAP}(n)) + \sum_{i=2}^{n} \overline{T}_{\underline{\texttt{Perc}}^{M}}((\underline{\texttt{Perc}}^{M})^{i-1}((\mathcal{TREAP}(n-1), n))$$

Repeated application of Proposition 8.2 yields:

$$(\underline{\texttt{Perc}}^{M})^{i-1}((\mathcal{TREAP}(n-1), n)) =$$
$$(\underline{\texttt{Perc}}^{M})^{(i-1)-1}(\underline{\texttt{Perc}}^{M}((\mathcal{TREAP}(n-1), n))) =$$
$$(\underline{\texttt{Perc}}^{M})^{(i-1)-2}((\mathcal{TREAP}(n-2), n(n-1))) =$$
$$(\underline{\texttt{Perc}}^{M})^{(i-1)-3}((\mathcal{TREAP}(n-3), n(n-1)(n-2))) = \ldots$$
$$(\underline{\texttt{Perc}}^{M})^{(i-1)-(i-2)}((\mathcal{TREAP}(n-(i-2)), n(n-1)\ldots(n-(i-3)))) =$$
$$\underline{\texttt{Perc}}^{M}((\mathcal{TREAP}(n-(i-2)), n(n-1)\ldots(n-(i-3)))) =$$
$$(\mathcal{TREAP}(n-(i-1)), n(n-1)\ldots(n-(i-2))) =$$
$$(\mathcal{TREAP}(n-(i-1)), \frac{n!}{(n-(i-1))!})$$

Note $\overline{T}_{\underline{\texttt{Perc}}^{M}}(\mathcal{TREAP}(n)) = \overline{T}_{\underline{Del}^{M}}(n, \mathcal{TREAP}(n))$ where we delete the n-th smallest label, i.e. the largest label, of the label set $\mathcal{L}$ for $\mathcal{TREAP}(n)$, since $\underline{\texttt{Perc}}^{M}$ acts similarly to $\underline{Del}^{M}$ when taking into account the comparisons carried out by both operations. Hence:

$$\overline{T}_{Treap\text{-}sort}(n) = 2(n+1)ln(n) + \overline{T}_{\underline{Del}^M}(n, \mathcal{TREAP}(n)) +$$

$$\sum_{i=2}^{n} \overline{T}_{\underline{Del}^M}(n-(i-1), ((\mathcal{TREAP}(n-(i-1)), \tfrac{n!}{(n-i)!}))).$$

However, by Theorem 1.3:

$$\overline{T}_{Treap\text{-}sort}(n) = 2(n+1)ln(n) + \overline{T}_{\underline{Del}^M}(n, \mathcal{TREAP}(n)) +$$

$$\sum_{i=2}^{n} \overline{T}_{\underline{Del}^M}(n-(i-1), (\mathcal{TREAP}(n-(i-1))))$$

Conclusion:

$$\overline{T}_{Treap\text{-}sort}(n) = 2(n+1)ln(n) + \sum_{i=1}^{n} \overline{T}_{\underline{Del}^M}(i, \mathcal{TREAP}(i)).$$

We show the following result below: $\overline{T}_{\underline{Del}^M}(n, \mathcal{TREAP}(n)) \in O(ln(n))$. Hence we conclude that $\overline{T}_{Treap\text{-}sort}(n) \in O(nln(n))$.

9.6.0.1 Average-Case Analysis of $\underline{Del}^M$ on $\mathcal{TREAP}(n)$ It remains to determine the actual average time of the $\underline{Del}^M$ operation on Heap-Ordered Treaps of a given size where the deletion is carried out on the largest label a placed at the root note of the Treap.

We recall that the average-case time for the basic $\mathcal{MOQA}$ operations on SP-orders has been analyzed in Chapter 6. Here we apply these formulas to analyze the average-case time of the delete operation for the particular case of Treaps, where we show that this operation, as one would hope, runs in logarithmic time.

Proposition 9.1. $\overline{T}_{\underline{Del}^M}(n, \mathcal{TREAP}(n)) \in O(ln(n))$.

Proof. Since Treaps form an inductively defined data type, preserved under the $\underline{Del}^M$ operation (cf. Proposition 8.1), the analysis is quite straightforward.

We consider the set of trees $\mathcal{TREAP}(n)$, where $n \geq 2$ and where we pruned as usual all branches leading from an internal node directly to a leaf labeled with $\emptyset$. The set of all trees from $\mathcal{TREAP}(n)$ with a left subtree of size i, where $i \in \{0, \dots, n-1\}$, is denoted by $\mathcal{TREAP}(n)[i]$. Also, the set of all binary trees of size n is denoted by $T(n)$.

By uniqueness of treaps, Section 2.3, it is clear that $|\mathcal{TREAP}(n)| = n!$ Moreover, a formula similar to the one for computing the number of heaps given in Section 2.3, yields that for $i \in \{0, \dots, n-1\}$,

$$|\mathcal{TREAP}(n)[i]| = \binom{n-1}{i} \times |\mathcal{TREAP}(i)||\mathcal{TREAP}(n-1-i)|$$

$$= \binom{n-1}{i} i!(n-1-i)!$$

Hence the probability of encountering a Treap of size n with a left sub tree of size i, and thus with a right sub tree of size $n-1-i$, is $\frac{|\mathcal{TREAP}(n)[i]|}{|\mathcal{TREAP}(n)|} = \frac{\binom{n-1}{i}i!(n-1-i)!}{n!} = \frac{1}{n}$.

Now, the average time taken to delete a label from a maximal node in a structure A all the way to the bottom is simply $\Delta(A, |A|)$, as defined in 6.3.1. In the following, whenever A and B are partial orders, $\mathcal{A}$ and $\mathcal{B}$ are the respective associated random structures.

We use the following notation: $i^* = n - i - 1$, so that the left subtree of size i corresponds to the right subtree of size i^*.

$$\overline{T}_{\underline{Del}}^{M}(\mathcal{TREAP}(n)) = \frac{1}{n}\sum_{i=0}^{n-1}\overline{T}_{\underline{Del}^M}(\mathcal{TREAP}(n)[i])$$

$$\overline{T}_{\underline{Del}^M}(\mathcal{TREAP}(n)[i]) = \frac{\sum_{A\in T(i)}\sum_{B\in T(i^*)}|A||B|\Delta(\bullet \otimes (A\|B), |A| + |B| + 1)}{\sum_{A\in T(i)}\sum_{B\in T(i^*)}|A||B|}$$

Here, the weighting is necessary because we want an average over all data-labelings, whilst Δ is a function of the underlying partial orders, not all of which have the same number of data-labelings. But now, the denominator can be simplified as $(\sum_{A\in T(i)}|A|)(\sum_{B\in T(i^*)}|B|) = |\mathcal{TREAP}(i)||\mathcal{TREAP}(i^*)| = i!(i^*)!$, and we can apply the series-parallel formulae for Δ^4 to the numerator to get

$$\frac{1}{i!(i^*)!}\sum_{A\in T(i)}\sum_{B\in T(i^*)}\left[|A||B|\left(|A||B_{max}| - 1 + \frac{|A|\Delta(A, |A|) + |B|\Delta(B, |B|)}{|A| + |B|}\right)\right],$$

where we have dropped the $\Delta(\bullet, 1) = 0$ term. Now, $|A| = i$, $|B| = i^*$ and $|A||B_{max}| = |A_{max}| + |B_{max}|$. Each of A and B will have exactly one maximal element unless they are empty orders (since they are both trees), so we have $|A||B_{max}| = 2 - \delta_{i,0} - \delta_{i^*,0}$, where $\delta_{m,n}$ is the Kronecker delta function, whose value is one when its arguments are equal and zero otherwise. Inserting all of these, and separating the A and B dependent terms in the sum, we get

$$1 - \delta_{i,0} - \delta_{i^*,0} + \frac{i}{n-1}\sum_{A\in T(i)}\frac{|A|\Delta(A, |A|)}{i!} + \frac{i^*}{n-1}\sum_{B\in T(i^*)}\frac{|B|\Delta(B, |B|)}{(i^*)!}$$

$$= 1 - \delta_{i,0} - \delta_{i^*,0} + \frac{i}{n-1}\overline{T}_{\underline{Del}^M}(\mathcal{TREAP}(i)) + \frac{i^*}{n-1}\overline{T}_{\underline{Del}^M}(\mathcal{TREAP}(i^*)),$$

---

[4] In the special case of deleting the largest label, the series parallel composition rules for Δ can be simplified to $\Delta(A\otimes B, |A|+|B|) = \Delta(A, |A|) + \Delta(B, |B|) + |A_{max}| - 1$ and $\Delta(A\|B, |A| + |B|) = \frac{|A|\Delta(A,|A|)+|B|\Delta(B,|B|)}{|A|+|B|}$ respectively.

since $\overline{T}_{DelM}(\mathcal{TREAP}(i)) = \dfrac{\sum_{A \in T(i)} |A| \Delta(A, |A|)}{\sum_{A \in T(i)} |A|} = \dfrac{\sum_{A \in T(i)} |A| \Delta(A, |A|)}{i!}.$

Inserting this back into the equation for $\overline{T}_{DelM}(\mathcal{TREAP}(n))$, we get (writing $h(n) = \overline{T}_{DelM}(\mathcal{TREAP}(n))$ for concision)

$$h(n) = 1 - \frac{2}{n} + \frac{1}{n(n-1)} \left(\sum_{i=0}^{n-1} ih(i) + \sum_{i=0}^{n-1} i^* h(i^*) \right) = 1 - \frac{2}{n} + \frac{2}{n(n-1)} \sum_{i=0}^{n-1} ih(i).$$

Rearranging, we get

$$n(n-1)h(n) - (n-1)(n-2) = 2\sum_{i=0}^{n-1} ih(i) = 2(n-1)h(n-1) + \sum_{i=0}^{n-2} ih(i).$$

But now,

$$\sum_{i=0}^{n-2} ih(i) = (n-1)(n-2)h(n-1) - (n-2)(n-3).$$

Inserting this and simplifying, we get

$$n(n-1)h(n) - (n-1)(n-2) = n(n-1)h(n-1) - (n-2)(n-3),$$

or

$$h(n) = h(n-1) + \frac{2n-4}{n(n-1)} = h(n-1) + \frac{4}{n} - \frac{2}{n-1}.$$

Developing this sum, and using the fact that $h(1) = 0$, we get

$$h(n) = 2\sum_{i=1}^{n} \frac{1}{i} - 4 + \frac{2}{n} = 2H_n - 4 + \frac{2}{n},$$

where H_n is the n-th Harmonic number. Hence $\overline{T}_{DelM}(\mathcal{TREAP}(n)) \in O(ln(n))$.

Remark 9.3. The formulae used to evaluate this time do not take into account the convention, mentioned above, that where one of the sub-trees is empty, one comparison is still assumed to be made in order to discover this. In order to correct for this, we would have to remove the two Kronecker delta functions (which each remove one comparison for the cases when each subtree is empty). If we then continue the analysis as before, we end up with

$$h(n) = h(n-1) + \frac{2}{n} = 2H_n - 2.$$

So the difference in running time between following the convention and not is $2 - \frac{2}{n} = O(1)$, which is clearly dominated by the order of growth of H_n.

9.7 Quickselect

We recall the pseudo-code and continue to use the notation of Section 8.8. The definition by product recursion, Case II), relying on a second-order conditional, for Quicksort in $\mathcal{MOQA}$ is the following:

Qselect[X: $\Delta, \underline{k}$]
Split$_1$(X,X);
If $|Y_1| \geq \underline{k}$ **then** Qselect(Y$_1, \underline{k}$)
    else if $|Y_1| = \underline{k} - \underline{1}$ **then** Qselect(Y$_2, \underline{1}$)
        else Qselect(Y$_3, \underline{k} - |Y_1| - \underline{1}$)

Here, the Split operation takes a pivot, and sorts the nodes in X into three categories: the pivot becomes Y_2, whilst those nodes with labels greater than the pivot become Y_3, and those with labels less than the pivot become Y_1. We assume that, when called on a list of length one, Qselect returns with no comparisons.

The average running time of Qselect on a discrete random structure of size n, where we seek the kth element is denoted by $\overline{T}_{Qselect}(n, k)$. We also let $H_n = \sum_{i=1}^{n} \frac{1}{i}$ be the nth harmonic number.

We show that

$$\overline{T}_{Qselect}(n, k) = n + \frac{k}{n} + \frac{1}{n}\left(\sum_{1 \leq j < k} \overline{T}_{Qselect}(n - j, k - j) + \sum_{k \leq j < n} \overline{T}_{Qselect}(j, k)\right).$$

We know that the initial Split will take $n - 1$ comparisons on a list of length n, and for each integer $j \in [0, n - 1]$, there is a $\frac{1}{n}$ chance that we will have $|Y_1| = j$ (since the operation is uniformly random bag preserving).

Now, let B_1 be the part of the pseudo-code starting from the first Boolean ($|Y_1| \geq \underline{k}$) and B_2 be the part starting from the second Boolean ($|Y_1| = \underline{k} - \underline{1}$). Also, let p_1 be the probability that the first Boolean is true, and p_2 be the probability that the second Boolean evaluates as true (given that it is called). We can apply Theorem 7.8 (4) to B_1 and B_2 to get

$$\overline{T}_{B_1} = 1 + p_1 \overline{T}_{Qselect}(|Y_1|, k) + (1 - p_1)\overline{T}_{B_2},$$

$$\overline{T}_{B_2} = 1 + p_2 \overline{T}_{Qselect}(|Y_2|, 1) + (1 - p_2)\overline{T}_{Qselect}(n - |Y_1| - 1, k - |Y_1| - 1).$$

Now, since Split is uniformly random bag preserving, it is easy to see that $p_1 = Prob(|Y_1| \geq \underline{k}) = \frac{n-k}{n}$, and hence $1 - p_1 = \frac{k}{n}$.

We can evaluate p_2 in a similar manner as a conditional probability:

$$p_2 = Prob(|Y_1| = \underline{k} - \underline{1}| |Y_1| \geq \underline{k}) = \frac{1}{k},$$

and hence $1 - p_2 = \frac{k-1}{k}$. So, if we let $j = |Y_1|$, we have

$$\overline{T}_{B_1} = 1 + \frac{k}{n} + \frac{n-k}{n}\overline{T}_{Qselect}(j,k) + \frac{k}{n}\cdot\frac{k-1}{k}\overline{T}_{Qselect}(n-j-1,k-j-1).$$

So, to get the overall average running time, we simply need to add on the $n-1$ comparisons from Split and express the values of $\overline{T}_{Qselect}(n,k)$ as averages over all possible cases:

$$\overline{T}_{Qselect}(n,k) =$$

$$n + \frac{k}{n} + \frac{n-k}{n}\left(\frac{\sum_{j=k}^{n-1}\overline{T}_{Qselect}(j,k)}{n-k}\right) + \frac{k-1}{n}\left(\frac{\sum_{j=0}^{k-2}\overline{T}_{Qselect}(n-j-1,k-j-1)}{k-1}\right).$$

Changing the index of summation on the second sum, this tidies up to the desired result:

$$\overline{T}_{Qselect}(n,k) = n + \frac{k}{n} + \frac{1}{n}\left(\sum_{k\le j<n}\overline{T}_{Qselect}(j,k) + \sum_{1\le j<k}\overline{T}_{Qselect}(n-j,k-j)\right).$$

Applying standard techniques from [Knu71], yields:

$$\overline{T}_{Qselect}(n,k) = n + \frac{k}{n} + \frac{1}{n}\left(\sum_{1\le j<k}\overline{T}_{Qselect}(n-j,k-j) + \sum_{k\le j<n}\overline{T}_{Qselect}(j,k)\right).$$

Contrast this to the result obtained in [Knu71] for a similar recurrence: if we have $\overline{T}'(1,1) = 0$ and

$$\overline{T}'(n,k) = n - 1 + \frac{1}{n}\left(\sum_{1\le j<k}\overline{T}'(n-j,k-j) + \sum_{k\le j<n}\overline{T}'(j,k)\right),$$

then we get

$$\overline{T}'(n,k) = 2n + 6 + 2(n+1)H_n - 2(k+2)H_k - (2n+6-2k)H_{n+1-k}.$$

(This is the recurrence which we would obtain for Qselect if we did not count the comparisons made in evaluating the two booleans).

The difference between the two is

$$\Delta(n,k) = \overline{T}_{Qselect}(n,k) - \overline{T}'(n,k) = 2H_k + H_{n+1-k} - 3.$$

It is known that the average running time of Quickselect (without counting the comparisons in the booleans, and over all values of k for a give value of n) is $O(n)$. Now, it is easy to derive directly from this that the same result holds for this variant, since

$$\Delta(n,k) \in O\left(\ln k + \ln(n+1-k)\right) \subseteq O\left(\ln n\right),$$

and so the order of growth of the difference between the two is dominated by the linear order of growth of the average running time.

Chapter 10
Distri-Track
Joint with D. Hickey and M. Boubekeur

The objective of the software tool *Distri-Track* is to automate the derivation of the average-case execution time (ACET) of $\mathcal{MOQA}$ programs. It is required to follow exactly the rules as set out in $\mathcal{MOQA}$ theory. It is also an evaluation of $\mathcal{MOQA}$ in that it explores how the language can be used in practice. In this chapter an overview of the design of *Distri-Track* is given and some preliminary evaluation results are reported.

A complete overview of *Distri-Track* and the $\mathcal{MOQA}$ language specifications in Java would exceed the scope of the current book. The overview sketched below is given to provide the main ideas underlying the approach to the implementation of the timing tool *Distri-Track*. $\mathcal{MOQA}$ code is provided on occasion as well as code used in the context of *Distri-Track*. Again, this is only for illustration purposes, without providing in every case full details on the codes meaning.

10.1 Analysable Code

Distri-Track analyses $\mathcal{MOQA}$[1] algorithms programmed in Java. The analysable code must obey the $\mathcal{MOQA}$ rules, as outlined in Chapters 5 and 7. This allows *Distri-Track* to accurately track data structures and generate ACET values.

As an example of such code and to aid our discussion in the remainder of this chapter, Listing 10.1 gives a simple example of $\mathcal{MOQA}$ code that implements the *Quickselect* algorithm. Quickselect is one of the simplest and most efficient algorithms in practice for finding specified order statistics (i.e. the k-th smallest/biggest element) in a given sequence. It was invented by Hoare [Hoa61] and uses the usual partitioning procedure of Quicksort: first choose a partitioning key, say x; regroup the given sequence into two parts corresponding to elements whose values are less than and greater than x, respectively; then decide, according to the size of the smaller part, which part to continue recursively on, or to stop if x is the desired order statistics.

---

[1] Beta Version 3.0 developed by J. Townley.

```
1   public class QuickselectTest {
2
3       @TimeDependsOn({0,1})
4       public <L extends Comparable,C> NodeInfo<L,C> method(
5           OrderedCollection<L,C> lpo, int k) {
6         return quickselect(lpo, k);
7       }
8
9       @TimeDependsOn({0, 1})
10      @Transform(param=0, rep=IDTBuild.DR, name="QSel")
11      private <L extends Comparable,C> NodeInfo<L,C> quickselect(
12          OrderedCollection<L,C> lpo, int k) {
13        NodeInfo<L,C> pivot = lpo.getDirectNodeInfoIter().next();
14        OrderedCollection<L,C> partition = lpo.split(pivot);
15        Iterator<OrderedCollectionSubset<L,C>> aboveAndBelow =
16            partition.getDirectSubsetIter();
17
18        OrderedCollectionSubset<L,C> top = aboveAndBelow.next();
19        OrderedCollectionSubset<L,C> bot = aboveAndBelow.next();
20
21        int bs = bot.size();
22        NodeInfo<L,C> result;
23
24        if (bs == k - 1)
25          result = partitionNI;
26        else if (bs >= k)
27          result = quickselect(bot, k);
28        else
29          result = quickselect(top, k - bs - 1);
30
31        return result;
32      }
33  }
```

Listing 10.1 Quickselect in $\mathcal{MOQA}$.

All $\mathcal{MOQA}$ *variables*, represented by OrderedCollection, Ordered-CollectionSubset and NodeInfo types in this code, are tracked by *Distri-Track* as random bags.

If the user chooses to begin the analysis at method, *Distri-Track* assumes the input parameter lpo, which is a $\mathcal{MOQA}$ variable with type OrderedCollection, is a random bag with a single random structure represented as a discrete partial order, i.e. an unsorted list, and assigns it a size, say n. For demonstration purposes n has a value of 4, in which case lpo will be as shown in Figure 10.1.

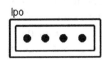

Fig. 10.1 The random bag for the variable lpo containing an discrete random structure.

The parameter k, which is the order of the element being searched for, is also assigned a value. Both lpo and k are passed to the method quickselect. Line 13 in the code stores a single node from lpo's discrete order and this is used in $\mathcal{MOQA}$'s split operation, the result of which is shown in Figure 10.2. We remark that `pivot` becomes the single node in the middle level with all nodes above having greater labels, which are referenced by `top` in Line 18, and all nodes below having lesser labels, which are referenced by `bot` in Line 19. The conditions in the `if` statements, which depend on the value of `k`, then determine if the algorithm recurses on `top` or `bot` or terminates with the desired result, i.e. the node containing the k-th smallest (in this case) label.

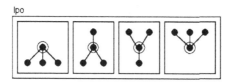

Fig. 10.2 The random bag for the variable `lpo` after `split`. The node associated with the variable `pivot` is circled in each random structure.

Note that when we depict the random bags and their random structures, the data-labelings are not shown. *Distri-Track* bases its analysis on the fact that a random structure will form all possible states, where we recall that the number of states can be derived directly from the underlying partial orders. In fact at no stage of the analysis does *Distri-Track* consider label values.

In the Quickselect code there are annotations attached to each of the methods. These are used to guide the analysis performed by *Distri-Track*. In the sections that follow, the function of these particular annotations will become clear.

10.2 *Distri-Track* Architecture

Figure 10.3 gives an overview of the design of *Distri-Track*.

10.2.1 Pre-Analysis

The $\mathcal{MOQA}$ code is pre-processed using a Java optimisation tool called Soot [Soo]. This transforms the Java code into an intermediate representation called *Jimple* which is a 3-address stackless language with 15 statements. Its features facilitate an analysis such as that performed by *Distri-Track*. Soot also builds a *call graph*, which reflects the invocations of methods, for the application being analysed and *control flow graphs* for each method. Figure 10.4 shows the control flow graph (CFG) for the body of `method` (left) and `quickselect` (right). As usual, the nodes in the CFG represent the *basic blocks* of code in a program that do not contain any *jump* statements. The edges correspond to jumps caused by Jimple statements such as `if` and `goto`. In the code for the method `quickselect` there are six blocks, approximately

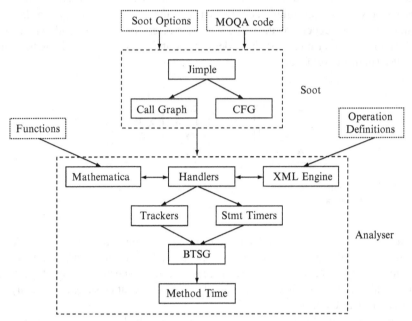

Fig. 10.3 *Distri-Track* architecture.

corresponding to the following - $B0$: Lines 13 to 24, $B1$: Line 25, $B2$: Line 26, $B3$: Line 27, $B4$: Line 29 and $B5$: Line 31.

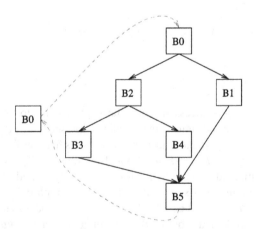

Fig. 10.4 CFG for method (left) and quickselect (right). The broken lines represent the edges of the call graph caused by Line 6.

10.2.2 The Analyser

The analyser traverses the call graph and CFGs to derive the ACET equations for the code. Its main processing engine incorporates *Handlers* which deal with the different Jimple statements and expressions which can be encountered in the nodes of the CFGs. Each handler contains a method called `handle` which takes a Jimple statement as input. *Trackers* track information on variable values, e.g. random bags, and other important aspects of the program, e.g. the number of times a loop will iterate. The `handle` method either creates new trackers or transforms a set of existing trackers according to the behaviour of the Jimple code.

When the handler for invoke expressions identifies a $\mathcal{MOQA}$ operation, the XML engine obtains a definition of the operation's behaviour. A simplified example of the XML definition of $\mathcal{MOQA}$'s `product` operation is shown in Listing 10.2. As can be seen, each input is assigned an *alias* which is used in processing the output, time, etc. The XML schema allows quite a lot of flexibility in the operation definitions. For example there can be overloaded definitions for the same operation name. Analogous to the way overloaded methods/functions are handled in programming languages, *Distri-Track* uses inputs to determine the appropriate definition. In the output definition of the product operation it can be seen how a random bag and its random structures are represented. Along with each random structure a multiplicity function can also be provided if the multiplicity is greater than 1. The final XML tag supplies the operation's ACET function. Currently *Distri-Track* incorporates definitions for all the $\mathcal{MOQA}$ operations. However it is likely that in the future other operations will be developed and their XML definitions can be included. This is why XML is used rather than hard coding the behaviour of the operations into *Distri-Track*'s Java code.

```
1   <operation>
2     <name>product</name>
3     <inputs>
4       <input>
5         <type> ... </type>
6         <alias>$a_3</alias>
7       </input>
8       <input>
9         <type> ... </type>
10        <alias>$a_4</alias>
11      </input>
12    </inputs>
13    <output>
14      <return>
15        <rb>
16          <rsrep>
17            <structure>
18              <series>
19                <component>$a_3</component>
20                <component>$a_4</component>
21              </series>
22            </structure>
23            <multiplicity>
24              <function>productMultiplicity</function>
25              <applyTo> ... </applyTo>
26            </multiplicity>
27          </rsrep>
28        </rb>
```

```
29        </return>
30      </output>
31      <time>
32        <function>productTime</function>
33        <applyTo>  ...  </applyTo>
34      </time>
35    </operation>
```

Listing 10.2 Product XML definition.

As the handlers manipulate trackers, they also interact with the Mathematica kernel [Mat] through J/Link [JLi] where necessary. As mentioned in the description of the XML definition of the product operation multiplicity and ACET functions are specified. These are found in a Mathematica package. Another package contains all the formulas used in calculating the ACETs over the series-parallel structures, as introduced in Chapter 6.

Behind the analysis a Branched Time State Graph (BTSG) is built for each method from its CFG. Like the CFG, the BTSG is a directed graph. Each path in a BTSG corresponds to one branch of execution in a method and must have its own set of trackers. A branch splits into two branches when a branching statement such as an if statement is encountered. Unlike a CFG however, paths do not merge. Attached to each statement is the set of branches which it affects. When a statement is being handled, the trackers which it modifies must be updated in each one of those branches. For example take Line 31 of the code in Listing 10.1. The return statement has three predecessors as can be seen in the CFG in Figure 10.4. The statement therefore has the union of its predecessor's branches associated with it. A graphical representation of the BTSG of the example code is shown in Figure 10.5.

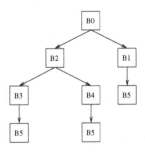

Fig. 10.5 BTSG for quickselect method.

Inevitably *Distri-Track* is affected by the state explosion that is a common problem in the static analysis of branching code. To offset this somewhat, *Distri-Track* efficiently manages how trackers for the different branches are stored in memory. For example after a path branches in the BTSG, only trackers for variables that are modified are copied into each of the new branches. However it is still possible that very large programs may become untraceable because of excessively large BTSGs.

Other information that needs to be tracked with each branch includes the condition that led to the branch, the probability of it executing (if possible to calculate) and the summation of the ACET of each of the statements in the branch reflecting the compositionality of $\mathcal{MOQA}$ programs.

Along with the control statements shown above *Distri-Track* can also handle `for` loops. `while` loops however are not supported because of the difficulty involved in potential non-termination and in determining the number of iterations in case of termination.

10.3 Random Bag Trackers

The most important tracker in *Distri-Track* tracks the random bags associated with $\mathcal{MOQA}$ variables. In this section an overview of the challenges involved in representing random bags and their random structures is presented.

It is assumed that all data structures in $\mathcal{MOQA}$ are series-parallel partial orders as discussed in Section 5.10. As shown in Listing 10.2 the output from a `product` operation produces a random bag with one random structure with two components in series. This gives a basic view of how *Distri-Track* represents structures: it lists the components and their relationship, i.e. series or parallel. With components allowed to be nested structure definitions, we get an inductive way of representing SP-structures and this means any random structure can be tracked.

10.3.1 Condensed Representations

Distri-Track represents the collection of random structures in a random bag in a much more concise way than specified in the theory. Firstly, as already noted, *Distri-Track* does not explicitly track data-labelings. Secondly, the fact that $\mathcal{MOQA}$ operations are only executed on isolated subsets is exploited to reduce the amount of repetition in the structure representations. Take the random bag in Figure 10.6a for example.

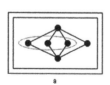 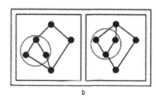

Fig. 10.6 a is the random bag before an operation on the circled isolated subset. b is the is the random bag after the operation.

Some operation on the circled isolated subset could give the random bag with two random structures in Figure 10.6b. In $\mathcal{MOQA}$ theory this is the usual way of depicting the output of an operation. However to store multiple structure representations for entire random structures after an operation in *Distri-Track* would be wasteful given that operations may only modify sub-structures. An example of the structure representation, called a *condensed representation*, *Distri-Track* uses to overcome this problem is shown in Figure 10.7. This greatly reduces the overhead on the trackers and simplifies the analysis.

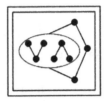

Fig. 10.7 *Distri-Track*'s condensed representation of random structures.

10.3.2 Collective Representations

The main issue representing random bags occurs when the number of random structures in a random bag is a function of a variable size, n. This in fact prevents a distinct representation of each random structure. Therefore a way to collectively represent the random structures is required. There are a number of methods of doing this. Two are discussed here.

Firstly, the output from $\mathcal{MOQA}$'s split operation needs such a *collective representation* when the atomic order it is executed on has variable size. This is achieved by specifying the number of times a structure occurs over a range of values. This generally leads to summations in the ACET functions output from *Distri-Track*. Figure 10.8 encapsulates the way in which this kind of structure is represented.

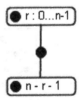

Fig. 10.8 *Distri-Track*'s collective representation of random structures using size ranges.

The top level equates to a discrete structure of size r, where r can range from 0 to $n - 1$. The bottom level is similar except its size will range from $n - 1$ to 0. This will work for example in defining the random bag in Figure 10.2 where $n = 4$.

Secondly, recursive algorithms can also produce random bags where distinct representations are not possible. In this case the idea of *inductively defined types* (IDT) is employed to alleviate the problem.

IDTs can be defined using a set of base cases and constructors. For example a list of integers is defined as follows:

$$< list - of - integers >::= ()|(< integer > . < list - of - integers >)$$

This defines a list of integers as being empty (base case) or an integer combined with a list of integers (constructor).

In $\mathcal{MOQA}$ the constructors are used to give an implicit representation of the random structures in a random bag and allow recurrence equations to be derived for the ACET based on the series-parallel formulas of Chapter 6. For example if the random bag contained Heap-Ordered Trees (HOTs) the following constructor would provide the necessary information:

$$< HOT >::= \phi| < x > \otimes(< HOT > || < HOT >)$$

This defines a HOT as being empty or a single node x in series with two HOTs in parallel. If the random bag contains all possible HOTs of size n then the size of the left and right HOT can be treated in a similar fashion to the value ranges discussed for the output from split.

For the Quickselect example shown in Listing 10.1 the annotation @Transform, used in line 10, instructs *Distri-Track* to generate an IDT definition called *QSel* to represent all possible outputs from the quickselect method. This process is completely automated and allows further operations on the output of Quickselect to be timed. *Distri-Track* outputs the IDT definitions it generates. Listing 10.3 shows the IDT definition generated for QSel.

```
1   IDT: QSel
2   ─────────
3   condition: Equal[r0,Plus[n2,Times[−1,n3]]]; case:
4     Group(series):
5       Group(parallel):
6         −
7           repeated Plus[n2,Times[−1,n3]]
8         −
9       Group(parallel):
10        −
11          repeated Plus[−1,n2,Times[−1,Plus[n2,Times[−1,n3]]]]
12  ─────────
13  condition: And[LessEqual[r0,Plus[−1,n2,Times[−1,n3]]],
14          Unequal[r0,Plus[n2,Times[−1,n3]]]]; case:
15    Group(series):
16      Group(parallel):
17        −
18          repeated r0, start: 0, end: Plus[−1,n2,Times[−1,n3]]
19        −
20      QSel[Plus[−1,n2,Times[−1,r0]]]
21  ─────────
22  condition: And[Greater[r0,Plus[−1,n2,Times[−1,n3]]],
23          Unequal[r0,Plus[n2,Times[−1,n3]]]]; case:
24    Group(series):
25      QSel[r0]
26      −
27      Group(parallel):
28        −
29          repeated Plus[−1,n2,Times[−1,r0]]
30  ─────────
```

Listing 10.3 Quickselect IDT definitions.

We do not give all the details of the definition here. The base case, as represented by the first case in the IDT definition, is the output of a single application of the `split` operation. This occurs when the k-th smallest label is found. Each of the remaining two cases correspond to one of the recursive calls being executed on the bottom or top levels of the output of `split`.

10.4 Calculating the ACET

When an operation is encountered *Distri-Track* retrieves the random bag trackers for the variables involved. Based on these it can calculate an ACET for the operation. First it calculates the ACETs for the operation on each random structure. It does this by processing the structure representations in the random bag tracker and then applying the series-parallel ACET formulas of Chapter 6. Also each random structure has a probability calculated as specified in Theorem 1.3 of Chapter 7. To do this *Distri-Track* uses the multiplicities which are attached to random structures as shown in Listing 10.2 and calculates the number of states based again on series-parallel functions. With this information the ACET for an operation on a random bag can then be obtained.

As each branch in the BTSG is analysed the ACET for the branch is stored adhering to the compositionality property of $\mathcal{MOQA}$. To obtain the ACET for the execution of a method there are two possibilities. If probabilities can be calculated for the conditions in the branching statements then the ACET for the method is the sum of the branch ACETs multiplied by their probabilities. There are a number of conditions which can have their probabilities calculated based on rules specified in $\mathcal{MOQA}$ theory as specified in Chapter 7. If probabilities cannot be calculated then the ACET for the method will be broken into cases depending on the branching statement conditions.

Recurrence equations for the ACETs are passed to Mathematica's `RSolve` function in an attempt to obtain a closed form. Taking the Quickselect code in Listing 10.1 and assigning size $n2$ to `lpo` and the value $n3$ to `k`, an ACET equation like the following is obtained:

$$qs[n2, n3] = (n2 - 1) + \frac{1}{n2} \sum_{r0=0}^{n2-n3} qs[n2 - r0 - 1, n3] +$$

$$\frac{1}{n2} \sum_{r0=n2-n3+1}^{n2-1} qs[r0, n3 - n2 + r0] \quad (10.1)$$

We remark that the recurrence matches the standard Quickselect recurrence. We recall that $n2 - 1$ is the ACET for split. The ACET for both recursive calls is multiplied by $\frac{1}{n2}$. This value represents the result of multiplying together the probabilities for the conditions with the probabilities for the random structures. Based on the condition bs >= k, $qs[n3...n2 - 1, n3]$ represents all possible invocations of the first

recursive call which takes the bottom component of the star produced by the split
($n2 - 1$ being the maximum size of the top and the bottom component.) In the recurrence equation, applying the sum bounds $0...n2 - n3$, $qs[n2 - r0 - 1, n3]$ can be
viewed as $qs[n2 - 0 - 1...n2 - n2 + n3 - 1, n3] = qs[n2 - 1...n3, n3]$. A similar
argument can be applied to show that the ACET for the second recursive call is also
correct.

The actual Mathematica package for the recurrence is shown in Listing 10.4.

```
1   BeginPackage["dtExUnits'"]
2
3   quickselect::usage  =  ""
4   method::usage  =  ""
5
6   Begin["'Private'"]
7
8   quickselect[n2_,n3_]  :=  Plus[-1,n2,
9     Times[Plus[-1,n2],Power[n2,-1],
10    Plus[Times[Plus[1,Times[-1,Power[n2,-1],n3]],-1],
11      Sum[Times[Power[Plus[n2,Times[-1,n3]],-1],
12        quickselect[Plus[-1,n2,Times[-1,r0]],n3]],
13        {r0,0,Plus[n2,Times[-1,n3]]}]],
14    Times[Power[n2,-1],n3,
15      Sum[Times[Power[n3,-1],
16        quickselect[r0,Plus[Times[-1,n2],n3,r0]]],
17        {r0,Plus[n2,Times[-1,n3],1],Plus[-1,n2]}]]]]];
18
19  method[n0_]  :=  quickselect[n0,n1];
20
21  End[]
22  EndPackage[];
```

Listing 10.4 Quickselect ACET Mathematica package.

10.5 Preliminary Evaluation Study

In this section we present a preliminary evaluation study of the RT-$\mathcal{MOQA}$ theoretical results for average-case timing by an experimental analysis of Quickselect.
We give a description of how the evaluation study is performed and we conclude by
giving the results.

10.5.1 Real-Time $\mathcal{MOQA}$

We incorporate the theoretical research in terms of modular quantitative analysis,
in particular timing analysis, into an RT environment by implementing $\mathcal{MOQA}$ as
an API in RT Java (RTJ) provided by Sun Microsystems. We call this RT-$\mathcal{MOQA}$.
RTJ is an implementation of the RTSJ [RTS] and is designed to allow programmers
to engineer large scale real-time systems in a modern, type-safe programming environment. Features such as memory safety, checked exceptions, and a rigorously
specified memory model, make Java a good programming language for developing

mission critical applications. In spite of these benefits, predictable ACET analysis tools are not available in RTJ.

We based the implementation of RT-$\mathcal{MOQA}$ on the original version of $\mathcal{MOQA}$ [TMS06]. As $\mathcal{MOQA}$ is implemented in Java 5 a number of changes had to be made. Features such as variable arguments and the use of generics are not supported in RTJ which is based on Java 1.4. Therefore these cannot be used in RT-$\mathcal{MOQA}$ programs.

The advantage of implementing RT-$\mathcal{MOQA}$ as an API is that we are not creating a new language. Programmers in general and in particular those in the real-time area are reluctant to add a new language to the large number that already exist. Also in RT-$\mathcal{MOQA}$ code all the features of RTJ are allowed.

An obvious concern for meeting hard real-time constraints in Java is the interaction of automatic memory management with real-time tasks. The strategy used in memory is also a key point for efficiently predictable real-time programs. In RTJ there is a strict memory model which offers memory areas called scoped and immortal memory which are free of the unpredictability associated with garbage collection.

We note that $\mathcal{MOQA}$'s features impose limitations and rules on the programmer. These guarantee a program executes in a very predictable way. Statically it can be determined at every stage of the execution what state the program's data structures are in. In turn we can determine the exact ACET of each operation.

Along with $\mathcal{MOQA}$ features, the predictability in terms of worst-case and average-case time also needs good control of the language structures, for instance iterative control statements (loops and recursion) should be managed. This is common in many RT languages. *Distri-Track* ensures that rules for control statements are not violated.

10.5.2 Evaluation Study Description

The experiments are undertaken using the RTJ JVM on a Sunfire V240 running Solaris 10. We measure the average, worst and best-case execution times of the algorithm executed on a sample of 10,000 randomly generated lists. The experiments are undertaken with lists of varying sizes. We compare the resulting average-case times with the number of comparisons calculated from the recurrence equations obtained by the RT-$\mathcal{MOQA}$ analysis tool.

10.5.2.1 Input Samples Generation   The generation of the inputs is a key issue. Indeed the quality of the experimental average-case time results is highly dependant on the distribution of the input data. For our study we used Jakarta Commons Math [Jak07] which is a library of lightweight, self-contained mathematics and statistics components addressing the most common problems not available in the Java programming language.

In Figure 10.9 we can see the timing results of the execution of RT-$\mathcal{MOQA}$ Quickselect on a sample of 10,000 lists of size 2048[2]. Figure 10.9 clearly reflects

---

[2] In the experiments, sizes have been selected which are powers of two, $2^{11} = 2048$.

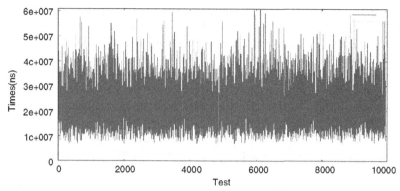

Fig. 10.9 Input data distribution

how well the sample input lists are distributed using the uniform random generation. We discuss the results for the Quickselect algorithm in the last section.

Since $\mathcal{MOQA}$ programs are RB-preserving, the ACET can be analysed in a modular manner. In such a situation, we can evaluate modular tasks separately within a program. Then combining the results we obtain the timing analysis of the entire program. In that case, the input could be different than a simple discrete list as in the Quickselect example. The samples need to be constructed with S-distributions, discussed in Chapter 1 in the context of random bags, and the output constraints of the previous modules. It is necessary for an efficient measurement based ACET analysis to have an automatic or semi-automatic method for the generation of well distributed random input samples. In the basic case, when the input is a simple discrete list, the probability to choose a list of n labels over a range of size m is

$$1/\binom{m}{n}.$$

We recall that a discrete list determines a single random structure with multiplicity 1 in $\mathcal{MOQA}$. In the general case however, where a module produces a random bag with more than one random structure with different multiplicities, the probability is more complex and depends on the shape of the random structure. The generation of such inputs and the calculation of the corresponding probabilities will be investigated for future experiments.

10.5.2.2 Measurements and Predictions   The recurrences representing the average number of comparisons executed in a program are generated using *Distri-Track*. The recurrence for quickselect is shown in Equation 10.1. In effect this corresponds to the average number of times the bodies of control statements are executed, i.e. *if* statements and loops. Of course this in general on its own will not give a sufficiently accurate running time. To achieve a more refined result, we need also to consider the number and nature of statements executed within each body. Therefore in order to effectively compare the experimentally derived results with those obtained using $\mathcal{MOQA}$ principles we use a *work-coefficient* in conjunction with the number of comparisons to reflect the amount of time to execute a body of code associated with a control statement.

Currently *Distri-Track* does not automatically generate information on the work-coefficient. However this capability will be added as the tool develops so that, for example, the average number of assignments per control-statement body will also be counted.

Here, for the purposes of the current experimental evaluation, we calculate the work-coefficient by taking the experimentally obtained ACET and dividing this by the average number of comparisons over many lists of different sizes. The final value of the coefficient is the average of the values obtained for each sample. For the algorithm discussed here this was not difficult given that there are not many control statements involved.

Then for an arbitrary list size we calculate the ACET of Quickselect in two ways:

- multiply the work-coefficient by the number of comparisons obtained by *Distri-Track*,
- experimentally obtain the ACET as explained above.

Comparing the consistency of these values for different list sizes validates the approach.

Note that this approach is similar to that taken in [Sar89] where ACET estimates are obtained through experimentation and control-flow analysis. Our method can yield more accuracy statically using the tight control offered by $\mathcal{MOQA}$.

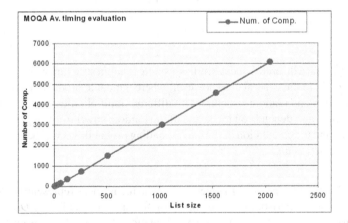

Fig. 10.10 RT-$\mathcal{MOQA}$ results in terms of number of comparisons

10.5.2.3 Results   Figure 10.10 shows the number of comparisons required by the Quickselect program corresponding to the size of each list as obtained by the

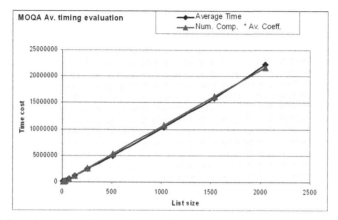

Fig. 10.11 Experimental results vs. RT-$\mathcal{MOQA}$ results

RT-$\mathcal{MOQA}$ tool. In Figure 10.11 the number of comparisons multiplied by the work-coefficient is plotted together with the experimentally obtained ACET.

The results of the evaluation study we have performed confirm the theoretical contributions of $\mathcal{MOQA}$. The graph shows that the results obtained by *Distri-Track* give good estimations of the actual ACET obtained experimentally. This can mainly be attributed to the exact ACET analysis achieved in $\mathcal{MOQA}$. Other contributing factors are the algorithm being comparison-based, the samples being well uniformly distributed and the RT-Java timing being very accurate.

Chapter 11
Conclusion and Future Work

Modular approaches to static analysis in general constitute a holy grail for Software Engineering. Approaches which allow one to exploit modularity for static timing are currently scarce and generally considered to be problematic. As pointed out in the preface to this work, a compositional calculus is needed to provide a foundation for modular static timing, the basis for which has been provided in the current work for the case of the average-case time measure.

The basic principles underlying the $\mathcal{MOQA}$ language have been outlined, providing a unified foundation for Average-Case Analysis. Our hope for this approach is that it will facilitate the discovery, design and analysis of new algorithms, the potential of which has been indicated to some extent in this work.

The unique features which ensure the modularity of $\mathcal{MOQA}$, include the use of random bag preservation and isolated subsets, where reliance on SP-orders greatly facilitates the average-case analysis. This framework may serve as a basis on which future modular static timing tools can be explored.

The formalization of randomness preservation, via the novel notion of a random bag, which was required to develop the modular approach, provides a foundation for the abstract study of randomness preservation in general.

An interesting problem which remains to be explored in this context is the classification of the random bag preserving functions computable via $\mathcal{MOQA}$ programs, as well as an investigation into $\mathcal{MOQA}$ extensions which might be complete, i.e. for which all random bag preserving functions are computable.

A related issue is the characterization of random bag preserving functions as formulated in the open problems in Chapter 4.

A functional language version of $\mathcal{MOQA}$ could be explored. Obviously, the language opens doors for a further exploration of semantic models which can incorporate complexity analysis. Existing models including those relying on monads, game theory and quantitative domains, as well as new models, could be explored in this context.

Further investigations are needed into relations with existing approaches to automated average-case analysis, such as the LUO language, to explore the use and incorporation of generating functions in the $\mathcal{MOQA}$ context. A somewhat related problem is to provide a characterization of recurrence equations obtained from $\mathcal{MOQA}$ programs.

The parallel aspect of $\mathcal{MOQA}$'s series-parallel data structures could be further exploited to include parallel constructs in the language. A case in point is the parallel recursion of the language, thus far incorporated in a sequential fashion. A similar approach could be explored for the product recursion.

The series-parallel nature of the $\mathcal{MOQA}$ data structures, typically a property arising at hardware level, raises the interesting question whether the underlying random bag preserving nature of $\mathcal{MOQA}$ can be consistently carried through from software to hardware level, to yield improved quantitative analysis of embedded systems.

Indeed, the effect of software on hardware is a crucial issue in the area of software/hardware co-design. This effect is currently quite elusive and clearly directly affects predictability of embedded systems, in particular regarding speed and power. The $\mathcal{MOQA}$ software enables the modular derivation of the average-case number of basic steps carried out during the execution of the program, which contributes useful information that can be related to speed and power use. Hence a consistent exploration of the $\mathcal{MOQA}$ approach in a software/hardware co-design context may open up new avenues for increased predictability.

In this context recent investigations, in collaboration with R. Agarwal and E. Popovici have yielded improved ways to estimate power by appropriate logic gate design, inspired by the approach to random bag preservation outlined in this work.

Moreover, links with cryptography have been obtained in a similar collaboration, which show that modulo operations can be interpreted as random bag preserving. Again, modulo operations are quite pervasive in Computer Science and Electrical Engineering and progress in this area has the potential to affect a variety of applications.

Obviously much work can be undertaken to expand the $\mathcal{MOQA}$ language further and investigate new applications. Some avenues being explored at CEOL are the potential extension of the data structures from partial orders to a more general graph based context and the potential inclusion of different basic operations and program constructs such as alternative approaches to conditionals and recursion.

Finally, we discuss some future work regarding the *Distri-Track* tool for the static average-case time analysis of $\mathcal{MOQA}$ programs. Constrained by the normal static analysis problems, *Distri-Track* manages to track $\mathcal{MOQA}$ data structures quite tightly allowing the ACET of the language operations to be calculated. To achieve this the system design is quite complex and a number of challenges in the representation of the random bags had to be tackled. The ultimate goal of this research is to produce a tool which can provide a programmer with accurate information on a $\mathcal{MOQA}$ program's ACET in order to complement WCET in scheduling tasks in a real-time system. In parallel with the development of $\mathcal{MOQA}$ there is also work being done on new ways of using ACET in this way [BHMS07a].

As $\mathcal{MOQA}$ develops further so must *Distri-Track*. More operations will be included and even new data structures which are more general than partial orders could be incorporated.

Currently *Distri-Track* relies on Mathematica's RSolve function to solve recurrence equations representing times, which, for very complicated recurrences, may not be sufficient. Other recurrence solving software could be used, e.g. PURRS: The Parma University's Recurrence Relation Solver [Pur], or recurrences could be solved using dynamic programming.

A technique developed in [BP02] overcomes the problems associated with analysing branched code, which could be explored in the $\mathcal{MOQA}$ context.

Following on from the evaluation study new measurement techniques will be incorporated in *Distri-Track* in order to bring the statically derived ACET results closer to the actual "real" average time values.

Appendix A
Appendix: Proof of the State Theorem

A.1 Depth-Levels

Given a finite partial order $(X, \sqsubseteq)$, then for any element $x \in X$, we define the *depth of x*, $depth(x)$, to be the number of elements strictly above x on a longest chain from x to a maximal element. Such a chain is referred to as a *maximal chain* from x to a maximal element.

Note that:
$$x \sqsubset y \Rightarrow depth(x) > depth(y)$$

Given a finite partial order $(X, \sqsubseteq)$, we let L denote the length of a longest chain in $(X, \sqsubseteq)$. Such a path of course connects a minimal to a maximal element. Let D denote the maximal possible depth of any element of $(X, \sqsubseteq)$, i.e. $D = L - 1$.

Given a state F of the partial order with range $\mathcal{L}$. For any label $a \in \mathcal{L}$, we define the depth of a, $depth(a) = depth(F^{-1}(a))$. Similarly, one can define the dual notion of height of an element and of a label.

We group the elements of X and their labels, for a given state F, by depth-level as follows: $\forall i: 0, 1, \ldots, D. \mathcal{D}_i^X = \{x \mid depth(x) = i\}$ and $\mathcal{D}_i^F = F(\mathcal{D}_i^X) = \{F(x) \mid x \in \mathcal{D}_i^X\}$. We refer to $\mathcal{D}_i^X$ as the *i-th depth-level* of the partial order $(X, \sqsubseteq)$ and to $\mathcal{D}_i^F$ as *the set of labels at depth i* for a state F.

It is easy to see that the collection of all depth levels $(\mathcal{D}_i^X)_{i \in \{0,1,\ldots,D\}}$ forms a partition of the set X. We denote the cardinality of each depth level $\mathcal{D}_i^X$ by d_i.

It is easy to see that in general $\mathcal{D}_0^X = M(X)$ and $\mathcal{D}_D^X \subseteq m(X)$.

Moreover, we use the following notation:

$$\mathcal{D}_{<i}^X = \cup_{0 \le j < i} \mathcal{D}_j^X \text{ and } \mathcal{D}_{>i}^X = \cup_{D \ge j > i} \mathcal{D}_j^X$$

$$\mathcal{D}_{\le i}^X = X - \mathcal{D}_{>i}^X \text{ and } \mathcal{D}_{\ge i}^X = X - \mathcal{D}_{<i}^X$$

We adopt the convention that $\mathcal{D}^X_{-1} = \emptyset$. This situation arises on occasion when $i = 0$ is chosen in $\mathcal{D}^X_{i-1}$. A similar convention is adopted for the other cases where the index is out of bounds, e.g. $\mathcal{D}^X_{<i} = \emptyset$ in case $i = 0$. Note that $\mathcal{D}^X_{<i} = \mathcal{D}^X_{\leq i-1}$ and $\mathcal{D}^X_{>i} = \mathcal{D}^X_{\geq i+1}$. We denote the cardinality of $\mathcal{D}^X_{<i}$ by $d_{<i}$ and similarly for the other cases. Clearly: $d_{<i} + d_{\geq i} = |X| = d_{\leq i} + d_{>i}$. For a state F of the partial order $(X, \sqsubseteq)$ we define: $\mathcal{D}^F_{<i} = F(\mathcal{D}^X_{<i})$ and similarly for the other cases.

Example A.1. We consider the labeled partial order represented by the Hasse diagram given below.

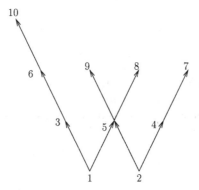

For the above state we obtain that $\mathcal{D}_0 = \{7, 8, 9, 10\}$, $\mathcal{D}_1 = \{4, 5, 6\}$, $\mathcal{D}_2 = \{2, 3\}$ and $\mathcal{D}_3 = \{1\}$.

We remark that a maximal chain from $(x_0, x_1, \ldots, x_n)$ from x_0 to x_n, where of course $depth(x_0) = n$, is such that for each $i \leq n$ we have that $(x_i, \ldots, x_n)$ from x_i to x_n is again a maximal chain. We remark that for $i < n$, $depth(x_{i+1}) = depth(x_i) - 1$. In particular $depth(x_i) = n - i$.

A.2 Canonical State

We define the important notion of a canonical state and will show the existence of canonical states among the states of a given random structure $\mathcal{R}_{\mathcal{L}}(X, \sqsubseteq)$.

Definition A.1. Given a state. A pair of labels a, b such that $b > a$ is called *depth-consistent* iff $depth(b) \leq depth(a)$. Otherwise the pair is *depth-inconsistent*. A state is *canonical* iff all its free pairs are depth-consistent.

We will provide alternative characterizations of canonical states. In order to achieve this, the technical notion of a segment and a segmented state is useful.

A segment is intuitively a depth-level for which labels have maximal possible value and, when ordered in decreasing order form a "consecutive list".

A *consecutive* subsequence of a decreasing sequence $(a_1, \ldots, a_n)$ is a subsequence of the form $(a_k, a_{k+1}, \ldots, a_{l-1}, a_l)$, where $1 \leq k \leq l \leq n$. A subsequence $(a_k, \ldots, a_l)$ which is not consecutive must have a *gap*, i.e. a pair (a_m, a_p) for which there is at least one element a_i which occurs strictly between a_m and a_p in the original sequence $(a_1, \ldots, a_n)$ but no elements occur strictly between a_m and a_p in the subsequence . The following sequences form consecutive sublists of the decreasing list $(22, 18, 7, 4, 2, 1)$: $(7, 4, 2)$, $(22, 18, 7, 4)$ and $(22, 18, 7, 4, 2, 1)$, while $(22, 7, 4)$ and $(22, 7, 4, 1)$ do not. We remark that $(22, 7, 4)$ has one gap, while $(22, 7, 4, 1)$ has two gaps.

Since the random structure $\mathcal{R}(X, \sqsubseteq)$ is an equivalence class (cf. Remark 4.3), we will simplify the presentation somewhat by focusing on states from the set of labels $\overline{n} = \{1, 2, 3, \ldots, n\}$. In this case a consecutive subsequence, when ordered in decreasing order, consists of a sequence of labels of the form: $k, k-1, k-2, \ldots, l, l-1$, while a gap consists simply of a pair of natural numbers for which the difference is greater than one.

For any sequence $A = (a_1, \ldots, a_n)$ and $0 \leq k \leq n$, we define the k-initial segment $A[k]$ to be the sequence $(a_1, \ldots, a_k)$ where, by convention, $A[0] = \emptyset$.

We recall that D is the maximal depth of the partial order under consideration. Given a state F then $\overline{\mathcal{D}}_i^F$ is defined to be $\mathcal{D}_i^F$ sorted in decreasing order. Then we define $\overline{\mathcal{D}}^F$ to be the sequence $Conc(\overline{\mathcal{D}}_0^F, \overline{\mathcal{D}}_1^F, \ldots, \overline{\mathcal{D}}_D^F)$. In other words the sequence $\overline{\mathcal{D}}^F$ is ordered as follows: $a \preceq_F b \iff (depth(a) = depth(b)$ and $a > b)$ or $depth(a) < depth(b)$.

We extend the order on pairs of labels by $(a, b) \preceq_F (c, d) \iff a \preceq_F c$ and $b \preceq_F d$.

Note that by the preceding notation $\overline{\mathcal{D}}^F[k]$ denotes the k-initial segment of $\overline{\mathcal{D}}^F$.

Definition A.2. Given a finite partial order $(X, \sqsubseteq)$, where say X has cardinality $n \geq 2$, $\mathcal{L} = \overline{n}$ and F is a state from $\mathcal{R}_{\mathcal{L}}(X, \sqsubseteq)$. For $k \in \{1, \ldots, n\}$, we say that F *induces a k-segment* if and only if $k = 1$ or $\overline{\mathcal{D}}^F[k] = (n, n-1, \ldots, n-k+1)$ for the case where $k \geq 2$.

When F induces a k-segment we define the *set* $\mathcal{R}_k^F$ to be the complement of the k-segment in $\overline{\mathcal{D}}^F$, i.e. $\mathcal{R}_k^F = \{1, \ldots, n-k\}$ when $1 \leq k \leq n-1$ and $\mathcal{R}_k^F = \emptyset$ in case $k = n$.

Remark A.1. If F induces a k-segment then F induces an l-segment for every $l \leq k$.

We introduce the following useful notion of the degree of segmentation.

Definition A.3. The *degree of segmentation* of F, $deg(F)$, is the maximum value k for which F induces a k-segment. We say that F is i-segmented in case $deg(F) \geq$

$\sum_{j \in \{0,1,\ldots,i\}} d_j$ and we say that F is *segmented* in case F is D-segmented, i.e. $deg(F) = n$ and $\overline{\mathcal{D}} = \{n, n-1, \ldots, 1\}$.

The element k referred to in the definition exists since F always induces a 1-segment.

Remark A.2. Let $deg(F) = k$ and let b be the $k+1$-th label of $\overline{\mathcal{D}}^F$. Of course there must be a gap between the k-th label and b and no prior gap occurs. Hence we refer to b as the label of F which *creates the first gap*. The element $a = n - k$ would be the $k+1$-th element in case we would have that $deg(F) = k+1$. Hence we refer to the element a as the *canonical replacement* of b. Note that $a > b$. If $depth(b) = i$ then it is clear that a must occur at a level j greater than i. Indeed, a can not belong to $\overline{\mathcal{D}}^F[k]$ and in particular $a \notin \overline{\mathcal{D}}^F[k] \cap \overline{\mathcal{D}}_i^F$. We note that a cannot occur at level i on the right of b in $\overline{\mathcal{D}}_i^F$ since we assume this list to be decreasing. Hence a does not belong to $\overline{\mathcal{D}}_i^F$ and thus a does not belong to $\mathcal{D}_i^F$.

Lemma A.1. *The following statements for a state F are equivalent:*

1) F is segmented
2) $\forall i: 0, 1, \ldots, D-1.\ \wedge \mathcal{D}_{\leq i}^F > \vee \mathcal{D}_{> i}^F$
3) $\forall i, j \in \{0, 1, \ldots, D-1\}.\ i < j \Rightarrow \wedge \mathcal{D}_i^F > \vee \mathcal{D}_j^F$

Proof. We verify the following sequence of results: $1 \Rightarrow 2$, $2 \Rightarrow 3$ and $3 \Rightarrow 1$.

The fact that $1 \Rightarrow 2$ follows directly from the definition of a segmented state. We remark that since $\mathcal{D}_i^F \subseteq \mathcal{D}_{\leq i}^F$ and since $i < j$ implies that $\mathcal{D}_j^F \subseteq \mathcal{D}_{> i}^F$, it is easy to verify that $2 \Rightarrow 3$.

Finally, we proceed to verify that F is not segmented implies that F does not satisfy 3. Assume that F is not segmented. Consider $k = deg(F)$ and let b be the $k+1$-th element of $\overline{\mathcal{D}}^F$ and let $a = n - k$ be the canonical replacement of b (cf. Remark A.2). We recall that $a > b$ and that $j = depth(a) > depth(b) = i$. We know that $a = n - k$ is greater than every label in $\mathcal{D}_j^F$. We conclude that $\vee \mathcal{D}_j^F = a$. Of course, since $b < a$ and $b \in \mathcal{D}_i^F$, we have that $\wedge \mathcal{D}_i^F < a$. Hence $\wedge \mathcal{D}_i^F < \vee \mathcal{D}_j^F$ where $j > i$, and thus F does not satisfy 3.

It is useful to state the following technical lemma that establishes the existence of a first depth-inconsistent pair for any state which is not canonical.

Lemma A.2. *A state F which is not segmented, where say b is the label creating the first gap and a is its canonical replacement, has a depth-inconsistent **free** pair $\{a', b\}$, such that $a' \in a \downarrow$, which is the first depth-inconsistent (b, a') free pair of F in the order $\preceq_F$ for which b creates the first gap. In particular, we know that a' is the largest label in $a \downarrow$ with this property.*

Proof. When F is not segmented we consider $k = deg(F)$, b be the $k + 1$-th label of $\overline{\mathcal{D}}^F$ that creates the first gap and $a = n - k$ the canonical replacement of b, where $a > b$ and $j = depth(a) > depth(b) = i$. We first show that there exists a label a' such that $b < a' \leq a$ and $\lfloor a' \rfloor \neq \emptyset \Rightarrow b > \vee \lfloor a' \rfloor$. We consider three cases.

1) When $\lfloor a \rfloor = \emptyset$, we obtain the result by choosing $a' = a$.

2) When $\lfloor a \rfloor \neq \emptyset$ and $b > \vee \lfloor a \rfloor$, we obtain the result by choosing $a' = a$.

3) When $\lfloor a \rfloor \neq \emptyset$ and $b < \vee \lfloor a \rfloor$, we consider any $a_1 \in \lfloor a \rfloor$ such that $b < a_1$.

In that case, we repeat the above three cases, with a_1 instead of a. Either this produces a suitable a' via 1 or 2, or the process returns to case 3). Hence we create a strictly decreasing sequence $a_0, a_1, a_2, \ldots, a_n$, where $n \geq 0$ and $a_0 = a$. This process has to terminate, since we obtain that $\forall n. \, depth(a_{n+1}) > depth(a_n)$. Hence, in cases the process did not terminate earlier at case 1 or case 2, at one point we must arrive at a situation where $\lfloor a_n \rfloor = \emptyset$ and the process terminates via 1. In that case, we select $a' = a_n$.

So we can assume that there is a label a' such that $b < a'$ and $\lfloor a' \rfloor \neq \emptyset \Rightarrow b > \vee \lfloor a' \rfloor$. Say this level occurs at depth $j' \geq j$. Note that since the state F is increasing, we know that $a' \leq a$.

We verify that $\{a', b\}$ is a depth-inconsistent *free* pair of labels. Clearly the pair is depth-inconsistent since $a' > b$ and by choice of a' we have $depth(a') \geq depth(a) > depth(b)$. Moreover, by construction, we have $\lfloor a' \rfloor \neq \emptyset \Rightarrow b > \vee \lfloor a' \rfloor$. Since $a' > b$, in order to prove the freeness, it remains to verify:

if $\lceil b \rceil \neq \emptyset$ then $a' < \wedge \lceil b \rceil$.

We assume that $\lceil b \rceil \neq \emptyset$. Since the depth function is strictly decreasing we know that $\lceil b \rceil \subseteq \mathcal{D}^F_{< i}$.

We remark that F is $(i - 1)$-segmented since F induces a k-segment. Hence we know that every element of $\mathcal{D}^F_{\leq i-1}$ is greater than every element in $\mathcal{R}^F_k$. Since $a' \in \mathcal{R}^F_k$ we have in particular that $a' < \wedge \lceil b \rceil$.

Lemma A.3. *F is canonical $\iff$ F is segmented.*

Proof. It is clear that if F is segmented then F is canonical. We show that when F is not segmented, F is not canonical. By the previous lemma we know that when F is not segmented we can always find a label a' such that $b < a' \leq a$ such that the pair $\{a', b\}$ is a free pair which is depth-inconsistent. Hence we obtain that F is not canonical.

Note that Example A.1 of Section 4.1 displays a segmented state which is also a canonical state. This is no coincidence since the notions are equivalent as the following corollary shows.

Corollary A.1. *Levels of canonical states consist of pairwise free elements. Any permutation of labels on a same level yields a new canonical state.*

Proof. The two statements follow from 3) of Lemma A.1 and the definition of a free pair.

Corollary A.2. *A canonical state is "unique" up to permutations of labels at equal depth. In other words, all canonical states can be generated from a given canonical state by carrying out all possible permutations on its pairs of labels occurring at equal depth. The cardinality of the set of all canonical states is:*

$$\Pi_{i=0}^{D} d_i!$$

Proof. Combining Corollary A.1 with the fact that by the definition of segmented states, all levels are segments and hence consist of fixed sets of labels, we obtain the result.

Definition A.4. For a given finite connected partial order $(X, \sqsubseteq)$ and its chosen Hasse diagram representation. Then for any set of states $\mathcal{R}_{\mathcal{L}}(X, \sqsubseteq)$, we define *the* canonical state F_C to be the canonical state determined by $\overline{\mathcal{D}}^F$, where F is any canonical state, and where the labels of F_C are assigned to the Hasse diagram representation consistently with the state order $\preceq_F$. I.e. on the Hasse diagram representation, we systematically assign the labels of $\overline{\mathcal{D}}^F$ in left to right order in this sequence (i.e. consistent with the way they occur with respect to the order $\preceq_F$) to the elements of the Hasse diagram as they occur on the chosen Hasse diagram *representation*: first in left to right order at level 0, then in left to right order at the next level, if there is one, and so on.

Example A.2. If we swap the labels 1 and 2 in the state of the Hasse diagram representation of Example A.1, we obtain a canonical state of this Hasse diagram representation.

We show in the following that every state can be transformed to a canonical state via suitable permutations on depth-inconsistent free pairs.

A.3 Canonical State Algorithm

We will show that Random Structures on a finite connected partial order can be generated from a single canonical state on this finite connected partial order.. First, we discuss the following algorithm, which allows one to generate a canonical state from any given state.

Canonical State Algorithm
The proof of Lemma A.2 provides an algorithm for detecting the first depth-inconsistent free pair of a non-canonical state. It is easy to see that one can design an algorithm from this which produces for any given state F a canonical state associated with F, via a sequence of swaps on depth-inconsistent free pairs, which systematically closes all gaps.

The algorithm proceeds as follows: given a state F. If F is canonical, then return F. Otherwise, we can always select the first depth-inconsistent free pair $\{a', b\}$ in F, where b is the first element creating a gap, a is its canonical replacement and $a' \in a\downarrow$. We recall that a' is the largest label in $a\downarrow$ forming a depth-inconsistent free pair with b. Swap b with a'.

In case $a' = a$, we have closed the gap. This creates a new state F' on which we recall the canonical state algorithm in order to systematically close all remaining gaps.

In case $a' \neq a$, we rename a' to b' and repeat the above, i.e. we locate the first depth-inconsistent free pair $\{a', b'\}$, where $a' \in a\downarrow$. Either we obtain $a' = a$, in which case we can close the gap as above. Otherwise, we note that $b < b'$ since prior to renaming of a' to b', we had $b < a'$. This creates a sequence $b < b' < b'' < \ldots$. The process hence must stop since the sequence consists of elements from the finite set $a\downarrow$. Hence the process must terminate with some $a = a'$, where we can close the gap.

Finally, this creates a new state F' on which we recall the canonical state algorithm in order to systematically close all remaining gaps.

We obtain the following immediate corollary.

Corollary A.3. *For a chosen Hasse diagram representation, every state can be transformed to the unique canonical state F_C via a sequence of permutations on free pairs of labels.*

We illustrate the Canonical State Algorithm in the Example displayed on the next page.

Corollary A.4. *For every pair of states F_1, F_2 there exists a sequence of permutations $\sigma_1, \ldots, \sigma_n$ on free pairs of labels such that $F_2 = \sigma_n \circ \sigma_{n-1} \circ \ldots \sigma_2 \circ \sigma_1 \circ F_1$.*

Proof. We remark that for every pair of states, F_1, F_2, we can find a sequence of swaps on depth-inconsistent free pairs which reduce each of the given states to the canonical state F_C. We remark that it is easy to see that a sequence of swaps on depth-inconsistent free pairs of F_2 leading to F_C can be reversed into a sequence of swaps on free pairs leading from F_C to F_2. Hence, in order to obtain the result, one simply has to carry out the sequence of swaps leading from F_1 to F_C followed by the reversed sequence leading from F_C to F_2 in order to transform F_1 into F_2.

Example A.3. The following example illustrates the Canonical State Algorithm

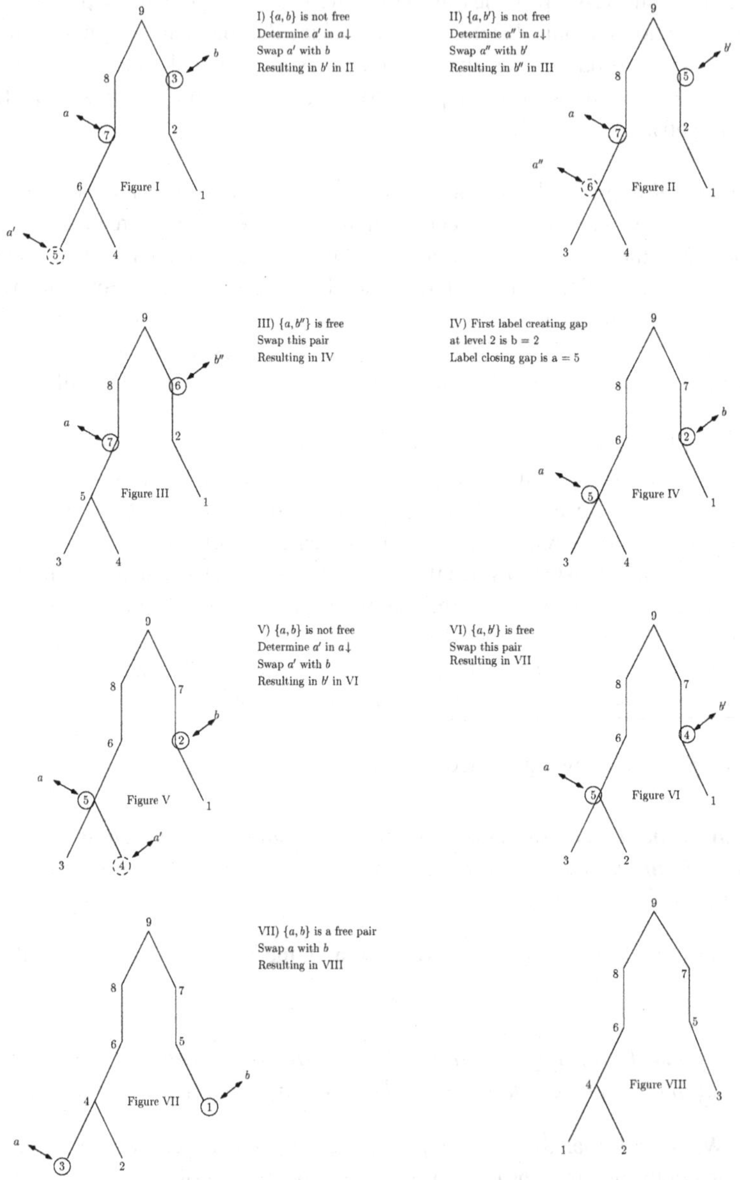

I) $\{a,b\}$ is not free
Determine a' in $a\downarrow$
Swap a' with b
Resulting in b' in II

II) $\{a,b'\}$ is not free
Determine a'' in $a\downarrow$
Swap a'' with b'
Resulting in b'' in III

Figure I

Figure II

III) $\{a,b''\}$ is free
Swap this pair
Resulting in IV

IV) First label creating gap
at level 2 is $b = 2$
Label closing gap is $a = 5$

Figure III

Figure IV

V) $\{a,b\}$ is not free
Determine a' in $a\downarrow$
Swap a' with b
Resulting in b' in VI

VI) $\{a,b'\}$ is free
Swap this pair
Resulting in VII

Figure V

Figure VI

VII) $\{a,b\}$ is a free pair
Swap a with b
Resulting in VIII

Figure VII

Figure VIII

From the above corollary, we obtain the following immediate result.

Theorem A.1. *(State Theorem) Each random structure on a finite connected partial order can be generated from any given state, by exhaustively carrying out all possible swap sequences on free pairs of labels, where a sequence terminates when a state is repeated.*

References

[AJM02] S. Abramsky, R. Jagadeesan, and P. Malacaria, Full abstraction for PCF, *Information and Computation* 163, 409-470, 2000.

[AHU87] A. Aho, J. Hopcroft and J. Ullman, *Data Structures and Algorithms*, Addison-Wesley Series in Computer Science and Information Processing, Addison-Wesley, 1987.

[BR92] J. de Bakker, J. Rutten (editors, CWI, Amsterdam), *Ten Years of Concurrency Semantics*, Selected Papers of the Amsterdam Concurrency Group, World Scientific, 1992.

[Bar84] H. P. Barendregt, *The Lambda Calculus: Its Syntax and Semantics*, North Holland, Amsterdam, 1984.

[BNS] S.J. Bellantoni, K.-H Niggl, H. Schwichtenberg, Higher type recursion, ramification and polynomial time, *Annals of Pure and Applied Logic*, 104(1), 17-30, 2000.

[BHS06] M. Boubekeur, D. Hickey and M. Schellekens, *Evaluation of $\mathcal{MOQA}$ Average-Case Timing Results on a Real Time Platform*, Proc. of the conference Information-MFCSIT'06, Electronic Notes in Computer Science, Cork, August 2006, to appear.

[BHMS07a] M. Boubekeur, D. Hickey, J. McEnery and M. Schellekens, A new Approach for Modular Average-Case Timing of Real-Time Java Programs, in *WSEAS Transactions on Computers*, 3(5), 361-368, 2006.

[BHMS07b] M. Boubekeur, D. Hickey and J. McEnery, M. Schellekens, *Towards Modular Average-Case Timing in Real-Time Languages: An Application to Real-Time Java*, in Proceedings of the 6th WSEAS International Conference on Applied Computer Science (ACS'06), Tenerife, December, 2006.

[BPS96] G. Brightwell, H.-J. Promel and A. Steger, The average number of linear extensions of a partial order, *J. Combinatorial Theory* (A) 73, 193-206, 1996.

[BW90] A. Burns, A. Wellings, *Real-time systems and their programming languages*, Addison Wesley, 1990.

[BP02] A. Burns, P. Puschner, *Writing Temporally Predictable Code*, 7th IEEE International Workshop on Object-Oriented Real-Time Dependable Systems WORDS02, 85-94, 2002.

[Coh74] J. Cohen, C. Zuckerman, Two Languages for Estimating Program Efficiency, *Communications of the ACM*, 17(6), 301-308, 1974.

[Coo91] S. Cook, *Computability and complexity of higher type functions*, in Logic from Computer Science (Y.N. Moschovakis, ed.), Springer-Verlag, 51-72, 1991.

[CLR96] T.H. Cormen, C. E. Leiserson, R. L. Rivest, *Introduction to Algorithms*, MIT Press, 1996.

[DP90] B. A. Davey, H. A. Priestley, *Introduction to Lattices and Order*, Cambridge University Press, 1990.

[Don04] M.R.C. van Dongen, *Computing the Frequency of Partial Orders*, in Proceedings CP'2004, LNCS 3258, Toronto, Canada, 772- 776, 2004.

[Dut92] R.D. Dutton, Weak-Heapsort, *BIT* 33, 372-381, 1993.

[Ede96] S. Edelkamp, *Weak-Heapsort, ein schnelles sortierverfahren*, Diplomarbeit Universität Dortmund, 1996.

[Erm03] A. Ermedahl, *A Modular Tool Architecture for Worst-Case Execution Time Analysis*, PhD thesis, Uppsala University, 2003.

[Fin03] S. Finch, *Mathematical Constants*, Cambridge University Presss, 2003 (Or: Series-Parallel Networks, http://pauillac.inria.fr/algo/bsolve/).

[FSZ89] P. Flajolet, B. Salvy and P. Zimmermann, *Lambda-Upsilon-Omega the 1989 cookbook* (RR 1073), 1989.

[FSZ91] P. Flajolet, B. Salvy, P. Zimmerman, Automatic average-case analysis of algorithms, *Theoretical Computer Science* 79, 37-109, 1991.

[FS95] P. Flajolet, R. Sedgewick, *An Introduction to the Analysis of Algorithms*, Addison Wesley, 1995.

[FS08] P. Flajolet, R. Sedgewick, *Analytic Combinatorics*, to be published by Cambridge University Press, 2008.

[FV90] P. Flajolet, J. S. Vitter, Average-Case Analysis of Algorithms and Data Structures, *Handbook of Theoretical Computer Science*, Volume A: Algorithms and Complexity, Elsevier, 431-524, 1990.

[Flo64] R.W. Floyd, Algorithm 245, treesort 3. *Commun. ACM* 701, 1964.

[Gis88] J.L. Gischer, The equational theory of pomsets, *Theor. Comput. Sci.* 61, 199-224, 1988.

[Gra81] J. Grabowski, On partial languages, *Fundamenta Informaticae* 4, 427-498, 1981.

[Gre97] J. Greiner, *Semantics-based parallel cost models and their use in provably efficient implementations*, CMU PhD thesis, 1997.

[Gun92] C. A. Gunter, *Semantics of Programming Languages*, MIT Press, Cambridge, MA, 1992.

[Gur91] D. Gurr, *Semantic frameworks for complexity*, Ph.D. thesis, University of Edinburgh, 1991.

[GKP94] R. L. Graham, D. E. Knuth, O. Patashnik, *Concrete Mathematics: A Foundation for Computer Science, 2/E*, Addison Wesley Professional, 1994.

[Ham88] A. G. Hamilton, *Logic for Mathematicians*, Cambridge University Press, 1988.

[HC88] T. Hickey, J. Cohen, Automating Program Analysis, *Journal of the ACM*, 35(1), 185-220, 1988.

[Hey05] M. Heyer, *Randomness Preserving Deletions on Special Binary Search Trees*, MSc Thesis, 2005.

[Hic07] D. Hickey, *Distritrack: Automated Average-Case Analysis*, Proceedings of the Fourth International Conference on the Quantitative Evaluation of SysTems, QEST2007, Edinburgh, Scotland, UK, IEEE Computer Society Press, 213-214, 2007.

[Hic08] D. Hickey, *Tracking Data Structures for Automated Average Time Analysis*, PhD thesis, National University of Ireland, Cork, June 2008 (in preparation).

[Hof98] M. Hofmann, *A mixed modal/linear lambda calculus with applications to Bellantoni-Cook safe recursion*, in: Proc. CSL'97. LNCS 1414. Springer-Verlag, Berlin, 275-294, 1998.

[Hof99] M. Hofmann, Linear types and non-size-increasing polynomial time computation, *Information and Computation* 183(1), 57-85, 2003.

[Hof00] M. Hofmann, Type systems for polynomial-time computation, Habilitation thesis, Darmstadt, 1999. Appears as LFCS Technical Report ECS-LFCS-99-406.

[HJ99] K. Hrbacek, T. Jech, *Introduction to Set Theory*, Marcel Dekker, Inc., 1999.

[Hoa61] C. A. Hoare, *Commun. ACM*, 4(7), 321-322, 1961.

[HBW02] E. Yu-Shing Hu, G. Bernat, A. Wellings, *A Static Timing Analysis Environment Using Java Architecture for Safety Critical Real-Time Systems*, Seventh IEEE International Workshop on Object-Oriented Real-Time Dependable Systems (WORDS'02), 77-84, 2002.

[IKR01] On Characterizations of the Basic Feasible Functionals, Part I, R. Irwin, B. Kapron and J. Royer, *Journal of Functional Programming* 11, 117-153, 2001.

[Jak07] The Apache Software Foundation, The Apache Commons Project, http://jakarta.apache.org/commons/math/

[JK78] A. T. Jonassen, D. E. Knuth, A trivial algorithm whose analysis is not, *J. Comput. System Sci.* 16, 301-322, 1978.

[JLi] *J/Link*, Wolfram Research Inc, www.wolfram.com/solutions/mathlink/jlink

[JP89] C. Jones, G. Plotkin, *A probabilistic powerdomain of evaluations*, in LICS '89, IEEE Computer Society Press, 186-195, 1989.

[Jon97] N. Jones, *Computability and Complexity from a Programming Perspective*, MIT Press, 1997.

[Kno75] G. D. Knott, *Deletions in Binary Storage Trees*, PhD Thesis, Computer Science Department, Stanford University, 1975.

[Koz81] D. Kozen. Semantics of probabilistic programs, *Journal of Computer and Systems Sciences*, 22, 328-350, 1981.

[KC96] B. Kapron, S. Cook, A new characterization of type 2 feasibility, *SIAM Journal on Computing* 25, 117-132, 1996.

[Knu71] D. Knuth, *Mathematical Analysis of Algorithms*, in Information Processing '71, Proc. of the 1971 IFIP Congress, North-Holland, Amsterdam, 19-27, 1971.

[Knu73] D. Knuth, *The art of computer programming* vol.3, Addison-Wesley, 1973.

[Knu77] D. Knuth, *Deletions That Preserve Randomness*, IEEE Transactions on Software Engineering, Vol SE-3, No. 5, 351-359, 1977.

[KFG93] H. Kopetz, G. Fohler, G. Grunsteidl et al., *Real-Time Systems Development: The Programming Model of MARS*, in Proceedings of the International Symposium on Autonomous Decentralized Systems, Kawasaki, Japan, March, 190-199, 1993.

[KS97] C. M. Krishna, K. G. Shin, *Real-time systems*, McGraw-Hill International Series, Computer Science Series, 1997.

[Lev84] L. A. Levin, Randomness Conservation Inequalities, *Information and Control* 61(1), 15-37, 1984.

[Lev03] A. Levitin, *Introduction to the Design & Analysis of Algorithms*, Addison Wesley, 2003.

[LV93] M. Li and P. Vitanyi. *An introduction to Kolmogorov Complexity and its applications*, Texts and Monographs in Computer Science, Springer Verlag, 1993.

[Mai00] T. Maibaum, *Mathematical foundations of software engineering: a roadmap*, International Conference on Software Engineering, Proceedings of the Conference on The Future of Software Engineering, Limerick, Ireland, 161-172, 2000.

[MR98] C. Martínez, S. Roura, Randomized binary search trees, *Journal of the Association for Computing Machinery*, 45(2), 288-323, March 1998.

[Mat] Mathematica, Wolfram Research Inc, Www.wolfram.com.

[Mis03] M. Mishna, Attribute grammars and automatic algorithm analysis, *Advances in Applied Mathematics* 30, 189-207, 2003.

[MA] E. Moggi, D. Archieri, *Monadic approach and complexity*, preprint.

[MP97] D. Mittermair and P. Puschner, *Which Sorting Algorithms to Choose for Hard Real-Time Applications*, in Proc. Euromicro Workshop on Real-Time Systems, Toledo, Spain, 250-257, 1997.

[MR95] R. Motwani, P. Raghavan, *Randomized Algorithms*, Cambridge University Press, 1995.

[Naa00] M. Naatz, The Graph of Linear Extensions Revisited, *SIAM Journal on Discrete Mathematics* 13 (3), 354 - 369, 2000.

[Nie84] H. Nielson, *Hoare Logics for Run-time Analysis of Programs*, Ph.D. thesis, CST-30-84, Edinburgh University, 1984.

[Par95] I. Parberry. *Problems on Algorithms*, Prentice Hall, 1995.

[Plo97] G. Plotkin, LCF considered as a programming language, *Theoretical Computer Science* 5, 223-255, 1977.

[Pra86] V. Pratt, Modelling Concurrency with Partial Orders, *International Journal of Parallel Programming* 15(1), 33-71, 1986.

[Pur] *Purrs: The Parma University's Recurrence Relation Solver*, Parma University, www.cs.unipr.it/purrs

[PK93] P. Puschner and C. Koza. *Calculating the Maximum Execution Time of Real-Time Programs*, Reprint in IEEE tutorial: Advances in Real-Time Systems, IEEE Computer Society Press, 322-339, 1993.

[Pus03] P. Puschner, *Hard Real-Time Programming is Different*, 17th IEEE Int'l Parallel and Distributed Processing Symposium, 11th Int'l Workshop on Parallel and Distributed Real-Time Systems, 117-118, 2003.

[QND04] G. Quan, L. Niu, P. Davis, Power Aware Scheduling for Real-Time Systems with (m,k)-Guarantee, *CNDS*, 18-21, 2004.

[Ram96] K. Ramamritham, Real-Time Databases, *International Journal of Distributed and Parallel Databases*, 28(2-3), 179-215, 1996.

[Ram 79] L. Ramshaw, Formalizing the Analysis of Algorithms, Ph.D. Thesis, Stanford University, 1979. (Also available as Report SL-79-5, Xerox Palo Alto Research Center, Palo Alto, California, 1979).

[RTS] *Real-Time Specification for Java*, http://www.rtsj.org/

[RS98] S. Romaguera, M. P. Schellekens, On the structure of complexity spaces: the general case, *Extracta Mathematicae* 13, 249-253, 1998.

[RS99] S. Romaguera, M. P. Schellekens, Quasi-metric properties of Complexity Spaces, *Topology and its Applications* 98, 311-322, 1999.

[RS03] S. Romaguera, M. P. Schellekens, *Norm-weightable Riesz spaces and the dual complexity space*, ENTCS 74, Elsevier, Proceedings MFCSIT2002, 2003.

[Sar89] V. Sarkar, Determining average program execution times and their variance, *SIGPLAN Not.* 24(7), 298-312, 1989.

[SS93] R. Schaffer and R. Sedgewick, The analysis of Heapsort, *Journal of Algorithms* 15(1), 76-100, 1993.

[Sch95] M. P. Schellekens, *The Smyth-completion: a common topological foundation for Denotational Semantics and Complexity Analysis*, PhD thesis, Carnegie Mellon University, 1995.

[Sch95a] M. P. Schellekens, *The Smyth-completion: a common foundation for Denotational Semantics and Complexity Analysis*, Electronic Notes in Theoretical Computer Science I, Proc. 11th Conf. on the Mathematical Foundations of Programming Semantics, Elsevier, 211-232, 1995.

[Sch99] M. P. Schellekens, Complexity Spaces: Lifting and Directedness, *Topology Proceedings* 22, 403-425, 1999.

[Sch03] M. P. Schellekens, A characterization of partial metrizability, Domains are quantifiable, *Theoretical Computer Science* 305, 409-432, 2003.

[Sch04] M. P. Schellekens, The correspondence between partial metrics and semivaluations, *Theoretical Computer Science* 315, 135-149, 2004.

[Sch08] M.P. Schellekens, *A randomness preserving product operation*, Proc. of the conference Information-MFCSIT'06, Elsevier series Electronic Notes in Theoretical Computer Science, 2008, to appear.

[Sch09] M. Schellekens, $\mathcal{MOQA}$; unlocking the potential of compositional static average-case analysis, *Journal of Logic and Algebraic Programming*, accepted for publication, to appear, 2009.

[SHB04] M. P. Schellekens, D. Hickey, G. Bollella, $\mathcal{MOQA}$, *a Linearly-Compositional Programming Language for (semi-)automated Average-Case Analysis*, WIP Proceedings, 25th IEEE International Real-Time Systems Symposium (RTSS 2004), Lisbon, Portugal, 2004.

[SS71] D. S. Scott and C. Strachey, *Toward a mathematical semantics for computer languages*, Proc. Symp. on Computers and Automata, 1971.

[Sco72] D. S. Scott, *Continuous Lattices, Toposes, Algebraic Geometry and Logic*, Lecture Notes in Mathematics 274, Springer Verlag, Berlin, 97-136, 1972.

[SA96] R. Seidel, C. Aragon, Randomized search trees, *Algorithmica* 16, 464-497, 1996.

[SL04] I. Shin and I. Lee, *Compositional Real-Time Scheduling Framework*, Proceedings 25th IEEE International Real-Time Systems Symposium (RTSS 2004), Lisbon, Portugal, 57-67, 2004.

[Smy87] M.B. Smyth, *Quasi-uniformities: Reconciling domains with metric spaces*, LNCS 298, Springer Verlag, 236-253, 1987.

[Smy91] M.B. Smyth, Totally bounded spaces and compact ordered spaces as domains of computation, in G. M. Reed, A. W. Roscoe and R. F. Wachter, editors, *Topology and Category Theory in Computer Science*, Oxford University Press, 207-229, 1991.

[Soo] Soot, A Java Optimization Framework, Sable McGill university, www.sable.mcgill.ca/soot.

[Stan99] R.P. Stanley, *Enumerative Combinatorics*, v 2., Cambridge University Press, 1999.

[Sto77] J. Stoy, *Denotational Semantics: the Scott-Strachey approach to Programming Language Theory*, MIT Press, 1977.

[TMS06] J. Townley, J. Manning, M. Schellekens, *Sorting Algorithms in* $\mathcal{MOQA}$, Proc. of
    the conference Information-MFCSIT'06, accepted for publication, Elsevier series, Electronic
    Notes in Theoretical Computer Science, 2008, to appear.

[UK03] O. Unsal, I. Koren, *System-Level Power-Aware Design Techniques in Real Time Systems*,
    Proceedings of the IEEE 91(7), 1055-1069, 2003.

[VM07] T. Vallee, J. Manning, *Reconstruction of Partial Orders*, preprint.

[VTL79] E.L. Lawler, R.E. Tarjan and J. Valdes, The recognition of series parallel digraphs, *SIAM
    Journ. Comput.* 11, 298-313, 1982.

[Vui80] J. Vuillemin, A Unifying Look at Data Structures, *Commun. ACM 23*, 229-239, 1980.

[Weg 75] B. Wegbreit, Mechanical Program Analysis, *Commun. ACM*, 18(9), 528-538, 1975.

[Weg90] I. Wegener, BOTTOM-UP-HEAPSORT, a new variant of HEAP SORT, beating on an
    average QUICKSORT (if n is not very small), *Theoretical Computer Science* 118, 81-98,
    1993.

[Wil64] J.W.J. Williams. Algorithm 232. *Commun. ACM* 7(6), 347-348, 1964.

Index